From Creation
to
NEW
CREATION

ESSAYS IN HONOR OF G. K. BEALE

From Creation to NEW CREATION

Biblical Theology and Exegesis

Daniel M. Gurtner & Benjamin L. Gladd, eds.

HENDRICKSON PUBLISHERS

From Creation to New Creation: Biblical Theology and Exegesis

© 2013 by Hendrickson Publishers Marketing, LLC
P. O. Box 3473
Peabody, Massachusetts 01961–3473

ISBN 978–1-59856–837–0

Scripture quotations marked CEB are taken from the Common English Bible®, CEB® Copyright © 2010, 2011 by Common English Bible.™ Used by permission. All rights reserved worldwide. The "CEB" and "Common English Bible" trademarks are registered in the United States Patent and Trademark Office by Common English Bible. Use of either trademark requires the permission of Common English Bible.

Scripture quotations marked ESV are from The Holy Bible, English Standard Version® (ESV®), copyright © 2001 by Crossway, a publishing ministry of Good News Publishers. Used by permission. All rights reserved.

Scripture quotations marked NASB are from the New American Standard Bible®, Copyright © 1960, 1962, 1963, 1968, 1971, 1972, 1973, 1975, 1977, 1995 by The Lockman Foundation. Used by permission. (www.Lockman.org)

Quotations marked NETS are taken from *A New English Translation of the Septuagint*, ©2007 by the International Organization for Septuagint and Cognate Studies, Inc. Used by permission of Oxford University Press. All rights reserved.

Scripture quotations marked NIV are taken from the Holy Bible, New International Version®. Copyright © 1973, 1978, 1984, 2011 by Biblica, Inc. All rights reserved worldwide. Used by permission.

Scripture quotations marked NRSV are taken from the New Revised Standard Version of the Bible, copyright © 1989 by the Division of Christian Education of the National Council of the Churches of Christ in the United States of America, and are used by permission.

Scripture quotations marked RSV are taken from the Revised Standard Version of the Bible, copyright © 1946, 1952, 1971 by the Division of Christian Education of the National Council of the Churches of Christ in the USA. Used by permission. All rights reserved.

Scripture quotations marked TNIV are taken from the Holy Bible, Today's New International Version®. Copyright © 2001, 2005 by Biblica, Inc. All rights reserved worldwide. Used by permission.

The photograph of G. K. Beale is copyright © Michael Hudson Photography, Wheaton, IL, and used with permission.

Printed in the United States of America

First Printing — October 2013

Library of Congress Cataloging-in-Publication Data

From creation to new creation : Biblical theology and exegesis / Daniel M.
    Gurtner and Benjamin L. Gladd, editors.
        pages cm
    Includes bibliographical references and indexes.
    ISBN 978-1-59856-837-0 (alk. paper)
    1. Bible—Criticism, interpretation, etc. I. Gurtner, Daniel M., editor of
compilation.
    BS511.3.F775 2013
    220.6—dc23
                            2013000399

TABLE OF CONTENTS

CONTRIBUTORS

Richard J. Bauckham Professor of New Testament Emeritus. University of St. Andrews—Scotland; Senior Scholar at Ridley Hall, Cambridge—England

Christopher A. Beetham Associate Professor of Biblical Studies. Evangelical Theological College—Addis Ababa, Ethiopia; Associate Professor of New Testament. Ethiopian Graduate School of Theology—Addis Ababa, Ethiopia

Daniel I. Block Gunther H. Knoedler Professor of Old Testament. Wheaton College—Wheaton, Illinois

C. Hassell Bullock Franklin S. Dyrness Professor of Biblical Studies Emeritus. Wheaton College—Wheaton, Illinois

D. A. Carson Research Professor of New Testament. Trinity Evangelical Divinity School—Deerfield, Illinois

Roy E. Ciampa Professor of New Testament. Gordon-Conwell Theological Seminary—South Hamilton, Massachusetts

John D. Currid Carl W. McMurray Professor of Old Testament. Reformed Theological Seminary—Charlotte, North Carolina

Benjamin L. Gladd Assistant Professor of New Testament. Reformed Theological Seminary—Jackson, Mississippi

Daniel M. Gurtner Associate Professor of New Testament. Bethel Seminary—St. Paul, Minnesota

Gordon P. Hugenberger Senior Minister. Park Street Church—Boston, Massachusetts. Ranked Adjunct Professor of Old Testament. Gordon-Conwell Theological Seminary—South Hamilton, Massachusetts

L. K. Larson   Research Assistant in Old Testament. Reformed Theological Seminary—Charlotte, North Carolina

Douglas J. Moo   Kenneth T. Wessner Chair of Biblical Studies. Wheaton College—Wheaton, Illinois

Nicholas Perrin   Franklin S. Dyrness Professor of Biblical Studies. Dean of the Graduate School. Wheaton College—Wheaton, Illinois

Rikk E. Watts   Professor of New Testament. Regent College— Vancouver, British Columbia, Canada

David F. Wells   Distinguished Senior Research Professor. Gordon-Conwell Theological Seminary—South Hamilton, Massachusetts

Joel R. White   Professor of New Testament. Freie Theologische Hochschule—Giessen, Germany

FOREWORD

David F. Wells

A fresh breeze is blowing in biblical studies today. It is felt in the desire, expressed in many different ways, to read the Bible as a whole, to see it as having a self-consistent narrative. How to describe that narrative, whether it has one central theme or multiple themes, is a matter of discussion. That there is a self-contained story, with a beginning and an end, is the important point that is being freshly articulated.

This new interest is, in one sense, very old. It would be foolish to think that the early fathers, like Irenaeus or even Tertullian, had no understanding of the Bible's connecting narrative. Nor would it make any sense to say that Calvin and Luther did not grasp the overall structure of Scripture. Calvin, after all, is among the very few to have commented on virtually the entire Bible.

However, it is true that the pursuit of the connecting ligaments of Scripture has taken its own path and has its own particular history in the modern period. It became ensconced in its own discipline, biblical theology, in the eighteenth century, and it has gone in and out of fashion ever since then. Mostly, though, it has been out of fashion.

This has been especially true in more recent times. Henning Graf Reventlow's *Problems of Biblical Theology in the Twentieth Century* gives the reader a good sense of the massive literature that has emerged and the major issues that have been engaged. It has been a checkered story. Brevard Childs, himself a practitioner in this discipline, had to lament its demise in *Biblical Theology in Crisis*. He was, of course, taking up just one of its episodes, the crash-and-burn end to the movement in the United States that had been rooted in the fresh interest in the Bible that had grown out of European neo-orthodoxy. This phase of biblical theology began in the 1950s and had ended by the 1970s.

Despite these difficulties, there has emerged a growing belief more recently that this enterprise must be continued. What has emerged in recent decades, then, is a fresh emphasis on the thought that the Bible's books do not stand conceptually alone, isolated from one another like silos in a field, but that they are bound together by a common story, redemptive in nature, whose chief actor is God himself. Reading these books for this narrative—dare we call it a metanarrative?—and this narrative for what we learn of God has emerged with fresh insistence. It is at least in this sense that we may speak of a theological reading of the Bible. It is what explains which OT texts are used in the NT, and it explains the way in which they are used. And the existence of this narrative tells us why there are OT texts to be used at all. It is that the NT is giving us a theological perspective on the OT. A significant contributor to this new turn is Greg Beale.

It is an honor to have this opportunity to express my great regard for him as well as my appreciation for his friendship. Indeed, for a time we were also colleagues. No one, I know, is more focused on his work than he, no one more relentless in the pursuit of textual detail, and no one more passionate about biblical truth. Furthermore, I know of no one else who would even think of doing what he did: he read the 750 pages of dense and complicated argument in N. T. Wright's *The Resurrection of the Son of God* while brushing his teeth morning and evening! He has made an extraordinary contribution within the academy as well as to the next generation of young scholars and of young pastor-scholars.

Greg's particular interest has been the use of the OT by the NT authors. This is not a narrow interest if one assumes, as he does, that all of this takes place within a coherent and identifiable narrative that links the parts. If that is so, then it is possible, using conventional exegetical norms, to lay bare the underlying meaning that links the texts. And that is what he has done most fully in his recent *A New Testament Biblical Theology: The Unfolding of the Old Testament in the New.* This volume picks up on the embedded typology, and this leads into a comprehensive way of reading the whole Bible, all its parts are connected together in its eschatological structure of the already/not yet.

This certainly places Greg alongside a scholar from an earlier time, Geerhardus Vos. However, Vos's *Biblical Theology: Old and New Testaments,* despite the subtitle, is more about the Old than the New, and more about how themes unfolded in the Old than about how they reached their fulfillment in the New. That is what Greg has done. He has, in a way, completed what Vos started.

The essays in this volume are grouped into three sections that reflect Greg's preoccupations in his work: he has worked on the OT, from the vantage point of a NT scholar, thereby creating a biblical theology. However, I should not attempt to summarize these essays here. I would do their authors a disservice. They must be read completely for their richness, intricate detail, and many insights. However, it is striking to see how much first-rate work, such as these essays represent, is now forging these narrative links within the OT and between the OT and the NT.

The church is all the richer for it!

PREFACE

Daniel M. Gurtner
Benjamin L. Gladd

Both editors of the present volume have studied under Professor Beale and worked as his teaching assistant. Through his years of teaching, Dr. Beale has developed a reputation among students as being intense, rigorous, even intimidating. For those of us who know him best from working closely with him, it is strikingly apparent that such enthusiasm in the classroom is deeply rooted in his faith in Jesus Christ, his love for the life-transforming power of the gospel of Jesus Christ through careful study of the Scriptures, and his pursuit—using every intellectual fiber of his being—to engage the most important of labors known to humanity: the service of Christ's church.

An academic? Yes. But some of us recall his passionate threat to jettison from the classroom anyone who was not engaged in some capacity of pastoral ministry. Another time Dr. Beale was red-faced with fury when a student requested of him a lowering of academic standards since the student was "only" going to be a pastor. For him, being a pastor is not a license for less rigor and care in one's study but a motivation, even responsibility, to pour all the energies of one's mind into engaging the Scriptures and relating them faithfully in preaching and teaching. Whether Dr. Beale is breaking a sweat in class over a word study or draining a ballpoint pen of most of its ink on a student's written work, students willing to be challenged are forever changed.

Professor Beale's enthusiasm for the life-changing truths of the Word of God and passion for others to join him on his journey of plumbing the richness of Scripture is an other-worldly, even apocalyptic experience. Dr. Beale both demands and exemplifies the joys of worshipful exegesis—using every skill available to engage carefully and critically but humbly and respectfully the Word of God in its original languages. Those of us still unearthing the riches Greg poured into us are enthusiastic to offer this collection of essays in appreciation of the goodness of God granted to us in the life and ministry of G. K. Beale.

Thanks are due to Allan Emery of Hendrickson Publishers for his immediate interest in this project and able guidance in seeing it to completion. Thanks are also due to Seth Ehorn, who provided remarkable service in proofreading, formatting, indexing, and tracking down numerous references with exemplary competence and expediency. Without Seth's efforts, this volume would not have been completed.

INTRODUCTION

Daniel M. Gurtner
Benjamin L. Gladd

Few evangelical scholars today have the skill to publish leading scholarship in both New Testament and Old Testament studies. Professor Beale's career has been marked by some of the best of both, employing the energies of his exegetical rigor in these areas toward fresh and innovative contributions to biblical theology. He is best known for his work on how the two Testaments are related to one another, particularly the use of the Old Testament in the New Testament. Laying the foundation for future projects, his dissertation at Cambridge focused on the use of Daniel in Second Temple Judaism and Revelation. Professor Beale's Revelation commentary, a demonstration of his fastidious exegesis and theological acumen, is hailed as one of the best commentaries ever written on John's Apocalypse. The academy has also lauded his other monographs, *The Temple and the Church's Mission* and *We Become What We Worship*, along with his commentary on 1 Thessalonians. With D. A. Carson, he co-edited the award-winning *Commentary on the New Testament Use of the Old Testament*. Dr. Beale's tireless work has culminated in the recent publication of his biblical-theological *magnum opus, A New Testament Biblical Theology: The Unfolding of the Old Testament in the New* (Baker, 2012).

Perhaps one of Professor Beale's greatest accomplishments lies in the indelible mark he leaves upon his students in the classroom. He not only takes his writing seriously but also his teaching. His students bear witness to his passion and conviction with which he presents the material. Professors rarely spend as much time preparing and intensely laboring over their lecture material. It is well known that he arrives at his office several hours before class to review his lecture notes. With his Hebrew and Greek text open, he meticulously combs over seemingly minute exegetical details. Many of the contributors of this volume can readily attest to the personal sacrifice he makes in discipling his students, as he is far more concerned with training men and women of the church than the academy.

Taking time out of his day to pray with and spiritually encourage a student is not an uncommon occurrence.

In honor of Dr. Beale's extensive contributions to Christ's church and the academy, we would like to present him with this volume as a small token of our appreciation. All of the contributors readily admit their understanding of Scripture has been deeply enriched because of his refreshing insights and detailed exegesis. Paying tribute to Professor Beale is an impressive gathering of his peers and students, touching on subjects as far reaching as his scholarship has itself gone. *From Creation to New Creation* exhibits some of evangelicalism's leading scholarship.

This volume is organized into three discreet sections: Old Testament, the Use of the Old Testament in the New, and Biblical Theology. The Old Testament essays address various exegetical and intertextual issues on the use of the Old Testament in the Old Testament. This field of study has received an increasing amount of attention in recent years and still remains fertile for continued investigation. Complementing the Old Testament essays is a series of essays on the use of the Old Testament in the New Testament. One of Professor Beale's lasting contributions is his interest in the relationship between the Testaments. He contends that the New Testament authors cited the Old Testament contextually and carefully contemplated their application of it. Several essays follow suit, investigating the use of the Old Testament in the New. The remaining essays, like the previous section, interact with the use of the Old Testament in the New, but will tease out the significance of intertextual relationships and construct a biblical theology of a particular theme. These essays on various aspects of biblical theology honor Dr. Beale's passion and interest in biblical theology.

Biographical Sketch

After earning his doctorate in New Testament from Cambridge University, Dr. Beale began his teaching career at Grove City College. Four years later, he moved to Gordon-Conwell Theological Seminary, where he would spend the next sixteen years. During that time, he and a fellow parent founded Covenant Christian School. He was head master of the school for ten years. The school grew to include kindergarten through eighth grade and, eventually, added a high school.

Wheaton College then appointed him the Kenneth T. Wessner Chair of Biblical Studies in 2000. He played a key role in the founding of Wheaton's PhD program. While at Wheaton, many of Dr. Beale's former students started their own ministries and began inviting him to come and teach. He and his wife, Dorinda, traveled throughout the United States and the world, affording him the opportunity to teach and preach. Currently, he teaches at Westminster Theological Seminary as the J. Gresham Machen Professor of New Testament.

Not only is Dr. Beale an accomplished scholar, he has lived a life in service to the local church. Throughout his career he has regularly taught Sunday school and preached in many churches. He currently holds ordination in the Orthodox Presbyterian Church.

Dr. Beale holds a number of prestigious memberships, such as *Studiorum Novi Testamenti Societas* and the Tyndale Fellowship at the Tyndale House at Cambridge University. He also served as the president of the Evangelical Theological Society in 2004.

A complete list of Dr. Beale's publications is provided beginning on p. 275.

ABBREVIATIONS

General Abbreviations

AB	Anchor Bible
ABD	*Anchor Bible Dictionary*. Edited by D. N. Freedman. 6 vols. New York, 1992
ABRL	Anchor Bible Reference Library
ACCSNT	Ancient Christian Commentary on Scripture: New Testament
AGJU	Arbeiten zur Geschichte des antiken Judentums und des Urchristentums
AJEC	Ancient Judaism and Early Christianity
AnBib	Analecta biblica
ANE	Ancient Near East(ern)
ANET	*Ancient Near Eastern Texts Relating to the Old Testament*. Edited by J. B. Pritchard. 3rd ed. Princeton: Princeton University Press, 1969
ANEP	*The Ancient Near East in Pictures Relating to the Old Testament*. Edited by J. B. Pritchard. Princeton: Princeton University Press, 1954
ANF	Ante-Nicene Fathers
AOAT	Alter Orient und Altes Testament
AOTC	Apollos Old Testament Commentary
Aq.	Aquila
ArBib	The Aramaic Bible
ASORDS	American Schools of Oriental Research Dissertation Series
ATD	Das Alte Testament Deutsch
ATANT	Abhandlungen zur Theologie des Alten und Neuen Testaments
BAR	*Biblical Archaeology Review*
BBR	*Bulletin for Biblical Research*
BDAG	Bauer, W., F. W. Danker, W. F. Arndt, and F. W. Gingrich. *Greek-English Lexicon of the New Testament*

	and Other Early Christian Literature. 3rd ed. Chicago: University of Chicago Press, 1999
BDB	Brown, F., S. R. Driver, and C. A. Briggs. *A Hebrew and English Lexicon of the Old Testament*. Oxford: Oxford University Press, 1907
BDF	Blass, F., A. Debrunner, and R. W. Funk. *A Greek Grammar of the New Testament and Other Early Christian Literature*. Chicago: University of Chicago Press, 1961
BDS	Bibal Dissertation Series
BECNT	Baker Exegetical Commentary on the New Testament
BETL	Bibliotheca ephemeridum theologicarum lovaniensium
BHS	*Biblia Hebraica Stuttgartensia*. Edited by K. Ellinger and W. Rudolph. Stuttgart, 1983
BHT	Beiträge zur historischen Theologie
Bib	*Biblica*
Bijdr	*Bijdragen: Tijdschrift voor filosofie en theologie*
BIS	Biblical Interpretation Series
BJS	Brown Judaic Studies
BN	*Biblische Notizen*
BNTC	Black's New Testament Commentaries
BWANT	Beiträge zur Wissenschaft vom Alten und Neuen Testament
BZ	*Biblische Zeitschrift*
BZNW	Beihefte zur Zeitschrift für die neutestamentliche Wissenschaft
ca.	circa
CAD	*The Assyrian Dictionary of the Oriental Institute of the University of Chicago*. Chicago: University of Chicago, 1956–
CBC	Cambridge Bible Commentary
CBET	Contributions to Biblical Exegesis and Theology
CBQ	*Catholic Biblical Quarterly*
cent.	century
ch(s).	chapter(s)
CNTTS	Center for New Testament Textual Studies
CCSA	Corpus Christianorum: Series Apocryphorum
CEB	Common English Bible
d.	died
DNWSI	*Dictionary of the North-West Semitic Inscriptions*. J. Hoftijzer and K. Jongeling. 2 vols. Leiden: Brill, 1995
DSD	*Dead Sea Discoveries*
DSS	*Dead Sea Scrolls*
EBib	Études bibliques

EDSS	*Encyclopedia of the Dead Sea Scrolls.* Edited by Lawrence H. Schiffman and James C. VanderKam. 2 vols. New York: Oxford University Press, 2000
ErIsr	*Eretz-Israel*
esp.	especially
EstBib	*Estudios bíblicos*
ESV	English Standard Version
FAT	Forschungen zum Alten Testament
FB	Forschung zur Bibel
GGBB	Wallace, Daniel B. *Greek Grammar Beyond the Basics: An Exegetical Syntax of the New Testament.* Grand Rapids: Zondervan, 1996
Gk.	Greek
GKC	*Gesenius' Hebrew Grammar.* Edited by E. Kautzsch. Translated by A. E. Cowley. 2d. ed. Oxford: Oxford University Press, 1910
HALOT	Koehler, L., W. Baumgartner, and J. J. Stamm. *The Hebrew and Aramaic Lexicon of the Old Testament.* Translated and edited under the supervision of M. E. J. Richardson. 5 vols. Leiden: Brill, 1994–1999
HB	Hebrew Bible
Heb.	Hebrew
HNT	Handbuch zum Neuen Testament
HNTC	Harper's New Testament Commentaries
HCSB	Holman Christian Standard Bible
HSS	Harvard Semitic Studies
HTKNT	Herders theologischer Kommentar zum Neuen Testament
HUCA	*Hebrew Union College Annual*
ICC	International Critical Commentary
IDB	*The Interpreter's Dictionary of the Bible*
IEJ	*Israel Exploration Journal*
JAAR	*Journal of the American Academy of Religion*
JANES	*Journal of the Ancient Near Eastern Society*
JB	Jerusalem Bible
JBL	*Journal of Biblical Literature*
JETS	*Journal of the Evangelical Theological Society*
JJS	*Journal of Jewish Studies*
JNES	*Journal of Near Eastern Studies*
JR	*Journal of Religion*
JSHJ	*Journal for the Study of the Historical Jesus*
JSNT	*Journal for the Study of the New Testament*
JSNTSup	Journal for the Study of the New Testament: Supplement Series

JSOTSup	Journal for the Study of the Old Testament: Supplement Series
JSS	*Journal of Semitic Studies*
JTS	*Journal of Theological Studies*
KEK	Kritisch-exegetischer Kommentar über das Neue Testament (Meyer-Kommentar)
KJV	King James Version
KNT	Kommentar zum Neuen Testament
LCL	Loeb Classical Library
LD	Lectio divina
lit.	literally
LHB/OTS	Library of Hebrew Bible/Old Testament Studies
LNTS	Library of New Testament Studies
LSJ	Liddell, H. G., R. Scott, H. S. Jones. *A Greek-English Lexicon*. 9th ed. with revised supplement. Oxford: Oxford University Press, 1996
LSTS	Library of Second Temple Studies
LXX	Septuagint
MS(S)	Manuscript(s)
MT	Masoretic Text
n(n).	note(s)
NA^{27}	*Novum Testamentum Graece*, Nestle-Aland, 27th ed.
NAC	New American Commentary
NASB	New American Standard Bible
NCB	New Century Bible
NCBC	New Cambridge Bible Commentary
NEB	New English Bible
Neot	*Neotestamentica*
NET	New English Translation
NETS	New English Translation of the Septuagint
NIBC	New International Biblical Commentary
NICNT	New International Commentary on the New Testament
NICOT	New International Commentary on the Old Testament
NIDOTTE	*New International Dictionary of Old Testament Theology and Exegesis*. Edited by W. A. VanGemeren. 5 vols. Grand Rapids: Zondervan, 1997
NIGTC	New International Greek Testament Commentary
NIV	New International Version
NIVAC	New International Version Application Commentary
NLT	New Living Translation
NovT	*Novum Testamentum*
NovTSup	Novum Testamentum Supplements
NRSV	New Revised Standard Version
NSBT	New Studies in Biblical Theology
NTL	New Testament Library

NTS	New Testament Studies
OEANE	The Oxford Encyclopedia of Archaeology in the Near East. Edited by E. M. Meyers. New York, 1997
OED	Oxford English Dictionary. Oxford: Oxford University Press, 2000–
OG	Old Greek
ÖTK	Ökumenischer Taschenbuch-Kommentar
OTL	Old Testament Library
OTP	Old Testament Pseudepigrapha. Edited by J. H. Charlesworth. 2 vols. New York, 1983
par.	parallels
p(p).	page(s)
PNTC	The Pillar New Testament Commentary
PTMS	Pittsburgh Theological Monograph Series
PTSDSS	Princeton Theological Seminary Dead Sea Scrolls
RB	Revue biblique
RevQ	Revue de Qumran
RGG	Religion in Geschichte und Gegenwart. Edited by K. Galling. 7 vols. 3rd ed. Tübingen, 1957–1965
RNT	Regensburger Neues Testament
RS	Ras Shamra
RSV	Revised Standard Version
SBEC	Studies in Bible and Early Christianity
SBLABib	Society of Biblical Literature Academia Biblica
SBLDS	Society of Biblical Literature Dissertation Series
SBLEJL	Society of Biblical Literature Early Judaism and Its Literature
SBLGNT	Society of Biblical Literature Greek New Testament
SBLMS	Society of Biblical Literature Monograph Series
SBLSymS	Society of Biblical Literature Symposium Series
SBM	Stuttgarter biblische Monographien
SC	Sources chrétiennes. Paris: Cerf, 1943–
Scr	Scripture
SEAug	Studia ephemeridis Augustinianum
SemeiaSt	Semeia Studies
SHCANE	Studies in the History and Culture of the Ancient Near East
SJ	Studia judaica
SJT	Scottish Journal of Theology
SNTSMS	Society for New Testament Studies Monograph Series
SP	Sacra pagina
SRB	Supplementi alla Rivista biblica
SSEJC	Studies in Scripture in Early Judaism and Christianity
STDJ	Studies on the Texts of the Desert of Judah
StPatr	Studia patristica
StPB	Studia post-biblica

SUNT	Studien zur Umwelt des Neuen Testaments
SVTP	Studia in Veteris Testamenti pseudepigraphica
Syr.	Syriac
Sym.	Symmachus
TANZ	Texte und Arbeiten zum neutestamentlichen Zeitalter
TDNT	*Theological Dictionary of the New Testament*. Edited by G. Kittel and G. Friedrich. Translated by G. W. Bromiley. 10 vols. Grand Rapids: Eerdmans, 1964–1976
Tg.	Targum
Theod.	Theodotion
TJ	*Trinity Journal*
TLZ	*Theologische Literaturzeitung*
TNIV	Today's New International Version
TNTC	Tyndale New Testament Commentaries
TOTC	Tyndale Old Testament Commentaries
TPINTC	TPI New Testament Commentaries
TSAJ	Texte und Studien zum antiken Judentum
TWOT	*Theological Wordbook of the Old Testament*. Edited by R. L. Harris, G. L. Archer Jr. 2 vols. Chicago: Moody Press, 1980
TynBul	*Tyndale Bulletin*
TZ	*Theologische Zeitschrift*
UBS⁴	*The Greek New Testament*, United Bible Societies, 4th ed.
v(v).	verse(s)
VC	*Vigiliae christianae*
Vg.	Vulgate
VT	*Vetus Testamentum*
VTSup	Supplements to Vetus Testamentum
WAC	Wise, Michael, Martin Abegg Jr., and Edward Cook. *The Dead Sea Scrolls: A New Translation*. New York: HarperCollins, 2005
WBC	Word Biblical Commentary
WMANT	Wissenschaftliche Monographien zum Alten und Neuen Testament
WTJ	*Westminster Theological Journal*
WUNT	Wissenschaftliche Untersuchungen zum Neuen Testament
ZAW	*Zeitschrift für die alttestamentliche Wissenschaft*
ZECNT	Zondervan Exegetical Commentary on the New Testament
ZIBBC	*Zondervan Illustrated Bible Backgrounds Commentary*. Edited by John H. Walton. 5 vols. Grand Rapids: Zondervan, 2009
ZNW	*Zeitschrift für die neutestamentliche Wissenschaft und die Kunde der älteren Kirche*
ZTK	*Zeitschrift für Theologie und Kirche*

Textual Abbreviations

Old Testament

Gn	Genesis
Ex	Exodus
Lv	Leviticus
Nm	Numbers
Dt	Deuteronomy
Jo	Joshua
Jgs	Judges
Ru	Ruth
1–2 Sm	1–2 Samuel
1–2 Kgs	1–2 Kings
1–2 Chr	1–2 Chronicles
Ezr	Ezra
Neh	Nehemiah
Est	Esther
Jb	Job
Ps(s)	Psalm(s)
Prv	Proverbs
Eccl	Ecclesiastes
Sg	Song of Songs
Is	Isaiah
Jer	Jeremiah
Lam	Lamentations
Ez	Ezekiel
Dn	Daniel
Hos	Hosea
Jl	Joel
Am	Amos
Ob	Obadiah
Jon	Jonah
Mi	Micah
Na	Nahum
Hb	Habakkuk
Zep	Zephaniah
Hg	Haggai
Zec	Zechariah
Mal	Malachi

New Testament

Mt	Matthew
Mk	Mark
Lk	Luke
Jn	John
Acts	Acts
Rom	Romans

1–2 Cor	1–2 Corinthians
Gal	Galatians
Eph	Ephesians
Phil	Philippians
Col	Colossians
1–2 Thes	1–2 Thessalonians
1–2 Tm	1–2 Timothy
Ti	Titus
Phlm	Philemon
Heb	Hebrews
Jas	James
1–2 Pt	1–2 Peter
1–3 Jn	1–3 John
Jude	Jude
Rv	Revelation

Apocrypha and Septuagint

Add Esth	Additions to Esther
Ep Jer	Epistle of Jeremiah
1–4 Esd	1–4 Esdras
Jdt	Judith
1–2 Mc	1–2 Maccabees
Pr Man	Prayer of Manasseh
Sir	Sirach/Ecclesiasticus
Tb	Tobit
Wis	Wisdom of Solomon

Pseudepigrapha

Apoc. Ab.	*Apocalypse of Abraham*
2 Bar.	*2 Baruch*
1–3 En.	*1–3 Enoch*
4 Esd.	*4 Esdras*
4 Ezra	*4 Ezra*
Jub.	*Jubilees*
L.A.B.	*liber antiquitatum biblicarum (Pseudo-Philo)*
L.A.E.	*Life of Adam and Eve*
Liv. Pro.	*Lives of the Prophets*
Mart. Ascen. Isa.	*Martyrdom and Ascension of Isaiah*
Pss. Sol.	*Psalms of Solomon*
Sib. Or.	*Sibylline Oracles*
T. Benj.	*Testament of Benjamin*
T. Jud.	*Testament of Judah*
T. Levi	*Testament of Levi*
T. Naph.	*Testament of Naphtali*
T. Zeb.	*Testament of Zebulun*

Philo

Abr.	*De Abrahamo*

Agr.	*De agricultura*
Conf.	*De confusione linguarum*
Congr.	*De congressu eruditionis gratia*
Mut.	*De mutatione nominum*
Opif.	*De opificio mundi*
Virt.	*De virtutibus*

Josephus

A.J.	*Antiquitates judaicae*
B.J.	*Bellum judaicum*
C. Ap.	*Contra Apionem*
Vita	*Vita*

Mishnah, Talmud, Targums, and Related Rabbinic Literature

Abod. Zar.	*'Abodah Zarah*
'Abot R. Nat.	*Abot of Rabbi Nathan*
b. B. Meṣ.	*Baba Meṣiʻa*
b. Ber.	*Berakot*
b. Ketub.	*Ketubbot*
b. Mak.	*Makkot*
b. Meg.	*Megillah*
b. Šabb.	*Šabbat*
b. Sanh.	*Sanhedrin*
b. Soṭah	*Soṭah*
b. Yoma	*Yoma*
Cant. Rab.	*Canticles Rabbah*
m. Hor.	*Horayot*
m. Meg.	*Megillah*
m. Qidd.	*Qiddušin*
m. Soṭah	*Soṭah*
Mek.	*Mekilta*
Midr. Exod.	*Midrash Exodus*
Midr. Lam.	*Midrash Lamentations*
Midr. Lev.	*Midrash Leviticus*
Midr. Tanḥ.	*Midrash Tanḥuma*
Pesiq. Rab.	*Pesiqta Rabbati*
Pesiq. Rab Kah.	*Pesiqta de Rab Kahana*
Sipre Num.	*Sipre Numbers*
Tg. Ez	*Targum Ezekiel*
Tg. Gn	*Targum Genesis*
Tg. Is	*Targum Isaiah*
Tg. Jl	*Targum Joel*
Tg. Lv	*Targum Leviticus*
Tg. Neof.	*Targum Neofiti*
Tg. Onq.	*Targum Onqelos*
Tg. Ps.-J.	*Targum Pseudo-Jonathan*

Dead Sea Scrolls
1QIsaᵃ	*Isaiahᵃ*
1QIsaᵇ	*Isaiahᵇ*
1QpHab	*Pesher Habakkuk*
1QapGen (= 1Q20)	*Genesis Apocryphon*
1QS	*Rule of the Community*
1QM	*War Scroll*
1QHᵃ	*Thanksgiving Hymns*
4Q174 (= 4QFlor)	*Florilegium*
4Q181 (= 4QAgesCreat)	*Ages of Creation*
4Q256 (= 4QSᵇ)	*Rule of the Community*
4Q258 (= 4QSᵈ)	*Rule of the Community*
4Q259 (= 4QSᵉ)	*Rule of the Community*
4Q379 (= 4QPssJoshᵇ)	*Psalms of Joshuaᵇ*
4Q385ᵃ (= 4QpsMoses)	*pseudo-Mosesᵃ*
4Q387 (= 4QpsEzek)	*pseudo-Ezekielᵇ*
4Q389 (= 4QpsMoses)	*pseudo-Mosesᵈ*
4Q390 (= 4QpsMoses)	*pseudo-Mosesᵉ*
4Q521 (= 4QMessAp)	*Messianic Apocalypse*
6QD	see CD
11Q13 (= 11QMelch)	*Melchizedek*
CD	*Cairo Genizahᵃ*

Apostolic Fathers
Barn.	*Barnabas*
1–2 Clem.	*1–2 Clement*

Greek and Latin Sources
Aristotle (contested authorship)

Eth. nic.	*Ethica nicomachea*
Mag. mor.	*Magna moralia*

Augustine

Enarrat. Ps.	*Ennarationes in Psalmos*
Faust.	*Contra Faustom Manichaeum*

Eusebius

Hist. eccl.	*Historia ecclesiastica*

Hippolytus

Antichr.	*De antichristo*

Irenaeus

Haer.	*Adversus haereses*

Martial

Epigr.	*Epigrammata*

Origen

Adnot. Exod.	*Adnotationes in Exodum*

Quintilian

Inst.	*Institutio oratoria*

Part 1

Old Testament

CHAPTER 1

EDEN: A TEMPLE?
A REASSESSMENT OF THE
BIBLICAL EVIDENCE

Daniel I. Block

Introduction

The contributors to this volume are deeply indebted to our friend and colleague Greg Beale for his significant contributions to the discipline of biblical theology.[1] Against the grain of increasing specialization and the barriers that exist between HB and NT scholarship, Greg has forced us to reflect deeply on the intertextual connections between the Testaments and the theological themes that bind the HB inextricably to the NT. It is a great privilege to participate in the conversation in his honor. Although my approach to the chosen subject differs somewhat from that of the honoree, I offer this essay as an expression of gratitude for his friendship and as a small contribution to a lively debate on a vital aspect of biblical theology. While limitations of space preclude full discussion of all the issues raised, I acknowledge at the outset that in presenting this response I am swimming against an overwhelming current of scholarly opinion, and even against positions I once held. However, regarding the relationship between the opening chapters of Genesis and Israel's temple traditions, it may be time to contemplate a slight course correction.[2] My musings in this essay are all in soft lead pencil, subject to revision, and they are offered here as part of an ongoing friendly dialogue.

Beale's work on the temple is fundamentally sound. First, it seems clear that Israel's sanctuaries were designed, constructed, and decorated

---

[1] I am indebted to my colleagues John Walton and Christopher Ansberry and to my assistants Carmen Imes and Austin Surls, who read earlier drafts of this essay and offered many insightful comments and suggestions for its improvement.

[2] Unless the context demands specificity, I use the term "temple" for Israel's central sanctuary, without distinguishing between the tabernacle—a portable temple—and the temple(s) in Jerusalem.

as microcosms of YHWH's heavenly temple. Whether or not Moses was able to gaze into the heavenly throne room on Mount Sinai, the tabernacle represented a replica תַּבְנִית; (*taḇnît*) built according to a divinely revealed plan (Ex 25:9, 40). While the temple in Jerusalem had the same basic structure as the tabernacle, it seems the plan revealed to David (1 Chr 28:9–19) also envisioned a replica of the heavenly temple,[3] complete with a throne room (represented by the Holy of Holies) and a throne (represented by the ark of the covenant).[4] Second, while functioning as replicas of YHWH's heavenly residence, both tabernacle and temple were also constructed as miniature Edens.[5] Decorated with images of cherubim and palm trees, lit by the menorah—a symbol of the tree of life[6]—and served by a priest decked out in royal colors and precious stones, these motifs hark back to the garden where God first put human beings.[7] But does this mean that the author of Gn 1–3 perceived either the cosmos or Eden as a temple? I used to think so,[8] but I now wonder if the case is as convincing

---

[3] The author of Hebrews suggests accordingly that the sacrificial actions, especially the sin and guilt offerings, represented replica actions of the true heavenly sacrifice of Jesus Christ.

[4] Cf. 1 Sm 4:4; 2 Sm 6:2; 2 Kgs 19:15; 1 Chr 13:6; Is 37:16; Pss 80:2[1]; 99:1. See further Daniel I. Block, *The Book of Ezekiel Chapters 25–48* (NICOT; Grand Rapids: Eerdmans, 1998), 580–81.

[5] See esp. Michael Fishbane, "The 'Eden' Motif/The Landscape of Spiritual Renewal," in *Biblical Text and Texture: A Literary Reading of Selected Texts* (Oxford: Oneworld, 1998), 111–20; T. Stordalen, *Echoes of Eden: Genesis 2–3 Symbolism and the Eden Garden in Biblical Hebrew Literature* (Contributions to Biblical Exegesis and Theology 25; Leuven: Peeters, 2000), 307–12; Dexter E. Callender Jr., *Adam in Myth and History: Ancient Israelite Perspectives on the Primal Human* (HSS 48; Winona Lake, IN: Eisenbrauns, 2000), 50–54.

[6] See Carol L. Meyers, *The Tabernacle Menorah: A Synthetic Study of a Symbol from the Biblical Cult* (ASORDS 2; Missoula, MT: Scholars Press, 1976), 180.

[7] For additional links, see G. K. Beale, *A New Testament Biblical Theology: The Unfolding of the Old Testament in the New* (Grand Rapids: Baker, 2011), 617–22; G. K. Beale, *Temple and the Church's Mission: A Biblical Theology of the Dwelling Place of God* (NSBT 17; Downers Grove, IL: InterVarsity Press, 2004), 66–75; Gordon J. Wenham, "Sanctuary Symbolism in the Garden of Eden Story," in *I Studied Inscriptions before the Flood* (ed. R. S. Hess and D. T. Tsumura; Sources for Biblical and Theological Study 4; Winona Lake, IN: Eisenbrauns, 1994), 399–404; Elizabeth Bloch-Smith, "Solomon's Temple: The Politics of Ritual Space," in *Sacred Time, Sacred Space: Archaeology and the Religion of Israel* (ed. B. M. Gittlen; Winona Lake, IN: Eisenbrauns, 2002), 83–94 (88), who characterizes the temple in Jerusalem as a "virtual garden of Eden"; Elizabeth Bloch-Smith, "Who Is the King of Glory? Solomon's Temple and Its Symbolism," in *Scripture and Other Artifacts* (ed. M. Coogan, J. C. Exum, and L. E. Stager; Louisville: Westminster John Knox, 1994), 18–31; Fishbane, "The 'Eden' Motif," 111–20.

[8] The literature on creation as a cosmic temple and Eden as the original earthly temple is vast and growing. See esp. Beale, *New Testament Biblical Theology*, 614–48; Beale, *Temple*, 29–122; G. K. Beale, "Eden, the Temple, and the Church's Mission in the New Creation," *JETS* 48 (2005): 5–31; Fishbane, "The 'Eden' Motif," 111–20; Jon D. Levenson, "The Temple and the World," *JR* 64 (1984): 275–98;

as I once thought. Questions concerning the equation arise from both the text of Gn 1–3 and the conceptual world represented by temples.

The Textual Evidence of Genesis 1–3

Genesis 1–3 introduces readers to a world that could be considered sacred space by virtue of its divine origin but that the narrator fails (or refuses) explicitly to place in that category, either by using special priestly vocabulary or by means of a conceptual framework. Apparently the functioning of the cosmos was to be secured by human vassals deputized by the Creator. If anything, this is a royal world, with the man being cast as a king, invested with the status of "image of God" (בְּצֶלֶם אֱלֹהִים; *bĕṣelem ʾĕlōhîm*, Gn 1:26–27), and charged to subdue (כבש; *kbš*) it and exercise dominion (רדה; *rdh*) over it.[9] This charge suggests that in the "super good" (טוֹב מְאֹד; *ṭôḇ mĕʾōḏ*, v. 31) world that God had made, creatures' freedom to resist divine authority needed to be checked. As the image of God, הָאָדָם (*hāʾāḏām*) did not have absolute or independent power; he was to govern as the viceroy and regent of the One in whose image he was created (cf. Ps 8).

The Eden Narrative (Gn 2:4b–3:24)

Despite critical scholars' general attribution of Gn 1:1–2:4a to "P," the only priestly element is the phrase וַיְקַדֵּשׁ אֹתוֹ (*wayĕqaddēš ʾōṯô*), "and he sanctified it." However, rather than applying the expression to created space, the object is time, the seventh day.[10] That YHWH should later expressly isolate the seventh day as a day of rest for humans is significant for

---

John M. Lundquist, "What Is a Temple? A Preliminary Typology," in *The Quest for the Kingdom of God: Studies in Honor of George E. Mendenhall* (ed. A. B. Huffmon, F. A. Spina, and A. R. W. Green; Winona Lake, IN: Eisenbrauns, 1983), 205–20; Stordalen, *Echoes of Eden*, esp. 307–12; Wenham, "Sanctuary Symbolism," 399–404. While most of these studies draw on extrabiblical parallels, these are highlighted in numerous recent works, most notably Manfried Dietrich, "Das biblische Paradies und der babylonische Tempelgarten: Überlegungen zur Lage des Gartens Eden," in *Das biblische Weltbild und seine altorientalischen Kontexte* (ed. B. Janowski and B. Ego; FAT 32; Tübingen: Mohr Siebeck, 2004), 281–323; Bernd Janowski, "Der Himmel auf Erden: Zur kosmologischen Bedeutung des Tempels in der Umwelt Israels," in *Das biblische Weltbild und seine altorientalischen Kontexte* (ed. B. Janowski and B. Ego; FAT 32; Tübingen: Mohr Siebeck, 2004), 229–60; John H. Walton, *Genesis 1 as Ancient Cosmology* (Winona Lake, IN: Eisenbrauns, 2011); John H. Walton, *Ancient Near Eastern Thought and the Old Testament: Introducing the Conceptual World of the Hebrew Bible* (Grand Rapids: Baker, 2006), 113–34.
[9] Even the sun, moon, and stars are cast in royal rather than priestly roles: note the verb משל (*mšl*), "to rule, govern," in Gn 1:18.
[10] On other supposedly priestly features, see below.

Israel's practice of the seventh-day Sabbath, but it says nothing about a temple metaphor underlying Gn 1.[11] While the Israelites celebrated many liturgical sabbaths (the annual festivals, new moon festivals, and so on), within the Pentateuch the seventh-day Sabbath was a domestic rather than cultic observance. Not only did Israel's observance of this Sabbath antedate the construction of the tabernacle and the establishment of its ritual (Ex 16:22–30), but the Sabbath ordinance was also embedded in the ten foundational principles of covenant righteousness, which are silent on temple and cult (Ex 20:8–11; Dt 5:12–15).[12] The difficulty of reconstructing from the Pentateuch and from the rest of the HB the cultic activities that people might have practiced on the seventh-day Sabbath makes an association with the temple even more unlikely.

Although Gn 2–3 is commonly attributed to the Yahwist rather than the Priestly source, ironically scholars have recognized more links to Israel's sanctuary traditions here than in Gn 1:[13] (1) the verb הִתְהַלֵּךְ (hiṯhallēḵ) (Gn 3:8; cf. Lv 26:12; Dt 23:15[14]; 2 Sm 7:6–7); (2) the כְּרֻבִים (kěruḇîm) guarding entrance to the garden (Gn 3:24; cf. Ex 25:18–22; 26:31; 1 Kgs 6:23–28); (3) the tree of life (Gn 2:9; cf. the menorah, a stylized tree of life, Ex 25:31–36); (4) YHWH's charge to Adam "to serve and to keep" (לְעָבְדָהּ וּלְשָׁמְרָהּ; lěʿoḇěḏāh ûlěšoměrāh) the garden (Gn 2:15; cf. Nm 3:7–8; 8:26; 18:5–6); (5) the garments (כָּתְנוֹת; koṯnōṯ) of skin provided for Adam and Eve (Gn 3:21; cf. Ex 28:40; 29:8; 40:14; Lv 8:13); (6) the river flowing from Eden to water the garden (Gn 2:10–14; cf. Ps 46:5[4]; Ez 47); (7) the reference to gold (Gn 2:12; cf. Ex 25:11, 17, 24, 29, 36); (8) the precious stones, בְּדֹלַח (běḏōlaḥ, Gn 2:12)[14] and שֹׁהַם (šōham, Gn 2:12; cf. Ex 25:7; 28:9–12, 20; 1 Chr 29:2), decorating tabernacle and temple and the high priestly vestments; (9) the lush arboreal imagery (Gn 2:9, 16–17);[15] (10) the garden as a mountain;[16] (11) the tree of the knowledge of good and evil, which was "good for food . . . a delight to the eyes . . . to be desired to make one wise" (Gn 2:9; 3:6; cf. Ps 19:8–9; cf. also Ex 25:16; Dt 31:26, referring to the law kept inside the Holy of Holies), and the illicit eating of which brought death (Gn 2:16–17; 3:3; cf. Nm 4:20; 2 Sm 6:7, touching

---

[11] Contra Walton, *Genesis 1 as Ancient Cosmology*, 180.

[12] See Daniel I. Block, "Reading the Decalogue Left to Right: The Ten Principles of Covenant Relationship in the Hebrew Bible," in *How I Love Your Torah, O Lord! Studies in the Book of Deuteronomy* (Eugene, OR: Cascade, 2011), 21–55.

[13] See Beale, *Temple*, 66–76.

[14] Cf. Nm 11:7, which compares the manna with בְּדֹלַח (běḏōlaḥ), an omer of which was stored in the ark of the covenant inside the Holy of Holies (Ex 16:32–33; Heb 9:4).

[15] Cf. 1 Kgs 6:18, 29, 32; 7:18–26, 42, 49, referring to palms, gourds, open flowers, pomegranates, and lilies that decorated the temple.

[16] Though not explicitly declared, that the rivers flowed downward in four directions suggests an elevated mountain (cf. Ez 28:14, 16; also Ex 15:17; Ez 40:2; and many references to Mount Zion).

the ark);[17] (12) the eastern entrance to the garden (Gn 3:24; cf. Ez 40:6); (13) the tripartite structure of the garden (Gn 2:10): Eden = the Holy of Holies; the garden = the holy place; the region outside the garden = the outer court.[18]

While admitting that Gn 2 does not develop the notion that Eden is the Holy of Holies of the cosmic temple or a place for God's presence, for some this impressive list of links suggests the author and the original audience assumed this notion.[19] But this conclusion seems unwarranted; every supposed link is either illusory or capable of a different interpretation. I shall consider the links in turn, beginning with the Eden narrative (Gn 2:4b–3:24) and then considering the first creation account (1:1–2:4a).

The use of the verb הִתְהַלֵּךְ *(hithallēk) (Gn 3:8).* None of the occurrences of this *hitpaʿel* form cited above speaks particularly of YHWH's residence in the sanctuary.[20] In Lv 26:11–12 YHWH promises to walk about among his people, to be their God, and to claim Israel as his people. The suffixed form, מִשְׁכָּנִי *(miškānî)*, may refer to the tabernacle elsewhere (Lv 15:31), but here "and I will grant my dwelling in your midst" וְנָתַתִּי מִשְׁכָּנִי בְּתוֹכְכֶם; *wěnātattî miškānî bětôkěkem)* functions periphrastically for "and I will dwell among you" (וְנָתַתִּי בְּתוֹכְכֶם; *wěnātattî bětôkěkem)* and speaks of YHWH's presence among his people.[21] Even if the tabernacle were in view, the point is not that it is a place in which YHWH may walk about but that the structure symbolized his presence with the people (cf. Ex 25:8). Deuteronomy 23:15[14] is not concerned about the purity of the tabernacle so YHWH may freely walk about in it but the sanctity of the Israelite camp. The presence of YHWH, the divine Commander-in-Chief, among the troops requires scrupulous maintenance of ritual purity. A superficial reading of 2 Sm 7:6 might suggest that in the past the tabernacle provided YHWH with a place to walk about and that he had not desired a permanent house as his home. However, 2 Sm 7:7 declares that the real issue is not a building in which he walks about but the means by which he relates to his people. Until now the tabernacle had symbolized his freedom to accompany Israel on their journeys; he had never asked for a permanent home.

---

[17] Many of these features are cited by Wenham, "Sanctuary Symbolism," 400–403.

[18] Beale adds numbers 10–12 (*Temple*, 66–74; *New Testament Biblical Theology*, 617–21). Levenson ("The Temple and the World," 275) has argued rightly that these paradisiacal features do not merely represent "the invasion of Canaanite culture right into the center of Israel's life and worship" but derive from Israel's own sacred traditions.

[19] Thus Walton, *Genesis 1 as Ancient Cosmology*, 186 n. 182; Walton, *Ancient Near Eastern Thought*, 125.

[20] A misinterpretation found in Wenham, "Sanctuary Symbolism," and repeated by Stordalen, *Echoes of Eden*, 458.

[21] For the use of the verb שׁכן *(škn)* with YHWH as the subject + בְּתוֹךְ *(bětôk)*, see Ex 29:45; 1 Kgs 13:2; Ez 43:9; Zec 2:11; cf. Rv 21:3.

If הִתְהַלֵּךְ (hithallēk) in Gn 3:8 does not allude to YHWH's activity within the sanctuary, to what does it refer? Based on the use of the *hitpaʻel* form elsewhere, three primary possibilities emerge. First, the expression may speak of random back-and-forth movement, like flashes of lightning (Ps 77:18[17]), though this sense seems unlikely. Second, it may speak of walking back and forth as claimant to space. In Gn 13:17 YHWH invites Abraham to walk about through the length and breadth of the land of Canaan, in effect, staking his claim to it.[22] Zechariah 6:7 uses the *hitpaʻel* of the four horses, who "patrol" the earth as agents of YHWH's sovereign rule. Third, the form may speak of free and friendly intercourse with those with and before whom one walks (Gn 24:40; 1 Sm 25:15). Genesis 3:8 reflects both YHWH's authority over the garden and his relationship with its inhabitants.[23] This applies particularly to its human inhabitants, to whom he calls out, "Adam, where are you?" However, having sinned, Adam and Eve hid from their friend and divine Suzerain; the confident relationship had been destroyed. If later texts speak of YHWH walking among his people, this is the reward for covenantal fidelity (Lv 26:11–12), which is a prerequisite to a return to Edenic circumstances.

The כְּרֻבִים *(kĕrubîm) guarding entrance to the tree of life (Gn 3:24).* The term כְּרֻבִים (kĕrubîm) occurs ninety-one times in the HB. Outside this context and Ez 28, which reflects on this text, the expression is always associated with Israel's sanctuary.[24] The Hebrew word appears to be related etymologically to Akkadian *kāribu/kuribu* (from *karābu*, "to bless, to pray"), which refers to a protective genus represented iconographically by sphinx-like composite figures, often human-headed bulls or lions with eagles' wings. Although often associated with temples,[25] these sculpted figures were not restricted to sacred space. Since they frequently appear supporting human thrones[26] and guarding royal palaces

---

[22] According to Donald J. Wiseman ("Abraham Reassessed," in *Essays on the Patriarchal Narratives* [ed. A. R. Millard and D. J. Wiseman; Leicester: Inter-Varsity Press, 1980], 155 n. 31), הִתְהַלֵּךְ (hithallēk) "denotes action according to the divine law expressed in judicial processes. Cf. 1 Sm 12:2; 25:15 and, referring to land tenure, Jo 18:4, 8; Jgs 21:24."

[23] See further below.

[24] Referring to sculptured images above the ark of the covenant (Ex 25:18–20; 37:7–9; Nm 7:89; 1 Chr 28:18), inside the Holy of Holies (1 Kgs 6:23–28, 8:6–7; 2 Chr 3:10–13), and beneath the massive sea (1 Kgs 7:29, 36); or decorations on the curtains of the tabernacle (Ex 26:1, 31; 36:8, 35; cf. 2 Chr 3:14, the veil of the temple) or the walls of the temple (1 Kgs 6:29, 32, 35; 2 Chr 3:7; Ez 41:18, 20, 25).

[25] According to Victor Avigdor Hurowitz, "YHWH's Exalted House—Aspects of the Design and Symbolism of Solomon's Temple," in *Temple and Worship in Biblical Israel* (ed. John Day; LHB/OTS 422; New York: T&T Clark, 2007), 87, "these cherubs were the private honor guard of the Temple's divine resident."

[26] E.g., the twelfth cent. B.C. cherub throne on the Megiddo Ivory; the sarcophagus carving of King Hiram of Byblos.

and gardens,[27] the presence of כְּרֻבִים (kĕrûḇîm) in Gn 3:24 and Ez 28 does not establish the garden as a sanctuary.

Ezekiel 28:11–19 combines motifs from several different sources. Admittedly, Eden is characterized as הַר קֹדֶשׁ אֱלֹהִים (har qōḏeš ʾĕlōhîm), "the holy mountain of God," and the pectoral decorated with gemstones recalls the Israelite high priest's breastpiece. However, several factors argue against a primarily priestly interpretation. First, the determinative title for this figure is מֶלֶךְ (melek), "king" (28:12), and when he is identified otherwise, he is a כְּרוּב (kĕrûḇ), whose role is fundamentally different from that of the כְּרֻבִים (kĕrûḇîm) in Gn 3:24.[28] Rather than guarding the entrance to Eden, in a creative adaptation of Gn 2–3, he is the principal human figure inside the garden. Second, this figure is renowned not for his cultic role but for his wisdom, which the HB never associates with priests but overtly links with kingship.[29] Third, although the LXX obviously connects him with the high priest in Jerusalem, the MT seems to have weakened the association deliberately by reducing the number of gemstones to nine and presenting them in an order that differs significantly from Ex 28:17–20 and 39:10–13.[30] While ancient heads of state often combined royal and priestly functions, this person is cast primarily as a royal figure; he is characterized as the signet of perfection (חוֹתֵם תָּכְנִית, ḥôṯēm toḵnîṯ), endowed with wisdom, perfect in beauty, and placed in the garden of God, apparently to govern it as God's vice-regent. This figure has been specially created and anointed;[31] YHWH dressed him with the symbols of office (the multigemmed pectoral, v. 13),[32] placed him in the garden to guard it,[33] and authorized him to "walk back and forth (הִתְהַלָּכְתָּ; hiṯhallāḵĕtā) among stones of fire" (v. 14) as YHWH had walked in the garden (Gn 3:8).

---

[27] E.g., the massive lamassus in front of Assyrian palaces: Ashurbanipal's human-headed winged lions in the Metropolitan Museum of Art and Sargon II's human-headed winged bulls in the British Museum.

[28] LXX's μετὰ τοῦ χερουβ ἔθηκά σε (meta tou cheroub etheka se), "With the cherub I placed you," drops מִמְשַׁח הַסּוֹכֵךְ (mimšaḥ hassôḵēḵ) and distinguishes this figure from the cherub, apparently reading MT's אַתְּ־כְּרוּב (ʾat-kĕrûḇ), "you are a cherub," as אֶת־כְּרוּב (ʾet-kĕrûḇ).

[29] See further below.

[30] Similarly, Moshe Greenberg, *Ezekiel 21–37: A New Translation with Introduction and Commentary* (AB 22; New York: Doubleday, 1997), 582, and Bernard Gosse, "Ézéchiel 28,11–19 et les détournements de malédictions," *BN* 44 (1988): 32.

[31] MT מִמְשַׁח (mimšaḥ), from משׁח (mšḥ), "to anoint." While the textual evidence is admittedly weak, some follow Vg.'s *extentus*, "extended," assuming משׁח II, "to stretch out, measure," hence "colossal." See Stordalen, *Echoes of Eden*, 342; Greenberg, *Ezekiel 21–37*, 583–84. Alternatively, the reference could be to "outstretched [wings]."

[32] In the iconography of Egypt and Mesopotamia, pectorals are more often associated with royalty than with priests.

[33] On this interpretation of הַסּוֹכֵךְ (hassôḵēḵ), see Block, *Ezekiel Chapters 25–48*, 100, 113.

Like Abraham, who was charged to "walk before" (הִתְהַלֵּךְ לְפָנַי; *hithallēk lĕpānay*) YHWH and be blameless (תָּמִים; *ṯāmîm*, Gn 17:1), so this כְּרוּב (*kĕrûḇ*) was blameless (תָּמִים; *ṯāmîm*) when he was installed as the guardian of the garden. The response of the כְּרוּב (*kĕrûḇ*) to his commission reinforces this royal interpretation: like many kings, he amassed great wealth, became autocratic and violent in his rule, was arrogant and corrupt in his administration, and profaned the sanctuaries within the garden.[34] His demise was not caused by failure to perform priestly duties but by his failure as YHWH's vice-regent and guardian of the garden.[35]

The tree of life (Gn 2:9). Although the tree of life in the garden probably inspired the shape of the menorah in the tabernacle (Ex 25:31–36), the context determines its function. The tree was situated in the midst of all sorts of beautiful fruit-bearing trees and juxtaposed with the tree of the knowledge of good and evil. Whereas outside Israel sacred rituals often involved caring for and feeding the gods, this tree existed for the benefit of human beings and symbolized the divine will for them. Despite the absence of a word for "covenant," Gn 2–3 seems to assume a suzerain-vassal covenantal relationship between YHWH and humankind. In an obviously preliterate world the two trees represented respectively the covenant blessings and curses (cf. Lv 26; Dt 28). Unlike the cosmic tree in extrabiblical iconography and mythology, apart from this symbolic significance the tree of life seems not to have served as the *axis mundi*, linking heaven and earth.

YHWH's charge to Adam "to serve and to keep" the garden (Gn 2:15). Many scholars have argued that the combination of the verbs עבד (*ʿbd*), "to serve," and שמר (*šmr*), "to keep, guard," in association with the tabernacle[36] suggests that the role of human beings in the garden was analogous to that of Levites, in which case the garden would be a sanctuary. Just as priests and Levites served and guarded sacred space, so the man was charged to serve and guard the garden. However, the use of the verbs in Gn 2:15 seems to point in a different direction. Indeed, many transla-

---

[34] The plural form suggests these sanctuaries are distinct from the garden itself.

[35] Ezekiel's association of a cherubic figure with Tyre is natural. Not only did Tyrian-style cherubs decorate Solomon's temple (1 Kgs 6:23–36), but also they figure prominently in ancient Phoenician ivories, many of which were richly decorated with gemstones. Note especially the carving of a king-cherub, whose face appears to be the portrait of the king and under whose feet are seen alternating patterns of stylized tulip flower gardens and mountains in M. E. L. Mallowan, *Nimrud and Its Remains* (London: Collins, 1966), vol. 2, figs. 504; 506, 538; R. D. Barnett, *Ancient Ivories in the Middle East and Adjacent Countries* (Qedem 14; Jerusalem: Institute of Archaeology, 1982), fig. 51. For discussion, see R. D. Barnett, "Ezekiel and Tyre," *ErIsr* 9 (1969): 9.

[36] Nm 3:7–8; 8:26; 18:5–6. See Wenham, *Genesis 1–15* (WBC 1; Waco, TX: Word, 1987), 67; Beale, *Temple*, 66–70; John H. Walton, *Genesis* (NIVAC; Grand Rapids: Zondervan, 2001), 192–93.

tions render עבד (*ʿbd*) as "till" or "cultivate," which would be nonsensical in the tabernacle context.[37] But a garden (גַּן; *gan*) is more than soil; this one consists of vegetation of all kinds (2:9), rivers (2:10–14), precious metals and gemstones (2:12), and all kinds of creatures of land and sky (2:19–20). Strictly speaking, the verb "to serve" assumes the subordination of the subject of the verb to its object.[38] Indeed, both verbs, "to serve" and "to keep, guard," demand that subjects expend their efforts in the interests of the object.[39] While the garden satisfied human aesthetic and utilitarian interests, the man was not placed in it merely to indulge himself with its resources. The purpose clause of v. 15 reverses the roles; he was placed in the garden to serve its interests and to guard it, presumably from inside and outside threats.

The text does not identify those threats. The earlier mandate to subdue and rule the earth (1:28) might suggest that the world outside the garden was "very good" (1:31), but it did not exhibit the *shalom* that characterized life within the garden.[40] It seems the man's function was to protect the garden from the encroachment of violence outside. However, Gn 3 suggests the greatest threats were not outside but inside the garden, in the forms of a serpent and the first human pair. While the feminine suffixes on לְעָבְדָהּ וּלְשָׁמְרָהּ (*lĕʿobdāh ûlĕšāmrāh*) are problematic for any interpretation, they seem to relate to the nearest antecedent, גַּן־עֵדֶן (*gan-ʿēden*), "the garden of Eden," which as a place is conceptually feminine.[41] The reference to guarding in 3:24 does not alter the situation, since the object to be guarded is access (דֶּרֶךְ; *derek*) to the tree of life. Lacking other clear signals it is inappropriate to read back into this collocation cultic

---

[37] This may be appropriate when its object is הָאֲדָמָה (*hāʾădāmā*), "the ground": Gn 2:5; 3:23; 4:2, 12; 2 Sm 9:10; Zec 13:5; Prv 12:11; 28:19. Cf. Tryggve N. D. Mettinger, *The Eden Narrative: A Literary and Religio-historical Study of Genesis 2–3* (Winona Lake, IN: Eisenbrauns, 2007), 13. But this use of עבד (*ʿbd*) is curious and may imply that humans work the soil for the sake of the soil. The closest analogue to the present construction occurs in Dt 28:39, where כֶּרֶם (*kerem*), "vineyard," is the object of this verb.

[38] Similarly, Terence E. Fretheim, *God and World in the Old Testament: A Relational Theology of Creation* (Nashville: Abingdon, 2005), 53.

[39] Rightly recognized by Steven Bouma-Prediger, *For the Beauty of the Earth: A Christian Vision for Creation Care* (Grand Rapids: Baker, 2001), 74, 154.

[40] Christopher J. H. Wright, *Old Testament Ethics for the People of God* (Downers Grove, IL: InterVarsity Press, 2004), 130–31, suggests the world outside was characterized by predation and death.

[41] While גַּן (*gan*) is always masculine elsewhere, here the gender of the suffix is influenced by its association with the toponym Eden, which is feminine. So also Claus Westermann, *Genesis 1–11: A Commentary* (Minneapolis: Augsburg, 1984), 184. Stordalen (*Echoes of Eden,* 460) objects, arguing that "the few instances implying a gender for עֵדֶן (*ʿēden*) point rather to the masculine." However, the only textually certain example he cites (Ps 36:9[8]) does not involve the place, and the other two involve conjectural readings and do not involve a toponym (Jer 31:34; 2 Sm 1:24).

significance derived from later texts (e.g., Nm 3:7–8; 8:26; 18:5–6). The conjunction of verbs עבד (ʿbd) and שׁמר (šmr) in association with the tabernacle suggests priestly functions were reminiscent of humankind's role in the garden, but the reverse is unwarranted.

The garments (כָּתְנוֹת; koṯnôṯ) of skin that YHWH provided for Adam and Eve (Gn 3:21). The garments of skin offer no evidence for ascribing a priestly role to Adam. While כָּתְנוֹת (koṯnôṯ) is used of priestly garments,[42] the word often referred to the dress of lay persons[43] and seems to have been a common term for a shirt-like tunic.[44] Furthermore, since YHWH clothed both Adam and Eve, consistency demands that both should be viewed as priestly figures. However, this would run against the grain of the entire HB. Although women often functioned as prophets, and female priests were common outside Israel, the patricentric world of the HB had no room for women priests.[45]

The river flowing out from Eden to water the garden (Gn 2:10–14). Genesis 2:10–14 speaks of four rivers flowing from Eden to water the garden:

A river flowed out of Eden to water the garden, where it divided and became four rivers. The name of the first is the Pishon; it is the one that flowed around the whole land of Havilah, where there is gold. . . . The name of the second river is the Gihon; it is the one that flowed around the whole land of Cush. And the name of the third river is the Tigris, it is the one that flows east of Assyria. And the fourth river is the Euphrates.[46]

The image is intriguing, as though a fountain flows continuously from an elevated place in Eden into the garden, where it divides to water the four quadrants of the earth.[47] We hear clear echoes of this text in Ps 36:9[8]:

---

[42] Ex 28:4, 39–40; 29:5, 8; 39:27; 40:14; Lv 8:7, 13; 10:5; 16:4; Ezr 2:69; Neh 7:69, 71; Sir 45:8.

[43] Joseph (Gn 37:3, 23, 31–33), Hushai the Archite (2 Sm 15:32), Eliakim (Is 22:21), Job (Jb 30:18), of women (2 Sm 13:18–19; Sg 5:3).

[44] Twelfth-century B.C. Canaanite ivory carvings from Megiddo depict men in long-sleeved robes over colored tunics (כָּתְנוֹת; koṯnôṯ?), decorated in geometric designs. See http://www.bible-archaeology.info/clothes.htm.

[45] The root כהן (khn) never occurs in a feminine form, either as a noun or as a verb. The closest the HB comes is the word קְדֵשָׁה (qĕḏēšā), "holy woman" (Gn 38:21–22; Dt 23:18; Hos 4:14). However, these were not priestesses but illicit cult prostitutes (HALOT, 3:1075). Compare this with Phoenician and Punic khnt, which occurs often in the inscriptions (DNWSI, 490–91), and Akkadian ēntu, "high priestess" (CAD 4 [E], 172–73), which figures prominently in Mesopotamian religious texts.

[46] Translations throughout are the author's own, unless otherwise stated.

[47] Dietrich ("Das biblische Paradies," 308–17) identifies the Pishon with the River Karun, whose source is in the Zagros mountains (modern Iran); Gihon with the Kharkheh River, also originating in the Zagros mountains, northwest of the Karun; Hiddekel with the Tigris; and Perat with the Euphrates. These identifications suggest the rivers are listed in an east-west order. Others argue that the Pishon and Gihon were significant rivers in Saudi Arabia that dried up more than four millennia ago. See J. Sauer, "The River Runs Dry," BAR 22/4 (1996): 52–57, 64.

They feast on the abundance of your house,
and you let them drink from the stream of your delights
  [lit., "the stream of your Edens"].
For with you is the fountain of life;
by your light do we see light.

Several prophetic texts speak explicitly of a river flowing from a sanctuary and transforming the surrounding landscape into a veritable garden.[48] However, these texts modify the tradition, envisioning a single river, or in the case of Zec 14:8–11, two: one flowing eastward to the Dead Sea and the other westward to the Mediterranean.[49] While these images derive from Gn 2:10–14, without the later adaptation we would not think of looking for a sanctuary here.

The reference to gold in the garden (Gn 2:12). Both the tabernacle (Ex 25:11, 17, 24, 29, 36) and the temple (1 Kgs 6:20–22, 28, 30, 32, 35) were lavishly decorated with gold, in keeping with the surpassing glory of the divine resident. However, decorations and vessels of gold were not limited to temples. Along with a wealth of other luxury items, Solomon accumulated vast amounts of gold through gifts from allies, tribute from vassal states, and international trade.[50] The gold in Gn 2:12 offers no reason to equate Eden with the temple.

The precious stones, בְּדֹלַח *(bĕḏōlaḥ) and* שֹׁהַם *(šōham) (Gn 2:12).* The first word occurs elsewhere only in Nm 11:7, which compares the appearance of manna with בְּדֹלַח *(bĕḏōlaḥ)*, generally translated "bdellium." The quadraliteral form suggests this is a loan word, cognate to Akkadian *budulhu*, which one text associates with bronze but others link with aromatic gum.[51] Apart from the fact that בְּדֹלַח *(bĕḏōlaḥ)* probably does not

---

[48] Ez 47:1–12; Zec 14:8–11; Jl 4:18, 20–21[3:18, 20–21]; cf. Rv 22:1–2. See also Ps 46:4–5: "There is a river whose streams make glad the city of God, the holy habitation of the Most High. God is in the midst of her; she shall not be moved; God will help her when morning dawns" (ESV).

[49] The closest analogue to the four rivers of Gn 2:10–14 is found on an Assyrian ivory carving portraying a mountain deity holding a vessel from which four streams of water flow in four different directions. See Othmar Keel, *The Symbolism of the Biblical World: Ancient Near Eastern Iconography and the Book of Psalms* (trans. T. J. Hallett; New York: Seabury, 1978), 118, fig. 153a. For discussion, see Dietrich, "Das biblische Paradies," 317–20; Larry Stager, "Jerusalem as Eden," *BAR* 26/3 (2000): 40–42. The traditions behind this image and the biblical tradition may derive from a common source.

[50] For a description of Solomon's gold, see 1 Kgs 10:2–25. On the historical plausibility of these accounts, see Alan R. Millard, "King Solomon's Gold: Biblical Records in the Light of Antiquity," *Society for Mesopotamian Studies Bulletin* 15 (1988): 5–18; Millard, "King Solomon in His Ancient Context," in *The Age of Solomon: Scholarship at the Turn of the Millennium* (ed. L. K. Handy; SHCANE 11; Leiden: Brill, 1997), 30–53.

[51] *CAD* 2 (B), 305–6. The Hebrew word probably refers to the odoriferous, yellowish, transparent gum of a South Arabian tree, *Commiphora mukul*. See further Ute Neumann-Gorsolke, "Bedolachharz," *Das Bibellexikon*, January 2006,

refer to a precious stone, the absence of this term from descriptions of both the breastpiece of Israel's high priest (Ex 28:17–20; 39:10–13) and the pectoral of the king of Tyre (Ez 28:13) eliminates a link with the tabernacle or the temple. The second word, שֹׁהַם (šōham), is more promising[52] because this word is associated with both the priestly vestments and the pectoral of Ezekiel's king of Tyre. Although the word occurs eight times in these descriptions,[53] שֹׁהַם (šōham) does not in principle bear priestly overtones. Job 28:15–19, a nonpriestly text, includes this item along with other precious commodities: gold of Ophir, sapphire, glass, jewels of fine gold, coral, crystal, pearls, and topaz. The reference to this gemstone in Gn 2:12 suggests no more than that this is a fabulous garden, analogous perhaps to the garden in Tablet IX of the Epic of Gilgamesh, which has trees bearing carnelian (sāmtu) and lapis lazuli as fruit[54] and is located at the mythic border between the human and supernatural world.[55] The garden of Eden was indeed a luxurious place, separated from the everyday world,[56] but this did not make it a temple.

The lush arboreal imagery (Gn 2:9, 16–17). Genesis 2–3 designates the space in Eden a garden (גַּן; gan) thirteen times.[57] The expression denotes fundamentally an (enclosed?) field, cultivated to produce either fruit or vegetables.[58] Like Hebrew פַּרְדֵּס (pardēs) in Eccl 2:5 and Sg 4:13, LXX's rendering of the term as παράδεισος (paradeisos, from Persian pairidaēza) rightly recognizes this space not simply as a plot that provides vegetables for a household but as a "park," perhaps even a royal garden.[59] Its location in Eden reinforces this impression. Whereas in the past Hebrew עֵדֶן ('ēden) was associated with Sumerian edinu, "plain, steppe," its derivation from a root 'dn, "to enrich, to give abundance," apparently because of access to abundant water, is now assured.[60] Ancient temples were often surrounded by gardens, and the gardens were thought to yield their fruit in response

---

http://www.bibelwissenschaft.de/nc/wibilex/das-bibellexikon/details/quelle/ WIBI/zeichen/b/referenz/10445/cache/bd8dbd8e00030e0d2b6901000fb- dae2a/; Manfred Görg, "Bdlh ('Bdellium'): zur Etymologie," *BN* 48 (1989): 12–16.

[52] Most translations render שֹׁהַם (šōham) as onyx, but it is probably cognate to Akkadian sāmtu, "carnelian," a red gemstone. So also *HALOT,* 4:1424. On the Akkadian word, see *CAD* 15 (S), 121–24.

[53] For the former, generally Ex 25:7; one on the breastpiece representing one of the twelve tribes (25:7; 28:20, 35:9, 27; 39:13), and two on the ephod, each inscribed with the names of six tribes (28:9; 39:6); for the latter, see Ez 28:13.

[54] *ANET,* 89; *CAD* 15 (S), 124.

[55] Thus Stordalen, *Echoes of Eden,* 161.

[56] Stordalen, *Echoes of Eden,* 286.

[57] Gn 2:8, 9, 10, 15, 16; 3:1, 2, 3, 8a, 8b, 10, 23, 24; see also 13:10.

[58] *HALOT,* 1:198.

[59] Like pardēsu in Akkadian. *CAD* 12 (P), 182. On royal gardens, see further, Dietrich, "Das biblische Paradies," 287–90; K. Gleason, "Gardens in Preclassical Times," *OEANE* 2:383.

[60] For discussion, see Stordalen, *Echoes of Eden,* 257–61; also Alan R. Millard, "The Etymology of Eden," *VT* 34 (1984): 103–6.

to divine forces, but the gardens themselves were not the sanctuary. Cornelius declared rightly that "theologically the garden of Eden represented the blissful state lost by humankind (Gen 3)."[61] Exhibiting features of ancient royal gardens (cf. Eccl 2:5),[62] this one was planned and planted by YHWH, the divine king, who committed it to the care of his vice-regent with the charge, "Serve it and guard it" (Gn 2:15).

The garden as a mountain. While the downward flow of the rivers of this garden in four directions suggests an elevated source, the absence of explicit reference to a mountain is striking. Either this text was composed before Mount Zion had been identified as YHWH's permanent residence (Dt 12:5, 11; Ps 132:13–16), or the author intentionally suppressed linkage of the garden with the sanctuary, perhaps to prevent association with Baal's residence on Ṣaphan.[63] Equally striking is the narrator's avoidance of any hint that YHWH may dwell at the source of the rivers, comparable to El's residence "at the headwaters of the two rivers, at the confluence of the deeps" in Ugaritic mythology.[64]

Wisdom and the tree of the knowledge of good and evil (Gn 2:9; 3:6). As noted earlier, while the HB never associates wisdom with the priesthood, its significance for kingship is explicitly declared in Prv 8:12–21 (especially vv. 15–16) and dramatically illustrated in Solomon's prayer as king in 1 Kgs 3:6–9 and the answer to that prayer in 1 Kgs 3:10–5:13[4:34].[65] Solomon's plea for wisdom to discern between "good" (טוֹב; *ṭôḇ*) and "evil" (רָע; *raʿ*; 3:9) echoes Gn 2:9 and 3:5–6, but note especially the people's response to his rule: "they stood in awe of the king, because

---

[61] I. Cornelius, "גַּן," *NIDOTTE* 1:876. While I question Cornelius's anthropocentric view of the garden, he adds significantly, "[t]he garden of Gen 2 was created for the human race (vv. 8, 15), not for God, although he strolled through it (3:8)."

[62] On ancient royal gardens and Adam's role as gardener, see Callender, *Adam in Myth and History*, 59–65; Manfred Hutter, "Adam als Gärtner und König (Gen 2:8,15)," *BZ* 30 (1986): 258–62. According to Dietrich ("Das biblische Paradies," 301), "Der Mensch wurde . . . erschaffen, um als Handlanger Gottes die Pflege des Paradieses zu übernehmen." For a helpful illustration of the relationships among the king, a secure source of water, and a royal garden, based on the sculptured relief from Ashurbanipal's North Palace at Nineveh, see fig. 89 by Paul Goodhead, in *Babylon: Myth and Reality* (ed. I. L. Finkel and M. J. Seymour; London: British Museum Press, 2008), 111.

[63] On the Israelite temple as an architectural embodiment of the cosmic mountain, see Lundquist, "What Is a Temple?" 207–8.

[64] RS 24.244, as translated by Pierre Bordreuil and Dennis Pardee, in *A Manual of Ugaritic* (Linguistic Studies in Ancient West Semitic 3; Winona Lake, IN: Eisenbrauns, 2009), 187. The link with the thirteenth-cent. B.C. ivory inlay from Aššur, portraying the mountain god framed by two trees and two "cherubim" (winged bulls) and holding a vase from which four streams of water flow out to four vessels, is even more tenuous. Cf. See Stager, "Jerusalem as Eden," 41.

[65] On the link between wisdom and rule, see also Gn 41:33, 39; Dt 1:13–15; 16:19; 2 Sm 14:17, 20; Is 11:2–3.

they recognized that the wisdom of God was in him to administer justice" (1 Kgs 3:28). Ezekiel 28 portrays the king of Tyre as a royal figure renowned for both his wisdom (28:2–5, 12) and his hubris—he claimed to have achieved that for which Adam was expelled from the garden (28:2–6; cf. Gn 3:5–6). However, the context seems to envision Adam as having possessed all the wisdom needed to fulfill his role as image of God without eating from the tree of the knowledge of good and evil (28:12–15).[66] To associate the wisdom motif with the law stored inside the Holy of Holies and eating the forbidden fruit with touching the ark[67] is farfetched and anachronistic, unless we assume a Persian date for the authorship of Gn 2–3.

The eastern entrance to the garden (Gn 3:24). The gate to the garden may have been located in the east, but the narrator does not speak of the entrance to the garden, either here or in the preceding description. He says simply that the garden was "in Eden in the east" (2:8).[68] If the guardian cherubs were stationed at the gate, Gn 3:24 has suppressed this fact; their primary function was to prevent access to the tree of life. That later sanctuary designs had entrances to the east may reflect a tradition that the gate to the garden was to the east, but the narrator of Gn 2–3 neither anticipated nor reflected those designs.

The tripartite structure of the garden (Gn 2:8–15). Read superficially, Gn 2:8–15 may suggest a three-tiered environment. However, the relationship between Eden and the garden is uncertain. Since YHWH "planted a garden toward the east, in Eden" (v. 8) and the river flowed from Eden to water the garden (vv. 10–14), Eden seems to have been larger than the garden, and if any part is to be associated with the Holy of Holies, it would be the garden. Although the luxurious features of the landscape were concentrated in the garden, the name Eden, "land of bliss," suggests that the surrounding space was also desirable. However, as noted earlier, the verb שׁמר (*šmr*) in v. 15 implies that the garden needed to be protected from outside threats, in which case the territory around the garden functioned as a buffer zone between the wider world that needed to be subdued and governed (1:28) and the garden itself. We may reconstruct the scene schematically as follows.

---

[66] From outside the HB, Stordalen (*Echoes of Eden*, 462) cites the characterization of Enkidu as "wise as a god" (*ANET*, 75). However, Andrew George's more recent translation (*The Epic of Gilgamesh: A New Translation* [London: Penguin, 1999], 8) translates the sentence, "You are handsome, Enkidu, you are just like a god!"

[67] Thus Wenham, "Sanctuary Symbolism," 402–3. According to Stordalen (*Echoes of Eden*, 461), the tree of life serves as a conventional symbol for either תּוֹרה (*tôrā*), which he translates as "Law," or חכמה (*ḥokmā*), "wisdom."

[68] Heb. מקדם (*miqqedem*), literally "from the east," i.e., as part of the eastern landscape. On the construction, see Westermann, *Genesis 1–11*, 184.

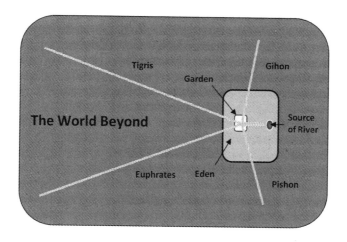

At first glance the three-tiered structure seems analogous to the structure of the tabernacle/temple environment. However, in the latter the sequence of concentric circles involves four tiers. More significantly, while it is possible these spheres represent increasing degrees of sanctity as one moves from the outside in, this does not render the entire structure a temple, unless a temple is defined more generally as "sacred space" rather than "the house/residence of the deity."[69] Furthermore, inasmuch as the garden was located in Eden (Gn 2:8), the "Eden-temple" interpretation reverses the prevailing relationship between temples and gardens; normally, temples (the *adytum* specifically) represented the most sacred spaces and sacred gardens surrounded the temples, rather than vice versa.

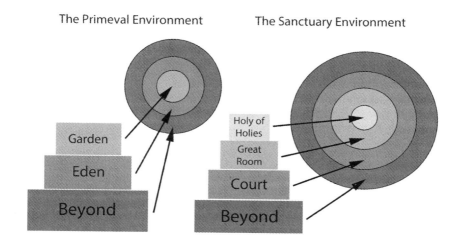

---

[69] See further below.

The Creation Narrative (Gn 1:1–2:4a)

Scholars have noticed numerous links between the tabernacle and the creation of the cosmos: (1) corresponding to the six days of creation marked by divine speech ("And God said"), the instructions for the tabernacle involved seven speeches, each introduced with "And YHWH spoke/said to Moses";[70] (2) six speeches deal with creative activity and the seventh with the Sabbath, which is explicitly grounded in creation (Gn 31:12–17); (3) the reference to "seasons" (מוֹעֲדִים; *môʿăḏîm*) in Gn 1:14 uses the expression applied to Israel's cultic festivals;[71] (4) both end with a reference to YHWH "finishing" (כלה; *klh*) his instructions for the new creation (Gn 2:1; Ex 31:18); (5) the seven lights of the menorah (Ex 25:31–40) recall the seven days of creation; (6) Lv 19:30 and 26:2 explicitly link the tabernacle with sabbaths: "You shall keep my sabbaths and revere my sanctuary; I am YHWH"; (7) the erection of the tabernacle on New Year's Day (Ex 40:2, 17) signals a new creation and the beginning of a new era in cosmic history; and (8) the symmetry and proportion in the design of the tabernacle reflect the symmetry and order built into the universe.[72]

The prominence of the number seven in the account of the later construction of the temple seems also to link this project intentionally with the creation accounts in Genesis: (1) the temple was seven years in construction (1 Kgs 6:38); (2) it was dedicated in the seventh month at Sukkoth (Festival of Booths), a seven-day observance (1 Kgs 8:2); and (3) Solomon's dedicatory prayer includes seven petitions (1 Kgs 8:31–53). Levenson concludes that creation and temple building were "congeneric" and that the cosmos itself is considered a temple.[73] He sees this interpretation reinforced by the declaration of the seraphim in Is 6:3: "YHWH Sebaoth is holy, holy, holy! His glory is the fullness of the whole earth."[74] Based on these links it is tempting to conclude that "creation in Genesis 1 uses the language of temple-building."[75] That extrabiblical accounts of

---

[70] Ex 25:1; 30:11, 17, 22, 34; 31:1, 12.

[71] Nm 10:10; 15:3; 29:39; Is 1:14; Ez 36:38; 46:9, 11; Neh 10:34; 1 Chr 23:31; 2 Chr 8:13; 31:3.

[72] We also hear verbal allusions to Genesis in the account of the construction of the tabernacle. Compare Ex 39:32 and Gn 2:1; Ex 39:43 and Gn 1:31; Ex 40:33 and Gn 2:2.

[73] Levenson, "The Temple and the World," 286–89. Others speak of the relationship between the cosmos and the temple as being homologous: "the cosmos is a temple; the temple is the cosmos." See Walton, *Genesis 1 as Ancient Cosmology*, 109, 178.

[74] The Heb. reads, קָדוֹשׁ קָדוֹשׁ קָדוֹשׁ יְהוָה צְבָאוֹת מְלֹא כָל־הָאָרֶץ כְּבוֹדוֹ (*qāḏôš qāḏôš qāḏôš yhwh ṣĕḇāʾôt mĕlōʾ kol-hāʾāreṣ kĕḇôḏô*).

[75] Mark S. Smith, *The Ugaritic Baal Cycle*, vol. 1: *Introduction with Text, Translation, and Commentary of KTU 1.1–1.2* (Leiden: Brill, 1994), 78; Beale, *Temple*, 60–63; cf. Walton, *Genesis 1 as Ancient Cosmology*, 181; claiming the support of Victor Avigdor Hurowitz, *"I have built you an exalted house": Temple Building in the*

cosmic creation follow divine defeat of chaos and creation of the world with divine rest in their temples appears to reinforce this interpretation.[76]

However, this understanding of the cosmos generally as a temple suffers from the same weaknesses as the interpretation of Eden in particular as a temple. When interpreting Genesis extrabiblical analogues should be used with caution. *Enuma Elish*'s association of the defeat of chaos with cosmic creation and the construction of a temple for the gods (including Marduk) has no parallel in Gn 1. The biblical text says nothing about chaotic forces resisting the work of God, let alone of a divine defeat of chaos.[77] Whereas extrabiblical texts speak of gods resting in the temples that have just been built,[78] neither Gn 2:2–3 nor any texts that look back on this moment (Ex 20:11; 31:17) has God dwelling in the structure just constructed. Rather, figuratively speaking, having completed the work of creation he will have retreated to his heavenly throne room. Although Ex 31:17 speaks anthropomorphically of YHWH "catching his breath"[79] and Ex 20:11 of him resting (נוח; *nwḥ*), the Genesis account speaks only of cessation of divine work. Technically, the Hebrew verb, שבת (*šbt*), does not mean "to rest" but "to cease." In the words of the narrator, "God ceased from his entire project, that is, what he had created by his actions,"[80] because the project was finished (כלה; *klh*) on the sixth day (v. 2).

Bible in the Light of Mesopotamian and Northwest Semitic Writings (JSOTSup 115; Sheffield: Sheffield Academic Press, 1992), 242. However, in fairness, in this context Hurowitz does not explicitly speak of creation as temple building; he speaks more generally of "the world as a building, the Creation as an act of building, and the Creator as a wise, knowledgeable and discerning architect." On the construction of the temple after Marduk's defeat of Tiamat, see Janowski, "Himmel auf Erden," 238–42.

[76] Beale, *Temple*, 60–66; Walton, *Genesis 1 as Ancient Cosmology*, 178–84; Moshe Weinfeld, "Sabbath, Temple, and the Enthronement of the Lord—The Problem of the Sitz im Leben of Genesis 1:1–2:3," in *Mélanges bibliques et orienteaux en l'honneur de M. Henri Cazelles* (ed. A. Caquot and M. Delcor; AOAT 212; Neukirchen-Vluyn: Neukirchener Verlag/Butzon & Bercker Kevelaer, 1981), 507–8. For extrabiblical evidence for the link between temple building and divine rest, see Hurowitz, *"I have built you an exalted house,"* 330–31.

[77] Opposition to the divine work does not surface explicitly until Gn 3. So also Richard Averbeck, "Ancient Near Eastern Mythography as It Relates to Historiography in the Hebrew Bible: Genesis 3 and the Cosmic Battle," in *The Future of Biblical Archaeology: Reassessing Methodologies and Assumptions* (ed. J. K. Hoffmeier and A. R. Millard; Grand Rapids: Eerdmans, 2004), 344–51. If the origins of "the world of tooth and claw" outside the garden is to be linked with a revolt of Satan and his minions against God, this might be located between the creation of the animals and humankind in Gn 1:25–26, but this motif is totally suppressed.

[78] For example, Ningirsu rests in the temple that Gudea of Lagash built for him in Gudea Cylinder B, xiv 21–24.

[79] Heb. וַיִּנָּפַשׁ (*wayyinnāpaš*). Cf. Ex 23:12 and 2 Sm 16:14, which speak of humans and draft/pack animals catching their breath.

[80] Heb. שָׁבַת מִכָּל־מְלַאכְתּוֹ אֲשֶׁר־בָּרָא אֱלֹהִים לַעֲשׂוֹת (*šābat mikkol-mĕla'ktô 'ăšer-bārā' 'ĕlōhîm la'ăśôt*).

When later texts speak of YHWH resting they are less concerned with the creation of the cosmos than with Zion theology, which views the temple in Jerusalem to be his dwelling place. Isaiah 66:1–2 is particularly notable:

> Thus says YHWH:
>> Heaven is my throne
>> and the earth is my footstool;
>> where is the house that you will build for me,
>> and where will my resting place (מְקוֹם מְנוּחָתִי; *māqôm mĕnûḥāṯî*) be?
>> All these things my hand has made,
>> and thus they came to be,
> The declaration of YHWH.

Rather than referring to a cosmos-sized temple,[81] v. 1 speaks merismically of the cosmos ("heaven and earth") as the realm over which YHWH rules. If anything, the cosmos is contrasted with the earthly temple that humans build as a place for this extra-cosmic deity's dwelling[82] and from which peace and well-being may radiate out to the world. The psalmist had this image in mind in Ps 132:7–8 and 13–14:

> Let us go to his dwelling place (לְמִשְׁכְּנוֹתָיו; *lĕmiškĕnôtāyw*);
> let us fall down at his footstool!
> Arise, O YHWH, and go to your resting place (לִמְנוּחָתֶךָ; *limnûḥāṯekā*),
> you and your mighty ark.
>
> For YHWH has chosen Zion;
> he has desired it for his dwelling (מוֹשָׁב; *môšāb*):
> This is my resting place (מְנוּחָתִי; *mĕnûḥāṯî*) forever;
> here I will dwell (אֵשֵׁב; *'ēšēb*), for I have desired it.

As for Is 6:3, rather than declaring, "The world in its fullness is the temple,"[83] the seraphim acknowledge that YHWH's holiness is concentrated in the temple. Like the psalmist in Ps 19:2[1], they declare that YHWH's glory is imprinted in all that he has created.[84]

In my response to reading Gn 1–3 as temple-building texts, I have hinted at the fundamental hermeneutical problem involved in this ap-

---

[81] Thus Walton, *Genesis 1 as Ancient Cosmology*, 179.

[82] The noun מְנוּחָה (*mĕnûḥâ*), "resting place," may denote a place where people rest and recover from their weariness (e.g., Is 28:12), but it usually refers to a secure retreat/base in the midst of a chaotic and threatening world. In the threatening desert YHWH went before the people seeking safe resting places for his people (Nm 10:33); the land of Canaan became the Israelites' resting place once the Canaanites had been defeated (Dt 12:9; 1 Kgs 8:56; cf. Is 32:18); Damascus as the security for Hadrach (Zec 9:1); a personal place of quiet (Ru 1:9; Ps 23:2; Mi 2:8–10); the temple as YHWH's secure base (Is 66:1; Ps 132:8, 14); and a place of security for his people (Ps 95:11).

[83] Contra Levenson, "The Temple and the World," 296.

[84] Cf. Rom 1:20.

proach. The question is, should we read Gn 1–3 in the light of later texts, or should we read later texts in the light of these? If we read the accounts in the order given, then the creation account provides essential background to the primeval history, which provides background for the patriarchal, exodus, and tabernacle narratives. By themselves and by this reading the accounts of Gn 1–3 offer no clues that a cosmic or Edenic temple might be involved. However, as noted above, the Edenic features of the tabernacle, the Jerusalem temple, and the temple envisioned by Ezekiel[85] are obvious.[86] Apparently their design and function intended to capture something of the original creation, perhaps even to represent in miniature the original environment in which human beings were placed. However, the fact that Israel's sanctuaries were Edenic does not make Eden into a sacred shrine. At best this is a nonreciprocating equation.

The Nature and Function of Temples in the HB and in the ANE

This assessment of interpretations that view Gn 1–3 as temple-building texts is reinforced by a conceptual consideration of the function of temples in the ANE. However, before we consider ancient understandings of "temple," we should reflect on modern understandings. The popular view, that a temple is "a building for religious practice,"[87] is problematic on two counts. First, although Gn 1 contains vocabulary that could be construed architecturally (e.g., רָקִיעַ; *rāqiaʿ*), it lacks explicit "architectural" cosmic features found elsewhere.[88] Second, whether or not one accepts that the world was created as a home for all creatures and that humankind was placed here to care for the earth in the interest of all its inhabitants, it is doubtful that the human activities mandated in Gn 1:26–28 and 2:15 represent "religious practice," especially if "religious

---

[85] Note especially the river that flows from the temple and transforms the landscape to Edenic lusciousness (Ez 47:1–12); similarly Zec 14:8–11; Jl 4:18, 20–21 [3:18, 20–21]. See further Fishbane, "The 'Eden' Motif," 118–20.

[86] See esp. Stordalen, *Echoes of Eden*, 307–10; Stager, "Jerusalem as Eden," 36–47; Stager, "Jerusalem and the Garden of Eden," in *ErIsr* 26 (ed. B. A. Levine et al.; Jerusalem: Israel Exploration Society, Hebrew University, Union College-Jewish Institute of Religion, 1999), 183–94; Bloch-Smith, "Solomon's Temple," 83–94 (88), who characterizes the temple in Jerusalem as a "virtual garden of Eden"; Bloch-Smith, "Who Is the King of Glory?" 18–31; Fishbane, "The 'Eden' Motif," 111–20.

[87] The first definition in the latest edition of Merriam-Webster, accessible at http://www.merriam-webster.com/dictionary/temple.

[88] E.g., "windows" (אֲרֻבֹּת; *ʾărubbāt*) of heaven (Gn 7:11; 8:2; Is 24:18; Mal 3:10), "foundations" (מוֹסְדוֹת; *môsĕdôt*) of the earth/heaven (2 Sm 22:8; Is 24:18; Jer 31:37; Mi 6:2; Ps 82:5; Prv 8:29); "pillars" (מְצֻקִים; *mĕṣṣuqîm*) of the earth/heaven (1 Sm 2:8; Jb 9:6; 26:11; Ps 75:4[3]).

practice" means liturgical actions performed in a cultic context before a deity. There is nothing overtly cultic or even religious about being fruitful, filling and subduing the earth, and ruling over the creatures (1:29), or serving and guarding the garden (2:15)[89]—unless one redefines "religious practice" more broadly as "reverential performance of one's duties in honor of a deity." However, this definition requires no building.

To interpret the cosmos or Eden as a temple becomes even less likely if one follows the more restricted definition of temples represented in the *Oxford English Dictionary*: "An edifice or place regarded primarily as the dwelling-place or 'house' of a deity or deities; hence, an edifice devoted to divine worship."[90] The narratives of Gn 1–3 are silent on either the earth or Eden as a dwelling place for God, and they are silent on divine worship, if the latter means veneration of a divine being "with appropriate acts, rites, or ceremonies."[91] A broader definition of "worship" as "reverential actions of homage in honor of a deity" could include the actions mandated in Gn 1:26–28 and 2:15, but again, the performance of these tasks requires no temple.

Finally, one could define a temple vaguely as "sacred space marked by the presence of deity."[92] We may indeed view the world as originally created and Eden in particular as sacred space, space that has been desecrated by human sin. In a sense, God is everywhere, and everything God touches is holy. However, this does not mean that either the cosmos or Eden was a temple, any more than calling the land of Israel "the holy land" (גְּבוּל קָדְשׁוֹ; *gĕbûl qodšô*, Ps 78:54; אַדְמַת הַקֹּדֶשׁ; *'admat haqqōḏeš*, Zec 2:16[12]) makes it a temple. Furthermore, rather than emphasizing divine presence in the cosmos or Eden, and in contrast to pantheistic and panentheistic perspectives of many ancients, Gn 1–3 highlights God's separation from the created world. Apparently the first humans did not eat the forbidden fruit in the direct presence of God; the fact that his arrival in the garden in the evening caused them to hide cautions against interpreting הִתְהַלֵּךְ (*hithallēk*) in Gn 3:8 in a durative sense.

In the end, we must read Gn 1–3 not through the lenses of modern views of temple but within the text's ancient conceptual environment. Unlike Christian sanctuaries, which are often designed to satisfy the interests of worshipers, the primary function of ancient temples was to provide an earthly residence for the deity (Pss 84:2, 3, 5, 8[1, 2, 4, 7];

---

[89] This interpretation is rendered even less likely by Gn 2:5 and 3:5, which speak of the man "serving the land" (לַעֲבֹד אֶת־הָאֲדָמָה; *la'ăbōd 'et-hā'ădāmā*).

[90] Accessible at http://www.oed.com/search?searchType = dictionary&q = te mple&_searchBtn = Search.

[91] Note the full definition of the *Oxford English Dictionary*: "To honour or revere as a supernatural being or power, or as a holy thing; to regard or approach with veneration; to adore with appropriate acts, rites, or ceremonies." Accessed at http://www.oed.com/view/Entry/230346?rskey = XZXVff&result = 2#eid.

[92] John Walton, in private conversation.

132:13–14).[93] This meant that when devout Israelites made pilgrimages to the temple, they knew they were in God's real, immediate presence.[94] Outside Israel people celebrated the completion of a temple construction project by bringing images of the deities into their cellae, where they could rest and from where their rule would extend throughout the land. Similar principles applied to Israelite temples. The tabernacle, a portable temple, was designed by YHWH himself (Ex 25:1–31:11). After inspired Israelite craftsmen, supervised by Bezalel (Ex 35:30–36:8), had produced the components needed for the structure, and Moses had assembled the prefabricated materials and installed the ark of the covenant inside the *adytum* (40:18–33), the cloud—the symbol of YHWH's presence—covered the tabernacle and his כָּבוֹד (*kāḇôḏ*) filled the building. No human transported YHWH into his palace; he entered of his own free will and in his own time.

The phenomenon was repeated when Solomon had completed the temple project in Jerusalem. Having installed the ark of the covenant in the Holy of Holies, as soon as the priests emerged from the sanctuary, the כָּבוֹד (*kāḇôḏ*) of YHWH filled the building, whereupon Solomon declared, "I have built you an exalted house, a place for you to dwell in perpetuity" (1 Kgs 8:13). Psalm 132:7–8 and 13–14 (cited above) declare unequivocally the eternality of YHWH's choice of Zion as his dwelling place. The destruction of the temple in 586 B.C. cast doubts on the veracity of YHWH's word.[95] However, in Ez 43:1–12 the exiled prophetic priest observes the return of the כָּבוֹד (*kāḇôḏ*) and hears the divine voice affirming the temple as "the place of my throne [מְקוֹם כִּסְאִי; *mĕqôm kisʾî*], and the place for the soles of my feet [מְקוֹם כַּפּוֹת רַגְלָי; *mĕqôm kappôṯ raglay*], where I will dwell [אֶשְׁכָּן; *ʾeškān*] in the midst of the descendants of Israel forever" (v. 7). A generation later, after the reconstruction of the temple, the failure of the כָּבוֹד (*kāḇôḏ*) to reappear caused the community of returned exiles to despair, necessitating YHWH Sebaoth's reassurance: "I will shake all the nations, so that the treasure of all nations shall come, and I will fill this house with כָּבוֹד [*kāḇôḏ*]. . . . Indeed the latter כָּבוֹד [*kāḇôḏ*] of this house will be greater than the former" (Hg 2:7, 9).[96]

---

[93] Cf. Hurowitz, "YHWH's Exalted House," 96–101. On the archaeological evidence for the nature and function of ancient Syro-Palestinian temples, see Beth Alpert Nakhai, "Syro-Palestinian Temples," *OEANE* 5:169–74.

[94] See further Ian Wilson, *Out of the Midst of the Fire: Divine Presence in Deuteronomy* (SBLDS 151; Atlanta: Scholars Press, 1995).

[95] Cf. Ezekiel's vision of the departure of the כָּבוֹד (*kāḇôḏ*) in Ez 8–11.

[96] Many understand the rending of the curtain in Herod's temple when Jesus was crucified (Mt 27:51; Mk 15:38; Lk 23:45) to signal the end of the old sacrificial order—even though Christians continued to worship in the temple after the death of Christ (Acts 2:46; 3:1–10; 21:26–30; 22:17). However, we may also interpret the event as exposing the sanctuary's lack of integrity; having been constructed by a pagan for political reasons, it never received the divine seal of approval and the כָּבוֹד (*kāḇôḏ*) never returned.

The opening chapters of Genesis lack any hints of these notions. God does not create the world because he is homeless or needs a place for his throne. His real residence is in heaven, as the Torah, the Psalter, and the Prophets declare:

> Look down from your holy habitation (מִמְּעוֹן קָדְשְׁךָ; *mimmĕ'ôn qodšĕkā*), from heaven [מִן־הַשָּׁמַיִם; *min-haššāmayim*], and bless your people Israel and the ground that you have given us, as you swore to our ancestors—a land flowing with milk and honey. (Dt 26:15 NRSV)

> Turn again, O God of hosts; look down from heaven [מִשָּׁמַיִם; *miššāmayim*], and see; have regard for this vine. (Ps 80:15[14] NRSV)

> Look down from heaven [מִשָּׁמַיִם; *miššāmayim*] and see, from your holy and glorious habitation [מִזְּבֻל קָדְשְׁךָ וְתִפְאַרְתֶּךָ; *mizzĕbul qodšĕkā wĕtip'artekā*]. Where are your zeal and your might? The yearning of your heart and your compassion? (Is 63:15 NRSV)

At the dedication of the temple, after asking, "Will God actually reside with humankind on earth?" (2 Chr 6:18; cf. 1 Kgs 8:27), Solomon recognized where YHWH's true dwelling place is: "When they pray to this place, listen from your residence, from heaven."[97] References to YHWH's heavenly throne reinforce this notion:

> YHWH is in his holy temple [בְּהֵיכַל קָדְשׁוֹ; *bĕhêkal qodšô*]; YHWH—in heaven is his throne. (Ps 11:4)

> YHWH has established his throne in the heavens, and his kingdom rules over all. (Ps 103:19)

> Heaven is my throne, and the earth is my footstool;
> what is the house that you would build for me,
> and what is the place of my rest? (Is 66:1)

Whatever God's reason for creating the world, it was not to provide a home for himself. As suggested earlier, the reference to YHWH walking about (הִתְהַלֵּךְ; *hithallēk*) in the garden (Gn 3:8) does not contradict this conclusion. Unlike ישב (*yšb*), "to dwell," the verb does not speak of residence but suggests occasional presence. As the creator of the garden, YHWH exercises authority over it; it is his domain. But the verb also contributes to an extraordinary domestic image. In ancient times, people would relax and go for a walk in "the cool of the day" (רוּחַ הַיּוֹם; *rûaḥ hayyôm*), when the evening breezes blow. YHWH's appearance in the garden reflects his confidence and openness to its inhabitants. However, instead of welcoming their "extraterrestrial" Suzerain, the man and his wife hid from him. Because of sin, an evening visit was transformed into a call to account and ended in a tragic disturbance of all relationships. In Israelite thought the temple was a symbol of the fallen world on the one hand and the divine

---

[97] 2 Chr 6:21; cf. 1 Kgs 8:30; also vv. 32, 34, 36, 39, 43, 45, 49.

desire to continue to relate to that world on the other. A pre-fall world needed no temple; relationship with God was free and open. Whatever the significance of temples elsewhere, in the HB it represents a brilliant and gracious divine solution to alienation caused by sin.

Since the temple of Baal at Ugarit was a replica of his heavenly temple on Ṣaphan,[98] we should not be surprised that the HB presents the tabernacle and temple as microcosms of YHWH's heavenly abode.[99] This was obvious to the author of Hebrews, whose perception of the relationship between the two is reflected in the expressions used to characterize the two.

Designations for the Heavenly Dwelling of God	Designations for the Earthly Dwelling of God
"type" (τύπος; *typos*, Ex 25:40; Acts 7:44; Heb 8:5)	"replica" (ὑπόδειγμα; *hypodeigma*, Heb 8:5; 9:23) "antitype" (ἀντίτυπος; *antitypos*, Heb 9:24)
"true" (ἀληθινός; *alēthinos*, Heb 8:2; 9:24)	"shadow" (σκιά; *skia*, Heb 8:5; 10:1)
"heavenly" (ἐπουράνιος; *epouranios*, Heb 8:5; 9:23)	"earthly" (κοσμικός; *kosmikos*, Heb 9:1) "of this creation" (κτίσις; *ktisis*, Heb 9:11) "hand-made" (χειροποίητος; *cheiropoiētos*, Heb 9:11, 24)

But this conception is anticipated by several HB texts. Exodus 25:8–9, 40 has YHWH instructing the Israelites to construct a residence for him, according "to the structure of the dwelling place" (תַּבְנִית הַמִּשְׁכָּן; *taḇnît hammiškān*) and the structure of all the furniture and utensils (תַּבְנִית כָּל־כֵּלָיו; *taḇnît kol-kēlāyw*) that he would show Moses. Although תַּבְנִית (*taḇnît*) is usually translated "pattern," apparently Moses saw more than a blueprint or model.[100] Since elsewhere the word usually refers to the object itself,

---

[98] See Loren R. Fischer, "Creation at Ugarit and in the Old Testament," *VT* 15 (1965): 318–19.

[99] As recognized by Josephus in *A.J.* 3.7.7 (§§178–82) (cited from *Josephus* [trans. H. St. J. Thackeray; 10 vols.; LCL; Cambridge, MA: Harvard University Press, 1926–1965]), though his allegorization is excessive. Many find stark contrasts between Deuteronomic and Priestly views of divine presence, with the former perceiving YHWH transcendentally as dwelling only in heaven and causing his "name" to reside in the temple, and the latter perceiving him imminently; his presence is concretized in the כָּבוֹד (*kāḇôḏ*) (cf. Hurowitz, "YHWH's Exalted House," 97–101). However, as was the case at Sinai, YHWH was simultaneously present in heaven and at the place where he would stamp his name. So also Michael Hundley, "To Be or Not to Be: A Reexamination of Name Language in Deuteronomy and the Deuteronomistic History," *VT* 59 (2009): 539–40.

[100] 1 Chr 28:19 suggests YHWH revealed to David in writing all the structural details of the temple (כֹּל מַלְאֲכוֹת הַתַּבְנִית; *kōl malʾăḵôṯ hattaḇnît*).

rather than a copy or plan of the object,[101] it seems that YHWH opened the windows of heaven, allowing Moses a glimpse into the heavenly reality, of which the tabernacle to be constructed would be a replica. The LXX translation of תַּבְנִית (*taḇnît*) as "paradigm" (παράδειγμα; *paradeigma*) in Ex 25:9 and as τύπος (*typos*) in 25:40 reinforces this interpretation.[102] In the only other occurrence of τύπος (*typos*) in the OG the word clearly refers to an idolatrous image, and not to a plan for an image (Am 5:26).[103]

However, tabernacle and temple also represent microcosms of Eden, and herein lies the key to the relationship between Gn 1–3 and Israel's sanctuaries. It is doubtful we should characterize the creation accounts of Gn 1–3 as being built "on a platform of temple theology,"[104] but characterizing the temple-building accounts as being built "on a platform of creation theology" is legitimate. Indeed, the Eden narrative provides much of the conceptual vocabulary for Israel's sanctuary tradition: כְּרֻבִים (*kĕruḇîm*) guarding the way to the tree of life, reflected in the menorah; the charge to Adam "to serve and to keep" the garden; the river flowing out from Eden to water the garden; references to gold and precious stones; lush arboreal imagery, and the eastern orientation of the Edenic landscape.[105] This is significant for grasping the function of the temple in Israelite thinking. To be sure, the sanctuary provided an earthly dwelling for YHWH in the midst of a fallen people, and its rituals provided a means whereby covenant relationship with him could be maintained even in a fallen world. In its design as a miniature Eden the Israelite temple addressed both the alienation of humanity from the divine Suzerain and the alienation of creation in general. From Zion Eden-like prosperity would flow out to the land that YHWH had given Israel as their grant (Lv 26:1–13; Dt 28:1–14; Ez 34:25–31). While the rabbis surely went too far in suggesting that the heavens and the earth were created from Zion,[106] the temple represented the source of Israel's and ultimately the world's re-creation. The temple

---

[101] Jo 22:28 (the structure of an altar); Ps 144:12 (the structure of a palace); Dt 4:16–18 (the forms of idolatrous images); Is 44:13 (the form of a man); Ez 8:10 (the forms of all kinds of creatures); Ps 106:20 (the form of an ox); Ez 8:3; 10:8 (the form of a hand). According to 2 Kgs 16:10: "King Ahaz sent to Uriah the priest a model (דְּמוּת; *dĕmût*) of the altar, that is, its form/structure (תַּבְנִית; *taḇnît*) according to its entire construction." Here the depiction is represented by model דְּמוּת (*dĕmût*), "likeness," not תַּבְנִית (*taḇnît*), "structure, form."

[102] In classical Greek τύπος (*typos*) had a wide range of meanings, including "cast" or "replica" made in a mold. LSJ, 1835.

[103] If the tabernacle and temple represented replica objects of the heavenly residence of God, then the sacrifices, especially the sin and guilt offerings, represented replica actions of the heavenly sacrifice of Christ, slain before the foundation of the world. Cf. Mt 13:35; 25:31–34; Jn 17:24; Eph 1:3–10; 1 Pt 1:12–21; Rv 13:8; 17:8.

[104] Thus Walton, *Genesis 1 as Ancient Cosmology*, 187.

[105] For references, see p. 6 above.

[106] *B. Yoma* 54b; *Midr. Tanh.* 10. For discussion, see Levenson, "The Temple and the World," 282–84.

symbolized the gracious divine determination to lift the effects of the curse from the land and the people, and the place from which YHWH's blessing and rule (the delights of Eden) could radiate forth (Ps 50:2–4) to the land and nation of Israel.

But YHWH's commitment to Israel was not for Israel's own sake. The redeemed and restored people were to serve as a microcosm of a redeemed humanity, while a prosperous land of Canaan would be microcosmic of the world restored. In his dedicatory prayer, Solomon acknowledged that the temple was built with the world in view (1 Kgs 8:41–43, 59–60). Indeed, in the eighth century B.C., Isaiah and Micah looked forward to the day when peoples from all over the world would "stream"[107] to Zion to learn the way of YHWH and his peace would flow out and envelop the world (Is 2:1–4; Mi 4:1–4).

Conclusion

As a sort of *axis mundi*, the Israelite temple was a divinely revealed and authorized means whereby God in heaven could continue to communicate with the inhabitants of earth—even after the relationship had been ruptured through human rebellion.[108] The rich combination of features derived from the heavenly temple and the original earthly paradise symbolized YHWH's grace in response to sin. But this combination also prepared the way for developments of the temple motif in the NT.[109] When Jesus cleansed the temple, he announced not only its destruction but also its replacement with his own person:

"Destroy this temple, and in three days I will raise it up."

Then the Jews said, "This temple has been under construction for forty-six years, and will you raise it up in three days?"

But Jesus was speaking of the temple of his body. After he was raised from the dead, his disciples remembered that he had said this; and they believed the Scripture and the word that Jesus had spoken. (Jn 2:19–22)[110]

The incarnation, death, and resurrection of Christ rendered superfluous the temple's role as the link between a fallen world and a heavenly court

---

[107] The choice of verb, נהר (*nhr*), "to flow, stream," a denominative verb נהר (*nhr*), "stream, river," not only reverses the direction of the flow of the rivers in Eden but also applies the word metaphorically to people who will come from all over to learn the way of YHWH.

[108] In the ancient world, among other images, the role of *axis mundi* could be played by sacred places (esp. mountains) or sacred trees. For discussion, see Mircea Eliade, *The Sacred and the Profane: The Nature of Religion* (trans. W. R. Trask; New York: Harper & Brothers, 1959), 36–42.

[109] Beale's work on this subject is unsurpassed.

[110] Cf. other references to Jesus' statement: Mt 26:61; 27:40; Mk 14:58; 15:29.

reaching out to that world. As Jesus acknowledged to the Samaritan woman: "The time is coming when you will worship the Father neither on this mountain nor in Jerusalem" (Jn 4:21). Indeed, this entire conversation deflects attention away from the place of worship and focuses on the person who once sat enthroned above the כְּרֻבִים (*kĕrubîm*)[111] but is now present incarnationally in Jesus (v. 26), with the result that many from her town recognized that "this One is indeed the Savior of the world" (v. 42). John himself acknowledged Christ as the fulfillment of the hopes represented by the temple in his prologue to the Gospel. Jesus (the Word) is not only the Creator but also the source of life for a world under the curse of death (1:1–5), the true light for a world in darkness (1:9–10), and the one who came into the world to empower all who believe in his name to become children of God, that is, to make them fully functional as images of God like Adam (1:11–13).[112] John's ode to the Word climaxes in v. 14: "And the Word became flesh and lived (ἐσκήνωσεν; *eskēnōsen*, lit., "tabernacled") among us, and we have seen his glory, the glory as of a father's only son, full of grace and truth." This one, "God the only Son" (Gk. μονογενὴς θεός; *monogenēs theos*, v. 18), has revealed the Father more fully than any tabernacle or temple could.

While Paul's identification of Christian believers as the temple of God, indwelt by the Holy Spirit,[113] reinforces the irrelevance of the temple as the primary symbol of YHWH's desire to relate to his world, the Epistle to the Hebrews provides the fullest essay on the relationship between the temple and the incarnation. In light of the appearance of the Son of God— through whom the world was created, who embodies the radiant glory of God and the exact imprint of his being, who sustains all of creation by his strong word, who has solved the problem of human sin, and who is seated at the right hand of the Majesty on high (Heb 1:1–4)—shadow institutions like temple and sacrifices and Aaronic priesthood have been superseded by the reality. Through Jesus Christ's saving work the people of God participate in God's Edenic rest.

The movement away from the temple as the locus of divine presence to Jesus Christ climaxes in the vision of a restored cosmos in the book of Revelation. On the one hand, the Apocalypse highlights the heavenly temple, where God is seated on his throne and surrounded by worshipers, and from where he governs the world (Rv 7:15; 11:19; 14:15, 17; 15:5–16:1, 17). On the other hand, the book (and Scripture) closes with a vivid

---

[111] The same emphasis is evident in the book of Deuteronomy, which focuses not on the place but on the relationship between the worshipers and YHWH, who is present at the place he has chosen to establish his name. See further Daniel I. Block, " 'In Spirit and in Truth': The Mosaic Vision of Worship," in *The Gospel according to Moses: Theological and Ethical Reflections on the Book of Deuteronomy* (ed. Daniel I. Block; Eugene, OR: Cascade, 2012), 272–98.

[112] Cf. Luke's interpretation of Gn 5:1–2 in Lk 3:38.

[113] Individually in 1 Cor 6:19–20 and collectively in 2 Cor 6:16.

portrayal of the new heavens and the new earth, in the midst of which is the perfectly proportioned and gloriously designed New Jerusalem. John describes this city in magnificently Edenic terms (Rv 21–22). Although the throne of God and of the Lamb will be there, and his vassals (δοῦλοι; *douloi*) will serve him with due reverential awe (Rv 22:3),[114] John declares explicitly that since God is present in person, there is no need for a temple, "for its temple is the Lord God the Almighty and the Lamb." Nor is there need for "sun or moon to shine on it, for the glory of God is its light, and its lamp is the Lamb" (21:2–23). While the first statement repudiates Mircea Eliade's notion of the homologization of world and temple,[115] the second declares that this is not a return to the original Eden but signals a glorious transformation of the original home of humanity. The divine visits will not be limited to appearances "in the cool of the day"; the very presence of the throne of God and the Lamb will guarantee access to the tree of life, the well-being of the city, and the permanent removal of the curse and its effects. Furthermore, it will ensure that his delegated agents will "serve and keep" the earth according to the original divine mandate.

---

[114] Underlying the Gk. λατρεύω (*latreuō*), usually rendered "to worship," is the Heb. הִשְׁתַּחֲוָה (*hištaḥăwā*), which means literally "to prostrate" before a superior, but which may be used more broadly of reverential service and true vassalage under God. In the Pentateuch the word is repeatedly paired with עָבַד (ʿbd), "to perform vassal service." Ex 20:5; 23:24; Dt 4:19; 5:9; 8:19; 30:17; cf. Heb 12:28.

[115] Mircea Eliade, *Patterns in Comparative Religion* (New York: Sheed & Ward, 1958), 373–85; cf. Levenson, "The Temple and the World," 295.

CHAPTER 2

THE SHAPE OF THE TORAH AS REFLECTED IN THE PSALTER, BOOK 1

C. Hassell Bullock

Introduction

Recently I was reading some of the prayers of Charles Spurgeon and noticed how replete they are with the language and images of the King James Version of the Bible—quotations, terms, phrases, images.[1] Having spent the last three years in research on the Psalms, it struck me that Spurgeon's use of the KJV, except for the quotations, is analogous to the psalmists' familiarity with the Torah. Spurgeon's allusions to the KJV reveal how saturated he was in the language and content of the Bible as expressed by this version. Further, his use of its language and images was an instrument by which he expressed his faith and prayed for divine intervention in personal and human situations. This is not to impose a modern analogue on ancient Scripture but to recognize a modern analogue that illustrates an ancient phenomenon in the Psalter. Judging from the many allusions in the Psalms to the Torah (also to the Prophets and Writings, which is another study), I suggest that the psalmists were steeped in the language of those writings, especially the poetic sections, and the images of the Torah stories. Indeed, like the Mishnah that also rarely quotes from the Torah—although it is an interpretation of (the) Torah—the psalmists' method of using the Torah was basically allusion.[2]

Admittedly it is sometimes difficult to establish literary dependence, but when the language and the imagery are overwhelmingly evocative of Torah texts, it is difficult not to admit the connection, as is often done

---

[1] *C. H. Spurgeon's Prayers* (New York: Fleming H. Revell Company, 1906).

[2] Richard L. Schultz's helpful study on quotation in the prophets wisely resists establishing a word-number criterion for determining whether a verbal correspondence constitutes a quotation and expresses a preference for a more generic label, like *literary correspondence*. His conclusions on pp. 211–15 are helpful in thinking through this important issue. *The Search for Quotation: Verbal Parallels in the Prophets* (JSOTSup 180; Sheffield: Sheffield Academic Press, 1999).

in the commentaries on the Psalms. I will attempt to establish the verbal correspondence and draw out the interpretive implications, suggesting that the verbal correspondences become a rhetorical frame in which the psalmists express their message, much like our illustration from Spurgeon's prayers.

The Method

The Psalms afford us the opportunity to look through the portholes of their language and thought and see the larger theological canvas from which the poets often extracted their verbal expressions and pictures. It is another layer of meaning that, once perceived, gives fullness to the hermeneutical enterprise. The question of whether this was a conscious and intentional layer of meaning provided by the psalmists is an interesting one, and the answer we give will depend on several factors. For one thing, if we start with the assumption that the Torah, for the most part, was late (postexilic), then we may have a problem agreeing on what sources the psalmists had to work with, especially those psalms that are attributed to writers from the formative years of Israel's national history, like Moses and David. Even then, however, there is general agreement that the literary sources, like the Song of Moses (Dt 32) and the Song of the Sea (Ex 15), are early. Therefore, the psalmists could have had these at their disposal.

A second issue is whether the editing that occurred in the formation of the Psalter was, so far as the individual psalms are concerned, macro-structural rather than internal, or both. That is, did the editors work with psalms they had at hand in the various collections and resist making internal changes to the individual psalms to bring them into agreement with their editorial frame of reference? Very likely, both procedures were exercised, although I tend to think the internal changes were far less frequent than some redactional proposals assume. In reference to the macro-structural editing, Hendrik Koorevaar proposes that the psalm titles are a key to understanding the final editing of the Psalter. Noting the general agreement that Book 1 is a Davidic collection, he points to the psalm clusters in Books 2, 3, and 4, calling attention to the arrangement within the clusters, and the final shape of the book that, according to his accounting, makes Ps 86 the center of the book. It is of interest that Ps 86 is the only Davidic psalm in Book 3 and is made up largely of quotations from other Davidic psalms. Just how much internal editing of the individual psalms took place at this stage of the book's formation is difficult to determine. My opinion is that it was largely confined to titles and subscripts, the latter illustrated by Pss 72:20; 25:22 (prayer for Israel); 31:23–24; 131:7–8 (admonitions to Israel).

There is general agreement that each of the five books has a historical orientation. Book 1 is oriented to the formative era of David's kingship and Israel's ongoing struggle to live in their factious world and be governed by the Torah. Books 2 and 3 are oriented to the exile and Babylonian captivity, offering a future and a hope and exhorting this captive people to trust in YHWH, even though the Davidic covenant seems to have failed (Ps 89). That is, Books 2 and 3 seem to fall more in the early era of exile, offering hope and comfort, much like the prophecy of Jeremiah. Book 4, however, is oriented to life within exile, and, much like Ezekiel, offers hope of God's presence and sovereignty in the face of defeat and the humiliation of captivity (e.g., "The LORD reigns," Pss 93–100). Book 5 edges right up to the return from exile, even celebrating it (e.g., Ps 126).

The point of this discussion is to suggest that in the editorial process, the editors viewed themselves in the prophetic role of comforting and admonishing Israel, much like Isaiah (Is 40) and other prophets, and they stationed Israel's heroes at particular junctures of the book to call out their words of admonition and comfort—they "being dead, yet speak." The first indication of this comes at the beginning of the collection where the editor, perhaps the final editor, positions David, though unnamed, as the righteous person whose life is permeated by the Torah (Pss 1–2). He stands as the sentinel of righteousness and Torah faith, a faith for which he, in the editorial process of the book, will be shaped into the paradigm of the righteous person and the teacher of Torah faith (Ps 34:11). In this essay I will try to show how David, the paradigm of righteousness and Torah life, teaches the Torah to Israel by allusions to heroes, events, and the use of Torah language. That is to say, *the psalmists' knowledge of the biblical tradition forms an important part of their presentation, and the language, personalities, events, and practices of the Torah* describe *and* prescribe *the spiritual posture of the later community and the individual psalmist.* The result recorded in the Psalms is portraits of faith, conflict, and hope that are painted with colors from the easel of that mental treasury, in the case of our study, the Torah. Indeed, there is good reason to insist that the Prophets, much of Wisdom, and the Psalms, along with other material of the OT, are premised on the Torah legislation and the "primal events" of Israel's history.[3] These data—language, personalities, events, and practices—form a rhetorical frame that becomes both a repository of the information and a platform from which to comfort, admonish, and challenge the psalmist and his contemporary audience. The object of our study is to explore how the psalmists of Book 1 (Pss 1–41) present the theology and piety of their faith in the rhetorical framework of Torah.

Textual Warrant for the Method

Psalm 1, which probably postdates Book 1 (Pss 3–41) by several generations, sets the stage for our study. While it has a history of its own, we must nevertheless look at Book 1 within the larger shape of the Psalter

---

[3] Verne H. Fletcher, "The Fundamental Shape of Old Testament Ethics," *SJT* 24 (1971): 50.

as a whole. The literary history of Book 1 has become subservient to the wider editorial history of the book of Psalms as a whole. That means then that when the final editing of the book took place, the Torah was a written body of literature on which the readers were invited to meditate "day and night" (Ps 1:2). That does not exclude the idea that the psalmists were working from an oral knowledge of the Torah.

The method that identifies paradigms of offices and individuals has been demonstrated quite effectively by Jamie A. Grant in his study of the law of kingship in Dt 17:14–20 and its paradigmatic representation in the king figure of the Psalms, who also is a keeper of the Torah.[4] Prior to that, and on the heels of Gerald Wilson's seminal study of the shaping of the Psalter,[5] Leslie C. Allen published a brief but titillating article on David as the paradigm of spirituality in the editorial view of the Psalter.[6] All of these studies can be traced to the headwaters of Brevard Childs's article on the Psalm titles,[7] in which he proposed a redactional role of David "as a model for the individual's response to the conflicts, crises and victories of life." In other words, the language of the Torah often becomes the rhetorical frame in which the psalmist expresses his message to his audience. In that sense, it represents to some degree a transfer of the ancient voice of the Torah, its psychological force, and its moral persuasion to the contemporary scene. It is along these lines that this study proceeds.

The method this essay employs can be demonstrated in other OT literature, at least in its incipient form, and this literature was most likely at the disposal of the editors of the Psalter in the early postexilic era. First, it is reflected in the statement of Jo 1:5: "As I was with Moses, so I will be with you; *I will never leave you nor forsake you*" (emphasis added).[8] Thus the writer of Joshua proceeds to show how Joshua re-enacts the life of Moses, or functions as the new Moses. In fact, the book of Joshua is composed in the shadow of Dt 18:15 ("The LORD your God will raise up for you a prophet like me from among you, from your brethren"), and in the acknowledgement of Dt 34:10–11, that the "new Moses" has not yet come, which, in the light of Dt 18:15, is an implicit prediction that he will yet come:

> And there has not arisen a prophet since in Israel like Moses, whom the LORD knew face to face, none like him for all the signs and the wonders which the

---

[4] Jamie A. Grant, *The King as Exemplar: The Function of Deuteronomy's Kingship Law in the Shaping of the Book of Psalms* (Atlanta: Society of Biblical Literature, 2004).

[5] Gerald H. Wilson, *The Editing of the Hebrew Psalter* (SBLDS 76; Chico, CA: Scholars Press, 1985).

[6] Leslie C. Allen, "David as Exemplar of Spirituality: The Redactional Function of Psalm 19," *Bib* 67/4 (1986): 544–46.

[7] "Psalm Titles and Midrashic Exegesis," *JSS* (1971): 137–50; also *Introduction to the Old Testament as Scripture* (Philadelphia: Fortress, 1979), 520–22.

[8] Translations throughout this chapter are the author's own, unless otherwise stated.

L ORD sent him to do in the land of Egypt, to Pharaoh and to all his servants and to all his land.

That this motif of a new Moses is not an anomaly in the book is evidenced by two texts that further reflect the new Moses theme personified in his successor Joshua: (1) Joshua is elevated in Israel's eyes by the miracle at the Jordan, just as Moses was elevated by the miracle at the Red Sea (Jo 4:14/Ex 3:5); and (2) the commander of the Lord's army ordered Joshua to take off his shoes because he was standing on holy ground, just as happened to Moses at the burning bush (Jo 5:15/Ex 14:31). Even the miracle of crossing the Jordan River carried parallel features in the detail that Israel crossed over on dry ground, just as they did at the Red Sea (Jo 3:17/Ex 14:22). In fact, from time to time the OT resumes its search for the "prophet like you [Moses] from among their brothers" (Dt 18:18) and in reality finds him, particularly in the person of Elijah (1 Kgs 17–19);[9] and the prophetic canon closes with its sights set on the future appearance of the new Moses (Mal 4:5–6), a detail that Mark applies to John the Baptist (Mk 1:2/Mal 3:1).

Gesturing in the same direction as our study, however, Allen proposed that the Chronicler presented the life of David as "a model for Israel which the Chronicler surely intended his own generation to copy (1 Chr 29, 18)."[10] Applying that to the Psalms, Allen concludes: "[i]t is by no means unreasonable to posit that in the Psalter also the ancient hero *mutatis mutandis* became a standard of spirituality for members of each generation of God's people."[11] We turn now to our analysis.

Thesis 1: Torah Language as a Rhetorical Frame

By the use of Torah language, the psalmists form a rhetorical frame to transfer the circumstances and attributes of Israel's past events and heroes to their own personal and contemporary setting.

Psalm 16

In Ps 16 David alludes to the language of the conquest and Levitical tradition to affirm his special devotion to God. Specifically the psalmist

---

[9] See Frank Moore Cross, *Canaanite Myth and Hebrew Epic: Essays in the History of the Religion of Israel* (Cambridge, MA: Harvard University Press, 1973), 190–94.

[10] Allen, "David as Exemplar," 545. Also H. G. M. Williamson, *1 and 2 Chronicles* (Grand Rapids: Eerdmans, 1982), 389, insists that the story of Manasseh is a paradigm of Israel's history. He was an idolator who was resistant to repentance, and he was exiled and subsequently restored to his kingdom (2 Chr 33:1–13), which are all phases of Israel's history.

[11] Allen, "David as Exemplar," 545.

has in mind the Levites who were not assigned a landed inheritance because the LORD assured them that he was their inheritance.

Torah Texts	Psalm 16
Regarding Aaron and the priests, the Lord says: "I am your portion [אֲנִי חֶלְקֶךָ; *'ănî ḥelqĕkā*] (Nm 18:20) and your inheritance [וְנַחֲלָתְךָ; *wĕnaḥălātĕkā*]"	"LORD, you have assigned me my portion [מְנָת־חֶלְקִי; *mĕnāt-ḥelqî*] and my cup" (v. 5).
Regarding Joshua's division of the land, "their inheritances were **assigned** by lot [בְּגוֹרָל נַחֲלָתָם; *bĕgôral naḥălātām*] . . . but [Moses] had not granted the Levites an inheritance among the rest" (Jo 14:2, 3).	"my lot [גּוֹרָלִי; *gôrālî*] secure" (v. 5)
"The boundary lines of Manasseh [חַבְלֵי־מְנַשֶּׁה; *ḥablê-mĕnaššeh*] were ten [portions]" (Jo 17:5)	"boundary lines" [חֲבָלִים; *ḥăbālîm*] (v. 6)

Metaphorically speaking, YHWH is the psalmist's portion, cup, and lot (v. 5), meaning that what worldly possessions were to some, YHWH was that to him and more. Though not a Levite himself, David had found the religious status of the Levites an appropriate description of his own special relationship to YHWH.

Psalm 17

Psalm 17 draws upon the language of the Song of Moses (Dt 32:10–11) and applies its endearing terms for Israel to David. An individual lament, Ps 17 is a good illustration of the use of metaphor. Verse 8 borrows two images from the Song of Moses, "the apple of your eye" (כְּאִישׁוֹן בַּת־עָיִן; *kĕ'îšôn baṭ-'āyin*) and "the shadow of your wings" (בְּצֵל כְּנָפֶיךָ; *bĕṣēl kĕnāpêkā*). Not surprisingly, this points to a familiarity with the Song. Moreover, these images immediately follow the petition that God will "show the wonder" of his great love, perhaps calling to mind the LORD's mighty acts under Moses. It is significant that the individual psalmist sees himself, rather than Israel, or at least not merely Israel, as the precious object of YHWH's attention, the "apple of his eye" (כְּאִישׁוֹן בַּת־עָיִן; *kĕ'îšôn baṭ-'āyin*). This psalm illustrates the fact that OT texts sometimes transfer the images of corporate Israel to the individual, suggesting a fluidity between the corporate and individual aspects of OT anthropology. The following terms in Ps 17 constitute a rhetorical frame to describe YHWH's endearment of David.

Torah Texts	Psalm 17
Dt 32:10 refers to Israel as very precious to the Lord (יִצְּרֶנְהוּ כְּאִישׁוֹן עֵינוֹ; *yiṣṣĕrenhû kĕʾîšôn ʿênô*).	"the apple of your eye" (כְּאִישׁוֹן בַּת־עָיִן; *kĕʾîšôn baṯ-ʿāyin*) (v. 8)
Dt 32:11 refers to YHWH's protective presence (יִפְרֹשׂ כְּנָפָיו יִקָּחֵהוּ; *yiprōś kĕnāp̄āyw yiqqāḥêhû*).	"the shadow of your wings " (בְּצֵל כְּנָפֶיךָ; *bĕṣēl kĕnāp̄êkā*) (v. 8)
Nm 10:35 the prescribed prayer when moving the ark (קוּמָה יְהוָה; *qûmā yhwh*)	"Rise up, O LORD" (קוּמָה יְהוָה; *qûmā yhwh*) (v. 13).

So David, and not merely the nation, as is the case in the Song of Moses, has become the object of the prayer, thus a transfer from the corporate to the personal, from the primal benefits of the covenant to the ongoing life of the covenant people. That was precisely how the covenant was supposed to work. (We will consider below the prayer language of Nm 10:35 [Ps 17:13], which David uses to implore the Lord to act miraculously against his enemies [v. 7].)

Psalm 23

In Ps 23 the Lord leads David as he had led Israel in the exodus from Egypt. Just as David's experience as shepherd (1 Sm 16:11; 17:20) and king engraved its language on this psalm, so the archetypal story of the exodus is echoed in its verbal expressions. It is not a recounting of the exodus story as we find it in some psalms (e.g., Ps 106:7–8) but an echo of the story.

Torah Texts	Psalm 23
Dt 2:7 uses the same verb to describe God's care of Israel in the wilderness ("You have not lacked anything [לֹא חָסַרְתָּ דָּבָר; *lō' ḥāsartā dāḇār*]").	"I shall not want" (אֶחְסָר; *'eḥsār*) (v. 1).
Song of Moses (Ex 15:13): "In your unfailing love you will lead [נָחִיתָ; *nāḥîtā*] the people you have redeemed. In your strength you will guide (נֵהַלְתָּ; *nēhaltā*) them to your holy dwelling."	verbs for "guide" (נהל [*nhl*] and נחה [*nḥh*]) (vv. 2–3)
Ex 15:13 (נְוֵה קָדְשֶׁךָ; *nĕwē qoḏšekā*, lit., "your holy pasture")	"pastures" (בִּנְאוֹת דֶּשֶׁא; *bin'ôṯ deše'*) (v. 2)

Here again we move from the macrocosm to the microcosm, or from the corporate to the personal, and that is a massive application, as we saw in Ps 17. That God would lead David as he had led Israel in those historic years of becoming God's people is a momentous application of history. The very suggestion that YHWH as David's Shepherd would lead him personally as he had led Israel out of Egypt and through the wilderness supports the position that there was in ancient Israel, even as early as David's time, a genuine sense of individual personality.

Psalm 27

In Ps 27 David faces a Joshua-like dilemma and hears Moses' words of encouragement, just as Joshua did. The language and imagery of this psalm straddle the Torah and the book of Joshua. David speaks of his fear in the face of his enemies, just as Joshua and Israel encountered similar fears as they faced the challenge of the conquest, implied by the shared vocabulary of the conquest.

Torah Texts	Psalm 27
Dt 31:8/Jo 8:1; 10:8 The same verb (ירא; *yr*ʾ) expresses Joshua's fear in face of the conquest.	Ps 27:1 "whom shall I fear?" (מִמִּי אִירָא; *mimmî ʾîrāʾ*) David asks this question as he faces his personal enemies.
Dt 31:8, Moses says to Joshua: "Do not be afraid" (לֹא תִירָא; *lōʾ tîrāʾ*).	Ps 27:3, David says, "my heart will not fear" (לֹא־יִירָא; *lōʾ-yîrāʾ*).
Jo 1:5 YHWH says to Joshua: "I will never . . . forsake you" (וְלֹא אֶעֶזְבֶךָ; *wĕlōʾ ʾeʿezbekā*).	Ps 27:9 David says, "Do not . . . forsake me" (וְאַל־תַּעַזְבֵנִי; *wĕʾal-taʿazbēnî*).
Dt 31:7 Moses' words to Joshua: "Be strong and courageous" (חֲזַק וֶאֱמָץ; *ḥăzaq weʾĕmāṣ*). Jo 1:6, 7, 9 YHWH's words to Joshua: "Be strong and courageous" (חֲזַק וֶאֱמָץ; *ḥăzaq weʾĕmāṣ*).	Ps 27:14 David encourages Israel as Moses and YHWH had encouraged Joshua: "Be strong and take heart" (חֲזַק וְיַאֲמֵץ לִבֶּךָ; *ḥăzaq wĕyaʾămēṣ libbekā*).

David's fear of his enemies reflects the historical moment of Joshua's fear-laden contemplation of the conquest. The enemies in the latter case were national, whereas David's political enemies had re-created the same dilemma in personal and national dimensions, and now in the echoes of these ancient voices, David and his contemporaries receive an installment of courage.

Psalm 31

Using the formulaic language of the Song of the Sea (Ex 15:13), Ps 31 personalizes YHWH's guidance of Israel. This psalm illustrates the personalization of the covenant faith in a way that is similar to Ps 23, as the psalmist prays "for the sake of your name lead and guide me" (תַּנְחֵנִי וּתְנַהֲלֵנִי; *tanḥēnî ûtĕnahălēnî*, v. 4[3]). The Song of the Sea affirms that God will lead and guide Israel (Ex 15:13), and David draws upon that language, as he did in Ps 23:2, 3, by using these same two verbs (נהל; *nhl* and נחה; *nḥh*) to petition YHWH's guidance. Moreover, the spirit of the Mosaic covenant that pervades this psalm takes formulaic expression in the personal confession of v. 15b[14b], "I say, 'You are my God'" (אָמַרְתִּי אֱלֹהַי אָתָּה; *'āmartî 'ĕlōhay 'āttā*), and gives assent to the first part of the trifold covenant formula, "I will be your God."[12] This provides further insight into how personal, as compared with corporate, the covenant faith had become. The covenant formula, which was a corporate confession, has now become a personal statement of faith in the mouth of the psalmist. He could even boldly ask for the effect of Aaron's benediction, "cause your face to shine upon your servant" (v. 16). Peter Craigie comments on this text: "[i]n a shortened form, he makes that blessing his own to quash the uncertainties within him."[13] Indeed, so absolutely had the psalmist committed himself to the covenant faith that he could pray, "into your hand I commit my spirit" (v. 6). The movement was not merely from the community to the individual, but also from the individual to the community, for David exhorts the community to "love the LORD," following his example and thus fulfilling the demands of the Torah (Dt 6:5/Ps 31:24[23]).

The Torah becomes the glossary of the psalmist's language of faith, and these allusions constitute a rhetorical frame in which he expresses his message, applying to him personally and to his contemporary community the spiritual legacy of Israel's history and heroes.

Thesis 2: Torah Texts as Prayer Language

The psalmist uses the terminology of Torah texts as prayer language and thus draws the ancient worthies into his prayers of intercession for Israel and for himself, silhouetting the spiritual posture of the ancients.

---

[12] Lv 26:12 contains all three components of the covenant formula: "I will walk among you [Part C], and be your God [Part A], and you will be my people" [Part B].

[13] Peter C. Craigie, *Psalms 1–50* (WBC 19; Waco, TX: Word, 1983), 81.

Perhaps the basis for this pattern is found in the ancient notion of the fluidity of personality in which the individual merged into the community, and the community's experience was reflected, perhaps even duplicated, in the individual's. The psalmists, in fact, could not see themselves as individuals apart from the corporate consciousness of the community. The individual was defined and understood within the context of the community, and the community was reflected in the life and experience of the individual. David's deliverance and Israel's were inextricably linked. To put it another way, the individual was validated within the community, and the psalmist's personal redemption, if Israel's did not happen, remained incomplete. One of the clearest illustrations of this latter view of the individual is found in the closing invocation of several psalms. While some of these may be later additions to the psalm to which they are attached, they are nevertheless reflective of this personality theory. One example will have to suffice. At the end of Ps 25, which is an individual lament, the suppliant prays, "Redeem Israel, O God, out of all his troubles" (Ps 25:22; see also 3:8; 31:23, 24; 130:7, 8; 131:3). Even if this prayer is a later application of the psalm to Israel's redemption—which I am not at all sure of—the point is still valid: the individual's deliverance, apart from Israel's, was incomplete.

Psalm 9

Psalm 9 reflects Moses' prayer upon the moving of the ark, now reissued in David's prayer regarding his national enemies. The prayer Moses prayed when the ark set out for another location was a well-known entreaty (Nm 10:35) and gestured YHWH's rule and reign in history. In that sense, Moses' language in Nm 10:35 became a baseline of prayer, applied to the psalmists' new situation. As was the case with Moses' original prayer, Israel's national enemies are clearly the object of the petition in 3:7; 7:7[6]; 9:20[19]; and 82:8.[14] In Pss 10:12; 17:13; and 74:22 the object has shifted to the psalmists' personal enemies. Perhaps it is best to step outside of Book 1 in order to find a clear illustration that will illuminate this principle of prayer. In Ps 132:8–10[7–9] the worshiper celebrates God's oath to David and Solomon's subsequent construction of the temple, clearly alluding to Nm 10:35:

> Let us go to his dwelling place,
> let us worship at his footstool, saying
> "Arise, O LORD [קוּמָה יְהוָה; qûmā yhwh], and come to your resting place,
> you and the ark of your might.

---

[14] Note that Pss 74:22 and 82:8 use the generic name of God, אֱלֹהִים (ʾĕlōhîm), rather than יְהוָה (yhwh), since Book 3, in which they occur, predominantly employs אֱלֹהִים (ʾĕlōhîm) as the divine name.

May your priests be clothed with your righteousness;
may your faithful people sing for joy."

To reinforce our point, we may observe that the Chronicler employs the language of 132:8–9 in Solomon's dedicatory prayer of the temple (2 Chr 6:41), showing how one saint of history (Solomon) prayed the prayer of a previous saint (Moses) and thus drew the ancient worthy into his prayers of intercession for Israel. This prayer obviously bore repeating, and such a repetition in effect encored God's extraordinary action in history. That is, the saints of one age, in effect, issue their prayers in the words of the saints of another era, and thus use their password to the throne of grace. In varying degrees of application, this is precisely the point of other occurrences of this ancient petition in the Psalter.

Thus, in times of crisis David petitions God in the words of two great and wise voices of Israel's past, Aaron and Moses. In effect, the psalmist draws these heroes of faith into his petition on Israel's behalf. In addition to the occurrences of "Arise, O LORD!" we may note the following psalms that use the terms of the Aaronic benediction of Nm 6:24–26.

Psalm 4

In Ps 4, the suppliant utilizes the Aaronic benediction (Nm 6:24–26) to seek YHWH's favor for Israel and for him personally. In some instances the language may be more an echo than an allusion, but the language unmistakably reflects the language of the Aaronic benediction in Nm 6:24–26.

Torah Texts	Psalm 4
Nm 6:25 "the LORD make his face shine on you (פָּנָיו אֵלֶיךָ יְהוָה יָאֵר; *pānāyw ʾēlêḵā yhwh yāʾēr*)	Ps 4:7[6] "Let the light of your face shine upon us O LORD" (נְסָה־עָלֵינוּ אוֹר פָּנֶיךָ יְהוָה; *nĕsā-ʿālênû ʾôr pānêḵā yhwh*).

With some transposed terms, and plural pronouns for the nation, yet in the language of the Aaronic benediction, Pss 67, 80, and 119, although outside of the delineated territory of Book 1, record such a petition for Israel.

Numbers 6:24, 25	Psalm 67
"The LORD bless you . . . and be gracious to you" (Nm 6:24a, 25b) (וִיחֻנֶּךָּ . . . יְבָרֶכְךָ יְהוָה; *wîḥunnekā . . . yĕḇārekkā yhwh*). "The LORD turn his face toward you" (Nm 6:26a) (יִשָּׂא יְהוָה פָּנָיו אֵלֶיךָ; *yiśśāʾ yhwh pānāyw ʾēlêḵā*).	Ps 67:2[1] "May God be gracious to us and bless us" (אֱלֹהִים יְחָנֵּנוּ וִיבָרְכֵנוּ; *ʾĕlōhîm yĕḥānnēnû wîḇārĕkēnû*) "and make his face shine upon us" (יָאֵר פָּנָיו אִתָּנוּ; *yāʾēr pānāyw ʾittānû*).

Note that Ps 67 is part of the "Elohistic Psalter," which overwhelmingly uses אֱלֹהִים (*ʾĕlōhîm*), rather than יְהוָה (*yhwh*) as the divine name, thus the change. This blessing is used in a community lament as a refrain in Ps 80:

"Make your face shine [upon us], that we may be saved" (הָאֵר פָּנֶיךָ וְנִוָּשֵׁעָה; *wĕhāʾēr pānêkā wĕniwwāšēʿā*) (Nm 6:25/Ps 80:8[7], 20[19]).

The community application transfers the blessing from the ancient community to the psalmists' contemporary community, whereas Ps 119:135 makes a personal application:

"Make your face shine upon your servant" (פָּנֶיךָ הָאֵר בְּעַבְדֶּךָ; *pānêkā hāʾēr bĕʿabdekā*).

Psalm 4, an individual lament, is further supplied with three phrases that occur in the Blessing of Moses (Dt 33), sketching out a personal prayer that employs the language of the great lawgiver in his final blessing on Israel. By the use of this language the psalmist accomplishes two things: he places David within the bounds of the Mosaic covenant, which is natural enough; and he takes Moses' words upon his own lips, calling him into his exercise of prayer for himself and for his people (note plural, "upon us," v. 6b).

Dt 33:19 "offer there the sacrifices of the righteous" (יִזְבְּחוּ זִבְחֵי־צֶדֶק; *yizbĕḥû zibḥê-ṣedeq*).	Ps 4:6[5] "Offer the *sacrifices of the righteous*"(זִבְחוּ זִבְחֵי־צֶדֶק; *zibḥû zibḥê-ṣedeq*).
Dt 33:28 "Jacob will dwell secure in a land of *grain and new wine*" (דָּגָן וְתִירוֹשׁ; *dāgān wĕtîrôš*).	Ps 4:8[7] "Fill my heart with joy when their *grain and new wine* [דְגָנָם וְתִירוֹשָׁם; *dĕgānām wĕtîrôšām*] abound."
Dt 33:28 "So Israel *will live in safety*" (וַיִּשְׁכֹּן יִשְׂרָאֵל בֶּטַח; *wayyiškōn yiśrāʾēl beṭaḥ*).	Ps 4:9[8] "For you alone, LORD, *make me dwell in safety*" (לָבֶטַח תּוֹשִׁיבֵנִי; *lābeṭaḥ tôšîbēnî*).

Employing the language of the Blessing of Moses, David claims in prayer those same blessings for his own generation. We should note, however, that this principle, that the psalmists engage the ancients in their prayers, is not the same as the belief that the saints can pray for us. Rather, David prayed in their words, and in so doing, called them into the service of prayer, joining them at the throne of grace. It is the OT doctrine of the communion of saints.

Psalm 18

In Ps 18, by allusions to the Song of Moses and other Torah texts, David translates his faithfulness to God's law into terms of personal piety. The language of 18:32[31] echoes again the Song of Moses (Dt 32:4, 31, the Lord as "rock," (צוּר; *ṣûr*), holding the Lord up as Israel's Rock and declaring that there is no one else like him. In the Song of Moses the word "rock" (צוּר; *ṣûr*) occurs four times as a metaphor for YHWH, plus once in reference to the literal rock Moses struck and twice in reference to a pagan god (סֶלַע; *slʿ*). So the Song of Moses as the source of the metaphor seems quite certain. Further, even though this psalm does not explicitly take up the issue of idolatry, as does the Song of Moses (Dt 32:12, 21, 37–39), it nevertheless proclaims YHWH's uniqueness (18:32[31]) and distinguishes him as the saving God.

The affirmation, "I love you LORD, my strength" (18:2[1]) resonates as a response to the command of the *Shema* to "Love the LORD your God with all your heart" (Dt 6:5), except that the verb "love" is רחם (*rḥm*) rather than אהב (*ʾhb*), as it is in Dt 6:5. A link that suggests the two verbs were synonyms is found in the *Targum of Onkelos*, which uses this verb רחם (*rḥm*) to translate the verb אהב (*ʾhb*), in Dt 6:5. The fact that this term is taken from covenant vocabulary, involving the covenant stipulations and promises, affirms the thought that the moral commandments of the Torah are summed up and fulfilled in the piety of the suppliant. The psalmist's piety is matched by the Lord's delight in him (18:20[19]), and its outcome is that the Lord reached down from his lofty place and "drew me out of deep waters" (יַמְשֵׁנִי מִמַּיִם רַבִּים; *yamšēnî mimmayim rabbîm*), a figure of Moses' rescue from the Nile (Ex 2:10). Indeed, the rather impersonal description of the theophany in 18:8–16[7–15] (cf. Ex 19:16–19) is turned into a deeply personal experience for David in the remainder of the psalm (except for the ethical interlude of 18:26–28). The Lord's response to David was decisive when he cried out in his distress (18:5[4]), which was the direct opposite of God's response to David's enemies when they cried out to the Lord for help—"he did not answer" (18:42[41]). The psalmist's declaration that "all his laws [כָּל־מִשְׁפָּטָיו; *kol-mišpāṭāyw*] are before me; I have not turned away from his decrees [וְחֻקֹּתָיו; *wěḥuqqōtāyw*]" (18:23[22]) is the explanation for his "righteousness," that is, keeping God's laws. For that reason the Lord has not turned away from him. This combination of law and personal piety to which we are introduced in Ps 1 is a fitting conclusion to the psalm. And if this is the concluding psalm in an early Davidic collection, consisting of Pss 3–18, crowned with Ps 19, a Torah psalm, as James Luther Mays has proposed,[15] it is the editor's witness that David, at least the David of the Psalms, is truly the pious person described in Ps 1.

Thesis 3: Torah Language as a Teaching Instrument

The psalmists employ the language of Torah life and practices as symbols and metaphors of their own and Israel's religious piety. In so doing, the

[15] James Luther Mays, "The Place of the Torah-Psalms in the Psalter," *JBL* 106 (1987): 11.

rhetorical use of Torah language becomes a teaching instrument to promote the Torah life and a means of moral persuasion for the ongoing life of Israel.

Psalm 19

In Ps 19 David draws upon the imagery of creation and the gift of the Torah and reviews the power of sin. In the broad sweep, Ps 19 is a "little Torah," beginning with creation and balancing that with God's gift of the law ("the Torah of the LORD"), much like the Pentateuch in its broadest scope. The poet does not make an effort to duplicate exact phrases from the creation account, but he shares the vocabulary of Gn 1–3, much as Ps 27 employs the language of the conquest. In fact, while other terms are common Hebrew vocabulary, the word "skies" ("firmament," רָקִיעַ; *rāqîaʿ*) is distinctive to the creation narrative, and the other occurrences in Ezekiel, Daniel, and the Psalms likely belong to that semantic center, suggesting that the Genesis narrative is the palette from which the psalmist takes his colors. The duplicate terms are particularly impressive.

Genesis		Psalm 19
1:1, etc.	"heavens"	19:2[1] הַשָּׁמַיִם (*haššāmayim*)
1:1, etc. (אֱלֹהִים; *ʾĕlōhîm*)	"God"	19:2[1] אֵל (*ʾēl*)
1:6–8	"skies"	19:2[1] הָרָקִיעַ (*hārāqîaʿ*)
2:9; 3:5, etc.	"knowledge"	19:3[2] דַּעַת (*dāʿat*)
1:5	"day" and "night"	19:3[2] יוֹם (*yôm*) and לַיְלָה (*laylā*)
1:1, etc.	"earth"	19:5[4] הָאָרֶץ (*hāʾāreṣ*)
2:7	"soul"	19:8[7] נֶפֶשׁ (*nāpeš*)
2:5, etc. (יְהוָה אֱלֹהִים; *yhwh ʾĕlōhîm*)	"YHWH/LORD"	19:8–10[7–9], 15[14] יְהוָה (*yhwh*)
3:5–7	"eyes"	19:9[8] עֵינָיִם (*ʿênāyim*)
3:6 (singular)	"precious"	19:11[10] הַנֶּחֱמָדִים (*hanneḥĕmādîm*)
2:11	"gold"	19:11[10] זָהָב (*zāhāḇ*)
3:8 (synonym, וַיִּתְחַבֵּא; *wayyithabbēʾ*)	"hidden"	19:13[12] מִנִּסְתָּרוֹת (*minnistārôt*) "hidden"
4:7	"rule"	19:14[13] משׁל (*mšl*)

A further theological parallel is the fact that Ps 19 duplicates the two views of God found in Gn 1–3. The first portrait is that of the transcendent God who speaks the world into existence (Gn 1), with a corresponding portrait in Ps 19:2–7 [1–6] not of the creation process as such but of creation itself, now proclaiming the glory of God the Creator. The second view of God is introduced by a focus on the immanent God in Gn 2–3, who, with his own hands, forms man from the dust of the ground, and the woman from his side, and comes "walking" in the garden to investigate how the new couple is getting along. In Ps 19 (vv. 8–10, 15[7–9, 14]), using the tegrammaton (יְהוָה; *yhwh*, YHWH/LORD—the divine name in Gn 2–3 is LORD God, יְהוָה אֱלֹהִים; *yhwh ʾĕlōhîm*) the corresponding view is articulated in terms of the "law of the LORD" that enters into Israel's world and exercises its transforming grace on the people of God. The suppliant describes God's personal involvement with the world, as does Gn 2–3, but in this case the Lord's instrument of creating human society for which he made the world is by the special instrument of Torah, which is just as personal as YHWH's using his own hands to form man and woman. The Torah in its domination of human life corresponds to the sun in its domination of the daytime sky, for "it is the Torah of God alone that reveals to mankind that he has a place in the universal scheme of things."[16] In a similar way, the immanent God of Gn 2–3 dominates the created order with his personal appearance and adds his "human" touch to creation.

Further, the reflections of 19:13–14[12–13], interestingly enough, focus on the story of the psalmist's sin, which is the center of the story in Gn 2–3; and as David contemplates the power of sin, he even employs the verb "rule" (משל; *mšl*) that came to describe sin's overpowering force in the early history of the human family (Gn 4:7). The hidden faults (נִסְתָּרוֹת; *nistārôt*, a synonym of וַיִּתְחַבֵּא; *wayyithabbēʾ*—Ps 19:14/Gn 3:8), the willful sins (זֵדִים; *zēdîm*), and the great transgression (פֶּשַׁע רָב; *pešaʿ rāb*),[17] may be echoes of the primordial fall, which the psalmist faces again on a personal scale.

While the psalmist is quite alert to his message and literary style, he may very well draw from a vocabulary that is imbedded in his subconscious mind, much as Spurgeon does in his prayers mentioned above. The shift from the cosmos to humankind at 19:8[7] is no accident but represents the centering of the Genesis story on humanity, beginning with Gn 2, and the eventual redeeming factor of the Torah that is the major emphasis of the Pentateuch.

Psalm 20

Psalm 20 contains an implicit reference to Dt 17:16 (against amassing horses) and portrays David as the true keeper of the Torah, because as

---

[16] Craigie, *Psalms 1–50*, 183.

[17] The term "great transgression" may refer to adultery (J. J. Rabinowitz, "The 'Great Sin' " in Ancient Egyptian Marriage Contracts," *JNES* 18 [1959]: 73). It could also refer to sin in general, or to the fall of Gn 3 (Craigie, *Psalms 1–50*, 183).

king, he keeps the Law of the King as set forth in Dt 17:14–20.[18] Psalm 20 is a royal psalm because it concerns the king and his success in battle (Ps 20:7[6], 10[9]). Indeed, the psalm is concerned with the king's obedience to the law of kingship, which forbids Israel's kings to "acquire great numbers of horses" (Dt 17:16), lest they trust in their own military resources rather than God's power to save Israel. David seemed to have kept this policy, seeing that he hamstrung the captured horses of Hadadezer, king of Zobah, and saved only enough of them for a hundred chariots (2 Sm 8:3–4), implying David's limited use of horses and chariots. Psalm 20:8 is thus an affirmation of David as the keeper of Torah, thus connecting Ps 20 to Ps 19.

Psalm 25

In the context of YHWH's character description drawn from the Torah (Ex 34:6), Ps 25 makes the drama of worship a symbol of personal devotion. There is no question that the covenant context is critical to understanding Ps 25. In 25:10 the Lord's ways are a reflection of his love (חֶסֶד; ḥesed) and truth (אֱמֶת; ʾĕmet), and this divine character shapes the covenant he has made with Israel and the relationship he has with the keepers of the covenant. These two terms are also found together in the second revelation to Moses on Mount Sinai, "abounding in love and faithfulness" (וְרַב־חֶסֶד וֶאֱמֶת; wĕrab-ḥesed weʾĕmet, Ex 34:6).

Further, two terms in v. 18 (עָנְיִי וַעֲמָלִי; ʿonyî waʿămālî) belong to the response Israel made when they brought the first fruits to the sanctuary (Dt 26:7): "and the LORD . . . saw our affliction and our suffering, and our oppression [וַיַּרְא אֶת־עָנְיֵנוּ וְאֶת־עֲמָלֵנוּ וְאֶת־לַחֲצֵנוּ; wayyarʾ ʾet-ʿonyēnû wĕʾet-ʿămālēnû wĕʾet-laḥăṣēnû]." Here David personalizes the "affliction" and "distress" as the psalmists often do of national experiences.

In 25:22 this personal psalm clearly turns toward Israel's corporate well-being. It is possible that it grows out of the suppliant's love for his nation, which ought to be part of a king's passion for his people, or that of any noble patron, for that matter. Indeed, it contributes an excellent balance to the psalm's personal orientation. While it is possible that v. 22 is a gloss, as suggested by Franz Delitzsch[19] and others, it nevertheless illustrates how David or his glossator applies this psalm to his own situation, much as the ancient words of the Mosaic covenant are applied to the psalmist's personal life in 25:18 ("look on my affliction and my distress").

---

[18] See Grant, *The King as Exemplar*.

[19] Franz Delitzsch, *Psalms* (trans. James Martin; 3 vols.; 1888; repr., Grand Rapids: Eerdmans, 1949), 1:347.

Psalm 26

Referring to cultic practice, Ps 26 uses the ritual of washing the hands as a metaphor for moral innocence. The psalmist washes his hands to symbolize his innocence (v. 6), a practice also observed by Israel's elders with the same objective (Dt 21:6–7).[20] The priests, too, as preparation for service at the altar of burnt offering, washed their hands in the great laver that sat in the tabernacle/temple court (Ex 40:30–32).[21] Here we have a camera-ready view of the court in front of the sanctuary, which contained both the altar of burnt offering and laver. Moreover, in 26:6–7 the service itself appears in minuscule with the washing of the hands (moral innocence), attendance at the altar (either as priest or worshiper), and proclaiming the wonderful deeds of YHWH in Israel's history, which were written into the temple liturgy. Thus the practices of the sanctuary have become for the psalmist symbols of the moral life of Torah.

Psalm 28

Similar to the metaphor in Ps 25, the lifting up of one's hands in Ps 28 is a metaphor of devotion; in this psalm, devotion to God and his temple. As Pss 26 and 27 include allusions to worship activities in the temple,[22] so Ps 28 alludes to the lifting up of one's hands toward the Holy of Holies (v. 2, דְּבִיר קָדְשֶׁךָ; *dĕbîr qodšekā*), a practice that is attested both in Israel (e.g., Ex 9:29; 1 Kgs 8:38) and in other ANE cultures.[23] No sweeter prayer than that of 28:9 occurs anywhere in the Psalter: "Save your people and bless your inheritance; be their shepherd and carry them forever." The theological frame of this prayer is the covenant, for which Israel's enemies cared nothing, and which even its own members had violated. In v. 9 the term "inheritance" (נַחֲלָתֶךָ; *naḥălāṭekā*) may recall the Song of Moses (Dt 32:9), as it does in other instances in the Psalms, where Moses identified the nation as the Lord's "allotted inheritance" (חֶבֶל נַחֲלָתוֹ; *ḥebel naḥălāṯô*). The personal perspective of the psalm ("I," "my," "me") is set in the light of the covenant relationship between Israel and YHWH ("his people," v. 8a; "your people," "their shepherd," v. 9) and the king and YHWH ("a fortress of salvation for *his anointed one*," v. 8b). The theological effect is to bring the king's conflict with his enemies under the overarching covenant, praying for their defeat and the Lord's shepherding care of the nation, expressed in covenant language.

---

[20] John W. Hilber, "Psalms," *ZIBBC*, 5:344.

[21] Hilber cites evidence of ritual washings in ANE temples: Hilber, "Psalms," 343, citing E. M. C. Groenewoud, "Use of Water in Phoenician Sanctuaries," *JANES* 38 (2001): 149–50, and *ANEP*, no. 619.

[22] Pss 26:6; 27:6.

[23] Hilber, "Psalms," 344.

Psalm 33

In Ps 33 the language of creation and redemption, the latter drawn from the Song of the Sea, brings those two concepts together as a single theological continuum. The "new song" (v. 3, שִׁיר חָדָשׁ; *šîr ḥāḏāš*) that the congregation sings (vv. 4–19) begins with creation, drawing upon Gn 1 and Moses' Song of the Sea (Ex 15). The vocabulary of Gn 1 forms a template for this description of creation: heavens, breath (spirit) of his mouth (Gn 1:2, "spirit/breath of God"), the deep, "God said . . . and there was" (here in v. 6, "the word of the LORD"). Yet, the imagery is a bit more poetic than Gn 1, and in that sense closer to the Song of the Sea, which says, "by the breath of your nostrils (וּבְרוּחַ אַפֶּיךָ; *ûḇĕrûaḥ ʾappêḵā*, Ex 15:8; cf. Ps 33:6, וּבְרוּחַ פִּיו; *ûḇĕrûaḥ pîw*, "by the breath of his mouth") the waters piled up in a heap [וּבְרוּחַ אַפֶּיךָ נֶעֶרְמוּ מַיִם; *ûḇĕrûaḥ ʾappêḵā neʿermû mayim*]."[24] In comparison, our poem describes the Lord as bringing the "starry host" (צְבָאָם; *ṣĕḇāʾām*) into being "by the breath of his mouth" (v. 6b). In any event, the miraculous event at the Red Sea elicited from Israel the fear of the Lord (Ex 14:31), the same response to which the psalmist calls "all the earth" (33:8). By its combination of terms from the creation narrative (Gn 1) and the story of redemption from Egypt at the Red Sea (Ex 14, 15), the psalm brings together the theological notions of creation and redemption, implicitly linking the Lord's work of creation to the miracle of redemption. God is Redeemer precisely because he is Creator. Isaiah 40–43 develops this concept, as does John in the Prologue to his Gospel (Jn 1). By linking creation and redemption, collapsing both the miracle of the Red Sea and the Jordan into a single reference (Ex 15:8; Jo 3:13, 16—the waters at the Red Sea and the Jordan River stood up in "a heap"; see also Ps 78:13), the psalmist accomplishes another virtual "miracle" for his audience that rehearses this "new song" and includes his audience in the narrative of creation and redemption.

In addition to making the story of creation and redemption a single narrative, our psalmist in vv. 10–19 breaks this subject out to include the particulars of history. In broadest outline, the Lord is sovereign over the plans and purposes of the nations, foiling their designs while making his own firm and secure (vv. 10–11), a normal outgrowth of his authority over the creation (v. 9, "he spoke, and it came to be; he commanded, and it stood firm"). At the center of this essay on history is the one model nation who best illustrates God's power and control, his chosen inheritance (v. 12). This God is not only omnipotent but also omniscient, observing all humankind and their actions (vv. 13–15). If there is any doubt about these attributes, one has just to look at Israel whose history illustrates the fact that salvation is not attained by great strength but by his "unfailing

---

[24] In Ps 33:7 NIV prefers נֹאד (*nōʾḏ*), "jar," rather than נֵד (*nēḏ*), "heap," but note the same expression in Ps 78:13 and Jo 3:13, which seems to favor "heap."

love" that delivers from death and saves in time of famine (vv. 16–19). This hope, secured by God's "unfailing love," constitutes the basis of Israel's present and future (vv. 10–22).

Psalm 37

In keeping with the Torah's stipulation that Israel's security in the land of Canaan was contingent upon moral obedience, Ps 37 applies that principle to a new climate of moral decline in the psalmist's day. Judging from the sustained emphasis on dwelling in the land (37:9, 11, 18, 27, 29, 34), the audience was obviously on the precipice of moral decline, and continued occupation of the land was contingent upon moral revision. The threat was real, and the psalmist phrased it in the legal language of the Torah: they will be "cut off" (37:9, 22, 34, 38; see Ex 30:33, 38; Lv 7:20, 21, for examples of the legal language). The psalmist reissues to his contemporaries this frightful prospect of being cut off from their ancestral land and being isolated from the society. But the benefits of life in the land were the same as those they had inherited from the Canaanites (37:3, 9b, 11, 22, 29, 34). In fact, the symbolism involves faith as a journey, symbolized by the use of the word "way" (37:5, 7, 23, 34), perhaps recalling the imagery of the wilderness era, and signified by their dwelling in the land (vv. 3, 27, 29). Israel's life in the land was dependent upon their obedience to God's laws (Dt 28:15–24), and the curses and blessings that Moses pronounced against them (Dt 27–28) governed their security there: "those the LORD blesses will inherit the land, but those he curses will be destroyed" (37:22). Twice in the psalm the speaker steps forth and makes his personal observations about life (37:25, 35) as he offers his moral advice. The consequence of ignoring it will be exclusion from the land, and the result of heeding it will be possession of the land. As suggested, this is likely a metaphor applied to a morally degenerate society, although the physical reality was that Israel constantly faced the threat of expulsion from their land. The story of history, with the potential for curses and blessings, has become a parable of moral persuasion.

The Shape of the Torah as Reflected in Book 1

In the widest terms the Psalms, Book 1, is a collection of poems whose composers show a deep familiarity with the Torah, at least certain portions of it. They know and use the language of biblical stories, including creation, the exodus, the fall, Sinai, the wilderness, apostasy at Sinai, and the conquest. While not inclined to use names of the ancient heroes, they nevertheless reflect their actions and words, among them Moses, Aaron, and Joshua. Yet their familiarity extends beyond story and personality to liturgical and legal language, such as the prayer upon the removal of the ark (Nm 10:35), the Aaronic benediction (Nm 6:24–26), the *Shema* (Dt 6:4–9), and the Ten Commandments (Ex 20/Dt 5). At the same time, the reader of Book 1 cannot ignore the familiarity with particular poetic texts of the Torah, including the Song of the Sea (Ex 15), the Song of Moses (Dt 32), and the Blessing of Moses (Dt 33). While a more explicit definition of the shape of the Torah is difficult, the broad range of familiarity is expansive, leading us to surmise that the Torah with which they were familiar was itself quite an expansive document, even in the earliest era of psalmic composition.

Conclusion

Our study has been an exercise in the history of interpretation, and the Psalms are the best example of that continuum that we have in the Bible, particularly since they represent several centuries of composition and application. First, we have identified the movement from the nation as the macrocosm of God's covenant grace in the Torah to the individual as the microcosm of that grace, although the macrocosmic application is also frequent in the Psalter. Second, we have pointed to the use of the prayer language of the Torah and the psalmists' tendency to reissue the ancient prayers of the heroes of the faith in the threatening and challenging circumstances of their own world. The psalmists and their community are connected to God's redeeming acts of history and to his servants by means of the covenant. They are always, without exception, acting within and on the basis of the covenant. Thus they can expect God to repeat his mighty deeds in their ongoing history, and they can summon the language of the ancients' prayers to petition the throne of grace. Third, we have seen some examples of how the poets of the Psalter have used the language of Israel's life and worship as metaphors of personal piety, and thus we have drawn attention to the developing sense of personal piety in ancient Israel, completing the circle that was constituted and formulated by the introduction to the Psalter with the installation of Ps 1 as the call to Torah piety. Fourth, we have drawn attention to the use of Torah language as an instrument of ethical persuasion, summoning Israel to moral action in critical circumstances that reflect Israel's ancient events and moral challenges. The point we have made and attempted to demonstrate is that Torah language often becomes the rhetorical frame in which the psalmists express their message. The purpose of that is to transfer by inference the Torah's theological and moral force of persuasion to the ongoing life of the people of God.

CHAPTER 3

NARRATIVE REPETITION IN
1 SAMUEL 24 AND 26: SAUL'S
DESCENT AND DAVID'S ASCENT

John D. Currid
and
L. K. Larson

Introduction

It has long been recognized that the two incidents of 1 Sm 24 and 26 are clearly parallel.[1] The parallels are many and significant in areas of vocabulary, syntax, and motif. The question that has engaged scholars for decades is, what is their relationship? A common interpretation is given by Klaus Koch, who says:

> These similarities are only explicable if the two narratives go back to the same source. The conformity between the two is in fact quite great. On both occasions David is in the wilderness of Judah fleeing from Saul. On both occasions he has the opportunity to kill the king. On both occasions there is the suggestion that it has been ordained by God, but though he is tempted to murder Saul, David strongly resists the impulse: he cannot violate the sanctity of the Lord's Anointed. But on both occasions he takes some material evidence with him. In the conversation which follows Saul recognizes David's superiority, and departs as he came. All this supports the assumption that it must be two versions of the same story, both of which developed in oral form quite independently of each other. How will the source of the story have looked?[2]

---

[1] For early scholarly work on this parallel, see K. Budde, *Die Bucher Richter und Samuel, ihre Quellen und ihre Aufbau* (Giessen: Ricker, 1890), 228; H. P. Smith, *A Critical and Exegetical Commentary on the Books of Samuel* (Edinburgh: T&T Clark, 1899), 229–30; and, J. Wellhausen, *Prolegomena to the History of Ancient Israel* (1883; repr., Cleveland: World Publishing, 1957), 264–65.

[2] K. Koch, *The Growth of the Biblical Tradition: The Form-Critical Method* (New York: Charles Scribner's Sons, 1969), 142–43.

Ralph Klein sums up the position more succinctly when he says, "It needs to be noted that the two chapters are probably alternate memories of one event."[3]

> Those who hold this position focus primarily on which chapter is older and better reflects the original tradition. It appears to be a toss-up, as Klein notes: "Koch, Veijola, Budde, and Schulte believe chap. 24 to be older; Wellhausen, Smith, Nubel, Mowinckel, Caird, and McCarter believe chap. 26 to be older."[4] Wellhausen's remarks on the issue are a good example of the details of the debate. He comments: There is a good deal of verbal coincidence between the two, and we are entitled to regard the shorter and more pointed version (chap. xxvi.) as the basis. But the sequence (xxvi. 25, xxvii. 1) shows beyond a doubt that chap. xxvi does not belong to the original tradition.[5]

Although many of these commentators disagree regarding the sequence of the two chapters, they still affirm that this doublet reflects different traditions of the same event. This interpretation has almost become a shibboleth in biblical studies.

In his commentary on 1 and 2 Samuel, Robert Alter offers a possible alternative solution to the understanding of the relationship of the two chapters. He does not take a strong stand on the issue, but he does say: "[s]cholarly consensus assumes that these doublets reflect different sources or traditions bearing on the same events, though the possibility cannot be rejected out of hand that the original writer may have deliberately composed his story with paired incidents. In any case, the pairings need to be read as part of the purposeful compositional design of the redacted version of the narrative we have."[6] It is our intention in this essay to do a detailed literary analysis of the two passages in order to determine what, in fact, is the relationship between them.

Narrative Repetition

Literary analysis is a field of study that deals with what Alter calls "the artful use of language" within a particular genre.[7] This includes such conventions of Hebrew writing as puns, plays on ideas, imagery, sound,

---

[3] R. W. Klein, *1 Samuel* (WBC 10; Waco, TX: Word, 1983), 236.

[4] Klein, *1 Samuel*, 237.

[5] Wellhausen, *Prolegomena*, 264–65.

[6] R. Alter, *The David Story: A Translation with Commentary of 1 and 2 Samuel* (New York: Norton , 1999), 162.

[7] R. Alter, *The Art of Biblical Narrative* (New York: Basic Books, 1981), 12. Other important works to introduce the reader to the topic include S. Bar-Efrat, *Narrative Art in the Bible* (Sheffield: Almond Press, 1989); A. Berlin, *Poetics and Interpretation of Biblical Narrative* (Sheffield: Almond Press, 1983); and, M. Sternberg, *The Poetics of Biblical Narrative* (Bloomington: Indiana University Press, 1985).

syntax, and various other things. One important artistic device employed by biblical writers is literary repetition. In other words, the authors of the HB often used verbal repetition as a standard literary convention. In narrative literature, the writer not only used repetition "to emphasize and re-emphasize significant words, but also concepts and central themes concerned with theological and socio-political ideologies."[8]

Narrative Repetition within a Text

Narrative repetition often occurs within a pericope to give shape to the plot and message of the story. As Beck comments, "Repetition can be used to structure the plot of the story, to develop a theme within the story, to develop the reader's view of a character, to create suspense, or mark a point of emphasis."[9] By observing the repetitions closely, the reader may derive the meaning and significance of a text in a more striking manner. There are various stages or tiers of the "artful" use of language in biblical literature like the book of 1 Samuel. We will consider these stages briefly, beginning with the most basic layer and proceeding to the larger and more complex levels.

Leitwort

The German term *Leitwort* (lit., "lead or guide word") refers to a word or root word that appears repeatedly throughout a pericope, and it is one of the most common components of narrative art in the OT. The role of a *Leitwort* is to highlight and to develop the principal theme of a narrative. Martin Buber defined it as follows:

> By *Leitwort* I understand a word or word root that is meaningfully repeated within a text or sequence of texts or complex of texts; those who attend to these repetitions will find a meaning of the text revealed or clarified, or at any rate made more emphatic. As noted, what is repeated need not be a single word but can be a word root; indeed the diversity of forms often strengthens the overall dynamic effect. I say "dynamic" because what takes place between the verbal configurations thus related is in a way a movement; readers to whom the whole is present feel the waves beating back and forth. Such measured repetition, corresponding to the inner rhythm of the text—or rather issuing from it—is probably the strongest of all techniques for making a meaning available without articulating it explicitly.[10]

---

[8] J. Yeo, "A Literary Approach to Biblical Interpretation: An Introduction to Biblical Repetition" (paper, Reformed Theological Seminary, Jackson, 2005), 1.

[9] J. A. Beck, "Why Do Joshua's Readers Keep Crossing the River? The Narrative-Geographical Shaping of Joshua 3–4," *JETS* 48/4 (2005): 689–99.

[10] M. Buber, "Leitwort Style in Pentateuch Narrative," in *Scripture and Translation* (ed. M. Buber and F. Rosenzweig; trans. L. Rosenwald and E. Fox; Bloomington: Indiana University Press, 1994), 114.

For example, Alter demonstrated that the repetition of the word קוֹל (qôl; "voice") serves to highlight the thematic exposition of 1 Sm 15:1–31.[11] In this passage there occurs a symphony of voices: the Lord speaks; the animals speak; the Israelite people speak; and Samuel speaks. The heart of the story is, which voice will Saul listen to? The author's use of the קוֹל (qôl) Leitwort drives home his point. Bruce Waltke argues that the account of Isaac uses two Leitworter that provide thematic purpose to the narrative of Gn 25–27. The words that occur repeatedly are צַיִד (ṣayid; "game," ten times) and מַטְעַמִּים (maṭʿammîm; "tasty food," six times). Waltke observes that "Isaac is said to 'love tasty food' by Rebekah, Isaac himself, and the narrator. This repetition makes clear the story's message: Isaac's cupidity has distorted his spiritual taste. He has given himself over to an indulgent sensuality."[12]

Leitphrase

Sometimes a phrase or a clause, rather than a single word, may dominate a text. For example, in Gn 1 the clause "And there was evening and there was morning, the . . . day" appears six times (vv. 5, 8, 13, 19, 23, 31). That Leitphrase (German for "lead/guide phrase") provides the temporal framework for the entire creation account. In another story, Samson's spectacular deeds prior to his arrest and martyrdom are introduced by the clause "then the Spirit of the Lord rushed upon him" (Jgs 14:6, 9; 15:14). That Leitphrase underscores the repeated source of Samson's victories over the Philistines.

Narrative Repetition between Texts

Leitwort and Leitphrase

Repetition also occurs between different pericopes in a narrative, and it can occur in both stages of Leitwort and Leitphrase. For instance, in Gn 39:1–6 a number of Leitworter and one Leitphrase appear in the account. The leading words are כֹּל (kōl; "all," 5x), בַּיִת (bayit; "house," five times), יָד (yād; "hand," four times), and מַצְלִיחַ (maṣlîaḥ; "success," twice). The leading phrase in the passage is "the Lord was with Joseph" (twice). The storyline describes Joseph's servitude to Potiphar, his Egyptian master. Later in the chapter we read about Joseph's imprisonment and how he is treated by the Egyptian jailer (Gn 39:19–23). The same leading words appear in this story as in the earlier account: כֹּל (kōl; "all," three times), בַּיִת (bayit; "house," four times), יָד (yād; "hand," twice), and מַצְלִיחַ (maṣlîaḥ;

---

[11] Alter, Art of Biblical Narrative, 93.
[12] Bruce K. Waltke, An Old Testament Theology (Grand Rapids: Zondervan, 2007), 116–17.

"success," once). In addition, the key phrase "the Lord was with Joseph," is twice present.[13] The point of these repetitions is to underscore a pattern: because the Lord is with Joseph, the human master places everything in Joseph's hands, and he is successful with it. This essential pattern prevails to the greater degree when Pharaoh places all the house of Egypt into Joseph's hands (Gn 41:37–45).

Another example of how a *Leitphrase* crosses various pericopes and thus ties them together thematically is the repetition of the clause in Jgs 17–21: "in those days there was no king in Israel" (17:6; 18:1; 19:1; 21:25). That recurrent phrase underscores the lack of a central political, social, and religious structure at the time in Israel; it highlights a sense of anarchy prevailing in the land. And, finally, that *Leitphrase* sets up the soon-to-be drama of the establishment of kingship in Israel (1 Sm 8). An additional repetitive phrase is "these are the generations of" (called the *toledot* formula) in the book of Genesis. It is a common heading that announces a new block of narrative material (Gn 2:4; 5:1; 6:9; 10:1; 11:10, 27; 25:12, 19; 36:1, 9; 37:2). This *Leitphrase* provides the structure for the entire book of Genesis.

Leitmotif

When considering narrative repetition between texts a perplexing issue for commentators is the fact that the same story, more or less, appears repeatedly. For example, a similar betrothal scene appears in Gn 24:10–61 and 29:1–20. The first text relates the episode of Abraham's servant being sent to Aram to find a bride for Isaac. At a well, the servant meets Rebekah. She draws water for the servant and his camels, and he responds by loading her with jewelry. Rebekah runs home to tell Laban of the encounter, and he welcomes the servant, sets a meal before him, and concludes a betrothal agreement between his family and Abraham's family. It is a slow-moving story with lots of verbal repetition. Genesis 29 also depicts a betrothal scene in which Jacob encounters Rachel at a well. There are many parallels between the two scenes, and even specific language is the same. This thematic doublet is a *Leitmotif* that appears a third time in Ex 2:11–22, and it could be dubbed the "meet the bride at the well" scenario!

Although there exist many parallels between Genesis 24 and 29, there are also some crucial dissimilarities that underscore the teaching points of the texts. In regard to Jacob's journey in Gn 29, Nahum Sarna states, "the scene depicting his arrival at the well and the ensuing events is reminiscent of what occurred many years ealier, in ch. 26, when Abraham's servant came to this same place intent on finding a wife for Isaac. But what a glaring contrast between the well-laden camel train of the grandfather

---

[13] Translations throughout are from the ESV unless otherwise stated.

and the lonely, empty-handed Jacob who arrives on foot!"[14] In the earlier incident, it is Rebekah who draws water for the servant's camels (24:19–20), in the later it is Jacob who draws water by overcoming an obstacle of a stone covering the well (29:9–10).

Let us give another example. Genesis 19:1–29 records the story of Sodom and Gomorrah. It tells the tale of the wicked Sodomites who attempt to do harm to the angels assisting Lot. Almost the exact same storyline appears in Jgs 19:22–30, in which the tribe of Benjamin deals with a traveling Levite in the city of Gibeah. Numerous *Leitworter* and *Leitphrasen* tie the two stories together (see, for instance, Gn 19:4 and Jgs 19:22; Gn 19:7 and Jgs 19:23; Gn 19:8 and Jgs 19:24). Why would the writer of Judges purposefully relay the historical episode in Gibeah in such a way as to remind the reader of the historical event of Sodom? "The answer is like a thunderclap: the Benjaminites are acting just like the pagan Sodomites! The morality of the people of Israel has really sunk to an all-time low by the later stages of the book of Judges."[15]

One final example will suffice. A common *Leitmotif* in Scripture is the barren wife. The motif is that of an Israelite woman unable to bear children, and then by miraculous means she conceives and bears a son. The son then becomes a leader or deliverer of the people of God. This leading scene first appears in Gn 11:27–30 with barren Sarah; Isaac is born miraculously to the aged Abraham and his wife. This theme repeats in Gn 25:20–21 (Rebekah); Gn 29:31 (Rachel); Jgs 13:2 (Samson's mother); and 1 Sm 1:2 (Hannah). The *Leitmotif*, of course, reaches its climax in the virgin birth of Jesus in the NT.

Narrative Repetition in 1 Samuel 24 and 26

The various stages of narrative repetition discussed thus far evidence a relationship between 1 Sm 24 and 26. In this section we will detail the many similarities between the two narratives with respect to the tiers of repetition. Then we will evaluate the purpose of the parallelism in these narratives in regard to their context in 1 Samuel.

The Leitwort *Stage*

The similarity of vocabulary in regard to both specific word usage and the number of occurrences indicates a close relationship between the two chapters. Our analysis gives consideration to only nouns and verbs that

---

[14] N. M. Sarna, *Genesis: The JPS Torah Commentary* (Philadelphia: The Jewish Publication Society, 1989), 201.

[15] J. Currid, *Strong and Courageous: Joshua Simply Explained* (Welwyn Commentary Series; Darlington, UK: Evangelical Press, 2011), 15.

appear in the two pericopes. The following table details the nouns and verbs that occur five times or more in each passage.

Chapter 24	Chapter 26
דָּוִד (*dāwiḏ*, 16x)	דָּוִד (*dāwiḏ*, 23x)
שָׁאוּל (*šā'ûl*, 14x)	יהוה (*yhwh*, 16x)
יהוה (*yhwh*, 12x)	שָׁאוּל (*šā'ûl*, 15x)
יָד (*yāḏ*, 11x)	אמר ('*mr*, 13x)
אמר ('*mr*, 9x)	בֵּן (*bēn*, 8x)
דבר (*dbr*, 5x)	מֶלֶךְ (*meleḵ*, 8x)
יוֹם (*yôm*, 5x)	בוא (*bô'*, 7x)
מֶלֶךְ (*meleḵ*, 5x)	יוֹם (*yôm*, 6x)
קוּם (*qûm*, 5x)	יָד (*yāḏ*, 6x)
ראה (*r'h*, 5x)	ראה (*r'h*, 5x)

As can be seen from the table, eight out of the ten leading words in each chapter overlap, accounting for 169 out of 194 occurrences from both lists. Furthermore, the top three leading words are identical in each list, although the second and third top occurrences appear in reverse order in 1 Sm 26. The top three words are the primary characters in the two narratives: David, Saul, and YHWH.

Additionally, rare words tie the two chapters together. For example, the word פַּרְעֹשׁ (*par'ōš*; "flea") occurs only twice in the OT, once in 1 Sm 24:15[14] and again in 1 Sm 26:20. In both instances, David uses the word "flea" as a form of self-abasement, calling himself a flea when he argues his innocence with Saul.

The Leitphrase *Stage*

While the parallelism of leading words in the two episodes is striking, the relationship between the chapters is shown more clearly by an examination of phrases that are identical or nearly identical in the two chapters. The following table includes the parallel phrases from the two narratives.

Chapter 24	Chapter 26
v. 2 Saul raises an army of "three thousand chosen men out of all Israel."	v. 2 Saul raises an army of "three thousand chosen men of Israel."
v. 2 Saul's purpose is "to seek David."	v. 2 Saul's purpose is "to seek David."
v. 4 David's men quote the Lord as saying, "Behold, I will give your enemy into your hand."	v. 8 Abishai says to David, "God has given your enemy into your hand this day."
v. 6 David says, "The Lord forbid that I should do this thing to my lord, the Lord's anointed, to put out my hand against him."	v. 11 David says, "The Lord forbid that I should put out my hand against the Lord's anointed."
v. 10 David states, "I will not put out my hand against my lord, for he is the Lord's anointed."	v. 23 David states, "I would not put out my hand against the Lord's anointed."
v. 16 Saul responds by saying, "Is this your voice, my son David?"	v. 17 Saul responds by saying, "Is this your voice, my son David?"

The Leitmotif *Stage*

The parallelism of leading words and phrases demonstrate a close connection between the two chapters. This relationship is further established by the outline these two narratives share. In both episodes David flees from Saul in the wilderness. Informers tell Saul of David's whereabouts. While Saul pursues David, it is David who is given the opportunity to kill Saul. David's subordinates encourage the future king that YHWH himself has given Saul into his hand, arguing that David should kill Saul. However, David refuses on both occasions to kill Saul because the king is the Lord's anointed. Here, David shows great respect for the kingship and trust that YHWH will establish David's own kingship in the proper way and time. Although David refuses to take Saul's life, he does take evidence from the scene as a sign that he had the occasion to kill Saul. At the end of both episodes Saul and David meet and the king recognizes David's innocence. They then depart to go their own way. The following table details that the two chapters unfold according to this basic storyline. While scholars recognize their similarities, the purpose of these parallels is greatly debated.

Chapter 24	Chapter 26
v. 1 Saul receives intelligence about David's location.	v. 1 Ziphites inform Saul of David's whereabouts.
23:19 Ziphites, Gibeah, Hachilah, and Jeshimon	v. 1 Ziphites, Gibeah, Hachilah, and Jeshimon
v. 2 Saul selects three thousand chosen men to chase down David.	v. 2 Saul selects three thousand chosen men to chase down David.
v. 3 David and his men are "sitting" in a cave.	v. 3 David and his men are "sitting" (ESV translates "remain") in the wilderness.
v. 4 David's men tell him that the Lord has given him an opportunity to kill Saul.	v. 8 Abishai tells David that God has given him an opportunity to kill Saul.
v. 4 David cuts off a piece of Saul's robe.	v. 12 David takes Saul's spear and jug.
v. 6 David will not raise a hand against the Lord's anointed.	v. 9 David will not raise a hand against the Lord's anointed.
v. 7 David restrains his men.	v. 9 David restrains Abishai.
v. 8 David reveals his identity to the king.	v. 14 David reveals his identity.
v. 9 David accuses Saul of listening to men.	v. 19 David suggests that certain men may have stirred Saul against him.
v. 11 David holds up the corner of Saul's robe as evidence he could have killed the king.	v. 16 David shows Saul's spear and water jug as evidence that he could have killed the king.
v. 14 Who does Saul pursue? A flea.	v. 20 Who does Saul pursue? A flea.
v. 16 Saul recognizes David's voice.	v. 17 Saul recognizes David's voice.
v. 22 David and Saul part ways.	v. 26 David and Saul part ways.

Few, if any, scholars question that there is a close relationship between the two chapters. Robert Bergen is correct about biblical scholars when he says about 1 Sm 24: "The predominant opinion of modern OT scholarship is that this account represents the first of two retellings of an event modified in its details in chap. 26."[16]

---

[16] R. D. Bergen, *1, 2 Samuel* (NAC; Nashville: Broadman & Holman, 1996), 237 n. 112.

Placement of 1 Samuel 25

Our study has detailed parallelism in vocabulary, phrases, and the story outline of the two chapters. Before we consider the purpose of these parallels, we must examine the placement of 1 Sm 24 and 26 and their relationship to 1 Sm 25.

The parallel episodes of 1 Sm 24 and 26 are separated by a fairly lengthy account (forty-four verses) that primarily records the story of Nabal and Abigail. However, 1 Sm 25 is not a mere interruption of the adjoining chapters but, in reality, helps to build the themes and motifs of those two chapters.[17] It is our opinion that the function of the Nabal/Abigail interlude is a foil to the surrounding chapters; David's actions in 1 Sm 25 are set in contrast to how he acts in 1 Sm 24 and 26.[18] We agree with Levenson on this point, who comments:

> The difference between 1 Samuel 25 and its neighbors is that in the latter, David seeks out Saul solely in order to demonstrate his good will, whereas in our tale, only the rhetorical genius of Abigail saves him from bloodying his hands. In short, the David of chaps. 24 and 26 is the character whom we have seen since his introduction in chap. 16 and whom we shall continue to see until 2 Samuel 11, the appealing young man of immaculate motivation and heroic courage. But the David of chap. 25 is a man who kills for a grudge.[19]

In other words, 1 Sm 25 pictures David as one who is quite capable of violence; he does not shy away from taking vengeance on Nabal (v. 22). This portrait of David serves as a contrast to 1 Sm 24 and 26, in which the character of David is one of having great restraint in his dealings with Saul. Such a variation "can point to an intensification, climactic development, acceleration of the actions and attitudes initially represented, or, on the other hand, to some unexpected, perhaps unsettling, new revelation of character or plot."[20] Because of the placement of the Nabal/Abigail episode between the parallel accounts of David's avoidance of blood-guilt against Saul, David's restraint toward Saul is greatly intensified and highlighted.[21]

---

[17] See, in particular, the studies of J. D. Levenson, "1 Samuel 25 as Literature and History," *CBQ* 40 (1978): 11–28; R. P. Gordon, "David's Rise and Saul's Demise: Narrative Analogy in 1 Samuel 24–26," *TynBul* 31 (1980): 37–64.

[18] Robert B. Chisholm, *Interpeting the Historical Books: An Exegetical Handbook* (Grand Rapids: Kregel, 2006), 228, defines foil as "[a] character that stands in contrast to another character, thereby highlighting one or more of the latter's characteristics or traits." In the account before us, David serves as a foil to himself.

[19] Levenson, "1 Samuel 25," 23.

[20] Alter, *Art of Biblical Narrative*, 63.

[21] Gordon's argument that 1 Sm 25 is similar to 1 Sm 24 and 26, rather than in contrast to them, and that Nabal is Saul's alter ego completely misses the foil angle that we would argue is at the hub of the relationship. See Gordon, "David's Rise and Saul's Demise," 43.

Purpose of the Parallel Accounts in 1 Samuel 24 and 26

The parallels we have noted in 1 Sm 24 and 26 advance the overarching theme of 1 Sm 16:1–31:13, which is Saul's fall from power and David's rise to the throne. The biblical author draws a deliberate contrast between the lives of Saul and David. Their lives run parallel in many ways. In both men we witness early success, but it is followed by grievous sin. The two lives, however, diverge at the point of how the two men deal with their iniquity. Saul's sin leads to bitterness, vengeance, and anger directed against David and others. David, to the contrary, has genuine sorrow and repentance for his actions. Although the lives of the two men run parallel, the stages of their lives are not concurrent. Thus, while Saul's fortunes are on the descent in 1 Sm 24–26, David is in process of acquiring the throne in those same chapters.

The purpose of the narrative repetition of the two episodes is to heighten the antithesis between the two characters. It intensifies the conflict, and it increases the dramatic tension of the storyline. In other words, the doublet fuels the development of the theme of 1 Sm 16:1–31:13 which, again, is the rise of David and the demise of Saul. At this point, we will attempt to give detail to the parallel and how it intensifies from 1 Sm 24 into 1 Sm 26.

The first matter to note is the fact that the account in 1 Sm 26 is more elaborate than the episode in 1 Sm 24. Much of this amplification can be accounted for because the structure of the speeches in 1 Sm 26 is much more complex. For example, David's dialogue with his men regarding whether to kill Saul is a mere three verses (24:4, 6–7), whereas the discussion with Abishai regarding the same matter is six verses (26:6–11). Also, when David reveals his identity to Saul, the second story includes a discussion between David and Abner (26:13–16) not present in the previous one. Such additional complexity adds to the literary development and intensity of the storyline.

The accentuation of the parallel narratives as one moves from 1 Sm 24 to 1 Sm 26 can be measured in various other ways as well. For example, there is a heightened protection of Saul in 1 Sm 26. In 24:3, Saul is on his own without any military protection. But in 26:5 he lays next to Abner, the commander of the army, and he is surrounded by his entire army. Saul is much less vulnerable to potential harm from David and his men. Where he is lying perhaps reflects his increased fear and suspicion. These circumstances highlight that David is more heroic in the later episode: he is quite bold, as he and Abishai sneak into Saul's camp and steal Saul's spear and water jug. In the first encounter David had merely cut off a corner of Saul's robe (24:4). The robe is a symbol of kingly authority, and this act is perhaps a sign that Saul's kingdom is being "cut off" from him (cf. 1 Sm 15:27–28; 1 Kgs 11:29–31). In the second episode, David robs Saul not of a mere patch of robe, but he steals his spear and water jug. The spear is a symbol of royal authority, and Saul had used it in the attempted murder of David (1 Sm 18:10–11; 19:10). David now has the opportunity to exact ironic justice on Saul with the king's own spear.

In 1 Sm 26, Saul is much more explicit about his guilt in regard to his mistreatment of David. In the first episode Saul had admitted to David that "I have repaid you evil" (24:17). But in the later account he confesses "I have sinned . . . I have acted foolishly, and have made a great mistake" (26:21). The reader rightfully wonders whether Saul is merely posturing, but that does not take away from the increasing intensity evident from the one incident to the next.[22]

In each circumstance David treats Saul with utmost respect and honor as befits the king of Israel. He employs various honorific titles for Saul in his speech. In 1 Sm 24 three primary epithets are used: "lord" (vv. 6, 8, 10), "the Lord's anointed" (vv. 6 [twice], 10), and "king" (vv. 8, 14). David's attitude toward Saul and his submission to him increase in 1 Sm 26 as these same epithets are used again, but more frequently: "lord" (vv. 15 [twice], 16, 17, 18, 19), "the Lord's anointed" (vv. 9, 11, 16, 23), and "king" (vv. 15 [twice], 16, 17, 19, 20, 22). First Samuel 25 may have helped to fuel that development. In the episode of Nabal, David perhaps became more resolved to spare Saul because he had become more aware of the violence he was capable of.

Conclusion

When all is said and done, it is difficult not to conclude that there is a purposeful compositional design of the two narratives. The character development of both Saul and David is clearly in evidence as the text moves along from 1 Sm 24 to 1 Sm 26. David becomes more honorable, bolder, generous, and God-fearing; Saul becomes less so. The king is dogged by failure, fear, and suspicion. The two of them are moving further apart: the biblical author's statement that there was "a great space between them" (26:13) is not merely geographical but perhaps also relational, moral, and spiritual. The development of the story underscores the lack of reconciliation between the two men. Ultimately, the heightened movement makes David's claim to the throne of Israel much more credible. As Ralph Klein correctly comments, the biblical author "incorporated both accounts to strengthen his defense of David and his critique of Saul."[23]

---

[22] Pharaoh has a similar response to the plague of hail that the Lord brings on Egypt, by saying, "This time I have sinned; the Lord is in the right, and I and my people are in the wrong" (Ex 9:27). His confession, like Saul's, does not ring true.

[23] Klein, *1 Samuel*, 260.

CHAPTER 4

SAMSON AND THE HARLOT AT GAZA (JUDGES 16:1–3)[1]

Gordon P. Hugenberger

Introduction

In spite of modern psychological speculations about Samson's loneliness after being jilted at Timnah, his insecure sexual identity, or his alleged irrepressible libido, the biblical text nowhere states why Samson went down to the city of Gaza (Jgs 16:1)—a trip of about fifty miles from his hometown of Zorah on the trade routes of his day.[2] The text merely reports that once Samson arrived at Gaza, whatever his motive may have been for coming, "he saw a prostitute there, and he came to her [וַיַּרְא־שָׁם אִשָּׁה זוֹנָה וַיָּבֹא אֵלֶיהָ; *wayyar'-šām 'iššā zônā wayyābō' 'ēlêhā*]."[3] If Samson had come to Gaza in order to avail himself of this woman's services, the reader

---

[1] Few scholars, if any, have done as much as G. K. Beale to demonstrate the value of giving careful attention to the NT's use of the OT as a key to fresh exegetical and biblical-theological insight. It is a pleasure to submit in his honor this modest essay, which builds on a close examination of a frequently overlooked example of the OT's own use of a prior OT text.

[2] See, e.g., James L. Crenshaw, who suggests that Samson, disappointed by a marriage based on physical attraction, was seeking the safety of an uncommitted relationship ("The Samson Saga: Filial Devotion or Erotic Attachment?" *ZAW* 86 [1974]: 472, 497). For a similar view, see J. Alberto Soggin, *Judges: A Commentary* (OTL; Philadelphia: Westminster Press, 1981), 256. Mieke Bal goes further in her psychoanalysis of Samson. She considers that Samson's actions were propelled by insecurity in his sexual identity (*Death and Dissymmetry. The Politics of Coherence in the Book of Judges* [Chicago: University of Chicago Press, 1988], 117–18, 226). According to the more traditional approach, Samson was impelled by a characterological ("wayward, sensual nature") rather than a psychological defect. See, e.g., Arthur E. Cundall, *Judges: An Introduction and Commentary* (TOTC; Downers Grove, IL: InterVarsity Press, 1968), 173.

[3] Translations throughout are the author's own, unless otherwise indicated.

might well be tempted to echo the complaint of Samson's parents in Jgs 14:3: Are there no prostitutes among his kinsmen or among all the Israelites closer to home that Samson needed to travel such a great distance into Philistine territory in order to find one?

As is well-known, the common expression "he came to her" (וַיָּבֹא אֵלֶיהָ; *wayyābō' 'ēlêhā*) or "he went in to her," which appears in 16:1, is ambiguous. It may allow the inference that Samson had sexual relations with this woman, especially since she is identified as a prostitute, but it does not require it.[4] The syntagm בוא (*bw'*; "come" or "go in") + אֶל ('*el*; "to") + a person (as the object of the preposition) appears hundreds of times in the HB, including Jgs 16:1. In the vast majority of cases the expression refers to one entering into the company of another without any sexual implication.[5] Within the book of Judges alone, there are fifteen other examples of this expression (3:20; 4:21, 22; 6:18; 8:15; 11:7, 12; 13:6, 8, 9, 10, 11; 15:1; 18:8, 10), and in five of these (4:22; 13:6, 9, 10; 15:1) a woman is the object of the preposition, as is the case in 16:1. In only one of these fifteen examples, namely 15:1, can the expression be understood as an explicit reference to sexual intimacy, and even here, a majority of modern English translations and commentaries do not favor this option.[6] In support of this consensus, if "come to" (בוא + אֶל; *bw'* + '*el*) in 15:1 is understood as an explicit reference to sexual intimacy, then Samson's specification that this take place in the "inner room" (חֶדֶר; *ḥeḏer*) or "bedroom" appears redundant or irrelevant. It is more likely that Samson mentions the "bedroom" as the meeting place in order to make clear his intention for approaching his wife: he intends to consummate their mar-

---

[4] A sexual reference for בוא (*bw'*; "come") + אֶל ('*el*; "to") is unambiguous in a case like Gn 16:4, "he came to [= he had sexual relations with] Hagar, and she conceived." It seems likely that בוא אל (*bw' 'el*) came to refer to sexual intercourse by extension from its more literal sense of a reference to the attendant approach of the man, rather than as a description of the sexual act itself.

[5] Cf. Gn 7:9, 15; 24:30; 26:27; 27:18; 32:7[6]; 33:14; 41:14; 42:29; 46:31.

[6] The NET in 15:1 is almost alone among modern English translations in its rendering of בוא (*bw'*; "come") + אֶל ('*el*; "to") as an explicit reference to sexual intimacy: "I want to have sex with my bride in her bedroom!" Against this, cf., e.g., the NIV, "I'm going to my wife's room," and most other modern translations. The majority of recent commentaries similarly favor a nonsexual reference, although typically without argument.

A few scholars have argued for a sexual reference in Jgs 13:6, such as Lillian R. Klein, *The Triumph of Irony in the Book of Judges* (Sheffield: Almond Press, 1988), 114, and Philippe Guillaume, *Waiting for Josiah: The Judges* (JSOTSup 385; New York: T&T Clark, 2004), 166. This suggestion is unconvincing, however, since Manoah's wife, who reports, "a man of God came to me [אֶל + בוא; *bw'* + '*el*]," is referring to what the narrator has already described in 13:3 as merely an appearance: "the angel of the LORD appeared [וַיֵּרָא; *wayyērā'*] to her." Furthermore, Manoah reuses and thereby interprets this same idiom in 13:8 in its ordinary, nonsexual sense: "O Lord, please let the man of God whom you sent come again to us [אֶל + בוא; *bw'* + '*el*] and teach us what we are to do with the child who will be born."

riage. As the CEB translates 15:1, "He said, 'Let me go into my wife's bedroom.'" In conclusion, although "he came to her" (וַיָּבֹא אֵלֶיהָ; *wayyābōʾ ʾēlêhā*) in 16:1 could have an explicit sexual reference, it certainly does not require it, and, apart from 16:1, everywhere else in Judges this expression has its more common meaning.

Furthermore, 16:1–3 offers no hint of moral rebuke for what Samson did at Gaza. Indeed, Samson's subsequent escape and his miraculous feat of removing the massive doors, doorposts, and bar of the city gates and carrying them up a hill in the direction of Hebron, or perhaps even to a hill that is opposite Hebron (a journey of about forty miles and a climb of more than three thousand feet), imply, if anything, divine approbation.[7]

The conventional understanding that Samson consorted with the prostitute at Gaza is challenged by this implied approbation and is problematic on almost any compositional theory for the book of Judges.[8] Jacob M. Myers, for example, writes:

> While at Gaza, Samson had relations with a harlot, a fact which throws light on the morals of the day and reveals the hero's waywardness and enslavement by passion. From our point of view, morals were exceedingly low. But the writer shows no disapprobation. Samson's morals were not out of the ordinary, and the storyteller obviously delighted in his prowess. The attitude

---

[7] Victor H. Matthews, among others, favors the latter option and provides these figures, based on his interpretation of עַל־פְּנֵי (*ʿal-pĕnê*) as "in front of [Hebron]" (*Judges and Ruth* [NCBC; Cambridge: Cambridge University Press, 2004], 156). For the alternative option of interpreting עַל־פְּנֵי (*ʿal-pĕnê*) as "in the direction of [Hebron]," cf. C. F. Keil, *Joshua, Judges, Ruth* (trans. J. Martin; 1863; repr., Grand Rapids: Eerdmans, 1982), 418–19.

[8] Perhaps the majority view among current scholars is that Jgs 16:1–3 derives from an etiological legend and was added, along with Jgs 16:4–31, to a pre-Deuteronomic/pre-Deuteronomistic collection of deliverer stories (3:7–15:20) by the Deuteronomic/pre-Deuteronomistic editor. See, e.g., John Gray, *Joshua, Judges, Ruth* (NCB; Grand Rapids: Eerdmans, 1986), 219; Robert G. Boling, "Judges, Book of," *ABD* 3:1107–17.

M. Noth expressed some uncertainty whether the Samson narrative ought to be excluded from the Deuteronomistic History. Noth's principal arguments are based on the absence of Samson from the seemingly comprehensive list of heroes offered in 1 Sm 12:11 and the overlapping judgeship of Samuel, contrary to the scheme of one specified savior figure for each specified period of foreign rule (*The Deuteronomistic History* [Sheffield: JSOT Press, 1981], 52–53.). Neither objection is compelling. Judges 13:5 is explicit that Samson would only "begin" to deliver Israel, thereby implying the necessity of a subsequent deliverer. Moreover, it is likely that the MT of 1 Sm 12:11, which is semantically awkward in its mention of "Samuel" (שְׁמוּאֵל; *šĕmûʾēl*) on the lips of Samuel, should be emended to "Samson" (שִׁמְשׁוֹן; *šimšôn*) with the LXX and Syr. The corruption to "Samuel" may have been facilitated by the graphic similarity of these names, the prevalence of Samuel's name elsewhere in the context, and the subsequent assertion that these heroes had been the means of deliverance from Israel's enemies—a fact that was perhaps more applicable to Samuel than to Samson. Accordingly, "Samson" should be restored as the *lectio difficilior*. Cf. P. Kyle McCarter Jr., *1 Samuel* (AB 8; Garden City, NY: Doubleday, 1980), 211.

of the Deuteronomic editor is reflected in what he did not say and, having been strongly influenced by the prophets, he would certainly have omitted the objectionable features of this and other Samson tales if they had not been so firmly grounded in the traditions of Israel.[9]

Such an approach, however, merely assumes what needs to be proven. It is hardly persuasive to build an argument on what an author or editor "did not say" or to pretend to know what the same source "would certainly have omitted" if he could. The fact that elsewhere in the Deuteronomic corpus sexual transgressions are viewed negatively, as Myers concedes, and typically provoke divine judgment raises serious questions about the unexamined assumption that Samson had sexual relations with the prostitute at Gaza and that God chose not only to overlook this moral lapse but also to rescue Samson from his enemies and empower him to dismantle the defenses of the city.

The remainder of this essay offers a postcritical reappraisal of this episode in the life of Samson and challenges the conventional view that Samson engaged the professional services of the prostitute at Gaza. Although it would be ideal to do so, it goes beyond the scope of this essay to set this reappraisal in the wider context of a much-needed reexamination of the entire Samson narrative and of the book of Judges as a whole.[10]

Here, however, it may help to address briefly, although of necessity without adequate defense, two important hermeneutical issues that bear on the interpretation of Jgs 16:1–3. First, the present attempt to resolve an apparent ethical ambiguity should not be dismissed as mere rationalism devoid of literary sensitivity. The Samson narrative is rich and complex, and the interpretation and ethical status of Samson's deeds are easily misunderstood and certainly open to debate. Some interpreters despair of making sense of the ethical stance of the narrator; others posit morals for the story that make for edifying preaching but find little support in the text. Nevertheless, the cautious search for a possible ethical and theological intention in a narrative is not a misguided effort by those who do not know how to enjoy a good story! It is instead an important part of the task of responsible biblical exegesis. Against the modern literary prejudice in favor of "openness" over against "moralism" and "didacticism," Wayne C. Booth wisely observes, "to pass judgment where the author intends neutrality is to misread. But to be neutral or objective where the author requires commitment is equally to misread."[11]

---

[9] Jacob M. Myers, "Judges, Introduction and Exegesis" in *The Interpreter's Bible* (ed. G. A. Buttrick et al.; 12 vols.; Nashville: Abingdon, 1953), 2:791.

[10] It is anticipated that this will be undertaken in the author's forthcoming commentary on the book of Judges in the Apollos Old Testament Commentary (AOTC) series.

[11] Wayne C. Booth, *The Rhetoric of Fiction* (Chicago: University of Chicago Press, 1961), 144. Cf. Stuart Lasine, "Judicial Narratives and the Ethics of Read-

A second hermeneutical issue, unique to the book of Judges, also deserves brief mention. Many scholars assume that the judges in this book are intended to reflect the Israelites as a whole. Accordingly, if there is a noticeable spiritual and moral decline in the people of Israel in the period of the judges, which appears to be the case, then readers should expect a parallel decline in the spiritual and moral qualities of the judges.

It is far from clear, however, that readers are intended to adopt this perspective regarding the judges. For one thing, to do so disregards the positive view of the judges which is articulated in the programmatic text of Jgs 2:6–23, where the judges are presented in sharp contrast to the people. The people are condemned because they "would not listen to their judges, but prostituted themselves to other gods" (Jgs 2:17 NIV). The verse implies that the judges speak for God, and as such they are the antithesis of their wayward idolatrous contemporaries. In Jgs 2:20, nearly the same complaint about the people is repeated, except that in this case they "do not listen" to the Lord, rather than to their judges, as in 2:17. Perhaps here is an important hint that, far from predisposing readers to expect the judges to resemble the people, readers should expect the judges to resemble the Lord, who raised them up (2:16, 18). Consistent with this more positive view of the judges, Jgs 2:19 explains that as long as the judges were alive, the Lord used them to deliver the people from their enemies and to restrain the people from idolatry and wickedness. "But when the judge died, the people returned to ways even more corrupt than those of their fathers" (Jgs 2:19 NIV).

Despite apparent inconsistencies and interpretive challenges, there are numerous examples throughout the book of Judges that support this more positive view of the judges.[12] Moreover, many of the texts assumed to offer incontrovertible proof of egregious moral failure or infidelity toward God on the part of the judges are often susceptible to less negative interpretations. These are often overlooked if the interpreter has decided in advance that the author intends to portray the judges as the disappointing leaders that rebellious Israelites deserve or as negative examples who warn readers about the perils of failing to live up to one's high calling.

Bernhard W. Anderson, for example, reflects a position regarding the Samson narrative that is common among recent interpreters. He explains

---

ing: The Reader as Judge of the Dispute Between Mephibosheth and Ziba," *Hebrew Studies* 30 (1989): 49–69.

[12] For an especially vivid example, cf. Jgs 10:6–11:11, where Jephthah is portrayed in ways that clearly mirror God rather than the people. In this passage, Israel's strained relationship with God mirrors their strained relationship with Jephthah. The resolution, which is prompted in both cases by the distress (צרר; *ṣrr*) caused by the Ammonite oppression (10:9; 11:7) and includes an initial rejection by both God and Jephthah (10:14; 11:7), is nearly identical in both cases (10:16; 11:6–11). For many other examples, see the author's forthcoming commentary on Judges in the AOTC series.

that the theme of these lusty stories is simply "the discomfiture of the Philistines by an Israelite Tarzan whose fatal weakness was women." At best, the moral of the story is what happens when "a person filled with charisma . . . disregards the guidance of Yahweh in a time of crisis to pursue whims of the moment."[13]

If Anderson is right, however, why in the Delilah account (Jgs 16:4–31) does the narrator, or the deity, allow Samson's hair to regrow (16:22) and his prayers to God to be recorded and heard (16:28, 30), so that his death is not simply a tragic end to a failed career, as one might expect, but the most triumphant victory of his life? By Samson's self-sacrificial death, with the implied help of God, he destroyed the temple of the pagan god Dagon and killed more Philistine enemies than he had killed during his lifetime (16:30).

Likewise, if Anderson is right, why does the author, or the deity, allow Samson to discover the plot against his life in the incident at Gaza (Jgs 16:1–3)? Why allow Samson to escape the trap of the Philistines and, for good measure, humiliate the city of Gaza on his way out by destroying and removing their defensive gate in such a dramatic fashion? Admittedly, Samson is a complex figure and the Samson narrative is rife with interpretive challenges. Nevertheless, if the account of Samson's visit to Gaza has a moral, it seems unlikely that it is the one posited by Anderson and many others.

Perhaps the time has come to question the overly facile assumption that Samson had a sexual relationship with the harlot at Gaza. Those who make that assumption are, understandably, inclined to disregard or minimize the positive view of Samson implied by the programmatic introduction to the judges in Jgs 2:6–23, the promising birth narrative of Samson in Jgs 13, numerous references to the Spirit coming upon Samson (13:5; 14:6, 19; 15:14), and the divine approbation of Samson implied by his many miraculous works.[14] Critical scholarship is not inclined to allow these texts to control the interpretation of Jgs 16, since the latter is typically viewed as coming from a later source, the Deuteronomic editor. As has already been noted, however, even if attention is restricted to the laconic text of Jgs 16:1–3 alone, it is still necessary to explain away, as does Myers, the lack of moral comment expected for a Deuteronomic text: "[t]he attitude of the Deuteronomic editor is reflected in what he did not say."[15]

---

[13] Bernhard W. Anderson, *Understanding the Old Testament* (3rd ed.; Englewood Cliffs, NJ: Prentice Hall, 1975), 154.

[14] For Jgs 13, see Benjamin J. M. Johnson, "What Type of Son Is Samson? Reading Judges 13 as a Biblical Type-Scene," *JETS* 53/2 (2010): 269–86.

[15] Myers, "Judges, Introduction and Exegesis," 791. Intriguingly, OT law includes no criminal sanctions against prostitution, so two prostitutes can have their case heard before Solomon without risk to their lives (1 Kgs 3:16–28). Nevertheless, the practice of prostitution is morally condemned and prohibited in many

Verbal and Situational Parallels between Joshua 2 and Judges 16:1–3—A Neglected Narrative Analogy

It is intriguing that many precritical scholars, such as John Marbecke (late sixteenth cent.), Edward Taylor (late seventeenth cent.), Paulus Cassel (mid-nineteenth cent.), and others, were disposed to argue that Samson had no sexual relations with this woman, whom they identify, with the *Targum Jonathan* and Josephus, as an innkeeper.[16] Since Josephus readily acknowledges Samson's wayward nature elsewhere, his interpretation of 16:1–3 is all the more impressive: he omits any mention of the woman and states that Samson came to Gaza and "lodged at one of the inns" (ἔν τινι τῶν καταγωγίων διέτριβε; *en tini tōn katagōgiōn dietribe*) (*A.J.* 5.8.10 [§304]). While the Targumic definition of זוֹנָה (*zônā*) as an "innkeeper" (פּוּנְדְּקִיתָא; *pûndāqîtāʾ*) is unnecessary, both the Targum and Josephus may have been influenced in their interpretation of 16:1–3 by the recognition of a narrative analogy between this text and the account of the spies coming to Rahab the harlot in Jo 2.[17]

---

texts (Gn 34:31; 38:23–24; Lv 19:29; 21:7, 9, 14; Dt 23:18–19 [17–18]; 1 Kgs 22:38; Am 7:17; Jer 3:3). The fact that religious apostasy is frequently described using the metaphor of prostitution implies that literal prostitution was viewed with revulsion. Cf., e.g., Dt 31:16; Jgs 2:17; 8:27, 33.

[16] See John Marbecke, *The lyues of holy sainctes, prophets, patriarches, and others, contayned in Holye Scripture* (London, 1574), 72; Edward Taylor, *Upon the Types of the Old Testament*, vol. 1 (ed. Charles W. Mignon; Lincoln: University of Nebraska Press, 1989), 200–201 [the sermon "Samson," 198–215, was preached in 1695]; and Paulus Cassel, "Judges," in *Commentary on the Holy Scriptures, Critical, Doctrinal and Homiletical* (ed. Johann Peter Lange; trans. P. H. Steenstra; 1865; repr., Edinburgh: T&T Clark, 1872 [German original 1865]), 212–13.

[17] The likelihood that the Targum recognized a parallel between Jo 2 and Jgs 16:1ff. is suggested by its description of both Rahab and the woman of Gaza as "an innkeeper" ([פּוּנְדְּקִיתָא; *pûndāqîtāʾ*), a term that the Targumim elsewhere employ only in 1 Kgs 3:16 and Ez 23:44. Cf. Bernard Grossfeld, *Targum Neofiti 1: An Exegetical Commentary to Genesis, Including Full Rabbinic Parallels* (New York: Sepher-Hermon, 2000), ch. 34, n. 26, for a summary of the distribution of terms employed in the Targumim for prostitutes, i.e., translation equivalents for זֹנָה (*zônā*): זָנְיְתָא (*zanyĕtāʾ*) the cognate term for Hebrew זֹנָה (*zônā*; *Tg. Jl* 4:3, etc.); נָפְקַת בְּרָא (*nāpqat bārāʾ*), lit., "one who goes outside" (*Tg. Gn* 34:31); תָּעְיָא (*taʿăyāʾ*), "one who goes astray" or מַתְעְיָא (*matʿăyāʾ*), "one who leads astray" (*Tg. Lv* 21:7); and פּוּנְדְּקִיתָא (*pûndāqîtāʾ*), "innkeeper."

Reflecting a view similar to the Targum, Josephus nowhere designates Rahab a harlot but refers to her house as an inn (καταγώγιων; *katagōgiōn*) (*A.J.* 5.1.2 [§5–15]). This parallels his treatment of the Gaza incident in Jgs 16:1–3: Samson "lodged at one of the inns" (ἔν τινι τῶν καταγωγίων διέτριβε; *en tini tōn katagōgiōn dietribe*) (*A.J.* 5.8.10 [§304–5]).

It is possible that Josephus and the Targum are merely being interpretive: these prostitutes may have been innkeepers. The Code of Hammurabi (CH) §109 stipulates that it is a capital offense if a female tavern keeper (*sābîtum*) fails to arrest felons who have banded together in her house. This law establishes the fact that there were female tavern keepers of questionable loyalty in Old Babylonian

Though largely ignored or overlooked in recent scholarship, there are numerous precise verbal and situational parallels between Jo 2 and Jgs 16:1–3. Given the evidence elsewhere for literary dependence between Joshua and Judges (cf. Jgs 1:1–2:9), the present case should not be deemed improbable. In particular, the following eight verbal parallels may be noted (listed in order of their appearance in Jgs 16).

(1) The narrative is introduced with the sequence of "went" (הלך; *hlk*) followed by "saw" (ראה; *rʾh*) to describe the activity of Samson and the spies (Jgs 16:1; Jo 2:1).

(2) The woman to whom they come is identified as "a woman, a prostitute" (אִשָּׁה זוֹנָה; *ʾiššā zônā*) (Jgs 16:1; Jo 2:1).

(3) The expression "came to" or "went into" (אֶל + בוא; *bwʾ* + *ʾel*) is used to describe what Samson and the spies did with respect to this woman (Jgs 16:1; Jo 2:3, 4).

(4) The report of the presence of Samson and the spies is expressed in almost identical terms (five lexemes are in common): "And it was told to the Gazites, 'Samson has come here [לַעַזָּתִים לֵאמֹר בָּא שִׁמְשׁוֹן הֵנָּה; *laʿazzātîm lēʾmōr bāʾ šimšôn hēnnā*]'" in Jgs 16:2 and "and it was told the king of Jericho, 'Men have come here [וַיֵּאָמֵר לְמֶלֶךְ יְרִיחוֹ לֵאמֹר הִנֵּה אֲנָשִׁים בָּאוּ הֵנָּה; *wayyēʾāmar lĕmelek yĕrîḥô lēʾmōr hinnê ʾănāšîm bāʾû hēnnā*]'" in Jo 2:2.[18]

(5) It is noted that Samson and the spies are in the city during "the night" (הַלַּיְלָה; *hallaylā*) (Jgs 16:2, 3; Jo 2:2).

(6) Mention is made of "the city gate" (הַשַּׁעַר; *haššaʿar*), which plays a prominent role in what prove to be futile plans to trap Samson in and the spies out of their respective cities (Jgs 16:2, 3; Jo 2:5, 7).

---

society and that their dwellings were places where unsavory characters might congregate. Since CH §110 stipulates burning as a penalty for any *nadîtum* or *entum* priestess who opens (the door of) or enters such a tavern, J. C. Miles infers that such women may have engaged in prostitution. On this assumption, Miles suggests that the decision whether Rahab, the זֹנָה (*zōnā*) in Jo 2, was a "prostitute" or an "innkeeper" may be "a distinction without a difference" (G. R. Driver and John C. Miles, *The Babylonian Laws* [2 vols.; Oxford: Clarendon Press, 1955], 1:205 n. 6, 206); see also the comment at *A.J.* 3.12.1 (§§274–75) in *Josephus* (trans. H. St. J. Thackeray; 10 vols.; LCL; Cambridge, MA: Harvard University Press, 1926–1965), 6:450–51. Miles may be correct, but the evidence of CH §110 is insufficient since lesser offenses attract the death penalty (cf., e.g., CH §108), and this law is explicit about the purpose of these women in entering the tavern: it is not in order to engage in sexual acts, but it is "for liquor" (*ana šikarim*).

On the importance of narrative analogy, see, e.g., Robert Alter, *The Art of Biblical Narrative* (New York: Basic Books, 1981), and Peter D. Miscall, *The Workings of Old Testament Narrative* (SemeiaSt; Philadelphia: Fortress Press; Chico, CA: Scholars Press, 1983).

[18] The MT of Jgs 16:2 is emended here to include וַיֵּאָמֵר (*wayyēʾāmar*) following the LXX καὶ ἀπηγγέλη (*kai apēngelē*). Cf. Jo 2:2 where LXX καὶ ἀπηγγέλη (*kai apēngelē*) similarly renders MT וַיֵּאָמֵר (*wayyēʾāmar*).

(7) Samson and the spies "lie down" (שָׁכַב; *škb*) in the home of the harlot (Jgs 16:3; Jo 2:1, 8).

(8) When they escape Jericho and Gaza, Samson and the spies leave for "the hill country" (הָהָר; *hāhār*) (Jgs 16:3; Jo 2:16, 22, 23).

With respect to situational parallels, in both texts Israelites go into an enemy city located within the promised land; upon arriving at the city, they immediately find a harlot and intend to spend the night in her house. This plan is interrupted, however, by the report of their unwelcome presence, which provokes the local citizenry to attempt to capture them. By the use of innuendo in both texts, it is apparent that the citizenry assume that both the spies and Samson have availed themselves of the professional services of their harlots. Despite the enemies' hope that this would work to their advantage, their plans to capture the spies and Samson are foiled. The spies and Samson escape from their respective cities and leave for nearby hill country. In the end, the walls of Jericho fall and the gates of Gaza are removed, thereby vividly exposing the weakness of these defenses against those who represent the Lord of Hosts.[19]

The Unlikelihood That the Spies in Joshua 2 Had Sexual Relations with Rahab

It appears unlikely that the spies in Jo 2 had sexual relations with Rahab the harlot, at least according to the final form of the text. This inference is based on several considerations. First, the text nowhere clearly states that they did, in fact, have sexual relations. Rather, the text implies that the spies came to Rahab for the sole purpose of fulfilling their commission from Joshua: "go, spy out the land, especially Jericho. So they went and entered the house of a prostitute" (Jo 2:1). Second, if the MT is maintained, the relative clause "who have come to your house" (אֲשֶׁר־בָּאוּ לְבֵיתֵךְ; *'ăšer-bā'û lĕbêtēk*) in Jo 2:3 appears to be intended to protect the reputation of the spies for the reader by defining the expression "the ones who have come (in) to you" (הַבָּאִים אֵלַיִךְ; *habbā'îm 'ēlayik*) precisely in a manner that excludes a sexual reference.[20] However, if the MT in 2:3 is emended with the LXX, then it is only Rahab in 2:4 who uses the expression בּוֹא אֶל (*bw' 'el*): "yes, the men came in to me [= had relations with

---

[19] Regarding the symbolism of gates, cf. the climactic curse of the Aramaic Azitawadda inscription against anyone who might replace the name of King Azitawadda of Adana on the city gate or who might remove the old and build a new gate bearing his own name, whether with good or evil intentions (*ANET*, 654).

[20] The LXX in Jo 2:3 fails to render הבאים אליך (*hb'ym 'lyk*) and thereby removes this ambiguity: Ἐξάγαγε τοὺς ἄνδρας τοὺς εἰσπεπορευμένους εἰς τὴν οἰκίαν σου τὴν νύκτα (*Exagage tous andras tous eispeporeumenous eis tēn oikian sou tēn nykta*).

me; כֵּן בָּאוּ אֵלַי הָאֲנָשִׁים; *kēn bāʾû ʾēlay hāʾănāšîm*]*." Since everything else that Rahab tells the men of Jericho is a deception ("I did not know where they had come from," "the men left," "I don't know which way they went," "quickly pursue them so that you may catch up with them"), it is likely that Rahab is deliberately using this ambiguous titillating language in order to mislead the men once again. As she well knows, in reality the spies had come to Jericho and to her for a very different purpose. Finally, given the larger context of holy war, within which the spies are functioning and according to which sexual relations are prohibited even between marital partners (cf. Dt 23:9–14; 1 Sm 21:4–5; 2 Sm 11:11, 13; see also Ex 19:15 and Lv 15),[21] the burden of proof would seem to lie with those who assume that the spies had sexual relations with Rahab. If then, as is generally conceded, there was no sexual misconduct on the part of the spies in Jo 2, it seems plausible that the same presumption of innocence should obtain for Samson at Gaza.[22]

Further Support That Samson Did Not Engage in Sexual Relations with the Harlot at Gaza

Offering support for this presumption is the remarkable coincidence that the men of Gaza are thrown off from capturing Samson by the same mistaken belief as the men of Jericho. The logic of their decision to wait in the city gate until dawn is transparent. They wrongly assume that Samson would spend the night engaging the professional services of their prostitute or recuperating from the same. They are positioned in the gates of the city, the official place where judgment was commonly rendered. Accordingly, their assumption constituted a gross misjudgment of the Nazirite.[23] Contrary to their expectation, Samson gets up at midnight and

---

[21] Gordon J. Wenham, *Leviticus* (NICOT; Grand Rapids: Eerdmans, 1979), 221–25.

[22] Marten H. Woudstra, *The Book of Joshua* (NICOT; Grand Rapids: Eerdmans, 1981), 69–70. For the opposing view (offered without proof) that the spies did have sexual relations with Rahab, see, e.g., Robert G. Boling and G. Ernest Wright, *Joshua: A New Translation with Notes and Commentary* (AB 6; Garden City, NY: Doubleday, 1982), 145. Pekka M. A. Pitkänen considers it impossible to be sure (*Joshua* [AOTC; Downers Grove, IL: InterVarsity Press, 2010], 123). Cf. M. L. Newman, "Rahab and the Conquest," in *Understanding the Word: Essays in Honor of Bernhard W. Anderson* (ed. J. T. Butler, E. W. Conrad, and B. C. Ollenburger; JSOTSup 37; Sheffield: JSOT Press, 1985), 167–81. Richard S. Hess provides historical background for the presence of inns or places of overnight accommodation unrelated to prostitution, which served the needs of travelers in the fourteenth to twelfth cent. B.C. ("West Semitic Texts and the Book of Joshua," *BBR* 7 [1997]: 63–76).

[23] For the city gates as the place of judgment, see, e.g., Dt 17:5; 21:19; 22:15, 24; 25:7; Jo 20:4; Ps 118:20; Prv 31:23; Ru 4:11.

judges them at the very place of their perverted judgment. In keeping with the general symbolism of Gn 22:17 and 24:60, the removal of the gates to the summit of a hill in the direction of Hebron was an unmistakable demonstration of the subjugation of Gaza before Samson and his Lord. It was perhaps also a sign of the consequent vulnerability of the inhabitants of the chief city of Philistia to the inhabitants of the chief city of Judah, which tribe was responsible to dispossess Gaza, if only they would accept the leadership of Samson (see Jgs 15:11–13).[24]

Less certain is the possibility that here is an instance of *lex talionis*. On this approach, Samson may have punished the city with a symbolic rape in response to their false judgment against him regarding his relationship to the harlot. In support, see *b. Ketub.* 10a, where the expression "tearing out the gate together with the bar" is used to describe a case of violent coitus.[25]

Theories Why the Spies Came to Rahab and Why Samson Came to the Harlot at Gaza

Of course, it may still be asked why the spies came to Rahab and why Samson came to the harlot at Gaza, if not to engage in sexual relations. Some have suggested that the spies sought out a harlot's quarters in the hope of securing anonymity or avoiding detection.[26] There is little to favor this hypothesis, however, given Rahab's immediate awareness of their identity as Israelites, for which reason she hid them in anticipation of the king's messengers, and given how quickly both Jericho and Gaza were informed of the presence of these unwelcome strangers (Jo 2:2; Jgs 16:2).

Others have imagined, perhaps based on modern analogies, that a brothel might provide useful military information for the taking of a city. It is doubtful, however, that the spies uncovered any information that was needed or could be incorporated in the eventual strategy that supernaturally caused the walls of Jericho to tumble. It is equally doubtful that Samson needed the harlot at Gaza to inform him how best to tear up and carry off the city gates.

---

[24] Gaza was assigned to Judah in Jo 15:47. See also Jgs 1:18, which, when emended with the LXX, asserts that Judah failed to take Gaza, demonstrating the later need for Samson to take this action. It is unnecessary to suppose that Samson carried these gates all the way to Hebron, forty miles to the east of Gaza. The phrase עַל־פְּנֵי (*'al-pĕnê*) can mean "in the direction of" or "facing," as it does in Gn 18:16. Hebron's prominence is evident from its patriarchal and Davidic associations: here is where David was first proclaimed king (2 Sm 2:4).

[25] James L. Crenshaw assumes that the Talmudic expression derives from Jgs 16 ("The Samson Saga," 490 n. 26). Whether this is so or not, the Talmudic usage proves an early understanding of the symbolism posited here.

[26] Cf., e.g., Richard D. Nelson, *Joshua* (OTL; Louisville: Westminster John Knox, 1997), 48, and Pitkänen, *Joshua*, 123.

Before proposing a further possible explanation for this uncanny interest in harlots, it may help to stress that whatever their intention, ethically the spies could not avail themselves of the alternative and more customary hospitality of the elders at the gate. To have done so, knowing that their ultimate intention was to destroy Jericho, would have constituted a grievous offense against the ancient conventions of hospitality and, in some circumstances, covenant making effected through shared meals.[27]

In any case, a number of texts that provide the theological justification for the conquest of Canaan may have some bearing on the spies' interest in Rahab. Leviticus 18:3, 24–30; 20:22–24; Dt 18:9–13; and 1 Kgs 14:24, for example, all stress that the Lord abhorred the Canaanites and caused them to forfeit their land to the Israelites precisely because of their detestable sexual practices.[28] Although the theory of cultic prostitution appears to be without foundation, it is possible that these sexual practices were at times related to their idolatry based on various evidences including the incident at Baal of Peor (Nm 25).[29] If so, these proscriptions may be subsumed under the condemnation of other texts such as Dt 20:16–18 and Lv 20:2ff., which stress the idolatrous practices of the Canaanites as a further justification for their annihilation.[30] If Joshua's spies shared a similar perspective, it is not surprising that their conversation with Rahab had less to do with the whereabouts of secret passageways in the walls of Jericho than with confirmation of God's impending judgment against its inhabitants. Indeed, in her person Rahab may have provided the requisite evidence (made only more forceful by her repudiation of her people) that

---

[27] See, e.g., Gn 26:30; 31:46–54; Jo 9:14; Ex 18:12; Pss 23:5; 41:10[9]; 69:23[22]; 1 Kgs 1:9, 25; 1 Chr 12:39–40; 29:22; 2 Chr 18:2. By contrast, note the prohibition against eating with those who are slated for destruction in 1 Kgs 13:9. Note also the offense of turning against one who has shared hospitality in Ps 41:10[9].

On the significance of shared meals, see Gordon P. Hugenberger, *Marriage as a Covenant* (VTSup 52; Leiden: Brill, 1994; repr., Grand Rapids: Baker, 1998), 205–11. See also Peter Farb, *Consuming Passions: The Anthropology of Eating* (New York: Washington Square Press, 1980); Paul Kalluveettil, *Declaration and Covenant: A Comprehensive Review of Covenant Formulae from the Old Testament and the Ancient Near East* (AnBib 88; Rome: Pontifical Biblical Institute, 1982), 11, 12–13, 118; Meir Malul, *Studies in Mesopotamian Legal Symbolism* (AOAT 221; Kevelaer: Butzon & Bercker; Neukirchen-Vluyn: Neukirchener, 1988), 176, 346, 353, 356, 376–78; Dennis J. McCarthy, *Treaty and Covenant: A Study in Form in the Ancient Oriental Documents and in the Old Testament* (AnBib 21a; Rome: Pontifical Biblical Institute, 1981), 254 n. 19; W. T. McCree, "The Covenant Meal in the Old Testament," *JBL* 45 (1926): 120–28; James F. Ross, "Meal," *IDB* 3:315–18.

[28] See also Lv 19:29 and Jer 3:1–2. In a manner analogous to the Canaanite experience, pre-exilic Israel was later condemned for its own sexual sins, which were among the offenses causing it to forfeit the land.

[29] See, e.g., Elaine Adler Goodfriend, "Prostitution," *ABD* 5:505–10; and Karel van der Toorn, "Cultic Prostitution," *ABD* 5:510–13.

[30] See also Gn 15:16; Ex 23:23–24; Dt 9:4–5; 18:9–13; 2 Kgs 16:3; 17:7–23; 1 Chr 5:25.

the land would soon vomit out its inhabitants (as predicted in Lv 18:24–30) and the Lord would soon give Jericho into Israel's hands because "the sin of the Amorites" had now "reached its full measure" (Gn 15:16).

Although nothing is said in Jgs 16 about Samson's purpose in relation to the harlot, it is possible that his interest was similar to that being proposed for Joshua's spies. If attention is given to the pervasive structural parallels between Jgs 16 and 14–15, as elucidated by J. Cheryl Exum, this would favor the assumption that Samson's intention at Gaza was the same as his intention at Timnah —namely, to take some divinely sanctioned action to dispossess the Philistines (see 14:4, 15).[31] If so, it is possible that his interest in this woman, as his interest in the Timnahite woman, was subservient to that desire.[32] In any case, it is clear that such a motive on Samson's part would be entirely at home in the book of Judges that elsewhere shows a particular concern to condemn the sexual sins of Canaan. A striking example of this concern is the anti-rape theme of Jgs 5, where Jael executes Sisera with a lethal thrust of a tent peg while he lies between her legs (5:27) in a manner correlating with his would-be rape of her (5:30).[33] In Jgs 19–21 the divinely sanctioned plan to annihilate Canaan's protégé, the Sodomite city of Gibeah, for the murderous

---

[31] J. Cheryl Exum, "Aspects of Symmetry and Balance in the Samson Saga," *JSOT* 19 (1981): 3–29. Exum's analysis of these chapters has been widely accepted. Cf., e.g., Klein, *The Triumph of Irony,* 109, and M. O'Connor, "Judges," in *The New Jerome Bible Commentary* (ed. R. E. Brown, J. A. Fitzmyer, and R. E. Murphy; Upper Saddle Rive, NJ: Prentice Hall, 1990), 142. The repeated closing formula of Samson's twenty-year term of judging Israel (Jgs 15:20; 16:31) is just one indication of this structure. Also alert to this parallel between Jgs 16 and Jgs 14–15, Cyril J. Barber makes the unlikely suggestion that Samson ravished this prostitute not because of lust but to show his power to defy the enemy (*Judges, A Narrative of God's Power* [Neptune, NJ: Loizeaux, 1990]).

Although Jgs 14:4 insists that Samson's marriage to the Timnahite woman has divine approval as a means for dispossessing the Philistines, as they themselves seem to recognize (Jgs 14:15), the details and ethics of this marriage are much debated among interpreters. Despite the objection of Samson's parents to the marriage, it is salutary to note that the Philistines are not included in the list of prohibited marriages in Jgs 3:5–6, or in any other comparable list in the OT (Gn 24:3, 37; 28:1, 6; Ex 34:11–16; Dt 7:1–4; Jo 23:12; 1 Kgs 11:1–2; Ezr 9:1–2, 14). Explaining how Samson's marriage could be useful to gain property in Timnah, see Jgs 1:11–15 for an example of property inheritance accomplished through marriage. For intermarriage as a means of dispossession in the postexilic community, see Ralph L. Smith, *Micah-Malachi* (WBC 32; Waco, TX: Word, 1984), 322; Norman K. Gottwald, *The Hebrew Bible: A Socio-Literary Introduction* (Philadelphia: Fortress, 1985), 510; and Joseph Blenkinsopp, *Ezra–Nehemiah* (OTL; Philadelphia: Westminster Press, 1988), 365.

[32] Just as the Philistines perhaps misjudged Samson's invulnerability as a Nazirite to the lure of alcohol in Jgs 14, which may have thwarted their original strategy for solving his riddle, so also perhaps they misjudged his attraction to the wiles of their harlot in Jgs 16.

[33] See M. Z. Levin, "A Protest Against Rape in the Story of Deborah [Hebrew]," *Beth Mikra* 25 (1979): 83–84.

rape of the Levite's concubine is another example. Indeed, the only recon-
naissance required was the determination of the facts of this abominable
act (20:3–7).

Judges 18 as a "Reflection Story" for Judges 16:1–3 (and Joshua 2): A Neglected Parallel

In further support of the present interpretation of Jgs 16:1–3, there is
a second narrative analogy of which the reader should be aware, namely,
one between this text and the account of the Danite spies in Jgs 18. Indeed, the episode of the Danite spies offers yet another example of what
Yair Zakovitch has termed a "reflection story."[34] Before examining this
reflection story in detail, however, it may be useful to review some of the
widely recognized thematic parallels and verbal links that exist between
the Samson narrative (Jgs 13–16) and the double epilogue (Jgs 17–18;
19–21) as a whole.

General parallels include the shared prominence of the tribe of Dan
(Samson of the tribe of Dan in 13:2 versus the migration of the tribe to
the north in 18:1ff.); a similar prominence accorded to the mothers of
Samson and Micah (13:1ff.; 17:1ff.); the motifs of the procurement of
a wife (14:1ff.; 21), the alienated affections of a wife (14:15ff.; 16:5ff.;
19:2); retaliation for the murder of a wife (15:7ff.; 19:29ff.); and perhaps
also the hostile intent of a Canaanite(-like) city's populace against a visi-
tor (16:2; 19:22ff.).

Explicit verbal connectors include the incidental detail of the eleven
hundred shekels mentioned in both 16:5 (the price promised by each Philistine ruler to Delilah for her treachery) and 17:3 (the amount stolen by
Micah from his mother), the mention of Mahaneh-Dan (13:25; 18:12),
and the repeated mention of Zorah and Eshtaol, from which Samson departed to go to Timnah (part of the designated inheritance for Dan) and
from which the Danites departed to abandon their tribal allotment in
favor of Laish (13:3, 25; 16:31; 18:2, 8, 11).[35]

Note that Ben-Sira condemns the wanton woman who is willing to squat be-
fore any "tent-peg," employing this term as a sexual euphemism (Sir 26:12). See
Patrick W. Skehan and Alexander A. Di Lella, *The Wisdom of Ben Sira* (AB 39; New
York: Doubleday, 1987), 350.

[34] "Reflection Story—Another Dimension of the Evaluation of Characters in
Biblical Narrative [Hebrew]," *Tarbiz* 54 (1984/1985): 165–76.

[35] One final verbal parallel, which has played a prominent role in the interpretation of Jgs 14, is a possible allusion in 14:3, 7, where the Timnahite woman
is described as "(up)right in the eyes of" (בְּעֵינָיו + יָשָׁר; *yāšār* + *bĕ'ênāyw*), to the
thematic refrain of the double epilogue in 17:6 and 21:25: "In those days Israel
had no king, everyone did what is right in his own eyes" (אִישׁ הַיָּשָׁר בְּעֵינָיו יַעֲשֶׂה;
'îš hayyāšār bĕ'ênāyw ya'áśeh). It goes beyond the scope of this essay to dispute

While some scholars have used these parallels to suggest that Samson, in his alleged disobedience, is typical of his fellow Danites, it is equally possible, and perhaps more likely, that the narrator employs these suggested literary connections precisely in order to highlight a radical dissimilarity between these protagonists. On this approach, the Danites provide a foil for Samson that underscores their abject failure to take their tribal allotment in the region of Zorah, Eshtaol, and Timnah, by contrast to the singular example of obedience offered by Samson, no thanks to his kinsmen. For all the well-rehearsed moral ambiguities of the Samson narrative, nothing about the account of Samson suggests an involvement in idolatry, while the account of Dan is inextricably linked with the sin of idolatry. Indeed, the text emphasizes the tainted history of Dan's idols, which were stolen by the tribe of Dan from Micah, who had fabricated them from silver he had previously stolen from his mother and returned to her only after being cursed by her.

Turning now to a closer examination of the account of the Danite spies in Jgs 18, it is remarkable that this narrative also offers clear parallels with Jo 2, precisely as has been argued with respect to Jgs 16.[36]

(1) In both Jo 2 and Jgs 18, the people have not yet come into their inheritance, and so they send out spies into land that they are hoping to conquer.

(2) At the outset of their exploration, the spies come to the house of a foreigner, where they plan to spend the night (Rahab's house in Jo 2:1; the house of Micah and Jonathan in Jgs 18:2).

(3) As far as is recorded, the spies gain no intelligence of direct military benefit, but their hosts do provide them with divine confirmation of the potential success of their mission (Jo 2:9–13; Jgs 18:5, 6).

(4) In the end, the hosts (Rahab and Jonathan) transfer their loyalty to the spies, who then take them in when they return for conquest (Jo 2:12–13; 6:22–25; Jgs 18:20).

If, as has been proposed, Joshua's spies came to Rahab the harlot because they were seeking confirmation of God's imminent judgment, it is not surprising that the Danite spies, functioning in their judicial capacity, should have a similar interest in the evidence of idolatry which they

---

the inference frequently drawn from this parallel, namely, that the narrator uses these similar, though not identical, expressions to suggest that Samson personifies Israel and that Samson's hoped-for marriage comes under the same condemnation (against the implication of 14:4) as any of Israel's clearly objectionable actions narrated in the double epilogue.

[36] There may also be parallels with the Nm 13 spy account. See, e.g., Cundall, *Judges*, 187. The inherent importance of the story of Rahab and the taking of Jericho, however, should prepare readers to find extensive parallels later, as is argued in this essay, as well as lesser echoes, as may be present in texts like Jgs 1:23–26 and 2 Sm 17:17–22.

discover at Micah's house. Judges 18:14 appears almost to tease the reader into expecting the appropriate response to this discovery: "then the five men who had gone to spy out the country of Laish said to their brethren, 'Do you know that in these houses there are an ephod, teraphim, a graven image, and a molten image? Now you know what you should do.'" Surely the Danites know that they must execute God's well-deserved judgment against the household of Micah for this gross idolatry, as required by Dt 13, a passage that also proves to be key for the interpretation of Jgs 19–21. Far from eradicating this idolatry, the Danites embrace it! They lure Jonathan away from Micah in order to become their priest, and they confiscate Micah's idols for their own use.

By contrast, in a perversion of justice the Danites proceed northward to dispossess the Laishites. The text appears to go out of its way to portray the Laishites in a sympathetic manner, thereby implicitly condemning the Danites' action. Nowhere had the Lord authorized the dispossession of the Laishites, whether by Dan or by any other tribe. The hostility of the Danites, it seems, was based not on any assessed guilt or on any perceived threat from the Laishites but merely on their vulnerability.[37]

In keeping with the many parallels that have been noted between the Samson narrative and this first epilogue (Jgs 17–18), the author may have intended one further contrastive parallel between 16:1–3 and Jgs 18. While the Danite spies fail to follow the pattern of Joshua's spies, the author of Judges suggests that the faithful Danite, Samson, who alone remained behind when the rest of his tribe had abandoned their inheritance, was replicating the stratagem of the spies meticulously. If so, Gaza was hardly Samson's downfall, as is so often alleged.

Conclusion

In conclusion, although modern scholars are virtually unanimous in the view that Samson had sexual relations with the harlot at Gaza, the evidence in support of this opinion is surprisingly limited. As has been stated, it rests mainly on the identification of the woman as a "harlot" (זוֹנָה; zōnā) in 16:1, on the appearance in the same verse of the syntagm בוא (bwʾ) + אֶל (ʾel) + a person, which sometimes refers to sexual relations, and on certain assumptions regarding Samson's moral character based on the wider narrative of Jgs 14–16. Despite modern unanimity, it is striking

---

[37] This negative appraisal of the Danite spies in the first epilogue to Judges and the assumed intertextuality with Jo 2 find a counterpart in the prologue to Judges, namely, the use of spies in the conquest of Bethel in Jgs 1:22–26. Unlike Rahab, their informant neither converts nor is assimilated into Israel. Instead, as a consequence of their misplaced mercy (cf., e.g., Dt 7:2; 1 Sm 15:8ff.), this Canaanite survives to transplant the accursed culture of Luz to the land of the Hittites.

that a substantial number of precritical interpreters, including those like Josephus who readily acknowledge Samson's wayward nature elsewhere, held that Samson had no sexual relations with the woman, whom they frequently identify as an innkeeper.

The present essay has sought to rehabilitate this earlier alternative interpretation, without requiring the posited definition of זנה (*znh*) as "innkeeper," mainly by an appeal to numerous situational and precise verbal parallels that exist between Jgs 16:1–3 and Jo 2 (the visit of Joshua's spies to Rahab the harlot). Although scholars commonly recognize quotations and allusions to Joshua elsewhere in Judges, the presence of these striking parallels in Jgs 16:1–3 has been all but neglected.

Further support for this alternative interpretation of Jgs 16:1–3 was sought in an examination of its immediate context. In particular, attention was given both to the well-established literary parallelism between Jgs 14 and Jgs 16 and to the generally neglected anti-parallelism between Jgs 16:1–3 and Jgs 18, which offers a possible "reflection story" for the episode at Gaza.

All three parallels strongly favor the conclusion that Samson did not, in fact, have sexual relations with the harlot at Gaza, as the citizens of Gaza wrongly assumed to the detriment of their own city, and that Samson's intention for coming to the harlot at Gaza was deliberately the same as the intention of Joshua's spies for coming to Rahab the harlot at Jericho: to take an appropriate step that would enable the divinely approved work of dispossession to begin.

Part 2

Use of the Old Testament in the New

CHAPTER 5

THE POWER AND THE GLORY: THE RENDERING OF PSALM 110:1 IN MARK 14:62

Richard J. Bauckham

Quotations of and allusions to Ps 110:1 (LXX 109:1) in the NT out-number those relating to any other OT text. Its importance for under-standing the origins and character of early Christology can hardly be exaggerated.[1] Early Christians understood it to mean that Jesus had been exalted to share the throne from which God rules the cosmos. The allusion to this text, combined with Dn 7:13, in Jesus' answer to the high priest (Mt 26:64; Mk 14:62; Lk 22:69)[2] is of special interest because, if it is an authentic word of Jesus, it would indicate that the early Christians' under-standing of him through exegesis of this text was rooted in his own use of this text to express his self-understanding. The present essay does not attempt to demonstrate the authenticity of the saying but focuses entirely on a verbal aspect of this allusion to Ps 110:1 that marks it out from all other such quotations and allusions, a matter that is not irrelevant to the issue of authenticity, though it cannot by itself establish that. In Mark's

---

[1] On Ps 110:1 in the NT, see David M. Hay, *Glory at the Right Hand: Psalm 110 in Early Christianity* (Nashville: Abingdon, 1973); Michel Gourgues, *Á la Droite de Dieu: Résurrection de Jésus et Actualisation du Psaume 110:1 dans le Nouveau Testament* (Ébib; Paris: Gabalda, 1978); Martin Hengel, "Sit at My Right Hand," in *Studies in Early Christology* (Edinburgh: T&T Clark, 1995), 119–225; Timo Eskola, *Messiah and the Throne: Jewish Merkabah Mysticism and Early Christian Exaltation Discourse* (WUNT 2/142; Tübingen: Mohr Siebeck, 2001); Richard J. Bauckham, *Jesus and the God of Israel: God Crucified and Other Studies on the New Testament's Christology of Divine Identity* (Milton Keynes: Paternoster; Grand Rapids: Eerdmans, 2008), 21–24, 152–81, 233–53.

[2] What is in effect another version of the saying, though doubtless based on Matthew or Mark, is in Hegesippus's account of the death of James the Lord's brother (Eusebius, *Hist. Eccl.* 2.23.13), where he has James say, "Why do you ask me about the Son of man? He is sitting in heaven at the right hand of the Great Power (τῆς μεγάλης δυνάμεως; *tēs megalēs dynameōs*), and he will come on the clouds of heaven."

version, the relevant words are "you will see the Son of man sitting at the right hand of the Power." (Matthew's text is identical apart from a difference of word order, but Luke has "the Son of man will be seated at the right hand of the Power of God." Other differences between the three versions of Jesus' answer to the high priest are not relevant to the present purpose.) In the psalm itself, YHWH addresses "my lord" with the words "sit at my right hand." Only in Jesus' answer to the high priest does an allusion to these words use the term "the Power" (τῆς δυνάμεως; *tēs dynameōs*) for God. Indeed, this designation of God is found nowhere else in the NT or in Second Temple Jewish literature. What accounts for it?

"The Power" הַגְּבוּרָה (*haggĕbûrâ*) as a Divine "Name" in Rabbinic Literature

Although it is not to be found in Second Temple Jewish literature, "the Power" (הַגְּבוּרָה; *haggĕbûrâ*) does occur as a designation for God, used in place of the divine Name or other ways of referring directly to God, in rabbinic literature, and commentators on Mark have often referred to this evidence. To the best of my knowledge, the only extended discussion of it is by Arnold Goldberg in an article published in 1964.[3] A number of Gospels scholars, in their comments on Mk 14:62 or Mt 26:64, have followed his conclusions.[4] He assembled and classified a comprehensive, though not exhaustive,[5] collection of rabbinic texts that refer to God as הַגְּבוּרָה (*haggĕbûrâ*), fifty-two in all,[6] though a considerable number of these are in late works that simply relay traditions already found in earlier works. In my view, valuable as Goldberg's study is, his conclusions about the function of הַגְּבוּרָה (*haggĕbûrâ*) as a designation for God are not entirely satisfactory. The evidence needs revisiting.

---

[3] Arnold M. Goldberg, "Sitzend zur Rechten der Kraft: Zur Gottesbezeichnung Gebura in der frühen rabbinischen Literatur," *BZ* 8 (1964): 284–93. See also Ephraim E. Urbach, "The Epithet *Gĕvûrā* and the Might of God," in *The Sages: Their Concepts and Belief*, vol. 1 (trans. Israel Abrahams; Jerusalem: Magnes Press, 1979), 80–96, who treats the term as a designation of God only briefly (pp. 83–85, 93–94) in the context of a broader synthesis of the rabbis' understanding of divine power.

[4] E.g., Raymond E. Brown, *The Death of the Messiah* (New York: Doubleday, 1994), 1:496–97; Simon Légasse, *L'Évangile de Marc* (LD; Paris: Cerf, 1997), 2:924 n. 53; Richard T. France, *The Gospel of Mark* (NIGTC; Carlisle: Paternoster; Grand Rapids: Eerdmans, 2002), 613–14 n. 45.

[5] Texts not listed by Goldberg include *b. Soṭah* 37a; *b. Mak.* 24a; *Sipre Num.* 112.

[6] There are smaller collections of texts in Arthur Marmorstein, *The Old Rabbinic Doctrine of God*: 1: *The Names and Attributes of God* (Jews' College Publications 10; London: Oxford University Press, 1927), 82; Hermann Leberecht Strack and Paul Billerbeck, *Kommentar zum Neuen Testament aus Talmud und Midrasch* (Munich: Beck, 1922), 1:1006–7; Urbach, 84–85; Darrell L. Bock, *Blasphemy and Exaltation in Judaism: The Charge against Jesus in Mark 14:53–65* (Tübingen: Mohr Siebeck, 1998; Grand Rapids: Baker, 2000), 217–18.

Goldberg points out that, if we are guided by the attributions to named rabbis in these texts (R. Yohanan b. Zakkai, R. Ishmael, R. Akiba, R. Joshua b. Hananiah, R. Eliezer b. Hyrcanus, R. Eleazar of Modiim), it appears that הַגְּבוּרָה (*haggĕbûrâ*) as a designation for God was current in the earlier Tannaitic period (i.e., down to about the mid-second century). Although such attributions cannot necessarily be considered reliable, the convergence of evidence pointing to a particular period is impressive, and so it is notable that the period indicated is relatively close to the time of the Gospels.

After the early Tannaitic period הַגְּבוּרָה (*haggĕbûrâ*) as a designation for God appears only in quotations from the early Tannaim and in very stereotyped expressions.[7] In fact, in a large majority of the texts it appears in the phrase "the mouth of the Power," more specifically in one of two expressions: "from the mouth of the Power" (מִפִּי הַגְּבוּרָה; *mippî haggĕbûrâ*) and "according to the mouth of the Power" (עַל־פִּי הַגְּבוּרָה; *ʿal-pî haggĕbûrâ*; i.e., "according to the command of the Power"). I have selected the following seven texts as representative of this usage in expressions that substitute it for references to "the mouth of God."

> (A) R. Ishmael says, "Scripture speaks in particular of idolatry, for it is said, '. . . because he has despised the word of the Lord' (Num 15:31), for he has despised the first word [the first of the Ten Commandments], as it is said to Moses according to the mouth of the Power: 'I am the Lord your God. You shall have no other gods before me' (Exod 20:23–3)." (*Sipre Num.* 112)[8]

> (B) [R. Yohanan, commenting on Ps 68:12, said] Every act of speech that came forth from the mouth of the Power was divided into seventy languages. (*b. Šabb.* 88b)[9]

> (C) [On Ex 4:30] Who indeed was qualified to speak, Moses or Aaron? Surely Moses! for Moses heard [the words] from the mouth of the Power, while Aaron heard them only from the mouth of Moses. (*'Abot R. Nat.* A 37)[10]

> (D) If he was a proselyte who has come to study the Torah, one may not say to him, "Look who's coming to study Torah which was given according to the mouth of the Power! One who ate carrion meat and *teref* meat, abominations and creeping things!" (*b. B. Meṣ.* 58b)[11]

---

[7] Goldberg, "Sitzend," 287.

[8] Translation (modified) from Jacob Neusner, *Sifré to Numbers: An American Translation and Explanation* (BJS 119; Atlanta: Scholars Press, 1986), 2:170.

[9] Translation (modified) from Jacob Neusner, *The Talmud of Babylonia: An American Translation*, vol. IIC: *Shabbat Chapters 7–10* (BJS 273; Atlanta: Scholars Press, 1993), 84.

[10] Translation (modified) from Judah Goldin, *The Fathers according to Rabbi Nathan* (Yale Judaica Series 10; New Haven: Yale University Press, 1955), 155.

[11] Translation (modified) from Jacob Neusner, *The Talmud of Babylonia: An American Translation*, vol. XXIIB: *Tractate Bava Mesia Chapters 3–4* (BJS 214; Atlanta: Scholars Press, 1990), 151–52.

(E) [On 1 Chr 15:11–15; 24:19] Where did he [God] give a commandment? He gave nothing at all to the sons of Kohath. So behold, the Levites in no way innovated, but everything was done according to the mouth of Moses, who did everything according to the mouth of the Power. (*Sipre Num.* 46)[12]

(F) [On Ex 15:22] R. Joshua said, "This journey did the Israelites undertake according to the mouth of the Moses, while all other journeys they undertook only according the mouth of the Power, as it is said, 'According to the commandment of the Lord they encamped, and according to the commandment of the Lord they journeyed' (Num 9:23)." (*Mek. Vayassa* 1)[13]

(G) There were three statements that Moses heard from the mouth of the Power, on account of which he was astounded and recoiled. (*Pesiq. Rab Kah.* 2)[14]

Texts that use הַגְּבוּרָה (*haggĕbûrâ*) otherwise than in the phrase פִּי הַגְּבוּרָה (*pî haggĕbûrâ*) are fewer, but I have selected six in order to illustrate the range of this more general usage.

(H) [On Ex 19:8] What did the Holy One, blessed be He, say to Moses, what did Moses say to Israel, what did Israel say to Moses, and what did Moses report before the Power? (*b. Šabb.* 87a)[15]

(I) [On Ex 15:24] R. Eleazar the Modiite says, "The Israelites were used to complaining against Moses. And not against Moses alone did they speak, but against the Power." (*Mek. Vayassa* 1)[16]

(J) Benjamin, the righteous, attained such merit as to be made the host of the Power, as it is said, "He dwells between his shoulders" (Deut 33:12). (*b. Soṭah* 37a)[17]

(K) And Moses said to Aaron, "Say to the whole congregation of the people of Israel, 'Come near'" (Exod 16:9). R. Joshua says, " 'Come near' because the Power is revealed." . . . "they looked toward the wilderness" (Exod 16:10). R. Joshua says, "They did not turn about until the Power had been revealed." (*Mek. Vayassa* 3)[18]

(L) Forthwith Moses agreed with him [Aaron], as it is said, "And when Moses heard that, it was well-pleasing in his eyes" (Lev. 10:20) and in the eyes of the Power too. (*'Avot R. Nat.* A 37)[19]

---

[12] Translation (modified) from Jacob Neusner, *Sifré to Numbers: An American Translation and Explanation* (BJS 118; Atlanta: Scholars Press, 1986), 1:211.

[13] Translation (modified) from Jacob Neusner, *Mekhilta according to Rabbi Ishmael: An Analytical Translation* (BJS 148; Atlanta: Scholars Press, 1988), 1:233.

[14] Translation (modified) from Jacob Neusner, *Pesiqta deRab Kahana* (BJS 122; Atlanta: Scholars Press, 1987), 1:29.

[15] Translation (modified) from Neusner, *The Talmud of Babylonia*, IIC:79.

[16] Translation (modified) from Neusner, *Mekhilta*, 1:236.

[17] Translation (modified) from Jacob Neusner, *The Talmud of Babylonia: An American Translation*, vol. XVII: *Tractate Sotah* (BJS 72; Chico, CA: Scholars Press, 1984), 209.

[18] Translation (modified) from Neusner, *Mekhilta*, 1:246.

[19] Translation (modified) from Goldin, *The Fathers according to Rabbi Nathan*, 155.

(M) He [Ezekiel] said to them [Hananiah, Mishael, and Azariah]: "If that is your idea, wait till I consult the Power"; and so it is written, "Certain of the elders of Israel came to inquire of the Lord, and sat before me" (Ezek 20:1). (*Cant. Rab.* 7:8:1)[20]

Goldberg's work is related to his much more extensive study of the Shekinah in rabbinic literature[21] in that he claims that גבורה (*gĕbûrâ*), like Shekinah and "Glory" (כָּבֹד; *kābōd*), is not a general circumlocution for the name of God but has specific meaning. It does not designate the Deity himself (the "being" of God) but only the appearing of the Deity, especially in revelation through Word.[22] It presents, in other words, only one aspect of God in his relation to his people.

While I do not wish to deny that הַגְּבוּרָה (*haggĕbûrâ*) has a specific meaning, designating God under the aspect of his power, just as even אֲדֹנָי (*'ădōnāy*), used as a substitute for the divine Name, does (referring to God's lordship),[23] I am not convinced by Goldberg's more specific argument that it has a special reference to God's revelation through Word. Clearly the stereotyped phrase "the mouth of the Power" refers to God's word or command, but we should notice that in some of the texts it obviously stands in for the biblical phrase "the mouth of YHWH." Among the texts quoted above this is the case in texts B (alluding to Dt 8:3) and F (alluding to Ex 17:1; Nm 9:18, 20, 23; 10:13; 13:3). It seems likely that the phrase originated as an anti-anthropomorphic substitution for "the mouth of YHWH." In the biblical text of Exodus and Numbers, the phrase "according to the mouth of YHWH" is clearly metaphorical (usually meaning "at/according to the command of YHWH"), but it is nevertheless an anthropomorphic idiom. The Targums render it as "according to the mouth of the decree of the Lord" or "according to the mouth of the Memra of the Lord" (these translations have the effect of making "according to the mouth" unavoidably a metaphor, virtually a preposition) or "according to the Memra of the Lord." Similarly, in Dt 8:3, "everything that proceeds out of the mouth of the YHWH" means "everything that YHWH commands," but *Targum Neofiti* depotentiates the anthropomorphism by rendering "everything that comes forth from the mouth of the decree of the Memra of the Lord."[24] The expression "the mouth of the Power" in our rabbinic texts has the same kind of anti-anthropomorphic effect, achieved

---

[20] Translation (modified) from Maurice Simon, *Midrash Rabbah: Song of Songs* (London: Soncino Press, 1939), 293.

[21] Arnold M. Goldberg, *Untersuchungen über die Vorstellung von der Schekhinah in der frühen rabbinischen Literatur—Talmud und Midrasch* (SJ 5; Berlin: de Gruyter, 1969).

[22] Goldberg, "Sitzend," 291–92.

[23] By contrast, "the Name" (הַשֵּׁם; *haššēm*), used by the rabbis, is a mere substitute for the name itself, having no specific meaning of its own.

[24] Cf. *Onqelos*: "everything that emanates from the Memra from before the Lord"; *Pseudo-Jonathan*: "everything that is created by the Memra of the Lord."

in this case by using an abstract term for God rather than a personal term (such as "the Holy One, blessed be he").[25]

That there is an anti-anthropomorphic purpose in the rabbinic use of הַגְּבוּרָה (haggĕbûrâ) can be confirmed by some of the texts where it is not part of the expression "mouth of God." Thus in text L the avoidance of anthropomorphism is obvious. Text J is an example of the rabbinic exegesis of Dt 33:12 as referring to the geographical location of the temple, but the suggestion that Benjamin hosts God as one would a human guest is protected from sounding too anthropomorphic by the use of הַגְּבוּרָה (haggĕbûrâ).[26] In other cases, the usage is perhaps not strictly speaking anti-anthropomorphic but does constitute a reverential circumlocution designed to protect the transcendence of God. Thus in text H the biblical text that is being explained says that "Moses reported [lit., returned] the words of the people to YHWH" (Ex 19:8), making God the direct object of Moses' speech-act, while in text I, R. Eleazar's comment would make God the object of Israel's complaints in just the same way as Moses was, were it not for his use of הַגְּבוּרָה (haggĕbûrâ). In these cases, the transcendence of God is being protected. Finally, in text K the biblical text to which R. Joshua alludes says that "the glory of YHWH appeared in the cloud" (Ex 16:10). The word הַגְּבוּרָה (haggĕbûrâ) is here evidently equivalent to "the glory of YHWH" (an equivalence to which we shall return later) and serves to avoid any implication of the visibility of God himself.

That there is an anti-anthropomorphic or transcendence-protecting purpose in the use of הַגְּבוּרָה (haggĕbûrâ) accounts for the whole range of usage that we find in the rabbinic texts more adequately than Goldberg's explanation. It remains true that the majority of texts relate to verbal communication, but this may be explicable by the fact that the phrase "the mouth of the Power" became a stereotyped expression in the usage of the rabbis whereas other usages did not. It is a mistake to conclude from this that הַגְּבוּרָה (haggĕbûrâ) itself necessarily has to do with revelation. It is also true that הַגְּבוּרָה (haggĕbûrâ) has a specific meaning: it refers to God under the aspect of his power. It is therefore useful to the rabbis in contexts where Shekinah, which refers to God under the aspect of his presence, would not be. But the specific meaning of גְּבוּרָה (gĕbûrâ) is one that differentiates God from all creation in a comprehensive way. It evokes God's all-powerful sovereignty to which all creatures are subject. It is therefore particularly useful for protecting the transcendence of God from language

---

[25] On anti-anthropomorphism in the rabbis, see Arthur Marmorstein, *The Old Rabbinic Doctrine of God: 2: Essays in Anthropomorphism* (Jews' College Publications 14; London: Oxford University Press, 1937). He argues that there are both anthropomorphic and anti-anthropomorphic traditions in the rabbis, often related to differences over literal or allegorical exegesis.

[26] It is easy to see why the versions of this tradition in *b. Meg.* 26a and *b. Yoma* 12a have Shekinah in place of גְּבוּרָה (gĕbûrâ) (Goldberg, "Sitzend," 289). Similarly the Targums, in rendering Dt 33:12, introduce the Shekinah.

that might otherwise seem to reduce him to the level of the creatures. By contrast, Goldberg does not really explain why the specific meaning of גְּבוּרָה (*gĕbûrâ*) should be especially appropriate to verbal revelation.

"The Power" הַגְּבוּרָה (*haggĕbûrâ*) as a Divine "Name" in *Merkavah* Literature

The term הַגְּבוּרָה (*haggĕbûrâ*) also occurs in the *Merkavah* literature, a term that I use here to include not only the *Hekhalot* texts strictly so-called, those which describe the ascent of the mystic through the heavenly "halls" to the throne of God, but also the *Visions of Ezekiel* (*Re'uyot Yehezke'l*), which is a midrash on the first chapter of Ezekiel, describing Ezekiel's vision of the seven heavens and the throne of God. The latter is probably the earliest of these texts, dating from the fourth or fifth century A.D.,[27] a fact that will be significant for our enquiry.

In the *Visions of Ezekiel* the first chapter of the book of Ezekiel is understood to mean that the prophet looked into the water of the river Chebar, in which the heaven was reflected. God opened the seven heavens so that Ezekiel could see the *Merkavah* of God in the highest heaven. Twice it is said that Ezekiel "saw the Power" (I:B, F),[28] while at one point it is said that "he saw God's glory, and the *hayyot*, angels, troops, seraphim, and sparkling-winged ones joined to the *merkabah*" (I:F).[29] Clearly the phrase "saw the Power" is here used interchangeably with "saw the Glory." As Scholem observed, "the Power" has "precisely the same meaning" as "the Glory of God."[30] In the second part of the *Visions of Ezekiel* the contents of the seven heavens are described, in each of which there is a *merkavah*. In the third heaven, Zebul, dwells "the Prince," and the text quotes Dn 7:9–10 and then several opinions of rabbis as to the name of this angelic Prince. They include: "Eleazar of Nadwad says: Metatron, like the name of the Power" (II:D2). This resembles the statement in *b. Sanh.* 38b that Metatron "is called by the name of his Master" (an exegesis of Ex 23:21: "For my name is in him"). Gruenwald considers that here the *Visions of Ezekiel* "may represent an older tradition than the one given in

---

[27] Ithamar Gruenwald, *Apocalyptic and Merkavah Mysticism* (AGJU 14; Leiden: Brill, 1980), 134. The dating of the *Hekhalot* texts is notoriously problematic, not least because, as Peter Schäfer has shown, they are shifting corpora of material that were frequently expanded and redacted.

[28] I refer to the divisions in the translation by David J. Halperin, *The Faces of the Chariot: Early Jewish Responses to Ezekiel's Vision* (TSAJ 16; Tübingen: Mohr Siebeck, 1988), 264–67. There is another English translation in Louis Jacobs, *The Jewish Mystics* (London: Kyle Cathie, 1990), 26–34.

[29] What Ezekiel saw is described as "the glory of God" in Ez 3:12; cf. 9:3; 10:18.

[30] Gershom G. Scholem, *Jewish Gnosticism, Merkabah Mysticism, and Talmudic Tradition* (New York: Jewish Theological Seminary of America, 1960), 67.

Bavli Sanhedrin."[31] In any case, here again we find the term "the Power" designating God on a heavenly throne. The quotation of Dn 7:9–10 (including the reference to plural "thrones," as well as to the throne of the Ancient of Days) may be intended to indicate that Metatron (whose name may mean that he is enthroned with God) has a throne alongside God's in the third heaven and therefore has a name resembling that of God.[32]

The three occurrences of הַגְּבוּרָה (*haggĕbûrâ*) in this short work indicate a preference for this term even over "the Glory," which is evidently equivalent. The statement that Ezekiel "saw the Power" is paralleled in one of the later *Hekhalot* texts, *Ma'aśeh Merkavah*:

> Rabbi Aqiva said: In the hour when I ascended and caught sight of the Power,[33] I observed all the creatures that are in all the pathways of heaven (§545).[34]

Only here in the *Hekhalot* literature do we find a reference to seeing "the Power."[35] The coincidence with *Visions of Ezekiel* may indicate that this is an old usage that has survived in this one instance in *Ma'aśeh Merkavah*.

I am aware of just four other occurrences of הַגְּבוּרָה (*haggĕbûrâ*) as a designation for God in the *Hekhalot* literature. In *3 En.* 28:2–3 (Schäfer §302) it is said of the four great heavenly Princes, the Watchers, that

> [t]heir abode is opposite the throne of glory, and their station is facing the Holy One, blessed be he, so that the splendour of their abode resembles the splendour of the throne of glory, and the brilliance of their image is as the brilliance of the Shekinah. (3) They receive glory from the glory of the Power,[36] and are praised with the praise of the Shekinah.[37]

---

[31] Gruenwald, *Apocalyptic*, 141 n. 34.

[32] It is tempting to wonder whether there is any connection with the "two powers in heaven" ideas opposed by the rabbis, in which interpretation of Dn 7:9–10 seems to have played a key part (Alan F. Segal, *Two Powers in Heaven: Early Rabbinic Reports about Christianity and Gnosticism*, chap. 2 [Leiden: Brill, 1977]). However, it should be noted that the word used for "power" in those discussions is רְשׁוּת (*rāšût*), not גְּבוּרָה (*gĕbûrâ*).

[33] Manuscript M40 has "the assembly," but this a late reworking of the text: see Peter Schäfer, *Übersetzung der Hekhalot-Literatur III §335–597* (TSAJ 22; Tübingen: Mohr Siebeck, 1989), 239 n. 1.

[34] The numbers with reference to this and other *Hekhalot* texts are those of Peter Schäfer's synoptic edition and translation of the *Hekhalot* literature. The translation of this passage is adapted from Naomi Janowitz, *The Poetics of Ascent: Theories of Language in a Rabbinic Ascent Text* (Albany: State University of New York Press, 1989), 31.

[35] The Merkavah mystics are more commonly said to see "the vision of the *merkavah*," as in *3 En.* 1:1: "Rabbi Ishmael said: When I ascended to the height to behold the vision of the chariot . . ."

[36] MSS E and F have "the Shekinah," clearly an assimilation to the following clause, perhaps because the scribes did not recognize the unusual term "the Power."

[37] Translation (adapted) from Philip Alexander, "3 Enoch," *OTP* 1:223–315 (282).

Here the association with the throne of glory is once again notable. "The Power" is God on his heavenly throne. Parallel here with "the Shekinah" and like "the Glory," it designates the visible manifestation of God on his *Merkavah*.[38]

The remaining three occurrences all occur in a statement that is the same in three different *Hekhalot* texts, presumably repeated from one to another. A mighty angelic figure is said to be "called to the Power six hours every day." In two cases this is Hasdri'el (*Hekhalot Rabbati* §302; *Hekhalot Zuṭarti* §419), while in the other case the identity of the figure is unclear, but may be Metatron.[39] This is the fullest of the three passages:

> For I am called to the Power six hours every day and a thousand times they drag me to my knees until I come before the throne of his Glory. (*Hekhalot Rabbati* §96)[40]

Once again "the Power" is obviously God on his heavenly throne of glory.

These rare references to הַגְּבוּרָה (*haggĕbûrâ*) in the *Hekhalot* literature, combined with its greater prominence in the *Visions of Ezekiel*, most likely indicate that it is an older usage that has survived only occasionally in these later texts. As a designation of God as manifested on his heavenly throne it is, of course, highly appropriate: the throne symbolized God's supreme power over all things. It is just as appropriate, in a different way, as "the Glory of God," with which it seems to be interchangeable in usage in the *Visions of Ezekiel*. But, like "the Glory," it can also serve an anti-anthropomorphic purpose in contexts in which a visionary is said to have "seen" God. Unlike the *Shi'ur Qomar* literature, the *Merkavah* literature in general does not take up the hints of an anthropomorphic divine figure in Ez 1:26–27.[41]

"The Power," "the Glory," and "the Majesty"

For our purposes it is of great interest that in both areas of literature in which we have observed the use of הַגְּבוּרָה (*haggĕbûrâ*) as a designation of God we found instances where it appears interchangeable with הכבוד

---

[38] For the Shekinah dwelling on the divine throne in *3 Enoch*, cf. 7:1; 18:19, 24; 22:13; 24:15; 28:2; 39:1. This usage is distinctive of *3 Enoch*. See Peter Schäfer, *The Hidden and Manifest God: Some Major Themes in Early Jewish Mysticism* (trans. Aubrey Pomerance; Albany: State University of New York Press, 1992), 123–26.

[39] See Peter Schäfer, *Übersetzung der Hekhalot-Literatur II §§81–334* (TSAJ 17; Tübingen: Mohr Siebeck, 1987), XXVII, 14 n. 2.

[40] This translation is dependent on the German translation in Schäfer, *Übersetzung der Hekhalot-Literatur II §§81–334*, 15.

[41] In *Hekhalot Rabbati* we learn that the face of God is exceedingly beautiful (Schäfer, *The Hidden and Manifest God*, 16–17), but the other texts do not even give this minimal description of his face.

(*hakkābôd*). In *Mekilta Vayassa* 3 (text K among the rabbinic texts) it substitutes for "the Glory of YHWH" in Ex 16:10. In the *Visions of Ezekiel*,
"the Power" is used just as "the Glory of God" is to designate what Ezekiel
saw. In all these cases (as also in *Ma'aśeh Merkavah* §545) it functions to
protect the transcendence of God in contexts where God is said to be revealed or to be seen. But, whereas "the Power" as a designation of God is
not extant in pre-rabbinic literature apart from Mk 14:62, "the Glory" is,
and is used in just the same way.

The oldest instance is in *1 En.* 14:20, where Enoch, taken up to heaven
in a vision, looks into the throne room of God,[42] "all of which so excelled
in glory and splendor and majesty that I am unable to describe for you its
glory and majesty" (14:16). He sees "a lofty throne" (14:18), and

> [t]he Great Glory sat upon it;
> his apparel was like the appearance of the sun
> and whiter than much snow.
> No angel could enter into this house and look at his face
> because of the splendor and glory,
> and no human could look at him. (14:20–21)[43]

There is an anti-anthropomorphic element in this description of God on
his heavenly throne. Unlike Ez 1:26–27 ("something like a human form,"
"what appeared like loins") and Dn 7:9 (which speaks of God's hair),
Enoch describes only clothing (like Is 6:1).[44] Reference is made to God's

---

[42] Some scholars, such as Gruenwald, *Apocalyptic*, 36–37, and Eskola, *Messiah*,
73, suppose that Enoch enters the throne room (and so is granted a privilege not
given to the angels), but this is pointedly *not* said. He enters the heavenly sanctuary building (14:13) and sees the door into the throne room open (14:15) but does
not enter. He sees the Great Glory on the throne through the open door. He stands
where angels stand (14:22) and sees what they see, which does not include the
face of God (14:21). Subsequently, he is brought right up to the entrance (14:25),
but still he does not enter. See George W. E. Nickelsburg, *1 Enoch 1* (Hermeneia;
Minneapolis: Fortress, 2001), 270.

[43] Translation from George W. E. Nickelsburg and James C. VanderKam,
1 Enoch: A New Translation (Minneapolis: Fortress, 2004), 35. The passage is not
present in the Aramaic fragments, but the phrase "the Great Glory" is found in
the Greek and the Ethiopic. Matthew Black, *The Book of Enoch or I Enoch* (SVTP
7; Leiden: Brill, 1985), 33, translates "the glory of the Great One," on the grounds
that "the Great One" is a designation of God elsewhere in *1 Enoch* (14:2) and "the
glory of the Great One" occurs three times (103:2; 104:1 *bis*; also in 9:3 Syncellus)
(Black, *The Book of Enoch*, 104–5, 149–50). But, given there are parallels to "the
Great Glory" (*1 En.* 102:3; *T. Levi* 3:4; *Mart. Ascen. Isa.* 9:37; 10:16; 11:32), this
seems an unnecessary emendation of the extant texts. One might suggest, instead,
the emendation of "the glory of the Great One" in *1 En.* 103:2; 104:1 to "the Great
Glory."

[44] Christopher Rowland, *The Open Heaven: A Study of Apocalyptic in Judaism
and Early Christianity* (London: SPCK, 1982), 257, claims that "1 Enoch carried on
the tendency already found in Ezekiel 1 of restrained anthropomorphism." The
Apocalypse of Abraham 18:13 carries this tendency away from anthropomorphism

face only to indicate that no one, angel or human, could look at it.[45] The term "the Great Glory" suggests that what could be seen was the radiance of the divine presence, a glory greater even than the indescribably glorious surroundings.[46] The phrase "the Great Glory" also occurs in *1 En.* 103:2, where (probably with allusion to Is 2:21), at the time of the last judgment, "all the sons of earth will seek to hide themselves from the presence of the Great Glory." This suggests the glory of God when he sets up his throne on earth for the final judgement.

A close parallel to *1 Enoch*'s location of the Great Glory on the throne in the heavenly throne-room is *T. Levi* 3:4:

> For in the highest [heaven] of all dwells the Great Glory in the holy of holies far beyond all holiness.[47]

Although the *Testaments of the Twelve* must be treated as, in their present form, Christian works, this passage is one for which an early Jewish *Grundlage* is very probable.

There is one other work where "the Great Glory" is used as a designation for God: the *Ascension of Isaiah*, an early Christian work that, in my view, should be dated towards the end of the first century,[48] though many scholars date it to the middle of the second century. Here, it is the prophet Isaiah who ascends in a vision to the highest heaven and describes what he saw:

> And I saw the Great Glory, while the eyes of my spirit were open, but I could not thereafter see, nor the angel who (was) with me, nor any of the angels whom I had seen worship my Lord [i.e., Christ]. (9:37)[49]

This passage reflects Is 6:1 ("I saw the Lord sitting on a throne"), which Isaiah's enemies have quoted in 3:9 in order to accuse him of claiming to have seen more than Moses, who said that no one can see the Lord and

---

to the extreme: Abraham sees the throne but nothing at all is said about the figure who is presumably seated on it.

[45] Differently, in *2 En.* 22:1 [J], Enoch says "I saw the face of the Lord."

[46] Cf. Hegesippus's use of the term "the Great Power" in the version of Jesus' words that he puts on the lips of James the brother of Jesus (Eusebius, *Hist. Eccl.* 2.23.13).

[47] Translation from H. W. Hollander and M. de Jonge, *The Testaments of the Twelve Patriarchs: A Commentary* (SVTP 8; Leiden: Brill, 1985), 136. Andrew Chester, *Messiah and Exaltation: Jewish Messianic and Visionary Traditions and New Testament Christology* (WUNT 207; Tübingen: Mohr Siebeck, 2007), 51, is mistaken in claiming that "the Great Glory" appears in *T. Levi* 5 as well as *T. Levi* 3.

[48] Richard J. Bauckham, "The Ascension of Isaiah: Genre, Unity, and Date," in *The Fate of the Dead: Studies on the Jewish and Christian Apocalypses* (NovTSup 93; Leiden: Brill, 1998), 363–90.

[49] This translation of the Ethiopic is from Michael A. Knibb, "Martyrdom and Ascension of Isaiah," *OTP* 2:143–76. I have also consulted the Italian translation by Enrico Norelli, *Ascensio Isaiae: Textus* (ed. Paolo Bettiolo et al.; CCSA 7; Turnhout: Brepols, 1995), 108.

live (Ex 33:20). So, again, we have a biblical narrative in which God is seen on his heavenly throne, interpreted as a vision of the radiance of the divine presence rather than of any anthropomorphic form of God.

Subsequently, from his vantage point in heaven, Isaiah has a vision of the incarnation. He hears "the Great Glory" giving Christ ("my Lord") a command to descend through the heavens to earth (10:16). Following his life, death and resurrection, Christ ascends through the heavens,

> [a]nd I saw that he sat down at the right hand of that Great Glory, whose glory I told you I could not behold. (11:32)

This, of course, is an example of the early Christian use of Ps 110:1. The phrase "the Great Glory" here designates God in an allusion to Ps 110:1, just as "the Power" does in Mk 14:62.

Another designation for God that has uses and associations similar to those of "the Glory" is "the Majesty." Again, this usage goes back to the earliest part of *1 Enoch*, where "the souls of men" ask the archangels to bring before God their petition for judgment in their favor and against the fallen Watchers:

> Bring in our judgment to the Most High,
> and our destruction before the glory of the Majesty,
> before the Lord of all Lords in majesty. (9:3)[50]

Here the three parallel phrases—"the Most High," "the glory of the Majesty," and "the Lord of all Lords in majesty"—all refer to the manifest presence of God on his heavenly throne. The context of judgment makes the second phrase appropriate, since it is probably borrowed from Is 2:10, 19, 21 ("from the glory of his majesty").[51]

Significantly, this phrase can also be found in early Christian allusions to Ps 110:1, this time in the epistle to the Hebrews. As well as directly quoting the words of God in that verse (1:13; cf. 10:12), Hebrews also alludes to them three times thus:

> He sat down at the right hand of the Majesty on high. (1:3)

---

[50] Translation from Nickelsburg and VanderKam, *1 Enoch*, 26, but I have capitalized "Majesty." Nickelsburg, *1 Enoch 1*, 208, suggests emending "before the glory of the Majesty" to "before the glory of the Great One" (as in 103:2; 104:1 *bis*), but since the phrase has a biblical source in Is 2:10, 19, 21, and God is called "the Majesty" in Heb 1:3; 8:1 and "the majestic Glory" in 2 Pt 1:17 (cf. "his majestic glory" in *1 Clem.* 9:2 in connection with Enoch), emendation seems unnecessary.

[51] Cf. 2 Pt 1:17: "a voice conveyed to him by the majestic Glory" (φωνῆς ἐνεχθείσης αὐτῷ τοιᾶσδε ὑπὸ τῆς μεγαλοπρεποῦς δόξης; *phōnēs enechtheisēs autō toiasde hypo tēs megaloprepous doxēs*). This is an elaborate way of protecting the transcendence of God by avoiding the idea that God speaks directly from heaven (cf. the rabbinic idea of the *bat qôl*). *First Clement* 9:2 uses the same periphrasis for God but adds αὐτοῦ (*autou*; "his majestic glory"), rather as Lk 22:69 adds τοῦ θεοῦ (*tou theou*) to Mark's τῆς δυνάμεως (*tēs dynameōs*).

[He] is seated at the right hand of the throne of the Majesty in the heavens. (8:1)

[He] has taken his seat at the right hand of the throne of God. (12:2)

Although the question of seeing God does not arise in these contexts, the concern to avoid anthropomorphism is clear. In Heb 12:2 the anti-anthropomorphic purpose is achieved, not by a periphrasis for God but by making the right hand not that of God but of the throne. (The meaning could be either that Christ sits to the right of the throne of God or, more likely [in view of other early Christian usage], that he sits on the right-hand side of the throne, beside God.) In 1:3 anthropomorphism is avoided by the use of the abstract term "the Majesty," while 8:1 combines the two strategies.

We conclude that in some early Jewish and early Christian texts the terms "the Great Glory" and "the Majesty" are used to designate God on his heavenly throne. In contexts where the throne and the radiance of the divine presence are seen, such a designation serves to avoid the implication that God himself is seen and/or to avoid anthropomorphism.[52] In the case of Christian allusions to Ps 110:1 such a designation defuses the anthropomorphic potential of the reference to (God's) right hand. It is easy, then, to see how in Mk 14:62, where there is reference both to seeing and to the right hand, the designation "the Power" serves the same two functions. In this particular context, where the reference is to judgment or vindication, "the Power" could be considered a more appropriate periphrasis than "the Glory" or "the Majesty."

Protecting the Divine Transcendence

We therefore arrive at a quite different conclusion from other studies that have considered the significance of "the Power" in Mk 14:62 in the light of Jewish usage of this term.[53] The term is not merely a substitute

---

[52] Note also the translation of Ex 24:10 ("they saw the God of Israel") in the Targums: "they saw the glory of the God of Israel" (*Tg. Onq., Tg. Ps.-J.*); "they saw the glory of the Shekinah of the Lord" (*Tg. Neof.*). For "glory" as a circumlocution for God in the Targums, see Paul V. M. Flesher and Bruce Chilton, *The Targums: A Critical Introduction* (Studies in the Aramaic Interpretation of Scripture 12; Leiden: Brill, 2011), 46; Andrew Chester, *Divine Revelation and Divine Titles in the Pentateuchal Targumim* (TSAJ 14; Tübingen: Mohr Siebeck, 1986), 313–22; Carmel McCarthy, "The Treatment of Biblical Anthropomorphisms in Pentateuchal Targums," in *Back to the Sources: Biblical and Near Eastern Studies: In Honour of Dermot Ryan* (ed. Kevin J. Cathcart and John F. Healey; Dublin: Glendale Press, 1989), 45–66 (54–55).

[53] E.g., Bock, *Blasphemy and Exaltation in Judaism*, 217–19; Brown, *The Death of the Messiah,* 1:496–97; Christiane Zimmermann, *Die Namen des Vaters: Studies zu ausgewählten neutestamentlichen Gottesbezeichnungen vor irhem frühjüdischen und*

for the divine Name, for which "God" would have sufficed, as it does in most early Christian allusions to Ps 110:1. Nor is the point simply to stress the Son of Man's participation in the exercise of God's supreme power over all things, though this may well be why "the Power" is preferred to "the Glory" or "the Majesty." Rather, in relation to the anthropomorphic reference to "the right hand" and to the suggestion that God could be seen, the use of this abstract term protects the transcendence of God. It is significant that the term used is not "his power" or "the power of God" (as in Lk 22:69),[54] which might suggest a "hypostatized divine attribute" (a notion not to be found in any of the Jewish texts discussed above),[55] but "the Power," meaning God manifested as power, God in his enthroned presence. The point is that only thus manifest as power will God be seen, while the "right hand" refers not to a literal body part of an anthropomorphic divine form but metaphorically to the Son of Man's participation in the cosmic sovereignty of God.

That the use of "the Power" functions, at least in part, to moderate the anthropomorphic implication of reference to God's hand becomes the more plausible when we recognize that, apart from the many allusions to Ps 110:1 and a few other quotations from the OT,[56] references to the hand or hands of God in the NT are almost confined to the Lukan writings, where they belong to Luke's "biblical" style (Lk 1:66; Acts 4:28, 30; 11:21; 13:11; elsewhere: Jn 10:29; Heb 10:31; 1 Pt 5:6). References to other body parts of God are even more rare. If we discount a small number of OT quotations,[57] Luke alone refers to the finger of God (Lk 11:20, whereas the parallel in Mt 12:28 has "the Spirit of God") and the arm of God (Lk 1:51; Acts 13:17) and only Hebrews to the eyes of God (4:13), while there are no references to the ears or the mouth of God that are not allusions to the OT.[58] In comparison with the many

---

paganen Sprachhorizont (AJEC 69; Leiden: Brill, 2007), 330–33; Richard T. France, *The Gospel of Matthew* (NICNT; Grand Rapids: Eerdmans, 2007), 1028. For the view that "the Power" is (merely?) a reverential substitute for the divine Name, see Craig A. Evans, *Mark 8:27–16:20* (WBC 34B; Nashville: Nelson, 2001), 452.

[54] Doubtless Luke is attempting to clarify the term for readers or hearers unfamiliar with the Jewish usage. Commentators on Mk 14:62 who merely accumulate references to God's power do very little to illuminate the text. Analysis and discrimination are required.

[55] Such a notion can be found in the early Christian and Gnostic texts cited by Jarl E. Fossum, *The Name of God and the Angel of the Lord: Samaritan and Jewish Concepts of Intermediation and the Origin of Gnosticism* (WUNT 1/36; Tübingen: Mohr Siebeck, 1985), 174 (on Simon Magus), 180–83; also Philo *Mut.* 28–29.

[56] Lk 23:46 (Ps 31:6[5]); Acts 7:50 (Is 66:2); Heb 1:10 (Ps 102:26[25]); 2:7 (Ps 8:7).

[57] Arm of God: Jn 12:38 (Is 53:1); eyes of God: 1 Pt 3:12 (Ps 33:16[34:15]); ears of God: Jas 5:4 (Is 5:9 LXX); 1 Pt 3:12 (Ps 33:16[34:15]; mouth of God: Mt 4:4 (Dt 8:3). Cf. also "footstool" (ὑποπόδιον; *hypopodion*): Mt 5:35; Acts 7:49 (Is 66:2).

[58] I am omitting consideration of the face of God here because it raises special issues of its own.

such references in the OT, especially to the hand of God, these statistics are striking. But they are probably not untypical of late Second Temple Jewish literature.

The extent to which this kind of anthropomorphism (reference to body parts of God) is avoided in the literature of this period has never been investigated. My analysis of some selected works of Palestinian Judaism has produced mixed results:

1 Maccabees (c. 100 B.C.):
  No references to divine body parts (but there is relatively little reference to God in this work)
2 Maccabees (c. 100 B.C.):
  hands: 6:26; 7:31[59]
  arm: 15:24[60]
Baruch (second–first cent. B.C.?):[61]
  hand: 2:11; 3:5
  arm: 2:11
  eyes: 1:22; 2:17
  ear: 2:16
Psalms of Solomon (first cent. B.C.):[62]
  hand(s): 2:22; 5:6, 12; 13:1 (*bis*); 18:1
  arm: 13:2
  eyes: 18:2
  ears: 18:2
Testament of Moses (first cent. A.D.):
  hand: 12:9[63]
Pseudo-Philo, *L.A.B.* (late first cent. A.D.):[64]
  hand(s): 19:16; 32:2; 55:4
  eye(s): 7:4; 22:4
  mouth: 11:14; 19:16; 25:3

---

[59] Both verses use the expression "to escape from the hands of" God. This is a biblical expression (e.g., Jer 34:3) but is not used in the Bible with reference to God.

[60] This text alludes to Ex 15:16.

[61] Many of these verses echo biblical phrases: 2:11 (hand and arm) (Dt 4:34, etc.); 1:22 (Nm 32:13); 2:17 (2 Kgs 19:16, etc.); 2:16 (2 Kgs 19:16, etc.).

[62] Most of these verses echo biblical phrases: 2:22; 5:6 (Ps 32:4); 5:12 (Ps 145:16); 18:1 (Ps 138:8); 18:2 (eyes) (Jer 24:6).

[63] The text is very uncertain, but there may be an allusion to Jer 22:24 and Hg 2:23. See Johannes Tromp, *The Assumption of Moses: A Critical Edition with Commentary* (SVTP 10; Leiden: Brill, 1993), 267–68.

[64] Most of these are scriptural allusions: 55:4 (1 Sm 5:7); 7:4 (Dt 11:12); 22:4 (cf. 1 Chr 21:23); 11:14 (Nm 12:8); 19:16 (mouth) (Dt 34:5). But 19:16 (hands) is a striking enhancement of a biblical anthropomorphism (God buried Moses "with his own hands"; contrast the way *Targum Neofiti* to Dt 34:6 avoids saying that God buried Moses), while 32:2 is also an anthropomorphism very deliberately devised (Abraham says to Isaac: "I am delivering you into the hands that gave you to me"). The author clearly does not object to anthropomorphisms as such.

4 Ezra (c. 100 A.D.):
   hands: 3:5; 5:30; 8:7, 44[65]
   eyes: 4:44; 5:56; 6:11; 7:102, 104; 12:7[66]
   ears: 8:24
Apocalypse of Abraham (c. 100 A.D.):
   eyes: 17:14[67]

Evidently none of these works, except perhaps the *Apocalypse of Abraham*, eschews reference to God's body parts altogether, but many of the references allude to Scripture and/or are stereotyped phrases (see the notes). For example, of the eleven references in *4 Ezra*, nine employ just two stereotyped phrases. In the case of Pseudo-Philo, there are only eight references in the course of sixty-five chapters, and some of these echo the biblical passages that underlie the text, but, on the other hand, two of the references are fresh and remarkable elaborations of the biblical texts (19:16; 32:2). (For a complete evaluation of anthropomorphism in Pseudo-Philo, it would be necessary to look for evidence of anthropomorphisms in the biblical text that Pseudo-Philo's rewriting has removed.) As far as this very preliminary investigation goes, it suggests a tendency away from reference to God's body parts at least in the first century A.D., though by no means an abandonment of such anthropomorphic expressions. Broadly, this accords with the evidence of the NT.

The Targums are well known for their anti-anthropomorphisms,[68] which include avoidance of reference to divine body parts such as eyes, ears, hand, and mouth.[69] Like the Second Temple period literature we have discussed, the Targums are not entirely consistent in this respect, but they exhibit a strong tendency to substitute other expressions for the Hebrew text's references to divine body parts.[70] Though the Targums are

---

[65] *4 Ezra* 3:5; 8:7, 44, all reflect Gn 2:7 but interpret it by making explicit that God created Adam with his hands. *4 Ezra* 5:30 probably reflects 2 Sm 24:14.

[66] All of these employ a stereotyped biblical phrase: "to find favor in the eyes of God." Some versions refer to God's eyes in 8:20, but the reading "heavens" is probably preferable: see Michael E. Stone, *Fourth Ezra* (Hermeneia; Minneapolis: Fortress, 1990), 269.

[67] Here God is addressed as "many-eyed," presumably with reference to Zec 4:10 (the seven eyes of God that "range through the whole earth"); 2 Chr 16:9. The epithet is in its own way anti-anthropomorphic since it means that God, unlike humans, sees everything everywhere. There are also, in 15:18–19 (and cf. 18:13), references to the light of God's face (doubtless dependent on Nm 6:25–26).

[68] Chester, *Divine Revelation*; Domingo Muñoz León, "Soluciones de los Targumim del Pentateuco a los antromorfismos," *EstBib* 28 (1969): 263–81; McCarthy, "The Treatment," 45–66; Flesher and Chilton, *The Targums*, 45–46.

[69] McCarthy, "The Treatment," 50–53 (many examples from *Targum Neofiti* and *Targum Onqelos*).

[70] For examples in which the Targums retain or even introduce anthropomorphisms of this kind, see Michael L. Klein, "The Translation of Anthropomorphisms and Anthropopathisms in the Targumim," in *Congress Volume Vienna 1980* (ed. John A. Emerton; VTSup 32; Leiden: Brill, 1981), 162–78 (168–70). Michael L.

not direct evidence for the Second Temple period, a widespread feature of their rendering of the biblical text, such as this kind of avoidance of anthropomorphism, may well reflect earlier practice, especially when, as in this case, the same usage is attested in literature of that period.

Protecting the Divine Transcendence in the Sayings of Jesus

In the words attributed to Jesus in all four Gospels, reference to divine body parts is even rarer than in the rest of the NT. As well as the quotation of Ps 110:1 in Mk 12:36 (par. Mt 22:44; Lk 20:42–43) and the allusion to that verse in Mk 14:62 (par. Mt 26:64; Lk 22:69), there are two other biblical quotations in Lk 23:46 (Ps 31:5) and Mt 4:4 (Dt 8:3; but the parallel in Lk 3:4 lacks the reference to God's mouth) and two biblical allusions in Mt 5:35 (Is 66:2) and Lk 11:20 (Ex 8:19; but the parallel in Mt 12:28 has "Spirit" rather than "finger"). The only reference to a divine body part that does not directly reflect a biblical source is Jo 10:29, and even here there is likely an echo of Ps 95[94]:7.

As well as such avoidance of anthropomorphism, a more general concern to protect the divine transcendence appears in the phenomenon known as the divine passive. For example, "the hairs of your head are all numbered" (Mt 10:30; Lk 12:7) means "God has numbered all the hairs of your head." The divine passive is not, as is sometimes said, simply a way of avoiding using the divine Name but a way of avoiding attributing an action directly to God as subject. We still lack an adequate study of this phenomenon, whether in the sayings of Jesus or in early Jewish literature.[71]

Klein, "The Preposition קדם ("Before"): A Pseudo-Anti-Anthropomorphism in the Targums," *JTS* 30 (1979): 502–7, shows that this preposition is used as an "expression of deference" in relation to eminent humans as well as to God and argues that therefore it is not an anti-anthropomorphism. McCarthy, "The Treatment," 50–52, responds that its use with reference to humans does not mean that it is not an anti-anthropomorphism when used with reference to God. Importantly, she points out that *Targums Neofiti* and *Onqelos* always substitute קֳדָם (*qoḏām*) for "in the eyes of" when the eyes are God's, but not when they are human. See also Chester, *Divine Revelation*, 286–87. Jonathan Shunary, "Avoidance of Anthropomorphism in the Targum of Psalms," *Text* 5 (1966): 133–44, shows that this type of anti-anthropomorphism is not common in the Targum of Psalms, but this late Targum evidently differs in this respect from the Pentateuchal Targums. Roger Le Déaut, *Targum du Pentateuque*, vol. 1 (SC 245; Paris: Cerf, 1978), 60, notes the inconsistency of the Targums' treatment of anthropomorphisms, attributing it to different attitudes at different periods and by different translators.

[71] In 1971 Joachim Jeremias, *New Testament Theology* (trans. John Bowden; NTL; London: SCM Press, 1971), 13, lamented the "complete lack of collections of material, much less special investigations." I am unaware of any attempts to supply the lack.

Following the brief treatment by Gustaf Dalman,[72] Joachim Jeremias drew attention to it as "one of the clearest characteristics of [Jesus'] ways of speaking."[73] He listed about a hundred instances (not counting parallels) in the Synoptic Gospels,[74] while stressing that there are "borderline cases in which it is not certain whether the passive is intended as a circumlocution for an action on the part of God or whether it is used without this consideration."[75]

Certainly, the use of the divine passive in short aphorisms such as "Judge not and you will not be judged" (Lk 6:37; cf. Mt 7:1) may well be more for the sake of epigrammatic brevity than for protection of the divine transcendence. The use of the divine passive in several of the first eight Matthean beatitudes (5:3–10) makes it possible for the second clause of all eight to begin with the same words (ὅτι αὐτοί [hoti autoi] or ὅτι αὐτῶν [hoti autōn]). Stylistic reasons of this kind may account for some of the divine passives, but probably not for the majority. Jeremias explained Jesus' usage as following the style of apocalyptic,[76] which he extended in order to indicate the hidden nature of the arrival of the kingdom in his ministry.[77] However, this explanation seems unlikely, because the use of the divine passive in Jewish literature, where examples of it have been adduced in the secondary literature, is not especially related to eschatology but seems to be one of a variety of ways of protecting the transcendence of God by not making him the direct subject (or, in some cases, object) of verbs connecting God and humans. It is true that the divine passive itself is rare in rabbinic literature,[78] where the use of the third person plural (equivalent to an English indefinite expression) is more common as a way of achieving the same effect, while Second Temple Jewish literature does not seem ever to have been searched for instances of the divine passive. The Targums use the divine passive along with a variety of other ways of avoiding a direct connection between God and an action.[79]

---

[72] Gustaf Dalman, *The Words of Jesus* (trans. D. M. Kay; Edinburgh: T&T Clark, 1902), 224–26.

[73] Jeremias, *New Testament Theology*, 14.

[74] Jeremias, *New Testament Theology*, 11–12 nn. 2–5. It is not clear whether Jeremias excluded John from the count or found no examples there.

[75] Jeremias, *New Testament Theology*, 12.

[76] Jacques Schlosser, *Le Dieu de Jésus* (LD 129; Paris: Cerf, 1987), 29, echoes Jeremias on this point. Jeremias pointed to the fact that the divine passive "occurs frequently for the first time" in Daniel (13). I have noted some possible occurrences in *2 Baruch* that suggest the continuation of Daniel's style in later apocalypses: 32:2–4; 33:2; 39:3, 4, 7; 40:1.

[77] Jeremias, *New Testament Theology*, 13–14.

[78] A few instances are collected in Dalman, *The Words*, 225, and Strack and Billerbeck, *Kommentar*, vol. 1, 443; a few more are added by Joachim Jeremias, *The Eucharistic Words of Jesus* (London: SCM Press, 1966), 202 n. 5.

[79] McCarthy, "The Treatment," 54–56.

That the use of the divine passive in the sayings of Jesus should be aligned with the occasional usage of the rabbis and the Targums, even though it is much more prevalent in the Gospels than in these later sources, can be supported by the fact that some of the other ways in which these later Jewish sources avoid making God the direct subject of an action can also be found in the Gospels. For example, in both Lk 6:38 and 12:48 the third person plural[80] is used actually in parallel with divine passives. In the former instance (6:38), we have a case of a proverbial saying that also occurs in the rabbis and the Targums. In the rabbinic citations of it the third person plural is used,[81] while in the Targums a divine passive is used to the same effect.[82] Another example is the use of prepositions meaning "before" (ἔμπροσθεν [emprosthen] and ἐνώπιον [enōpion]) in ways that parallel the use of "before" (קֳדָם; q°dām) in the Targums. Luke 12:9 says of the sparrows that "not one of them is forgotten before (ἐνώπιον; enōpion) God," immediately preceding a use of the divine passive (12:10). The expression "for such was good pleasure before you" (Mt 11:26; Lk 10:21: ὅτι οὕτως εὐδοκία ἐγένετο ἔμπροσθέν σου; hoti houtōs eudokia egeneto emprosthen sou) is equivalent to the expression "there is good pleasure before the Lord," frequent in the Targums.[83] In Mt 18:14 there is a different Greek rendering of the same idiom: "such is not (the) will before your Father who is in heaven" (οὕτως οὐκ ἔστιν θέλημα ἔμπροσθεν τοῦ πατρὸς ὑμῶν τοῦ ἐν οὐρανοῖς; houtōs ouk estin thelēma emprosthen tou patros hymōn tou en ouranois). These examples show the need for further study of the ways in which the sayings of Jesus deploy ways of protecting the divine transcendence that can be paralleled in other Jewish literature.

Enough has been said to demonstrate that the use of "the Power" to protect the divine transcendence from anthropomorphism in Mk 14:62 is consistent with ways of speaking of God that are well evidenced in the traditions of Jesus' sayings elsewhere in the Gospels. This does not prove the authenticity of Mk 14:62 but certainly helps to make it plausible.

---

[80] See also Lk 12:20.

[81] E.g., *m. Soṭah* 1:7; other examples are cited in Strack and Billerbeck, *Kommentar*, vol. 1, 444–45. This form also occurs in *Tg. Is* 27:8.

[82] *Targum Neofiti, Frg. Tg. Gn* 38:25: see Martin McNamara, *The New Testament and the Palestinian Targum to the Pentateuch* (AnBib 27; Rome: Pontifical Biblical Institute, 1966), 138–42.

[83] Martin McNamara, *Targum and Testament* (Shannon: Irish University Press, 1972), 95–96.

CHAPTER 6

GENESIS 1–3 AND PAUL'S THEOLOGY OF ADAM'S DOMINION IN ROMANS 5–6

Roy E. Ciampa

Introduction: Romans 5–8 in Context

Romans 5–8 has often been treated as the ugly stepsister of the family of major sections in the letter to the Romans. Chapters 1–4, so full of material of crucial importance for the central Protestant theme of justification by faith, have tended to receive the majority of scholarly attention.[1] Chapters 9–11 receive their fair share of attention thanks to the recent rediscovery of Paul's focus on the place of Jews and Gentiles in the gospel (and the theme of justification by faith is reprised in these chapters as well). Chapters 12–16 have received some attention thanks to the further material on the place of Gentiles in God's plan and due to some interest in the various practical issues addressed (e.g., the role of secular governments in Christian ethical thought, the issue of the weak and the strong, and further material on the law of Moses and the love command). Those of us who are especially interested in the use of the OT in the NT have also given much attention to the chapters preceding and following chapters 5–8 since they are full of quotations and these chapters are not.

Recently, however, these chapters have been described as containing the heart of Paul's gospel presentation to the Roman believers. Douglas Campbell has suggested that "Paul's account of sanctification [in Rom 5–8] *is* the gospel."[2] Unfortunately, his overall interpretation depends on his argument that most of Rom 1–4 does not reflect Paul's own views but those of his opponents. This radical rereading of Romans has not found many supporters. Even more recently Richard Longenecker has

---

[1] It is a privilege to offer this essay in honor of Greg Beale, whose work in biblical exegesis, biblical theology, and the use of the OT in the NT has provided such important insights and such an admirable model of academic excellence for those of us working in these same fields.

[2] Douglas A. Campbell, *The Deliverance of God: An Apocalyptic Rereading of Justification in Paul* (Grand Rapids: Eerdmans, 2009), 934.

also suggested that it is in Rom 5–8 that we find the heart of his gospel message. He suggests it is in these chapters that Paul presents "for the Christians at Rome what he had been proclaiming as the Christian gospel to Gentiles in his Gentile mission—that is, 'my gospel' as he calls it in 2:16 and 16:25."[3] Longenecker does not consider most of Rom 1–4 un-Pauline, but he thinks those chapters represent material that Paul "held in common with his addressees" and that he "often proclaimed . . . when addressing Jews or when addressing those who had been influenced by Jewish thought" for the better or the worse.[4] Unlike what we find in Rom 1:16–4:25, the material in Rom 5–8, Longenecker argues, is "what he proclaims in his Gentile mission—that is, to pagan Gentiles who had not been prepared for the gospel by Jewish or Jewish Christian teaching, and so did not think in Jewish categories."[5] Longenecker thinks Paul's Roman audience, although a mixed group, would have consisted primarily of people of this type for whom the material in these chapters would have been his primary spiritual gift offered in this letter.

The suggestion that Rom 5–7, in contrast to 1:16–4:25, was written for people who did not think in Jewish categories is based on several observations that cannot all be addressed here. One of those observations is that while "there are about eighteen quotations of Scripture in eight or nine places in 1:16–4:25 . . . only two biblical quotations appear in 5–8, and then somewhat tangentially."[6] In fact, Longenecker suggests that of numerous "striking differences between these two sections" the "most obvious is their difference in the use of Scripture."[7]

Longenecker's proposals merit the kind of serious attention that would require an extended essay just to review and engage the key arguments. For now I must limit myself to little more than confessing that I do not find his explanation of the relationship between the two major sections (1–4 and 5–8) persuasive. The space, energy, and polemical tone devoted to the argumentation in 1:16–4:25 seems to me to be a bit excessive for material that is thought to be completely uncontroversial. Not only does Longenecker think it is uncontroversial, but he suggests that "it was probably on the basis of their acceptance of the message of 1:16–4:25 that both they [i.e., the Romans] and he originally became believers in Christ."[8] It is remarkable that material which has been at the core of a traditional understanding of distinctively Pauline teaching is now thought to be so pre-Pauline as to have been the message that was taught by others to both Paul and the Romans (and thus was common pre-Pauline material).

---

[3] Richard N. Longenecker, *Introducing Romans: Critical Issues in Paul's Most Famous Letter* (Grand Rapids: Eerdmans, 2011), 400 (cf. 373–76).

[4] Longenecker, *Introducing Romans*, 373.

[5] Longenecker, *Introducing Romans*, 374.

[6] Longenecker, *Introducing Romans*, 369.

[7] Longenecker, *Introducing Romans*, 368.

[8] Longenecker, *Introducing Romans*, 373.

I have argued elsewhere[9] that proposals that find Paul's gospel in either Rom 1–4 or 5–8, rather than finding it expounded throughout 1–8 (and beyond), offer a truncated understanding of that gospel. I find persuasive the proposal of C. E. B. Cranfield and others that Rom 1–8 reflects a fulsome unpacking of the significance of Hb 2:4 with the first four chapters explaining what it means to be righteous by faith and Rom 5–8 explaining the "living" experienced by and expected of those who are righteous by faith. The good news that Paul proclaims includes justification by faith, the blessings of the life found within that faith, and even the complete renewal of creation by the Spirit and the ultimate vindication of all those who have found the life and righteousness that is ours thanks to God's love, as described in Rom 8.

So it seems to me to be a mistake to suggest one of these sections is more crucial to Paul's gospel message than the other. A few further clarifications are called for with respect to Longenecker's argumentation. First, it is true that the relationship with Scripture is different in Rom 5–8 than in Rom 1–4 (and 9–11): here we do not have the repeated and extensive use of quotations and explicit interpretation of OT texts. It is also true, as he suggests, that in parts of Rom 5–8 the focus is on "the universal, foundational story of sin, death and condemnation having entered the world by 'one man,' but grace, life and righteousness brought about 'through Jesus Christ our Lord'" (as in 5:12–21).[10] But the story Paul tells continues to be closely tied to and based upon his interpretation of Scripture. It is primarily a difference in the type of use of Scripture, not in its use elsewhere versus its non-use in Rom 5–8.[11] We should consider potential intertextual relationships with Greco-Roman discourses as well as Jewish discourses, but Paul is explicitly invoking scriptural themes and reflecting a Jewish rather than a Gentile metanarrative. Longenecker's point may still stand in that it may be easier for Gentiles to follow the lines of his biblically based summary of the metanarrative than to follow the intensive engagement of scriptural quotations in the earlier chapters. It is not

---

[9] See Roy E. Ciampa, "Paul's Theology of the Gospel," in *Paul as Missionary: Identity, Activity, Theology, and Practice* (ed. Trevor J. Burke and Brian S. Rosner; LNTS 420; London: T&T Clark, 2011), 180–91.

[10] Longenecker, *Introducing Romans*, 117.

[11] At one point Longenecker refers to Paul's "use (or non-use) of Scripture in [Romans] 5–8" (*Introducing Romans*, 404). Craig Blomberg's summary of Longenecker's argument reflects the impression left on an attentive reader: "A little-discussed observation with respect to Paul's use of the Old Testament is how seldom it appears in chapters 5–8 compared to the rest of the theological body of the epistle." It is suggested that these chapters were "written primarily for those in the church overemphasizing a law-free Gospel. Here Paul hardly roots his remarks in the Hebrew Scriptures, at all, because they won't be as appreciated, especially among the Gentile Christians in this group" (Craig Blomberg, review of *Introducing Romans: Critical Issues in Paul's Most Famous Letter* by Richard Longenecker, accessed April 11, 2012, http://www.denverseminary.edu/article/introducing-romans-critical-issues-in-pauls-most-famous-letter/).

clear, however, that he does not have the same readership in mind in both parts, namely, a readership that consists of a mixed group of Jews and Gentiles both of whom are (to different degrees) significantly formed by Christian discourse of a deeply Jewish and scriptural nature.

The Romans were familiar with a narrative of decline and collapse followed by the good news of the arrival of a savior whose coming constituted a source of joy, was considered the beginning of all things, and the turning point of restoration to society. Caesar's arrival was declared to mark the highest point to which history had arrived and which would never be exceeded. His coming and leadership were destined to result in universal peace and blessing as the nations submitted to Roman rule. But in that narrative the perceived decline was tied to the chaos following Caesar's assassination in 44 B.C., and the turning point was identified with the life and accomplishments of Augustus and the empire that he (and his heirs) established.[12]

While there are interesting parallels (and others could be found if we considered religious movements of the time), there are several elements that make it a distinctively Jewish narrative framework. Those elements include the universal nature of the underlying problem as expounded in Romans, its basis in details embedded in the narrative of origins in the first chapters of the Jewish Bible, the relationship with Jewish concepts of Adam, Moses, sin, judgment, and the Messiah.

There is no reference to Jews and Gentiles in Rom 5–8 and there are only a couple of scriptural quotes, but that is not unusual for Jewish discourse of the time. That would be true, for instance, of many (or most) cases of "rewritten Bible" in the Jewish world. There are significant differences between the *Community Rule* and the *pesharim* of Qumran in terms of how they relate to their underlying biblical texts, but both are distinctly Jewish discourses based on scriptural interpretation and both would be more comprehensible to those familiar with Jewish frameworks than with Greco-Roman modes of thinking.[13] Key differences between Rom 5–8 and the preceding and following chapters of the letter may be similarly understood.

Adam's Reign and the Reign of Death: A First Look

Before looking more carefully at Rom 5:14–6:14 and what we learn from Paul's use of the OT to describe the reign of sin and death (see the fol-

---

[12] See the first decree of the Asian League regarding the new provincial calendar (the Priene calendar inscription with the prefatory letter of the proconsul Paulus Fabius Maximus) and other evidence in Mark Forman, *The Politics of Inheritance in Romans* (Cambridge: Cambridge University Press, 2011), 33–36; cf. James R. Harrison, *Paul and the Imperial Authorities at Thessalonica and Rome: A Study in the Conflict of Ideology* (Tübingen: Mohr Siebeck, 2010), 63–66.

[13] This is not to ignore the fact that the "Jewish" and "Greco-Roman" worlds were not independent of each other or completely incomprehensible to each other. Jewish thought in particular was inevitably forced to develop within a world significantly defined by Greek and Roman cultures.

lowing section), we will first look at some of the key lexical information in this section of Romans and the OT understanding of Adam as one appointed to reign and how that understanding is reflected in some early Jewish texts.

We find an unusual density of verbs of reigning in this section of Romans compared with elsewhere in Paul's letters. There are six occurrences of βασιλεύω (*basileuō*; 5:14, 17[twice], 21[twice]; 6:12), and three occurrences of κυριεύω (*kyrieuō*; 6:9, 14; 7:1). But little attention has been given to unpacking the significance of these terms in Paul's argument. Of course, Christ's own kingly role had been clearly identified since the first four verses of the letter, which highlight his Davidic descent as well as his related identity as Son of God, Christ/Messiah, and Lord. That messianic royal identity is reinforced by references to Jesus as Christ and Lord throughout the letter and in 5:17 in particular with its reference to those who will "reign in life through the one man Jesus Christ."[14]

Romans 5:14 is not merely the first of the occurrences of these terms in this group of chapters; it is the first use of either term within the letter as a whole. Within Romans the only other occurrence of either term is that of κυριεύω (*kyrieuō*) in 14:9. The fact that these terms begin to appear in the context of Paul's rewriting of the Adam narrative has been neglected. Although most commentaries on Rom 5:12–21 refer to Gn 3 and its description of the sin in the garden and humanity's fall, it is extremely rare to find any scholar referencing Gn 1 and the theme of human dominion in Gn 1:26–28.

In Rom 5:14 Paul tells us that "death reigned from Adam [ἐβασίλευσεν ὁ θάνατος ἀπὸ Ἀδάμ; *ebasileusen ho thanatos apo Adam*] until Moses." As shown in the following chart, which compares the verbs (in lexical form) used for reigning in ancient Gk. versions of Gn 1:26, 28 and in Rom 5–6, the verb Paul uses here is not the same as found in Gn 1:26, 28, but there are several different verbs used in the early Gk. versions (ἄρχω [*archō*], χειρόω [*cheiroō*], ἐπικρατέω [*epikrateō*], παιδεύω [*paideuō*]), suggesting there was no one specific verb expected to be correlated to the Heb. רדה (*rdh*).

	MT	LXX	Symmachus	Aquila	Theodotion	Paul
Gn 1:26	רדה (*rdh*)	ἄρχω (*archō*)		ἐπικρατέω (*epikrateō*)		
Gn 1:28a	כבש (*kbš*)	κατακυριεύω (*katakyrieuō*)	ὑποτάσσω (*hypotassō*)	ὑποτάσσω (*hypotassō*)	ὑποτάσσω (*hypotassō*)	
Gn 1:28b	רדה (*rdh*)	ἄρχω (*archō*)	χειρόω (*cheiroō*)	ἐπικρατέω (*epikrateō*)	παιδεύω (*paideuō*)	
Rom 5:14, 17, 21; 6:12						βασιλεύω (*basileuō*)
Rom 6:9, 14						κυριεύω (*kyrieuō*) cf. Is 14:2 LXX

---

[14] Unless otherwise indicated, biblical citations are from the ESV.

The fact that a reign that starts with Adam is mentioned would seem to merit more careful attention in light of the fact that, according to the underlying narrative from which Paul is drawing, Adam himself was created to reign. According to Gn 1:26, when God created humanity it was so that they might "have dominion [רדה; *rdh*] over the fish of the sea and over the birds of the heavens and over the livestock and over all the earth and over every creeping thing that creeps on the earth." In case the point was missed, it is repeated two verses later in the form of a commission given to the created humans: "have dominion over the fish of the sea and over the birds of the heavens and over every living thing that moves on the earth" (1:28; they were also told to subdue [כבש; *kbš*] the earth).[15] Paul had already alluded to these texts from Genesis in Rom 1:23, where he references several of the items mentioned in Gn 1:24–28 (image, man, birds, four-footed animals, reptiles), and in 1 Cor 11:7 he had also alluded to Gn 1:27, so there is no doubt about his familiarity with these texts (and could there be doubt about his knowing the first chapter of the HB?).

That Gn 1:26–28 describes the appointment of humanity as God's vice-regent is reinforced by Ps 8, where the creation narrative of Gn 1 is taken up and elaborated on in a more deliberately poetic register. In vv. 6–8 we find fairly direct allusions to Gn 1:26–28, with its references to dominion over all the prior categories of living creatures (those in the sky, in the seas/waters, and on land). In Ps 8:6 the reference to having dominion is reinforced through the statement that God has "put all things under his feet"—a clear reference to subjugation under the authority of a sovereign king. It is also made explicit in the fifth verse of the psalm, where we are told he was "crowned with glory and honor." I take מֵאֱלֹהִים (*mēʾĕlōhîm*) in the first part of the verse to mean "than God" (with Aquila, Symmachus, Theodotion, and the most common meaning of אֱלֹהִים [*ʾĕlōhîm*] in the HB and against the LXX, Syriac, Targum, and Vulgate) and to reference the role of the human being as God's vice-regent (so, "a little lower than God," as with the NRSV). This canonical interpretation of the significance of Gn 1:26–28 in poetic form strongly reinforces the understanding that that earlier text described the creation of humanity as the coronation of God's vice-regent, intended to reign over all other living creatures.

Philo clearly understood Gn 1:26–28 in this way. Speaking of the creation account in Gn 1, Philo says God created man as "a natural ruler and master" (ἡγεμόνα φύσει καὶ δεσπότην; *hēgemona physei kai despotēn; Opif.* 83) and appointed him "king over all creatures under the moon" (καθίστη τῶν ὑπὸ σελήνην ἁπάντων βασιλέα; *kathistē tōn hypo selēnēn hapantōn*

---

[15] For further discussion of the OT background of Adam's kingship, see G. K. Beale, *A New Testament Biblical Theology: The Unfolding of the Old Testament in the New* (Grand Rapids: Baker Academic, 2011), 30–38, 63–85.

basilea; Opif. 84).[16] Furthermore, Adam named the animals because that is "the task of wisdom and royalty" (σοφίας γὰρ καὶ βασιλείας τὸ ἔργον; *sophias gar kai basileias to ergon; Opif.* 148), and the man "was, moreover, a king, and it befits a ruler to bestow titles on his several subordinates" (καὶ προσέτι βασιλεύς· ἐμπρεπὲς δ᾽ ἡγεμόνι προσαγορεύειν ἕκαστον τῶν ὑπηκόων; *kai proseti basileus; emprepes d᾽ hēgemoni prosagoreuein hekaston tōn hypēkoōn; Opif.* 148).

The evidence that Gn 1:26–28 described a reign conferred upon Adam and humanity in creation and that it was understood as such elsewhere in the HB and within Second Temple Judaism is fairly clear, I hope. More interesting and important for the thesis of this essay is the way in which Paul understands the consequences of the fall for that reign. The proposal of this essay is that in Rom 5:12ff., we find evidence of how Paul read Gn 3 in light of Gn 1 and vice versa.

Before examining Paul's text in light of that proposal, we should look at a different text from the period that also read Gn 1 and Gn 3 together, albeit in a slightly different way.

In the Greek *Life of Adam and Eve* (also known as the *Apocalypse of Moses*) we encounter an interpretation of Gn 3 that several scholars have found instructive for their understanding of parts of Paul's treatment of the downfall of humanity in the letter to the Romans.[17] Several of those scholars have suggested that Paul had either been influenced by *Life of Adam and Eve* or was a near contemporary of, "and moved in the same circle of ideas" as, the original author of the latter.[18] The parallels that others have found between Romans and *Life of Adam and Eve* are all encountered in Rom 1:18–32 and 3:23. In concluding his own discussion of parallels between Rom 1:18–32 and *Life of Adam and Eve*, John Levison mentions "other correspondences which we might also have productively explored" including "the portrayal of death as gaining rule over the human race in *GLAE* [*L.A.E.*] 14.3 (κατακυριεύειν) and Rom 5.12–14 (βασιλεύειν)."[19] Along the way he had pointed out "as an aside" that "the depiction of death in Rom 5 is similar to the *Life*. Paul writes that 'death reigned from Adam until Moses . . .' (5.14). Adam, in the *Life*, charges Eve with 'death's gaining mastery over our entire race' (14.2). In both texts, death is a ruler, a master, a tyrant."[20]

---

[16] Citations from Philo utilize *Philo* (trans. F. H. Colson and G. H. Whitaker; 10 vols.; LCL; Cambridge, MA: Harvard University Press, 1929–1962).

[17] See the discussion in John R. Levison, "Adam and Eve in Romans 1.18–25 and the Greek *Life of Adam and Eve*," *NTS* 50 (2004): 519–21.

[18] L. S. A. Wells, "The Books of Adam and Eve," in *The Apocrypha and Pseudepigrapha of the Old Testament in English* (ed. R. H. Charles; 2 vols.; Oxford: Clarendon, 1913), 2:130.

[19] Levison, "Adam and Eve in Romans 1.18–25," 534.

[20] Levison, "Adam and Eve in Romans 1.18–25," 527 n. 23.

The key texts include Greek *L.A.E.* 24:3, where God tells Adam, as part of his explanation of the curse of the ground, that "the wild animals whom you ruled [ἐκυρίευες; *ekyrieues*] will rise up against you in rebellion, because you did not keep my command."

Earlier, in Greek *L.A.E.* 10:3–11:2 we find an encounter between Eve and a wild beast that was attacking her son, Seth. Part of the encounter includes this dialogue explaining how it came about that the reign of humans was transformed or exchanged into a reign of beasts, due to the fall:

> "How could you not remember your subordination [τῆς ὑποταγῆς σου; *tēs hypotagēs sou*]—that in the past you were subordinate to the image of God [ὑπετάγης τῇ εἰκόνι τοῦ θεοῦ; *hypetagēs tē eikoni tou theou*]?" Then the wild animal shouted, saying, "Oh, Eve, your greed has nothing to do with us—nor your sobbing—but with you, since the rule of the wild animals [ἡ ἀρχὴ τῶν θηρίων; *hē archē tōn thēriōn*] has come about from you! How was your mouth opened to eat from the tree concerning which God commanded you not to eat from it? On account of this also our natures have been exchanged" [ἡμῖν ἡ φύσις μετηλλάγη; *hēmin hē physis metēllagē*].

As Levison puts it, "[t]he wild animal has entirely forgotten its subordinate place in the natural order—an order firmly established in Gen 1.26, to which Paul also alludes—and has begun to rule in humankind's stead."[21]

In Greek *L.A.E.* 39:1–3 God says:

> Adam, what have you done? If you had kept my command, those who brought you down [οἱ κατάγοντες; *hoi katagontes*] into this place would not have rejoiced. Nevertheless, I say to you that their joy I will turn to grief, and your grief I will turn to joy. And I will return you to your rule [τὴν ἀρχήν σου; *tēn archēn sou*], and I will make you sit upon the throne of the one who deceived you. And that one will be cast into this place, so that he may see you seated upon it [the throne]. Then he will be judged—and those who heard him—and he will be grieved when he sees you seated upon his throne.[22]

It seems, as Levison has argued, that according to the Greek *Life of Adam and Eve*, in Gn 3 an exchange of natures took place resulting in the inversion of the roles of humans and beasts. So by following the lead of the serpent rather than that of God, the rule of humans over beasts and all the other creatures has been transformed into a rule of beasts over humans, and God promises to reverse this travesty at some future time.

Levison thinks Paul reflects a similar idea in Rom 1:18–25, where he says humans "exchanged the glory of the immortal God for images resembling mortal man and birds and animals and creeping things" (v. 23) and "exchanged the truth about God for a lie and worshiped and served the creature rather than the Creator" (v. 25). I have found Levison's treatment quite stimulating and helpful but suggest Paul's thought points in a slightly

---

[21] Levison, "Adam and Eve in Romans 1.18–25," 532.
[22] See Levison, "Adam and Eve in Romans 1.18–25," 529.

different direction. Comparing what Paul says in Rom 1 with what we find in Rom 5–8, it seems that Paul agrees that starting in the garden we see an inversion of the proper direction of worship, so that humans worship creatures rather than the Creator, but rather than seeing a transfer of dominion from humanity to animals, he understands the human dominion to be transformed from what it was supposed to be to what it would inevitably be once humanity, through its rejection of God's leadership (in worshiping and obeying him), had given itself over to sin and death.

Reading Gn 1:26–28 in light of Gn 2:17 and 3:3–4 (where God promises death for disobedience and the serpent deceives Eve on that very point), Paul has concluded either that humanity abdicated the throne and transferred its authority to a reign of sin and death or that humanity continues to reign but, having chosen the route of sin and death, can do no other than extend a reign marked by sin and death rather than the reign of righteousness and life intended by God.

That is, I suggest that in Rom 1 Paul addresses an inversion in Adam's worship (worshiping and serving creation), but in Rom 5 Paul addresses the transfer in authority or dominion that resulted from that inverted worship. According to Rom 1 humans now worship creatures rather than God (based on Gn 1, 3), while according to Rom 5 humans have experienced the reign of sin and death (which they themselves inaugurated) rather than the reign of life and righteousness that was intended (again, based on reflection on Gn 1, 3).

In Rom 1:25, where Paul says humans "worshiped and served the creature," he uses religious terms rather than political ones (ἐσεβάσθησαν καὶ ἐλάτρευσαν; *esebasthēsan kai elatreusan*). And in Rom 8:19–23, he does not suggest that creation or creatures received a promotion in terms of a dominion over us but that all of creation was "subjected to humility" (v. 20) by what happened and groans to be "set free from its bondage to corruption" (v. 21; cf. v. 22). There is nothing in Paul to suggest that beasts or other creatures have been given a reign over humans (even if humans worship them in their foolishness).[23] Rather, creation was also made subject to a destructive bondage, as were we, and is awaiting our liberation (vv. 21–23).

Not only is death a key theme in Gn 2 and 3, but its ubiquitous presence and power is confirmed in the tag line applied to each person but one in the extended genealogy in Gn 5. It did not take long for it to become clear that outside the garden humans became "swift to shed blood" (Rom 3:15) in that the first death mentioned in the Bible is not a death by

---

[23] In Rom 16:20 Paul's promise that God "will soon crush Satan under your feet" may be alluding to the "proto-evangelium" of Gn 3:15, where it is promised that Adam or his seed will strike the serpent's head. This may well suggest that the reign of sin and death is a periphrasis for the reign of Satan, whom Paul rarely mentions by name (see the exceptions in Rom 16:20; 1 Cor 5:5; 7:5; 2 Cor 2:11; 11:14; 12:7; 1 Thes 2:18; 2 Thes 2:9; 1 Tm 1:20; 5:15; cf. Eph 2:2).

natural causes but by murder, as Cain shed the blood of his brother, Abel, blood which cried out to God from the ground (Gn 4:8–10).

I have referenced the Greek *Life of Adam and Eve* (and Levison's treatment of it) not because I assume Paul had contact with it or with its ideas or even moved in circles familiar with such an interpretation, but for the sake of comparison and contrast with another ancient Jewish author's way of reading Gn 1 and 3 together to understand the implications of the fall for the reign originally given to humanity. I think Paul's exposition is perfectly explicable as an interpretation of one text of Genesis in light of the other (and both in the light of Christ) as is the case in the Greek *Life of Adam and Eve*.

In the remainder of this essay I want (1) to see what we can discern about the reign of death from the verses in Rom 5–8 that refer to reigning (5:14, 17, 21; 6:9, 12, 14; 7:1) and their near co-texts; (2) to consider briefly the possible implications of this material for recent debates about Paul's concern or lack of concern for the Roman Empire in Romans; and (3) to consider (again, briefly) the implications for the scope of Paul's gospel and for Christian engagement in light of that gospel.

The Reign of Sin and Death in Romans 5–8: A Closer Look

In Rom 5:14 we find the first use in the letter of a verb for reigning. Here we are told that "death reigned" from Adam until Moses.[24] The reference to a reign in the same clause as a reference to Adam is what first suggests we may be dealing not only with a reign for which he is responsible but perhaps even (as suggested here) his own reign, perverted into a reign of death by his own choice of death over life. In light of this suggestion we may consider a possible relationship between the reign of death mentioned in 5:14 with the spread of death to all people that had been mentioned in 5:12. In his insightful treatment of the garden narrative in *The Temple and the Church's Mission*, Greg Beale provides some background that might equally apply to a reign of death starting from Adam. In his

---

[24] Note N. T. Wright's comment, "Paul does not speak here of the kingdom of Satan, but instead personifies 'sin' and 'death,' speaking of each as 'reigning' (5:14, 17a, 21a). He does not speak here, either, of the reign of God, or even of Jesus; rather, as in the admittedly ironic 1 Cor 4:8, he speaks of believers as reigning (5:17b), and then finally of the reign of grace itself (5:21b). The last, clearly, is a personification, a periphrasis for God. This theme of kingly rule, coming so soon after the grand statement of justice, peace, and lordship (5:1), cannot but be seen as a further indication of Paul's overall mission: to announce the kingdom of God in the face of all the principalities and powers of the world, not least those of Rome itself (cf. 8:38–39 and the pregnant conclusion of Acts 28:30–31)" ("Romans," *New Interpreter's Bible* [Nashville: Abingdon, 2002], 10:524).

view, "[b]ecause Adam and Eve were to subdue and rule 'over all the earth', it is plausible to suggest that they were to extend the geographical boundaries of the garden until Eden covered the whole earth."[25] Beale thinks it probable that Adam "was to spread God's luminescent presence by extending the boundaries of the original Edenic temple outward into the earth."[26] That is, "the presence of God, which was initially to be limited to the garden temple of Eden, was to be extended throughout the whole earth by his image bearers, as they themselves represented and reflected his glorious presence and attributes."[27] As it turned out, however, Adam "allowed the Serpent to 'rule over' him rather than 'ruling over' it and casting it out of the Garden. Rather than extending the divine presence of the garden sanctuary, Adam and Eve were expelled from it."[28]

Because Adam chose to disobey God rather than to represent and reflect his glorious presence and attributes and thus became a bearer of death wherever he went, it could be expected that as he was cast out of the garden he might still spread some type of reign. But in this case as humanity spread throughout the earth it brought death (and sin) wherever it went and thus fulfilled an antithetically parallel role to that which God had originally intended when he placed them in the garden to work it and fill the earth.

In the final clause of 5:14 Paul tells us that Adam was a "type" of the one who was to come (v. 14; Ἀδὰμ ὅς ἐστιν τύπος τοῦ μέλλοντος; *Adam hos estin typos tou mellontos*). Many church fathers and modern scholars have discussed the fact that both Adam and Christ have had similarly dramatic consequences for their people, with opposite effects and opposite inheritances coming from each of them. Discussions of the way Adam serves as a type of Christ consistently wrestle with the clear differences between them and consistently omit any reference to Gn 1 and the implication that Adam, like Christ, was to have dominion over the rest of creation as God's image and representative in human form.[29] That both

---

[25] G. K. Beale, *The Temple and the Church's Mission: A Biblical Theology of the Dwelling Place of God* (NSBT 17; Downers Grove, IL: InterVarsity Press, 2004), 81–82.

[26] Beale, *Temple*, 82.

[27] Beale, *Temple*, 83.

[28] Beale, *Temple*, 87.

[29] See, e.g., Gerald Bray, *Romans* (ACCSNT 6; Downers Grove, IL: InterVarsity Press, 1998), 137–38; Douglas J. Moo, *The Epistle to the Romans* (NICNT; Grand Rapids: Eerdmans, 1996), 334 ("The similarity between the two consists in the fact that an act of each is considered to have determinative significance for those who 'belong' to each"); James D. G. Dunn, *Romans 1–8* (WBC 38A; Dallas: Word, 1988), 277 ("each begins an epoch and the character of each epoch is established by their action"); C. E. B. Cranfield, *Romans* (2 vols.; ICC; London and New York: T&T Clark, 1975), 1:283. For a rare exception (in passing), see Robert Jewett, *Romans: A Commentary* (Hermeneia; Minneapolis: Fortress, 2006), 378: Paul's "primary interest appears to be in the idea of dominion: both Adam and Christ determine the fate of their subjects (βασιλεύω in vv. 14, 17 [twice], 21 [twice])."

Adam and Christ are understood as royal figures reigning on God's behalf over universal dominions is passed over, despite the fact that Paul explicitly develops some of these themes in 1 Cor 15:22–28.

The reign of death has resulted in the death of "many" people (which we know amounts to virtually all of them) since the beginning (5:15). The parallel in the language used for Adam and Christ in 5:17 suggests that death's reign did not replace Adam's reign but was a manifestation of the transformed nature of Adam's reign. Paul says "death reigned through the one [man]" and then that "those who receive the abundance of grace and the free gift of righteousness reign in life through the one man Jesus Christ" (5:17). When we compare διὰ τοῦ ἑνός (*dia tou henos*; "through the one") in the first part of the verse with διὰ τοῦ ἑνὸς Ἰησοῦ Χριστοῦ (*dia tou henos Iēsou Christou*; "through the one man Jesus Christ") at the end of the verse, it becomes clear that Paul has in mind not merely reigns that sequentially follow the actions of those two men but reigns that are manifestations of the character and achievements (negative and positive) of those two men. The references to "righteousness" and "life" in this verse also reinforce the understanding that the reign instituted by Christ (and which is a reflection of his own reign) is the antithetical counterpart to the "sin" and "death" that have come to reign through Adam. It also suggests the nature of the reign that Adam was supposed to manifest and extend: a reign of righteousness and life similar to, although possibly not quite the same as, the one that has been inaugurated by Christ.

The reference in v. 17 to many people reigning ("those who receive the abundance of grace and the free gift of righteousness") reminds us that it was not just Adam who was intended to reign in life, but all human beings. Christ brings about the ultimate realization of God's intention for humanity as suggested in Gn 1. The parallel between Christ and Adam indicates that for Paul, thanks to Adam, humanity had received condemnation (Rom 5:16) as well as sin and death, just as believers receive grace, righteousness, and life through Christ.

Romans 5:19, "as by the one man's disobedience the many were made sinners, so by the one man's obedience the many will be made righteous," suggests that part of what the reigns of death/sin and of life/righteousness do is constitute their subjects as those who are sinners or righteous people. In the broader context of this letter and especially its development in Rom 5–8, that role of each reign cannot be understood to consist merely in affecting one's legal status but would include both legal status and the manifestation of sinful or righteous living. Adam did not merely make people guilty of sin but turned them into practitioners of sin as well (one might say sin addicts). And Christ's reign brings about both the change of legal status from sinner to righteous and the ultimate realization of the righteous world that God had intended for humanity when he created it and us in the first place. This is part of Paul's "new creation" theology.[30] Christ is not just bringing about some new messianic reign but is restoring (an even improved version of) the reign that had been originally granted to humanity, the reign of life and righteousness that we were supposed to govern.

What had been characterized as a reign of death in 5:14, 17 is described as a reign of sin in, through, or leading to death (ἐβασίλευσεν ἡ ἁμαρτία ἐν τῷ θανάτῳ; *ebasileusen hē hamartia en tō thanatō*) in v. 21. According to the same verse, that reign is parallel to the reign of grace through righteousness which leads "to eternal life through Jesus Christ our Lord." I agree with Cranfield that "[b]y ἐν τῷ θανάτῳ is probably meant 'with death as its result and accompaniment.' For Paul, with Gen 2:17 not far from his mind, death is the result of sin. . . ."[31] That is to take ἐν (*en*) as equivalent to εἰς (*eis*) here, as those two prepositions are sometimes interchanged.[32] That also does justice, it seems, to the expected parallel between the two sides of the comparison: as we clearly have eternal life as the final result of the reign of grace through Christ in the second half, one would infer that the result of the reign of sin would be death. So on the one side of v. 21 we have a reign of sin leading to death and on the other side we have a reign of grace through righteousness leading to eternal life through Jesus Christ. The reference to Christ as "Lord" reinforces (along with the term "Christ" or "Messiah") the presence of the idea of a reigning king, empowering the reign of grace under his authority. It may be that there is an unspoken parallel which could be inferred in the first part of the verse such that it could be understood to speak of a reign of sin leading to death *through Adam our forefather.*

When we get to Rom 6 Paul turns to address more directly how the change of regimes came about and how it should affect our understanding of the power of sin in our lives and churches. He clarifies that the change from death to life came and comes about through Christ's own death and resurrection and our union with him in that death and resurrection. As James D. G. Dunn has put it, "God's purpose of salvation embraces death since it is through death that the epoch of Adam ends and the power of sin is broken (6:7–10)."[33] In 6:9 Paul explains that Christ's victory over death

---

[30] See the treatment of this with reference to Rom 6 in Beale, *New Testament Biblical Theology,* 836–38.

[31] Cranfield, *Romans,* 1:294.

[32] For the use of ἐν (*en*) where εἰς (*eis*) is expected (infrequent in the NT), see BDF §218. A strong argument may also be given for the view that Paul means sin reigned "in [the sphere of] death" in a way that is parallel to righteousness reigning "in life" in 5:17; see Thomas R. Schreiner, *Romans* (BECNT; Grand Rapids: Baker, 1998), 296.

[33] Dunn, *Romans 1–8,* 287. As Daniel Kirk has argued, "Because the problem of sin and death extends beyond the reach of the Torah, the solution is also beyond the reach of Torah; it is found in Jesus' one act of obedience in going to the cross; it is found in Jesus' own resurrection life and the reign in which it enables

through his resurrection brings the power or reign[34] of death to an end for him. He will never die again, having been loosed from death's power.

In vv. 12–14[35] the Romans are exhorted to live as those who have entered into Christ's reign of grace and to refuse to let sin reign over them any longer as it did when they were still under the law (which was unable to free them from such a reign and became an accomplice to that reign, it seems). Here the reign of sin is also reflected in its power to lead people to disobey God, but that power has been broken in those who have been brought from death to life by the death and resurrection of Christ.

According to the ESV, in 6:13–14 Paul tells the Romans, "Do not present your members to sin as instruments for unrighteousness, but present yourselves to God as those who have been brought from death to life, and your members to God as instruments for righteousness. For sin will have no dominion over you, since you are not under law but under grace." The word translated "instruments" (ὅπλον; *hoplon*) twice in v. 13 is most often used for instruments of war or battle, that is, weapons.[36] The words translated "unrighteousness" and "righteousness" in v. 13 (ἀδικία [*adikia*] and δικαιοσύνη [*dikaiosynē*]) could also be translated "injustice" and "justice" and include within their scope both upright personal behavior and social/community standards of equitability (what we tend to distinguish as righteousness and justice). The point is that no part of their bodies or beings should be offered up to sin to be used as weapons on the side of injustice or unrighteousness, but our whole being is to be offered to God as weapons in the service of justice and righteousness. There is a battle between the remnants of the regime Christ has defeated and the new regime he is establishing, and we are to be wholly engaged against the old regime and in the advancement of Christ's new regime, which is the establishment of the reign of righteousness, justice, grace, and life that was intended at the beginning.[37]

In Rom 7:1 we have the final use of a verb for reigning in Rom 5–8. In this case it is to make the point that the reign of the law of Moses, like

---

believers to share"; see J. R. Daniel Kirk, *Unlocking Romans: Resurrection and the Justification of God* (Grand Rapids: Eerdmans, 2008), 106.

[34] He switches here from βασιλεύω (*basileuō*) to κυριεύω (*kyrieuō*).

[35] In these verses Paul switches between βασιλεύω (*basileuō*) and κυριεύω (*kyrieuō*).

[36] See BDAG, 716.

[37] It must remain clear, as Paul points out in 2 Cor 10:4–5 (where he uses the same word for "weapon" [twice] that was used in Rom 6:13), that "[t]he weapons we fight with are not the weapons of the world. On the contrary, they have divine power to demolish strongholds. We demolish arguments and every pretension that sets itself up against the knowledge of God, and we take captive every thought to make it obedient to Christ" (NIV). That is, "our struggle is not against flesh and blood, but against the rulers, against the authorities, against the powers of this dark world and against the spiritual forces of evil in the heavenly realms" (Eph 6:12 NIV).

the reign of sin and death, comes to an end with life after death. It reigns (κυριεύει; *kyrieuei*) as long as one lives, and not beyond that. In this chapter Paul places the law and its reign within the reign of sin and death and shows it to be incapable of bringing the deliverance from it that is only found in Christ.

The Reign of Sin and the Question of Anti-Imperialism

In light of the fact that NT scholarship has engaged in a lively debate over the extent to which Paul's writings contain anti-imperial rhetoric,[38] it seems appropriate to reflect on the significance of the motif of reigning in this part of Romans for that topic. Neil Elliott's argument that Paul's declaration "that he was charged by God with securing 'faithful obedience among the nations'" must be understood in light of the fact that "'the obedience of nations' was also the prerogative claimed by the Roman emperor" deserves serious consideration.[39] It seems many of Paul's statements could easily provoke reflection on relationships with pagan imperial ideology, but Paul's evident lack of interest in making any such rhetoric explicit is remarkable, although perhaps not surprising, given the tendency of oppressed peoples to express their resistance to the dominant ideology in ways that are less likely to leave themselves fully exposed.[40]

Paul's theology of the gospel has critical implications for Roman imperial ideology and pretensions, even if they are indirectly expressed, but he seems much more concerned about the reigns of sin and death than he does about the Roman Empire and his argument in this letter in general and in Rom 5–8 in particular (and more especially in Rom 5–6) would seem to suggest that he thinks his readers should be focused more on the imperialism of sin and death than on Roman imperialism. In fact, I think that is the implicit message, and it is not unlike the message Jesus's Jewish compatriots might have been expected to infer from his evident lack

---

[38] See, e.g., Warren Carter, *The Roman Empire and the New Testament: An Essential Guide* (Nashville: Abingdon, 2006); N. T. Wright, *Paul: In Fresh Perspective* (Minneapolis: Fortress, 2005), 59–79; Richard A. Horsley, ed., *Paul and Empire: Religion and Power in Roman Imperial Society* (Harrisburg, PA: Trinity Press International, 1997); Richard A. Horsley, *Paul and the Roman Imperial Order* (Harrisburg, PA: Trinity Press International, 2004); Seyoon Kim, *Christ and Caesar: The Gospel and the Roman Empire in the Writings of Paul and Luke* (Grand Rapids: Eerdmans, 2008); and the Fortress Press monograph series, "Paul in Critical Contexts."

[39] Neil Elliott, "'Blasphemed among the Nations': Pursuing an Anti-imperial 'Intertextuality' in Romans," in *As It Is Written: Studying Paul's Use of Scripture* (SBLSymS 50; ed. Stanley E. Porter and Christopher D. Stanley; Atlanta: Society of Biblical Literature, 2008), 213–33 (214).

[40] On "public" and "hidden transcripts," see James C. Scott, *Domination and the Arts of Resistance: Hidden Transcripts* (New Haven: Yale University Press, 1990). Cf. Elliott, "Blasphemed among the Nations," 215–19.

of preoccupation with the Roman occupiers and the attention he gave instead to other powers that had invaded and taken control of territory where they were not wanted. When Jesus spent time casting demons out of those whose personal boundaries had been invaded by them rather than casting the Romans out of the national boundaries of Israel, it suggested that Israel's real or ultimate problem was not that of the geopolitical superpower but that of the pneuma-political superpower of Satan and his "legions." It is not that political oppression and subjugation were and are of no concern to Christ, but that the even deeper problem that needed to be recognized and addressed was the spiritual oppression and subjugation that underwrote those problems and other key challenges of the human race and creation in general.

So also for Paul's argument written to the churches living at the Roman Empire's center of power: The Roman Empire, with its own metanarrative in which it plays the key role of bringing salvation and peace to the world, finds itself completely marginalized in Paul's argument[41] where the metanarrative turns not on the good news of the coming of a Roman emperor to save a decaying world but on the good news of the arrival of the messianic seed of David and second Adam who comes to bring the universal reign of sin and death to an end and replace it with one of righteousness and grace as originally intended by God. For Paul, his readers' greatest problem did not consist of the Romans and their presence but of spiritual realities in our lives and world for which Roman occupiers served merely as good analogies and symptoms.

Somewhat similarly, Ann Jervis suggests "it seems reasonable to understand Paul's description of sin [in Rom 7] analogously to the colonizer, and the world and humanity as the colonized: sin came into the world and reigned over humanity (Rom 5:12–14)."[42] In a slight modification of Jervis's proposal, the thesis of this essay suggests that sin did not invade and conquer the world and humanity as foreign territory but was the cultural offspring of the one originally appointed to rule the other earthly crea-

---

[41] Paul's discussion of the law in Rom 7 suggests it is a good gift of God that had nevertheless served to demonstrate just how sinful and pernicious sin is by its ability to take even such a holy righteous and good thing (7:12) and turn even it into an instrument of death (7:13) and demonstrate the spiritual and moral plight of humanity. Paul's remarkably positive portrayal of governmental power and authority in Rom 13 may suggest that Paul understands both the Mosaic law and civil government as basically good gifts of God that still are ultimately ineffectual opponents of the reign of sin and death that even get co-opted by that reign. So again, the point remains that the real problem and enemy are sin and death (possibly as personifications pointing to the serpent [see in Rom 7 about being deceived] or Satan).

[42] L. Ann Jervis, "Reading Romans 7 in Conversation with Postcolonial Theory: Paul's Struggle toward a Christian Identity of Hybridity," in *The Colonized Apostle: Paul through Postcolonial Eyes* (ed. Christopher D. Stanley; Minneapolis: Fortress, 2011), 98.

tures. According to Paul's portrayal of the early narrative, sin and death were not foreign invaders but domestic innovations and forces wrongfully set loose by the rightfully appointed king. Still, there are significant parallels to a colonial or postcolonial situation, and Jervis is right to suggest we can learn from postcolonial theory and insights.

Reign of Sin and Death and the Issues of Perpetrators, Victims, and Suffering, and the Christian Response

The reign of sin and death is manifest not only in the universal experience of death but also in the various kinds of suffering that they cause leading up to death, just as Christ's passion began well before his death on the cross. The theme of suffering appears near the beginning and end of Rom 5–8 (5:3; 8:17–18), forming something of an *inclusio* around the unit. If Rom 1–4 deals with deliverance from the guilt of sin and from death, Rom 5–8 deals, among other things, with deliverance from the suffering that we cause and receive through the reign of sin and death.

Believers should recognize that their sufferings may be an essential part of their growth in character and Christian faithfulness (5:3), and as part of our participation in the sufferings of Christ himself it also leads us to anticipate our participation in his resurrection (8:17–18). Among other kinds of suffering that are experienced in this world due to the reign of sin and death, Paul mentions tribulation, distress, persecution, famine, nakedness, danger, sword, and death (8:35–36). In the first three chapters Paul had rehearsed a wide variety of sinful behaviors. Although those sins are usually (and rightfully) considered evidence of human guilt and our need for forgiveness and justification, they also point beyond those issues to God's intention to undo the empire of sin and death that makes both perpetrators and victims of all of us.

Among other things, Paul had cited Scripture to highlight the fact that we subject others to deceit and we ourselves are subject to being deceived by others, to experiencing curses and bitterness, to shedding others' blood, to bringing and experiencing ruin, misery, and a lack of peace (3:13–17). Thanks to the reign of sin and death the world is full of envy, murder, strife, deceit, maliciousness, gossip, slander, insolence, haughtiness, ever newer forms of evil, faithlessness, heartlessness, and ruthlessness (see 1:29–31). The reign of sin and death brings not just guilt and death but these and other kinds of pain, suffering, and brokenness that we inflict on others and that is inflicted on us by others.

When Paul comes to the end of Rom 12 he exhorts the Romans saying, "Do not be vanquished by evil but vanquish evil with good."[43] The

---

[43] My translation (cf. HCSB: "Do not be conquered by evil, but conquer evil with good"). Many translations render the text "Do not be overcome by evil, but

repeated verbs in this verse (forms of νικάω [*nikaō*]) have to do with achieving victory over an enemy or opponent.[44] This is fitting language for the conflict that must take place between the defeated but defiant reign of sin and death and Christ's victorious reign of grace and life, as was already indicated in 6:13. In the rest of Rom 12–15 Paul highlights some of the particular ways in which the Christians in Rome were to advance Christ's reign of life and righteousness at the expense of the vanquished reign of sin and death.

The reign of sin and death affects all people. All people sin, are sinned against, and die. But this reign ravages some people and places more than others. The reign of sin and death brings greater suffering, more frequent suffering, earlier death and death following a less dignified life in some places more than others. Richard Stearns reminds us that "26,575 children die each day of largely preventable causes related to their poverty."[45] That is one dramatic reflection of the reign of sin and death, one that believers have worked to mitigate over the centuries. We also know that girls and women suffer and die young in exponentially disproportionate numbers compared to men around the world. "It appears that more girls have been killed in the last fifty years, precisely because they were girls, than men were killed in all the battles of the twentieth century. More girls are killed in this routine 'gendercide' in any one decade than people were slaughtered in all the genocides of the twentieth century."[46] Furthermore, "[e]very year at least another two million girls worldwide disappear because of gender discrimination."[47] The gospel message Paul presents us with is one that should lead the church to seek to preach Christ and to bring his reign, the reign of grace, to bear in every sphere where we see the remnants of the reign of sin and death in the world today.

If we are to "reign in life" through Christ according to 5:17 and according to 6:12–14 must already refuse to let sin reign over us rather than

---

overcome evil with good," which is acceptable, but does not give quite the same sense of engagement in conflict in which there will be a winner and a loser.

[44] Cf. BDAG, 673, and the HCSB rendering of the verse.

[45] Richard Stearns, *The Hole in Our Gospel: What Does God Expect of Us?* (Nashville: Thomas Nelson, 2009), 114.

[46] Nicholas D. Kristof and Sheryl WuDunn, *Half the Sky: Turning Oppression into Opportunity for Women Worldwide* (New York: Alfred A. Knopf, 2009), xvii. See also the summary of some key issues by Carolyn Custis James, "Disposable Girls?" last modified April 15, 2012, http://www.whitbyforum.com/2012/04/disposable-girls.html: "Although in the West, the number of females exceeds males, males significantly outnumber females in the rest of the world. The reason behind declining numbers of females is directly connected to how they are devalued. As many have noted, 'It's a girl!' are three of the most dangerous words spoken in many parts of today's world, where gendercide snuffs out the lives of millions of little girls before they ever have a chance. Countless other girls die from neglect, malnourishment, and because they are deprived of basic medical care, for no other reason than they are not boys."

[47] Kristof and WuDunn, *Half the Sky*, xv.

being used as instruments of righteousness, it would seem to follow that we are to work in this present world, in this time between the times, to let Christ manifest through us the kind of reign that had been intended for Adam/humanity from the beginning, rather than that which Adam let loose in the world. The destructive power of sin and death is to be challenged in every sphere and at every opportunity. That happens through the proclamation of the Christ-centered gospel and through the incarnation of the gospel in ministry modeled upon Christ's own example of confronting the power of sin and death in all of its manifestations with the power of God's kingdom/Spirit.

Conclusion

The study suggests that like his argument in Rom 1–4, Paul's argument in Rom 5–8 is a very Jewish argument rooted in his theological interpretation of the Genesis narratives, especially his reading of Gn 3 in light of Gn 1:26–28. It is a different type of engagement with Scripture than what we find in the chapters preceding and following this section, but it is rich in scriptural interpretation nonetheless. His reading of Gn 3 in light of Gn 1 is different from and yet has some similarities to what we find, for example, in the Greek *Life of Adam and Eve*. In Paul's reading of Genesis, it seems that death is not merely a punishment for Adam's sin (or our own) but a reflection of the terrible turn taken in Adam's (that is, humanity's) reign in the choice of death over that of obedience and life.

Paul's reading of the early Genesis narratives reflects the relevance of his gospel message for the full depth of the problem of sin and death introduced by Adam and provides the foundation for the Christ-centered gospel of God's solution not just to the problem of human guilt requiring forgiveness and justification but also for the wider problems of human corruption requiring the overturning of all of Adam's corrupt reign and its replacement with the reign of righteousness intended by God from the beginning.

Paul's biblical narrative framework marginalizes the role of the Roman Empire by ignoring it and focusing our attention on the more basic problem of the power of sin and death in the world and Christ's solution to that more fundamental problem, bringing about a more holistic redemption as was required.

The framework of and broader context to Rom 5–8 should lead us to recognize the holistic calling on believers' lives that flows from this gospel message. It focuses our attention not only on the guilt associated with sin but also on the sufferings that the reign of sin and death brings into our lives and the lives of others. The recognition that we are to reign in life through Christ suggests that under his reign we are to work against the power of sin and death by proclaiming the life-giving gospel of Christ and to work—as Adam should have worked in the garden—in such a way that the destructive power of sin and death might be opposed in every sphere as Christ does his transforming work in the world in and through his church.

CHAPTER 7

LUKE'S ISAIANIC JUBILEE

Daniel M. Gurtner

Introduction

Isaianic influence on the formation of the synoptic tradition has been well noted.[1] Indeed, at its outset, in our earliest Gospel, widely agreed to be the source for Luke—namely, the Gospel of Mark—scholars have posited the priority of Isaiah,[2] even finding allusions in every chapter of Mark.[3] Moreover, Mark begins his entire narrative with a citation from this influential book:

> The beginning of the gospel of Jesus Christ, the Son of God. As it is written in Isaiah the prophet, "Behold, I send My messenger before Your face, Who will prepare Your way; The voice of one crying in the wilderness, 'Make ready the way of the Lord, Make His paths straight.'" (Mk 1:1–3)[4]

The quotation is important not simply because it places an Isaianic citation at the beginning of the earliest narrative account of Jesus of Nazareth but also because Mark's quotation is not exclusively from the book of Isaiah, despite the author's attribution. Instead, Mk 1:2 draws from Mal 3:1, which is itself drawn from Ex 23:20. Not until v. 3 does Mark cite from Isaiah (Is 40:3). While much could be said regarding the nature of what Mark intends here,[5] the importance of these few observations is

---

[1] This essay originated in a course taught by Greg Beale at Gordon-Conwell Theological Seminary in 1999.

[2] M. A. Beavis, *Mark's Audience: The Literary and Social Setting of Mark 4.11–12* (JSNTSup 33; Sheffield: JSOT Press, 1989), 10.

[3] R. Schneck, *Isaiah in the Gospel of Mark, I–VII* (BDS 1; Vallejo, CA: BIBAL, 1994).

[4] Translations throughout are from the NASB unless otherwise stated.

[5] See Joel Marcus, *The Way of the Lord: Christological Exegesis of the Old Testament in the Gospel of Mark* (Edinburgh: T&T Clark, 1992), 12–47; Rikk E. Watts, *Isaiah's New Exodus in Mark* (WUNT 2/88; Tübingen: Mohr Siebeck, 1997; repr., Grand Rapids: Baker, 2000), 53–90.

that at the outset the citation of prophetic texts from Israel's Scriptures in general, and Isaiah in particular, may contain conflations with other texts. This characteristic, well noted in Mark,[6] is immediately pertinent for our study of Lk 4, where Jesus begins his public ministry not with an announcement of the fulfillment of the καιρός (*kairos*) and nearness of the kingdom of God (Mk 1:15; cf. Mt 4:17) but with a citation from the book of Isaiah (Lk 4:18–19).

Isaiah's influence on Lukan writings is widely recognized.[7] Luke explicitly introduces readers to Isaianic prophecies with John the Baptist's depiction as the one to announce the arrival of the Messiah (Lk 3:4–6, citing Is 40:3–5). In the ensuing temptation narrative (Lk 4:1–13), Jesus speaks almost exclusively from the words of Scripture (Dt 8:3; 6:13, 16). Yet in the next scene (Lk 4:14–30) Jesus begins his public ministry, where his first public words—like his private words before—are from Scripture, this time from Isaiah:

> And He came to Nazareth, where He had been brought up; and as was His custom, He entered the synagogue on the Sabbath, and stood up to read. And the book of the prophet Isaiah was handed to Him. And He opened the book, and found the place where it was written, "The Spirit of the Lord is upon Me, Because He anointed Me to preach the gospel to the poor. He has sent Me to proclaim release to the captives, And recovery of sight to the blind, To set free those who are downtrodden, To proclaim the favorable year of the Lord." And He closed the book, and gave it back to the attendant, and sat down; and the eyes of all in the synagogue were fixed upon Him. And He began to say to them, "Today this Scripture has been fulfilled in your hearing." (Lk 4:16–21)

The citation is striking not simply because it presents the first public words of Jesus as exclusively from Scripture (4:18–19) but also because of the claim made later (4:21) that the aforementioned Scripture stands fulfilled in the hearing of those present in the synagogue. Moreover, the manner in which Isaiah is quoted here is intriguing. For while the majority of the citation is drawn directly from Is 61, there are portions of that text absent from Luke's citation, and some items found in Luke's citation are found not in Is 61 but in Is 58. A cursory comparison indicates the Evangelist's careful hand in his employment of the OT texts.

---

[6] H. C. Kee, *Community of the New Age* (NTL; London: SCM Press, 1977).
[7] David Seccombe, "Luke and Isaiah," in *Right Doctrine from the Wrong Texts? Essays on the Use of the Old Testament in the New* (ed. G. K. Beale; Grand Rapids: Baker, 1994), 249, cites Lukan quotations of Isaianic texts in support of this view: Lk 3:4–6 (Is 40:3–5); Lk 4:17–19 (Is 61:1–2); Acts 8:28–33 (Is 53:7–8); Acts 28:25–27 (Is 6:9–10). See also David W. Pao, *Acts and the Isaianic New Exodus* (WUNT 2/13; Tübingen: Mohr Siebeck, 2000; repr., Grand Rapids: Baker Academic, 2002).

Text Comparison		
Luke 4:18–19	**Isaiah 61:1–2**	
18a πνεῦμα κυρίου ἐπ᾽ ἐμὲ (*pneuma kyriou ep' eme*)	πνεῦμα κυρίου ἐπ᾽ ἐμέ (*pneuma kyriou ep' eme*)	61:1a
18b οὗ εἵνεκεν ἔχρισέν με (*hou heineken echrisen me*)	οὗ εἵνεκεν ἔχρισέν με (*hou heineken echrisen me*)	61:1b
18c εὐαγγελίσασθαι πτωχοῖς, ἀπέσταλκέν με (*euangelisasthai ptōchois, apestalken me*)	εὐαγγελίσασθαι πτωχοῖς ἀπέσταλκέν με (*euangelisasthai ptōchois apestalken me*)	61:1c
	ἰάσασθαι τοὺς συντετριμμένους τῇ καρδίᾳ (*iasasthai tous syntetrimmenous tē kardia*)	61:1d
18d κηρύξαι αἰχμαλώτοις (*kēryxai aichmalōtois*)	κηρύξαι αἰχμαλώτοις (*kēryxai aichmalōtois*)	61:1e
18e ἄφεσιν καὶ τυφλοῖς ἀνάβλεψιν (*aphesin kai typhlois anablepsin*)	ἄφεσιν καὶ τυφλοῖς ἀνάβλεψιν (*aphesin kai typhlois anablepsin*)	61:1f
18f ἀποστεῖλαι τεθραυσμένους ἐν ἀφέσει (*aposteilai tethrausmenous en aphesei*)	ἀπόστελλε τεθραυσμένους ἐν ἀφέσει (*apostelle tethrausmenous en aphesei*)	58:6d
19 κηρύξαι ἐνιαυτὸν κυρίου δεκτόν (*kēryxai eniauton kyriou dekton*)	καλέσαι ἐνιαυτὸν κυρίου δεκτὸν (*kalesai eniauton kyriou dekton*)	61:2a
	καὶ ἡμέραν ἀνταποδόσεως (*kai hēmeran antapodoseōs*)	61:2b
	παρακαλέσαι πάντας τοὺς πενθοῦντας (*parakalesai pantas tous penthountas*)	61:2c

Luke's citation is a conflation of two Isaianic texts, which naturally influences textual variation.[8] Most scholars recognize that both copyist activity and attention to the phrasing of the citation indicate its origin from Is 61:1–2 and Is 58:6. Analysis of Luke's conflation of these texts requires first an examination of their respective Isaianic contexts.[9]

---

[8] Consideration of the text of Luke here is far from comprehensive. Additional readings are noted in the CNTTS Apparatus. For convenience, I have primarily consulted those adduced in Reuben Swanson's *New Testament Greek Manuscripts: Luke* (Sheffield: Sheffield Academic Press, 1995), the NA²⁷, the UBS⁴, and *The Greek New Testament: SBL Edition* (ed. Michael W. Holmes; Atlanta: Society of Biblical Literature, 2010).

[9] For Luke's use of the OT in general and his sources in particular, see David W. Pao and Eckhard J. Schnabel, "Luke," in *Commentary on the New Testament Use of the Old Testament* (ed. G. K. Beale and D. A. Carson; Grand Rapids: Baker, 2007),

Isaianic Contexts of the Lukan Citation

Despite the rich tapestry of potential christological significance of the Isaianic contexts, Is 58:6 is cited only here in the NT[10] and Is 61:1–2 is cited (independently) only in *Barn.* 14:9.[11] Luke's citation draws from the final section of Isaiah (chs. 56–66) in which the prophet returns to the earlier emphasis (chs. 7–39) on human inability to achieve the much-needed deliverance. The problem, unfolded in the opening section of the book (chs. 1–6), is that though Israel is God's chosen means by which he intends to convey his blessings to the nations, the nation has failed to live up to its role as servant of the Lord. It is God's intent to make them into the Israel he intends them to be. God's gracious intervention through his Servant (chs. 40–55) stands in stark contrast to human inability to achieve deliverance (56:1–57:13; 58:1–59:14). God's empowerment brings unequivocal hope (57:14–21; 59:15–21). He has established his glory among his people (60:1–62:12). God is more than capable to achieve their deliverance (63:1–9; 65:1–66:24), whereas Israel is most decidedly not (63:10–64:12). Nevertheless, Israel is seen as "the repository of God's glory, to which all the nations will come" (e.g., 56:1–8; 60:1–3, 13–14; 66:18–23).[12]

The Context of Isaiah 58:6

The particular context of Is 58:6 is an extended section on Israel's failure and inability to achieve deliverance from exile (56:1–57:13; 58:1–59:14), in contrast to the unequivocal hope of God's empowerment (57:14–21; 59:15–21). Luke's quotation forms part of the beginning of a segment (58:6–14) that functions as the third of four elements describing characteristics of Israelite fasts that would please the Lord (Is 58:6a).[13] Yet the description (Is 58:6b–e) seemingly has nothing to do with fasting:

> 6a Is this not the fast which I choose,
> 6b To loosen the bonds of wickedness,
> 6c To undo the bands of the yoke,
> 6d And to let the oppressed go free,
> 6e And break every yoke?

251–53. See also Pao, *Acts and the Isaianic New Exodus*, 70–84; B. J. Koet, " 'Today This Scripture Has Been Fulfilled in Your Ears': Jesus' Explanation of Scripture in Luke 4:16–30," *Bijdr* 47 (1986): 368–94.

[10] François Bovon, *Luke 1: A Commentary on the Gospel of Luke 1:1–9:50* (trans. Christine M. Tomas; Hermeneia; Minneapolis: Fortress, 2002), 153, suggests Is 58 is used extensively in the NT, though 58:6 is cited only here.

[11] I. Howard Marshall, *The Gospel of Luke* (NIGTC; Grand Rapids: Eerdmans, 1978), 183.

[12] J. N. Oswalt, *The Book of Isaiah* (2 vols.; NICOT; Grand Rapids: Eerdmans, 1986, 1998), 2:11.

[13] This stands in contrast to a scathing rebuke of hypocritical fastings (Is 58:1–5).

John Oswalt suggests the prophet is employing Semitic hyperbole, illustrating in the opposite extreme that the observation of mere ceremonial legislation is of no value (cf. Is 1:10–20; Am 5:25–27; Mi 6:6–8). That is, Isaiah calls his hearers to express their piety in a manner less conducive to self-delusion than the act of fasting.[14] Luke's citation is from Is 58:6d, employing an expression which in Hebrew (חׇפְשִׁי + שׁלח; *šlḥ* + *ḥopšî*) is used for the manumission of slaves (Ex 21:26–27; Dt 15:12–13, 19; Jer 34:8–16).[15] Indeed, all four verbs in this context pertain to liberation (cf. Jer 34:8–22), an object of utmost importance in the ministry of the Servant of the Lord (cf. Is 42:7; 43:3–7; 45:13; 49:9; 61:1).

The Context of Isaiah 61:1–2

Isaiah 60 exalts in triumph, exhorting Israel to rise and shine, for its Light has come (60:1). The substance of the chapter juxtaposes, then, a darkness covering the earth (v. 2a) with the Lord rising upon his people (v. 2b), and escalating blessings of God upon Israel despite its oppressors, frailties, and sin: restoration, vindication, and peace. Israel will then know that the Lord is its Savior, Redeemer, and Mighty One of Jacob (60:16). Instead of destruction and violence, Israel's walls will be called Salvation and its gates Praise (60:19). Rather than the sun and moon for light, the Lord himself will be its light and glory (60:19–20). The Lord himself announces that he will do this, and swiftly (60:22). Isaiah 61 begins with another announcement, but it is not clear by whom:

> The Spirit of the Lord God is upon me, Because the LORD has anointed me To bring good news to the afflicted; He has sent me to bind up the brokenhearted, To proclaim liberty to captives, And freedom to prisoners; To proclaim the favorable year of the LORD, And the day of vengeance of our God; To comfort all who mourn, To grant those who mourn *in* Zion, Giving them a garland instead of ashes, The oil of gladness instead of mourning, The mantle of praise instead of a spirit of fainting. (Is 61:1–3a)

Whoever the speaker is, the result of this activity for Israel will be to devour the wealth of the nations (61:4–11), not the other way around (62:6–9), and to demonstrate to the nations that God has not forsaken Israel (62:1–5).

The speaker here makes a first-person announcement (61:1a): "the Spirit of the Sovereign Lord is upon me" (61:1a). The owner is identified as both אֲדֹנׇי (*'ădōnāy*),[16] my master (Ps 12:5), my king (Jer 22:18; 34:5),

---

[14] Oswalt, *Isaiah*, 2:503.

[15] Joseph Blenkinsopp, *Isaiah 56–66* (AB 19B; New York: Doubleday, 2003), 179.

[16] MSS^k LXX 1QIsa^a Vg omit אֲדֹנׇי ['*ădōnāy*]. Syr Tg support MT. Oswalt, *Isaiah*, 2:561, therefore denies its originality. However, its presence in 1QIsa, which

or, when God is the subject, my Lord (Ex 23:17; Ps 114:7; Mi 4:13). It is a
term denoting authority and utmost respect.[17] The inclusion of יְהוָה (yhwh)
affirms the certainty of God being the Lord in question. Isaiah's expression of the רוּחַ (rûaḥ) of God being upon (usually עַל ; ʿl) someone suggests
the conveyance of supernatural wisdom or capacity in some sense (Gn
41:38; Ex 31:3; Nm 11:17, 29).[18] In each case the Spirit's coming upon
someone involves several common, essential aspects. First, the recipient
of the Spirit is always a person in military and/or spiritual leadership
over God's covenant community. Second, the coming of the Spirit is in
conjunction with a specific task involving the leadership of God's people
to execute the task of deliverance for his people. Third, the coming of the
Spirit upon these men is done for deliverance from either a physical (e.g.,
political and military) threat or captivity to idolatry and/or to pronounce
judgment on his enemies (cf. 2 Chr 15:1; 24:20; Ez 11:5). In each case the
action of deliverance was a direct consequence of the coming of the Spirit.
In Isaiah (see 11:2), the Spirit is associated with the ability to impart righteousness and justice upon the earth.[19]

Though some scholars presume messianic claims for the speaker,[20] his
identity has been subject to discussion.[21] Some suggest it is the prophet
himself[22] perhaps receiving a metaphorical or figurative anointing.[23] Or
perhaps the speaker is not to be identified with the prophet himself, even
though his utterance occurs within a prophetic genre.[24] Others suggest it

---

predates all other MSS, supports the MT. Therefore אֲדֹנָי (ʾădōnāy) is probably
original.

[17] Robert L. Alden, "אָדֹן," TWOT 1:12.

[18] Oswalt, Isaiah, 2:564. It is said to come upon Balaam to bless Israel (Nm
24:2) and judges for their acts of deliverance, such as Othniel (Jgs 3:10), Gideon
(6:34), Jephthah (11:29), and Samson (13:25; 14:6, 19; 15:14), in these instances
serving a twofold purpose of deliverance from, and judgment upon, the Philistines.

[19] This is often done through the spoken word (Oswalt, Isaiah, 2:464). See also
Is 11:2; 32:15–16; 42:1; 44:3; 48:16; 59:21. John D. W. Watts, Isaiah 34–66 (WBC
25; rev. ed.; Nashville: Thomas Nelson, 2005), 871, emphasizes the similarity to
the theme of 11:2 where "the king is clearly in view," claiming the speaker to be
the Persian king (Oswalt, Isaiah, 2:301, 302).

[20] See E. J. Young, The Book of Isaiah (3 vols.; Grand Rapids: Eerdmans, 1965,
1969, 1972), 3:458; Oswalt, Isaiah, 2:464.

[21] Most recently surveyed in Randall Heskett, Messianism within the Scriptural
Scrolls of Isaiah (LHB/OTS 456; New York: T&T Clark, 2007), esp. 225–63.

[22] Donald Juel, Messianic Exegesis: Christological Interpretation of the Old Testa-
ment in Early Christianity (Philadelphia: Fortress, 1988), 9; Claus Westermann,
Prophetic Oracles of Salvation in the Old Testament (trans. Keith Crim; Louisville:
Westminster John Knox, 1991), 188.

[23] Douglas Jones, Isaiah 56–66 and Joel (London: SCM Press, 1964).

[24] Robert R. Wilson, Prophecy and Society in Ancient Israel (Philadelphia: Fortress, 1959), 26; David L. Petersen, Late Israelite Prophecy (Philadelphia: Fortress,
1980), 213–30. Hugenberger suggests the speaker here takes on a "prophetic
identification"; Gordon P. Hugenberger, "The Servant of the Lord in the 'Servant
Songs' of Isaiah," in The Lord's Anointed: Interpretation of Old Testament Messianic

is the Servant speaking here (cf. 42:1–9; 49:1–9; 50:4–9; 52:13–53:12).[25] Some have recognized the priestly dimension,[26] even a high-priestly consecration (Ex 28:41; 29:7; 30:30).[27] There are certain royal connotations (Jgs 9:8, 15; 1 Sm 9:16; 2 Sm 2:4).[28] But the role of the speaker is inconsistent with priestly or kingly tasks.[29] Strikingly, similar language is used of Cyrus as the Lord's servant (42:1–4). Perhaps the author is suggesting Cyrus's role has passed, and a new servant, one quite distinct from Cyrus, is in place.[30] The anointing may, as some have suggested, be metaphorical. Yet this does not remove the distinct connotation of the anointing in view—it is a decidedly commissioning effect, ambiguously, perhaps deliberately so, overlapping either priestly and/or kingly figures. The Isaianic speaker has clear affinities with his role elsewhere, such as the presence of the Spirit (42:1), the first-person address (49:1–12; 50:4–9), language of opening (42:7) and prisoners (49:9).[31] Moreover, there are additional clear affinities with the messianic figure of Is 11, including the presence of the Spirit of the Lord (11:2), the importance of speaking (11:4), the establishment of righteousness (11:5), and the exaltation of God (11:9–10). John Collins assesses the ambiguity by positing a prophet Messiah making proclamations in the name of God.[32] This is important as a messianic identification of the speaker, adopted also by others as a Servant Messiah[33] or messianic King.[34] Oswalt observes that in the OT, especially Isaiah, the Spirit's filling and anointing are mentioned together only in kingship texts (1 Sm 10:1, 6–7; 16:13; 2 Sm 23:1–7).[35] A striking parallel is found in Is 59:21, where the Lord announces his covenant (ἐμοῦ διαθήκη; *emou*

Texts (ed. Philip E. Satterthwaite, Richard S. Hess, and Gordon J. Wenham; Grand Rapids: Baker, 1995), 112.

[25] Notably Walter Zimmerli and Joachim Jeremias, *The Servant of God* (rev. ed.; Studies in Theology 20; Naperville, IL: Allenson, 1965), 26, 29; Oswalt, *Isaiah*, 2:564.

[26] J. Morgenstern, "Isaiah 61," *HUCA* 40 (1969): 109–21.

[27] See also P. Grelot, "Sur Isaïe lxi: La Première Consécration D'un Grand-Prêtre," *RB* 97 (1990): 414–31.

[28] See Richard L. Schultz, "The King in the Book of Isaiah," in *The Lord's Anointed: Interpretation of Old Testament Messianic Texts* (ed. Philip E. Satterthwaite, Richard S. Hess, and Gordon J. Wenham; Grand Rapids: Baker, 1995), 141–65.

[29] Blenkinsopp, *Isaiah 56–66*, 221.

[30] Similarly Blenkinsopp, *Isaiah 56–66*, 220.

[31] Oswalt, *Isaiah*, 2:562. Watts, *Isaiah 34–66*, 871, holds the speaker to be the Persian king.

[32] Citing a striking parallel in 4Q521. John J. Collins, *The Scepter and the Star: The Messiahs of the Dead Sea Scrolls and Other Ancient Literature* (ABRL; New York: Doubleday, 1995), 118–22, 205.

[33] C. C. Torrey, *Second Isaiah: A New Interpretation* (New York: Scribner, 1928), 452.

[34] Walther Eichrodt, *Theology of the Old Testament* (trans. J. A. Baker; 2 vols.; London: SCM Press, 1967), 2:59.

[35] Oswalt, *Isaiah*, 2:564.

diathēkē) with his people that entails his Spirit upon a singular individual (τὸ πνεῦμα τὸ ἐμόν ὅ ἐστιν ἐπὶ σοί; *to pneuma to emon ho estin epi soi*) and the enduring words of God within his mouth (τὰ ῥήματα ἃ ἔδωκα εἰς τὸ στόμα σου οὐ μὴ ἐκλίπῃ ἐκ τοῦ στόματός σου; *ta rhēmata ha edōka eis to stoma sou ou mē eklipē ek tou stomatos sou*). The connotation seems to be that the prophet is here employing the ambiguity of the identity of the speaker with clear thematic allusions made previously in the book, allocating a unique combination of messianic, kingly, and prophetic facets upon the enigmatic speaker in Is 61:1–2.

The reason for the Spirit being on the speaker (61:1b) is because the Lord has anointed him.[36] The language (יַעַן [*ya'an*]; οὗ εἵνεκεν [*hou heineken*]) is typically conjunctive with the perfect (cf. Nm 20:12; 1 Sm 15:23; 1 Kgs 14:13; 20:42; 2 Kgs 22:19; Hos 8:1, Is 61:1; 65:12; 66:4), suggesting that the Spirit of the Lord God is upon the recipient as a direct result of the act of anointing.[37] When YHWH is the subject, anointing (מָשַׁח [*mšḥ*]; ἔχρισέν [*echrisen*]) is received by kings Saul (1 Sm 10:1), David (2 Sm 12:7; Ps 89:20), Jehu (2 Kgs 9:3, 6, 12), and the figure of Ps 45:7. This suggests, likewise, a kingly anointing for the speaker by YHWH for the speaker of Is 61:1–2. Furthermore, the anointed figure in Isaiah is particularly directed and characterized by both the will (9:6[5]; 11:2; 40:13–14; 50:4) and the enabling power (9:6[5]; 11:4; 42:4; 49:5; 50:9) of YHWH.[38] Next Isaiah provides a series of infinitive phrases indicating the multiple purposes for the anointing.

The first purpose of the anointing is "to proclaim good news to the poor" (61:1c). Isaiah's verb (לְבַשֵּׂר [*lĕbaśśēr*]; typically εὐαγγελίζομαι [*euangelizomai*])[39] occurs in contexts of the hope of deliverance (Is 40:9; 41:27; 52:7; 60:6), particularly the message concerning the Lord's salvation and restoration of Zion (Is 52:7).[40] The recipients of this message, "afflicted ones" (עֲנָוִים; *'ănāwîm*), are humble, seemingly helpless people who are the special objects of God's attention (cf. Pss 9:13[12]; 10:17) and special salvific or redemptive provision (Pss 37:11; 76:10[9]) in reference to a future eschatological event. The term is often used in the Psalms for the faithful "who wait on YHWH in spite of their personal distress" (cf. 57:15).[41] This usage is continued in the preaching of the prophets, which

---

[36] Luke's citation, following the LXX, removes the Lord as the subject presumably seeing it as redundant.

[37] Bruce K. Waltke and M. O'Conner, *An Introduction to Biblical Hebrew Syntax* (Winona Lake, IN: Eisenbrauns, 1990), 640; also Ronald J. Williams, *Hebrew Syntax: An Outline* (2nd ed.; Toronto: University of Toronto Press, 1976), 61.

[38] So Oswalt, *Isaiah*, 2:564.

[39] See David Seccombe, "Luke and Isaiah," *NTS* 27 (1981): 252–59.

[40] Blenkinsopp, *Isaiah 56–66*, 223. It also recounts the central theme of Is 40 (cf. 40:9; 41:27; see also 60:6). Watts, *Isaiah 34–66*, 872–73. See also 1 Sm 31:9; 1 Chr 10:9; Is 61:1.

[41] Watts, *Isaiah 34–66*, 872.

proclaims God's future vindication of the downtrodden (Is 32:7; Am 2:7) at the future "day of the Lord" (Is 11:4; 29:19; Am 8:4; Zep 2:3).

The second purpose of the anointing is "to bind up the broken-hearted" (61:1d). Such binding (חבשׁ; *ḥbš*) can suggest the healing of a broken or wounded people (Jb 5:18; Ps 147:3) but in the prophets conveys a much more redemptive quality, such as the healing from the wounds of sin (Hos 6:1; cf. Is 1:6; 30:26; 61:1; Ez 16:10; 30:21; 34:4, 16).[42] The term "broken-hearted" (לְנִשְׁבְּרֵי־לֵב; *lĕnišbĕrê-lēb*) occurs only here and in Pss 51:19[17] and 147:3, where the repentant believer looks for deliverance from God. Here in Isaiah it recalls the dispirited Jewish people in Jerusalem before the return of Ezra (Is 57:15).[43] Importantly, of the statements quoted from Is 61:1–2 in Lk 4, the statement here about binding up the broken-hearted (61:1d) and the statement about vengeance (61:2b) are absent from his citation. The significance will be considered below.

The third purpose for the anointing is "to proclaim liberty to captives" (61:1e).[44] The prophetic proclamation here is one of deliverance (cf. Jer 34:8, 15, 17), with the announcer presumably authorized to make his announcement.[45] The recipients of the message are captives (לִשְׁבוּיִם; *lišbûyim*),[46] and in Isaiah's context, exiles (cf. 49:9).[47] Moreover, the Isaianic proclamation (לִקְרֹא לִשְׁבוּיִם דְּרוֹר; *liqrōʾ lišbûyim dĕrôr*) draws verbatim from the Levitical proclamation of liberty at the Year of Jubilee (Lv 25:10; cf. Jer 34:8; Ez 46:17), a theme common in prophetic expression for release from the burdens of exile (cf. Jer 34:8, 15, 17) and one that will surface again.

The fourth reason for the anointing is "to proclaim liberty to those who are bound" (61:1–2).[48] The "bound," like the "captives" (v. 1e), suggests captivity, even imprisonment (cf. Gn 39:20; 40:5; Ps 146:7; Is 49:9)[49] from which release is found in the sabbatical texts of the OT (Ex 21:2; Dt 15:1–11; Jer 34:8–22).

The fifth reason for the anointing is "to proclaim the year of the Lord's favor" (61:2a). The "Lord's favor" (1 Sm 13:12; 2 Kgs 13:4) is given even

---

[42] Oswalt, *Isaiah*, 2:565.

[43] Watts, *Isaiah 34–66*, 873.

[44] Isaiah switches from בשׂר (*bśr*, "to proclaim good news," 61:1c) to קרא (*qrʾ*, "to proclaim" or "to announce"). He repeats this theme, explicitly or implicitly, three additional times in 61:1, 2.

[45] So Oswalt, *Isaiah*, 2:565; Watts, *Isaiah 34–66*, 873.

[46] When שׁבה (*šbh*) occurs as a *qal* active participle (1 Kgs 8:46, 47, 50; 2 Chr 6:36; 30:9; Pss 106:46; 137:3; Is 14:2; Jer 50:33) it refers to a physical, political enemy who serves the role of captor or to those who carried someone away as captives.

[47] Watts, *Isaiah 34–66*, 873.

[48] MT's פְּקַח־קוֹחַ (*pĕqaḥ-qôaḥ*) is read as one word at Qumran (פקחקוח [*pqḥqwḥ*], 1QIsaᵃ). See Watts, *Isaiah 34–66*, 870.

[49] Here, again, the context of the reference in Is 49:9 is one of a future, eschatological restoration of the faithful remnant of Israel.

amid covenant infidelity, but in its Isaianic context, "favor" (רָצוֹן; rāṣôn) recalls two particularly pertinent texts.

First is one of eschatological restoration:

> Thus says the LORD, "In a favorable time [בְּעֵת רָצוֹן; bĕ'ēṯ rāṣôn] I have answered You, And in a day of salvation I have helped You; And I will keep You and give You for a covenant of the people, To restore the land, to make *them* inherit the desolate heritages." (Is 49:8)

Second, Isaiah recalls an unacceptable time made so by wanting cultic practices:

> "Is it a fast like this which I choose, a day for a man to humble himself? Is it for bowing ones head like a reed, And for spreading out sackcloth and ashes as a bed? Will you call this a fast, even an acceptable day to the LORD?" (וְיוֹם רָצוֹן לַיהוָה; wĕyôm rāṣôn layhwh) (Is 58:5)

The statement in Is 61:2a, then, is drawing on terminology that decidedly contrasts the unacceptable time based on the activity of God's people from a context with which Luke has already drawn connection in his citation (Is 58:5; cf. 60:7) with a favorable time in which God himself is the active agent in the restoration of his people (Is 49:8).

Here is where Luke's citation from Isaiah ends. Yet Is 61 continues additional purposes for the anointing, including the proclamation of a day of vengeance[50] for our God (61:2b), an antithetical parallelism with "year of . . . favor," and completing the dual nature to this day. Possible explanations for Luke's omission of the vengeance will be considered below. For the present, it is important to note that the role of the anointed speaker—whoever he may be—as rendered in Luke, is exclusively one of proclamation (61:1c, e, f, 2a). That is, the purpose of the anointing on this figure as Luke employs it is one of proclamation or announcement.

Luke draws from Isaianic contexts where eschatological restoration for God's people in exile is in view. The first (58:6) looks for a redemptive activity of loosening bonds in the thick of a context of Israel's utter iniquity. The second (61:1–2), on the lips of an ambiguous figure, makes a proclamation pertaining to an eschatological redemption for God's captive people. Both employ language of Jubilee redemption and restoration, which is expanded upon in several OT and early Jewish texts. In its OT context (Lv 25:8–55; cf. Lv 27:16–21; Nm 36:1–9), the Jubilee Year[51] pertained to the

---

[50] "Vengeance" (נָקָם; nāqām) is found most often in Isaiah (Is 34:8; 35:4; 47:3; 59:17; 61:2; 63:4) in the context of God executing judgment in his covenant lawsuit against the unfaithful among his people (six out of seventeen occurrences in the MT).

[51] Though Lv 25:10 suggests it is the "fiftieth year," it is often understood as a full year after the seventh sabbatical year. Michael A. Harbin, "The Manumission of Slaves in Jubilee and Sabbath Years," *TynBul* 63/1 (2012): 68; Baruch A. Levine, *Leviticus* (Philadelphia: JPS, 1989), 130; J. Milgrom, *Leviticus 23–27* (AB 3B; New York: Doubleday, 2001), 2163.

restoration of land that was sold,[52] people returning home (Lv 25:10, 13), rest (Lv 25:11–12), holiness (Lv 25:12), and inheritance (Nm 36:4). But, predominantly, the Year of Jubilee is mentioned in the thematic context of redemption, or release from an undesired captivity or ownership (Lv 25:28, 30, 31, 33, 40, 54; 27:21, 24). Yet the biblical development of the concept transcends pentateuchal law. Elsewhere in the OT, Jeremiah employs the related conception of "redemption" (גְּאֻלָּה [gĕ'ullā], Jer 32:1–15) for the return from exile and a final eschatological state (Ez 46:16–18; cf. Ez 40:10).[53] Its first messianic reinterpretation may be Is 61:1–3 (cf. Is 49:7–9),[54] where the prophet looks not backwards to financial transactions but forward to restoration, where the enigmatic figure "will proclaim and inaugurate a new age characterized by the freedom and restoration of the jubilee year."[55] We will see that the appropriation of Jubilee legislation is enhanced in early Judaism. Yet prior to examining the concept of Jubilee in these texts, we must examine the matrix through which the disparate writings of early Judaism interpreted the Isaianic texts (Is 58:6; 61:1–2).

Use of Isaiah 58:6 and Isaiah 61:1–2 in Early Judaism

Though Is 58:6 is not explicitly cited in early Judaism, an illuminating use of Is 61 is found in a document from Qumran, 11Q13 (= 11QMelch), best dated to the middle of the first century B.C.[56] Scholars have long recognized affinities between 11QMelch and Is 61.[57] M. Miller posits that the

---

[52] It was, as Harbin describes, a means by which a person in financial distress could "sell" (Harbin suggests it is more correct to say the land was "leased") his land in anticipation of its restoration at the next Jubilee.

[53] John Sietze Bergsma, *The Jubilee from Leviticus to Qumran* (VTSup 115; Leiden: Brill, 2006), 203.

[54] Bergsma, *Jubilee from Leviticus to Qumran*, 202.

[55] Bergsma, *Jubilee from Leviticus to Qumran*, 203. Bergsma also cites Dn 9:24–27 (see also Jer 25:11; 29:10; 2 Chr 26:20–21) where, after a prayer of confession, Daniel receives from Gabriel the announcement of a restoration of Jerusalem and the advent of the messiah in a period of "seventy weeks" (490 years; 10 Jubilees) followed by an implicit "inauguration of an eschatological jubilee year" (cf. Jer 29:12–13; Lv 25:39–42). Bergsma, *Jubilee from Leviticus to Qumran*, 232.

[56] Cf. É. Puech, "Notes sur le manuscript de XIQMelkîsédeq," *RevQ* 12 (1985–1987): 483–84 nn. 2–4; J. J. M. Roberts, "Melchizedek (11Q13 = 11QMelchizedek = 11QMelch)," in *Pesharim, Other Commentaries, and Related Documents* (PTSDSS 6B; Tübingen: Mohr Siebeck, 1994), 264. It is unclear whether the one to whom the text is applied is Melchizedek (lines 5, 8, 9) or to the Teacher of Righteousness, to whom the Qumran texts characteristically apply such redemptive qualities (see esp. 1QH 18:14; see also 1QH 7:6–7; 9:32; 12:12; 16:2, 3, 7, 10, 12).

[57] Y. Yadin, "A Note on Melchizedek and Qumran," *IEJ* 15 (1965): 152–54; M. de Jonge and A. S. van der Woude, "11QMelchizedek and the New Testament," *NTS* 12 (1965–1966): 301–26; J. A. Fitzmyer, "Further Light on Melchizedek from Qumran Cave 11," *JBL* 86 (1967): 25–41.

various citations from the HB in 11QMelch (Lv 25:13; Dt 15:2; Is 52:7; Pss 7:8–9; 82:1–2) are each related to Is 61:1–2, a text that "stands behind" 11QMelch as the linchpin of sorts to the *yaḥad's* self-identity in the end of days.[58]

The author begins with an interpretation of the Jubilee Year "for the latter days" (11Q13 ii 2a, citing Lv 25:13)[59] or of the tenth and final "Jubilee" (line 7). Melchizedek will proclaim emancipation (וקרא להמה דרור [*wqr' lhmh drwr*], 11Q13 ii 4–6; Is 61:1e) for those who are captives (השבויים; *hšbwyym*) to the burdens of sin (line 6; Is 61:1e).[60] Yet there will also be judgment (lines 10–13; Is 61:2b). All this will occur in a year of favor (לשנת הרצון [*lšnt hrṣwn*], line 9; Is 61:2a).[61] As Timothy Lim has observed, debates regarding whether Lv 25 or Is 61 is the main passage behind this text are unnecessary, as both are essential to the text.[62] This indicates that even prior to the composition of the Lukan account, Jews of the Second Temple period were recognizing the connection between the Levitical Jubilee and the Isaianic proclamation. Moreover, the text in 11QMelch is explicit about the identity of the central figure as an eschatological deliverer for God's people.[63]

Isaiah 61 is also referenced at Qumran in the so-called Messianic Apocalypse from Qumran (4Q521), where the activities of Is 61:1 are clearly carried out in a richly eschatological context by the Lord himself through the "agency" of the messiah:[64]

---

[58] M. Miller, "The Function of Isa. 61:1–2 in 11Q Melchizedek," *JBL* 88 (1969): 467–69 (467).

[59] The text is from PTSDSS 6B; the translation is from there also, with my own modifications.

[60] In 11QMelch, they are the "inheritance of Melchizedek" (מנחלת מלבי צדק; *mnḥlt mlby ṣdq*), perhaps a priestly inheritance (cf. Jo 18:7; 1QapGen 22:14). Fitzmyer, "Further Light," 34.

[61] This is a curious reading. It clearly draws from Is 61, yet the Isaianic reference is favor of the Lord (ליהוה; *layhwh*) (61:2). In Lv 25:10 דְּרוֹר (*děrôr*) is equated with יוֹבֵל (*yôḇēl*), prompting the Qumran script to link Lv 25:13 to Is 61:1–2. Roberts, "Melchizedek," 267 n. 4.

[62] Timothy H. Lim, "11QMelch, Luke 4, and the Dying Messiah," *JJS* 43 (1992): 90 n. 8; 11QMelch makes yet another important intertextual connection in Isaiah, here with the herald of Is 52:7. Lim suggests 11QMelch's exposition of Is 52:7 (11Q13 i 17ff) identifies the "herald" (מבשר [*mbšr*], Is 52:7; 11Q13 i 18) as "the anointed of the spirit" ([הונ]אה מ[שוח הרו[ח]; *hw['h m]šwḥ hrw[ḥ]*), associating him with the messiah prince of Dn 9.25 (מָשִׁיחַ נָגִיד; *māšîaḥ nāgîd*). What is striking here is 11Q13's association of the prince/messiah of Dn 9 with the herald of Is 52.7. It is the latter who is said to comfort the mourners of Zion (Is 61:2–3; 11Q13 i 20). Lim, "11QMelch, Luke 4, and the Dying Messiah," 91–92.

[63] Though his identity at Qumran, Melchizedek, is hardly less allusive than in Is 61:1.

[64] This is distinct from the view of Michael O. Wise and James D. Tabor ("The Messiah at Qumran," *BAR* 18/6 [1992]: 60–65), who reconstruct line 12 in such a manner as to distinguish between the agency of God and that of the messiah, which Collins suggests is unwarranted.

and the Lord shall do glorious things which have not been done, just as He said. For He shall heal the critically wounded, He shall revive the dead, *He shall send good news to the afflicted* (ענוים יבשר [*ʿnwym ybšr*]; Is 61:1), He shall sati[sfy the poo]r, He shall guide the uprooted, He shall make the hungry rich, and [. . .] disc[erning ones . . .] and all of them as the ho[ly ones . . .] and [. . .]. (4Q521 f2+4 ii 11–15 WAC)

The works of the messiah also correlate rather closely with aspects of Is 61,[65] particularly in lines 8 (releasing captives, giving sight to the blind) and 12 (healing, preaching good news to the poor). While no further explicit citations are extant from the Second Temple period,[66] messianic claimants employed aspects of Is 61. For instance, Josephus mentions a certain Simon bar Giora (Aramaic: בר גיורא [*br gywrʾ*], "son of the pros-elyte") who indicates, among other things, that his military insurrec-tion was accompanied "by proclaiming liberty for slaves and rewards for the free" (προκηρύξας δούλοις μὲν ἐλευθερίαν γέρας δὲ ἐλευθέροις τοὺς πανταχόθεν πονηροὺς συνήθροιζεν; *prokēryxas doulois men eleuthe-rian geras de eleutherois tous pantachothen ponērous synēthroizen; B.J.* 4.9.3 [§508] LCL).[67] Michael Bird further observes the heightened importance for those who perceived themselves as enslaved[68] and in quest of liberty.[69] For example, 2 Maccabees contains this exhortation: "Gather together our scattered people, set free those who are slaves among the Gentiles, look upon those who are rejected and despised, and let the Gentiles know that thou art our God" (2 Mc 1:27 RSV).

Within its Second Temple context, the appropriation of Is 61:1–2 finds explicit correlation with the Levitical Jubilee that is cast in

---

[65] John J. Collins, "The Works of the Messiah," *DSD* 1 (1994): 98–112.

[66] Later rabbinic interpretations are too late for influence here but bear men-tioning nonetheless. Some identify the Isaianic speaker as prophetic. *Targum Isa-iah* 61:1 adds אמר נביא (*ʾmr nbyʾ*) "the prophet said"; cf. *Midr. Lam.* 3:49–50, 59; Bruce D. Chilton, *Glory of Israel: The Theology and Provenience of the Isaiah Targum* (JSOTSup 23; Sheffield: JSOT Press, 1982), 52–56. Others cite Is 61 in reference to a general anointing of God's prophets (*Midr. Lev.* 10:2) or, more specifically, to the comforting ministry of Isaiah (*Pesiq. Rab.* 29/30A.5). This verse is also cited as one of three places where the Holy Spirit is mentioned in connection with redemp-tion (*Midr. Lam.* 3:49–50; cf. *b. ʿAbod. Zar.* 20; *Midr. Exod.* 15:23). *Testament of Levi* 17:1–11 indicates the years of Jubilees that will establish a messianic priest-hood, though the questionable provenance of this work inhibits its applicability to our analysis.

[67] Michael F. Bird, *Are You the One Who Is to Come? The Historical Jesus and the Messianic Question* (Grand Rapids: Baker, 2009), 51.

[68] Ez 9:8–10; Neh 9:36; Jdt 8:22–23; Add Est 14:8; 2 Mc 1:27; Josephus *B.J.* 5.9.4 (§§395–96); *A.J.* 18.1.1 (§4).

[69] Is 45:13; 61:1; Jer 34:8, 15; 1 Mc 10:13; 2 Mc 1:27; *4 Ezr* 12:34; Josephus *B.J.* 2.13.4 (§259); 5.16.4 (§396); *T. Jud.* 23:5; *T. Zeb.* 9:8; *Pss. Sol.* 11:1–9. Bird, *Are You the One?* 51; *1 En.* 48:4; Mark Adam Elliott, *The Survivors of Israel: A Reconsideration of the Theology of Pre-Christian Judaism* (Grand Rapids: Eerdmans, 2000), 497.

an eschatological outlook focusing on a messianic figure. This finds
congruence with other early Jewish texts,[70] where the "jubilee" becomes
a unit of time into which epochs of redemptive history are divided in a
solar calendar system.[71] The end of this Jubilee cycle constitutes the (future) entry into Canaan (*Jub.* 50:4–5; cf. *T. Levi* 14–18).[72] For such texts
the Jubilee charts Israel's redemptive history, at the end of which Israel
is "portrayed as experiencing liberation and restitution."[73] Similarly, at
Qumran biblical history is divided into Jubilee cycles (1Q21; 4Q181; cf.
4Q379), sometimes measuring from the time of the exile to the eschaton
in a final Jubilaic formulation (4Q385a, 4Q387, 4Q390; 11Q13).[74] In the
tenth and final Jubilee the sons of God and the people of Melchizedek's lot
will receive atonement (11Q13 ii 7–9, 25; cf. 4Q389 2; Lv 25:9).[75] After its
Levitical inception, through the prophets and early Jewish texts, the Jubilee is "spiritualized" into units of time of redemptive history culminating
in a final eschatological release and restoration. Perhaps what Luke does
with it, then, in combination with Is 58:6, is not entirely unexpected. Yet
what is unique is that in the Lukan context Jesus claims the fulfillment of
this anticipated conflation in himself.

Use of Isaiah 58:6 and 61:1–2a in Luke 4

Analysis of the Broad NT Context

In its NT context the Gospel of Luke contains a number of unique
features that are exhibited both in the Lukan pericope itself (Lk 4:16–
21) and in the context leading up to it (Lk 1:1–4:15). For example,
whereas Matthew's interest is directed to Israel (Mt 2:6; 10:6; 15:24),
Luke looks to the implications of the gospel more broadly to include
Gentiles. Simeon foresees Jesus as a light for revelation to Gentiles (Lk
2:32). Whereas Mark (1:3) and Matthew (3:3) both cite Is 40:3 in reference to John the Baptist as the voice of one calling out in the wilderness,
Luke alone (Lk 4:4–6) continues the Isaianic citation (Is 40:3–5) indicating that "all flesh shall see the salvation of God" (Lk 3:6). Furthermore,
Luke has regard for otherwise negative categories of people, such as Sa-
maritans (9:54; 10:25–37; 17:11–19), tax collectors (18:9–14; 19:1–10),
and the repentant thief on the cross (23:39). He is concerned with marginalized people, such as women (2:25–38; 7:36–50; 8:1–3; 10:38–42)

---

[70] Bergsma, *Jubilee from Leviticus to Qumran.*
[71] See Johann Maier, "Religious Beliefs, Qumran Sect," *EDSS*, 2:754.
[72] M. Testuz, *Les Idées religieuses du livre des Jubilés* (Geneva: E. Droz, 1960).
[73] Bergsma, *Jubilee from Leviticus to Qumran*, 249. Yet their respective chro-
nologies defy harmonization.
[74] Bergsma, *Jubilee from Leviticus to Qumran*, 293.
[75] James C. VanderKam, "Yom Kippur," *EDSS*, 2:1002.

and the poor (1:53; 6:20; 21:1–3; cf. 14:7–24; 16:19–31). Finally, Luke alone notes that Jesus is full of the Spirit as the Spirit leads him into the wilderness temptation (Lk 4:1) and that his public ministry begins in the power of the Spirit (4:14; see also 1:15, 41; 10:21–22; 24:49; Acts 2:4; 4:31).

In our context Jesus returns to Galilee "in the power of the Spirit" (4:14) and begins teaching in "their synagogues and was praised by all" (4:15). Luke 4:14–15 serves as a broad summary, while 4:31–44 illustrates specific examples of him carrying out his role in public ministry through healings and service. Luke 4:16–30 bears some distinct wording from its Synoptic parallels (Mk 6:1–6a; Mt 13:53–58; Aland §33). I. Howard Marshall observes that Mark's placement of the story occurs considerably later in his Gospel, suggesting that Luke's placement of it here is because of its "programmatic significance" and its contents of "many of the main themes of Lk-Acts *in nuce.*"[76] It is "a representative sample of Jesus' ministry, a paradigm for his ministry."[77]

Jesus comes to to Nazareth (16a) where he had been brought up (cf. 1:26; 2:4, 39–40, 51–52). It is not immediately clear whether Jesus' custom (κατὰ τὸ εἰωθὸς αὐτῷ; *kata to eiōthos autō*) was teaching in the synagogue,[78] attending the synagogue and teaching,[79] or generally going to the synagogue on the Sabbath.[80] The location of the prepositional phrase suggests attendance at the synagogue on the Sabbath.[81] Readers are then given a (unique) glimpse into its activities: Jesus stands in order to read.[82] Then he is handed the scroll of the prophet Isaiah (v. 17) and finds the text for his reading (vv. 18–19).

---

[76] Marshall, *Luke*, 177–78. Similarly Joel B. Green, *The Gospel of Luke* (NICNT; Grand Rapids: Eerdmans, 1997), 207.

[77] Cf. Darrell L. Bock, *Luke* (BECNT; 2 vols.; Grand Rapids: Baker, 1994, 1996), 1:394; J. A. Fitzmyer, *The Gospel of Luke I–IX: Introduction, Translation, and Notes* (AB 28; New York: Doubleday, 1982), 529.

[78] John Nolland, *Luke 1–9:20* (WBC 35A; Dallas: Word, 1989), 195.

[79] Green, *Luke*, 209.

[80] Robert H. Stein, *Luke* (NAC 24; Nashville: B&H, 1992), 155; Fitzmyer, *Luke*, 530; E. Earle Ellis, *The Gospel of Luke* (London: Nelson, 1966), 97; Bock, *Luke*, 1:402.

[81] Perhaps this is in keeping with a Lukan motif of "to the Jews first" (Acts 13:46; cf. 18:6; 26:20; 28:28; Fitzmyer, *Luke*, 529).

[82] This is the earliest account of a synagogue service (P. Billerbeck, "Ein Synagogengottesdienst in Iesu Tagen," *ZNW* 55 [1964]: 143–61; E. Schürer, *History of the Jewish People in the Age of Jesus Christ* [ed. M. Black et al.; 2 vols; Edinburgh: T&T Clark, 1984], 2:447–63). The precise order of service is otherwise only attested earliest in the Mishnah, where one finds that it was common for a reading of the Torah (in Heb.) in a standing position, followed by an Aramaic paraphrase (Neh 8:8–9; Acts 13:15, 27; 15:21; *m. Meg.* 4:1–5, 10). A reading from the prophets then followed (*m. Meg.* 4:1–2; *b. Meg.* 31a–b; Bock, *Luke*, 1:404).

Exegesis of Luke 4:18–19

Luke follows the LXX at the outset of his quotation (4:18a, πνεῦμα κυρίου ἐπ᾽ ἐμέ; *pneuma kyriou ep᾽ eme*, Is 61:1a).[83] As in the Isaianic context, the identity of the speaker as appropriated in Luke is likewise contested. For some, the speaker is a prophet,[84] a priestly messiah,[85] a servant with messianic connotations,[86] a merger of an eschatological prophet with a messiah, [87] or a messiah with "prophetic characteristics."[88] Joseph Fitzmyer advocates a prophetic reading in recognition that prophets were considered anointed servants of the Lord (citing CD 2:12; 6:1; 6QD 3:4)[89] and the "herald" of good news (מְבַשֵּׂר; *mĕbaśśēr*, Is 52:7), who can also be anointed with the Spirit (11QMelch 2:13).[90] As we have seen, the presence of the Spirit upon a figure may only suggest the person is one in leadership for an appointed task of deliverance for God's covenant people, such as elders (Nm 11:25, 29), judges (Jgs 3:10; 11:29), prophets (1 Kgs 19:12; 2 Kgs 2:16), and kings (1 Sm 10:6; 16:14). Yet it may not identify the person so endowed. So the Spirit's presence empowers the figure for his task but in itself does not clarify the identity of the figure or the task for which he is empowered. To establish the identity of the speaker, both in Isaiah and Luke, one must identify the purpose for the Spirit's presence and the outcome(s) it achieves.

Luke's citation of Isaiah is explicit about indicating the reason of the Spirit's presence, followed by purposes or intended outcomes, which cumulatively serve to identify the speaker. The reason the Spirit is upon the speaker is the anointing of the Lord upon him (4:18b, οὗ εἵνεκεν ἔχρισέν με; *hou heineken echrisen me*, Is 61:1b).[91] While figures such as priests or

---

[83] See also 1QIsaᵃ, 1QIsaᵇ. MT reads רוּחַ אֲדֹנָי יְהוִה עָלָי (*rûaḥ ʾăḏōnāy yhwh ʿālāy*) (so also 4QIsaᵐ). The NT reading varies only in the Syriac.

[84] James D. G. Dunn, "Messianic Ideas and Their Influence on the Jesus of History," in *The Messiah: Developments in Earliest Judaism and Christianity* (ed. James H. Charlesworth; Minneapolis: Fortress, 1992), 378.

[85] William H. Brownlee, "Messianic Motifs of Qumran and the New Testament," *NTS* 3/3 (1957): 195–210.

[86] Ellis, *Luke*, 97; E. Earle Ellis, *Eschatology in Luke* (ed. John Reumann; Biblical Series 30; Philadelphia: Fortress, 1972), xiii, 1–20.

[87] Marshall, *Luke*, 128.

[88] Bovon, *Luke*, 154.

[89] Fitzmyer, *Luke*, 529–30.

[90] Fitzmyer, *Luke*, 530, suggests the anointed figure is someone other than a political or kingly individual, which, he posits, accounts for the comparison to Elijah and Elisha later in the scene.

[91] The text exhibits slight variation in the Syr (σε [*se*] [ܠܝܟ; *ʾlyk*] for με [*me*] in Syrˢ) and some distinction in spelling, such as ἔνεκεν (*eneken*) for εἵνεκεν (*heineken*) (1346 τ) or ἔχρεισέν (*echreisen*) (B A D L) or ἔχρισέι (*echrisei*) (1346) for the more common ἔχρισεν (*echrisen*) (Δ 33 700 579 τ u w rell). The reading is Septuagintal from Is 61:1b. The MT's יַעַן מָשַׁח יְהוָה אֹתִי (*yaʿan māšah yhwh ʾōtî*) inserts the subject יהוה (*yhwh*) (so also Origen, Aq., and Theod., κύριος [*kurios*]). Luke's account, fol-

prophets may be anointed, only a king is anointed by the Lord (1 Sm 10:1; 2 Sm 12:7; 2 Kgs 9:3, 6, 12; Pss 45:7; 89:20). Furthermore, in the Isaianic context the anointed figure is directed and characterized by both the will (9:5[6]; 11:2; 40:13–14; 50:4) and the enabling power (9:5[6]; 11:4; 42:4; 49:5; 50:9) of YHWH.[92]

Here Luke, following his Isaianic source, enumerates a set of purposes for this anointing.[93] The first purpose for the anointing is to preach good news to the poor (4:18c, εὐαγγελίσασθαι πτωχοῖς; *euangelisasthai ptōchois*, Is 61:1c).[94] As we have seen, in its Isaianic context such proclamations connote hope of deliverance (Is 40:9; 41:27; 52:7; 60:6) and eschatological restoration (Is 52:7). The poor (πτωχός; *ptochos*) is a classification of people exploited by others but whose plight is not unnoticed by God. The poor are among those who are exploited by Israel's wayward leadership (Is 3:14), taken advantage of in their state of helplessness (3:15), and robbed of their rights (10:2; cf. 58:7). Yet they will have God himself as their advocate, providing them with provisions and security (14:30; 41:17; 61:1), and in turn offer praise to God (25:3; 29:19). In Luke's context, the πτωχός (*ptochos*) are recipients of the proclamation of good news (4:18; 7:22). They are compared with the prophets in terms of condemnation by people but future rewards in heaven (6:20, 23). They are contrasted with the rich (6:24) who, like false prophets, are in danger of judgment (6:25–26; cf. 16:20, 22). They are among those who are to be included in celebratory banquets (14:13, 21; cf. 18:22; 19:8), who are to experience vindication at the "day of the Lord" (Is 11:4; 29:19; 32:7; Am 2:7; 8:4; Zep 2:3).[95] Luke's inclusion of "He has sent me" (ἀπέσταλκέν με; *apestalken me*)[96] indicates

---

lowing the LXX, renders the preposition יַעַן (*ya'an*) with εἵνεκεν (*heineken*) and inserts a relative pronoun οὗ (*hou*). Aquila and Sym. read διότι (*dioti*); Theod. reads ἀνθ᾽ ὧν (*anth hōn*). Aquila and Theod. render the verb ἤλειψέ (*ēleipse*).

[92] So Oswalt, *Isaiah*, 2:564.

[93] So R. T. France, *Jesus and the Old Testament* (Vancouver: Regent, 1998), 149.

[94] MS τ spells the infinitive εὐαγγελίζεσθαι (*euangelizesthai*). The reading εὐαγγελίσασθαι πτωχοῖς, ἀπέσταλκέν με (*euangelisasthai ptōchois, apestalken me*) is adopted by UBS[4] NA[27] SBLGNT and supported by א B D L W C *f*[13] 33 579* 700 892* it[a, aur, b, c, d, ff2, 1, q, r1] vg[ww, st] syr[s] cop[sa, bo] arm eth Origen[gr, lat] Peter-Alexandria Eusebius Didymus Nestorius Ambrose Jerome Augustine; με (*me*) is omitted in D*. LXX א* reads ταπεινοις (*tapeinois*) also Q[mg] Sa Syh[mg]. MT reads לְבַשֵּׂר עֲנָוִים (*lĕbaśśēr 'ănāwîm*).

[95] In Judaism the poor were seen as a class of socioeconomic depression whose condition not only will cease in the eschaton (*Sib. Or.* 3:378; *T. Jud.* 25:4) but also will be in conflict with the rich and eventually be elevated above them (*4 Esd.* 14:13; *Jub.* 23:19).

[96] Luke's reading is Septuagintal (Is 61:1c, MT שְׁלָחַנִי [*šĕlāhanî*]). The common ἀπέσταλκεν (*apestalken*) is spelled ἀπέσταιλμαι (*apestailmai*) (D*) or ἀπέστελκέν (*apestelken*) (1071). I follow Marshall (*Luke*, 183), who observes the disputed punctuation in v. 18c. Some put a period after πτωχοῖς (*ptochois*) so that εὐαγγελίσασθαι (*euangelisasthai*) is dependent on ἔχρισεν (*echrisen*) (UBS[4]), while others place it after με (*me*), so that εὐαγγελίσασθαι (*euangelisasthai*) is dependent

the mission or purpose of the one sent, presumably as a messenger or envoy of the One sending (cf. 1:19, 26; 4:43; 7:27; 9:2).[97]

Both the LXX and MT of Is 61:1d continue a quotation, "to bind up the broken-hearted,"[98] omitted here by Luke. There is no consensus on the reason for the omission. Some suggest its absence in Luke's copy of the LXX, means that Luke reserves ἰάομαι (iaomai) for physical healings,[99] or that Luke offers a "targumic reading" of Is 61.[100] Others posit that it was originally present,[101] but they fail to account for its omission. Perhaps the Isaianic context provides some guidance. For in Is 61, the purpose of the anointing is both proclamation (61:1c, e, f, 2a) and binding up (61:1d). Yet Luke's citation omits the reference to "binding up" (61:1d). What is left, then, is that Luke draws on Is 61:1–2 exclusively for the proclamatory role of the speaker. Luke is concerned with the actual acts of deliverance themselves, but he draws that not from Is 61 but Is 58, as we will see below.

The second purpose for the anointing is "to proclaim release to the captives" (4:18d, κηρύξαι αἰχμαλώτοις ἄφεσιν; kēryxai aichmalōtois aphesin, Is 61:1e).[102] Again Luke draws from a prophetic proclamation of deliverance (cf. Jer 34:8). Luke's αἰχμαλώτοις (aichmalōtois) refers to prisoners of war or captives in exile (Nm 21:29; Ex 2:6; Tb 7:3; 13:12; 1 Mc 2:9; Jb 12:17, 19; 41:24; Am 6:7; 7:11, 17; Na 3:10; Is 5:13; 14:2; 23:1; 46:2; 52:2; Ep Jer 1:1; Ez 12:4; 30:18). As we observed above, the Isaianic proclamation is verbatim from the Levitical proclamation of liberty at the Year of Jubilee (Lv 25:10). In Luke-Acts, such release (ἄφεσιν; aphesin) is used exclusively in reference to those who are captive to sin as a release, or to forgiveness, from that state of captivity (Lk 1:77; 3:3; 7:47; 24:47; Acts 2:38; 5:31; 10:43; 13:38; 26:18).[103]

---

on ἀπέσταλκεν (apestalken) (NEB; JB; E. Nestle, "Luc 4, 18:19," ZNW 2 [1901]: 153–57). Marshall favors the latter for its agreement with the MT and LXX and coherence with Luke's interpretation of the quotation in 4:43.

[97] Alfred Plummer, A Critical and Exegetical Commentary on the Gospel According to St. Luke (ICC; 5th ed.; Edinburgh: T&T Clark, 1922), 121.

[98] ἰάσασθαι τοὺς συντετριμμένους τῇ καρδίᾳ (iasasthai tous syntetrimmenous tē kardia); לַחֲבֹשׁ לְנִשְׁבְּרֵי־לֵב (laḥăḇōš lĕnišbĕrê-lēḇ).

[99] T. Holtz, Untersuchungen über die alttestamentliche Zitate bei Lukas (Akademie: Berlin, 1968), 40.

[100] Bock, Luke, 1:404.

[101] For contextual reasons (cf. Lk 4:4; H. Schürmann, Das Lukasevangelium [HTKNT; 2 vols.; Freiburg: Herder, 1969], 1:229 n. 58) or its symmetrical rhythm (Bo Reicke, "Jesus in Nazareth—Lk 4,14–30," in Das Wort und die Wörter: Festschrift Gerhard Friedrich [ed. H. Balz and S. Schulz; Stuttgart: Kohlhammer, 1973], 48–49).

[102] Significant manuscripts (B D*c L W f13 33 579 700 u w) omit κηρύξαι αἰχμαλώτοις ἄφεσιν καὶ τυφλοῖς ἀνάβλεψιν (kēryxai aichmalōtois aphesin kai typhlois anablepsin).

[103] See also B. Charette, "'To Proclaim Liberty to the Captives': Matthew 11:28–30 in the Light of OT Prophetic Expectation," NTS 38/2 (1992): 290–97.

The third purpose for the anointing is to proclaim "recovery of sight for the blind" (Lk 4:18e, καὶ τυφλοῖς[104] ἀνάβλεψιν[105]; *kai typhlois anablepsin*, Is 61:1–2). Luke, following the LXX, is distinct from the MT, which reads "freedom to prisoners."[106] The LXX exploits the mixed metaphor of פקח (*pqḥ*), [107] a term invariably used in the MT for the opening of eyes[108] with clear connotations of understanding, and in almost all instances it is God who is the active agent[109] either directly (e.g., Ps 146:8) or through the agency of his servant (e.g., Is 42:7a). Luke's adoption of the LXX rendering exploits the ambiguity for his own theological purposes and draws attention to his often unique concern for the eschatological significance of Jesus' concern for the blind. Though what may come immediately to mind is Jesus' healing of the physically blind (7:21–22; 18:35–43), it should be taken in its more metaphorical sense of a healing from spiritual blindness, a parallel concept that Luke has already joined (1:77–80) and that he will refer to again (6:39; 8:10; 10:23–24; 18:41–43; cf. 4:33–41).[110]

Luke's emphasis on "blindness" finds expression elsewhere in his Gospel, such as in his parable of the blind man leading a blind man (Lk 6:39; cf. Mt 15:14). Like the poor, the blind are included in Lukan eschatology among those invited to participate in eschatological bliss (Lk 14:7–14). Similarly, in Luke's account of the parable of the great supper (Lk 14:15–24; Mt 22:1–14; Aland §216), servants are not simply to invite "as many as you find" (Mt 2:9 RSV) or "all whom they found, both good and bad" (Mt 22:10 RSV), as in Matthew, but "the poor and maimed and blind and lame" (Lk 14:21). While all the Synoptics report the healing of blind

---

[104] For Luke's τυφλοῖς (*typhlois*), Aq., Sym., and Theod. read τυφλοῖς τοῖς δεδεμένοις (*typhlois tois dedemenois*).

[105] For ἀναβεψιν (*anabepsin*), Aq. reads διάβλεψιν (*diablepsin*), Sym. reads ἀπόλυσιν (*apolysin*), Theod. διάνοιξιν (*dianoixin*).

[106] וְלַאֲסוּרִים פְּקַח־קוֹחַ (*wĕlāăsûrîm pĕqaḥ-qôaḥ*); followed by LXX (Sym., Theod.), the Latin, the Syr, and the Tg.

[107] For the verb פקח (*pqḥ*), LXX renders it most commonly with ἀνοίγω (*anoigō*) (Gn 21:19; 4 Kgs 19:16; Is 35:5; 37:17[B]; 42:7, 20). The LXX choice of ἀνάβλεψις (*anablepsis*) is unique in that it occurs only at Is 61:1 in the entire LXX. Strikingly, neither in Hebrew nor in the cognate languages is there evidence for its use for opening doors or prisons. The Hebrew is therefore a mixed metaphor; either we must see פקח (*pqḥ*) as used "figuratively as freeing from dark prison" (BDB), or we must see אסר (*'sr*) as figurative for "blind" (i.e., one whose eyes are bound). Either is unique. The Tg, sensing the difficulty, has produced a similar mixed metaphor in its version. See France, *Jesus and the Old Testament*, 252.

[108] Gn 3:5, 7; 21:19; 2 Kgs 4:35; 6:17, 20; 19:16; Jb 14:13; 27:19; Ps 146:8; Prv 20:13; Is 35:5; 37:17; 42:7; Jer 32:19.

[109] Once the reference is to opening of ears (Is 42:20), and once the request is made of God for his awareness (Dn 9:18; cf. Zec 12:4). In this reading, Luke varies from the MT connotation that alludes not to Jubilee but to sabbatical texts (Ex 21:2; Dt 15:1–11).

[110] G. K. Beale, *A New Testament Biblical Theology: The Unfolding of the Old Testament in the New* (Grand Rapids: Baker, 2011), 569. Similarly, Bock, *Luke*, 408; Green, *Luke*, 211.

Bartimaeus (Mt 20:29–34; Mk 10:46–52; Lk 18:35–43, though only Mark names him), only in Luke's account does the healed man not only follows Jesus (as in Mt 20:34; Mk 10:52) but also glorifies God, and a similar response is reported of witnesses (Lk 18:43; see also Acts 13:11). Perhaps the most important of these is in Lk 7:22, a text attested also in Matthew (11:3–5) but with some distinct features in Luke. Both Evangelists record the question of the imprisoned John the Baptist sending his disciples to inquire about the identity of Jesus as "he who is to come" (ὁ ἐρχόμενος; ho erchomenos, Mt 11:2–3; Lk 7:18–19). Luke's account alone has John's disciples repeat the question (7:20) and records Jesus' activities in that hour: "At that very time He cured many people of diseases and afflictions and evil spirits; and He granted sight to many who were blind" (7:21). Then both accounts report Jesus answering the disciples to go tell John what they have seen and heard: "the blind receive sight, the lame walk, the lepers are cleansed, and the deaf hear, the dead are raised up, the poor have the gospel preached to them" (7:22b). Luke's inclusion of the incidents of v. 21, absent in Matthew, heighten the association between Jesus' activities and his identity as the one to come. The healing of the blind in the OT context is done almost exclusively by YHWH himself or, as here, his Servant. As we will see, Luke conceives of Jesus, in his statement "Today this Scripture has been fulfilled in your hearing" (Lk 4:21), as the embodiment of both YHWH and the Servant.

The fourth purpose for the anointing is "to set free those who are downtrodden" (4:18–19; ἀποστεῖλαι τεθραυσμένους ἐν ἀφέσει; aposteilai tethrausmenous en aphesei).[111] This comes not from Is 61:1–2 but Is 58:6, which Luke follows (from the LXX) except that he renders its imperative (ἀπόστελλε; apostelle) as an infinitive (ἀποστεῖλαι; aposteilai), likely done to fit the phrase into the syntax of Is 61:1–2.[112] The insertion of the phrase from Is 58:6 seems to be linked to Is 61:1 by the common word ἄφεσις (aphesis), "liberty," rendered in the Hebrew by two distinct terms.[113] Presumably the inclusion of Is 58:6 contributes something not found in Is 61:1–2 alone.[114] As we observed above, Luke's citation of Is 61:1–2 employs only the proclamation role of the speaker and omits reference to the action of deliverance itself for which he turns in Is 58:6. That is, rather than Is 61's binding up of the broken-hearted, Luke looks to Is 58's

---

[111] Textual witness is consistent, except that D* reads τεθραυματισμένους (tethraumatismenous).

[112] Nolland, Luke, 193. The MT here reads וְשַׁלַּח רְצוּצִים חָפְשִׁים (wešallaḥ rĕṣûṣîm ḥāpĕšîm). Curiously, Luke's infinitive reflects more effectively the pi'el infinitive (שַׁלַּח; šallaḥ) of the MT. In the Isaianic context Hebrew infinitive absolutes are employed for all three verbs constituting the answer to the question of what kinds of fasts the Lord would choose (i.e., "I choose opening . . . loosing . . . sending"). Oswalt, Isaiah, 2:488, citing GKC §§113–14.

[113] Nolland, Luke, 193; Fitzmyer, Luke, 532.

[114] Pace Marshall, Luke, 184.

sending out in freedom of the oppressed (ἀποστεῖλαι τεθραυσμένους ἐν
ἀφέσει; *aposteilai tethrausmenous en aphesei*) for his appropriation of the
Isaianic function of Jesus in Lk 4. This cannot be done of a mere prophet,
and Jesus is clearly greater than a prophet in Luke's context (Lk 11:14–
23, 31–32; 18:38–39; 19:37–38).[115] These are activities of God alone (Is
40:9; 41:27; 51:16; 52:7)[116] and accomplished through Jesus' ministry,
specifically with regard to the binding power of Satan (Lk 13:10–17; Acts
10:38), the release from debts (Lk 11:4), and the forgiveness of sins (Lk
5:20–24; 7:47–50; cf. Lk 1:77).[117]

The fifth purpose for the anointing is to "to proclaim the favorable
year of the Lord" (Lk 4:19). Luke's reading[118] follows the LXX (Is 61:2a)
with one small adjustment;[119] he provides a rendering of the Hebrew לִקְרֹא
(*liqrōʾ*) with κηρύσσω (*kēryssō*) rather than the LXX καλέσαι (*kalesai*).[120]
The adjustment is unexpected, because of Luke's ten (eighteen total in
Luke-Acts) uses of the verb only one is unique to Luke's Gospel (24:47).
Much more common is καλέω (*kaleō*), which occurs forty-three times in
Luke (sixty-one in Luke-Acts). Moreover, LXX Isaiah uses καλέω (*kaleō*)
fifty-nine times but κηρύσσω (*kēryssō*) only once (61:1e). It seems that
Luke's unique adjustment in 4:19, while running contrary to extant LXX
witnesses, the predominance of the LXX Isaiah word usage, and even
his own Luke-Acts preferences, conforms the citation of Is 61:2a to that
of Is 61:1e just cited. Some suggest influence of the MT[121] or "Christian
affinities."[122] A more satisfactory explanation not only recognizes the
verb's suitability for preaching in Luke's context[123] but also underscores
the proclamatory role of the speaker for which Luke looks to Is 61 in
the first place. The object of what is proclaimed is the "favorable year
of the Lord" (ἐνιαυτὸν κυρίου δεκτόν; *eniauton kyriou dekton*).[124] As we
saw in the Isaianic context, such favor from the Lord resounds with a

---

[115] Bock, *Luke*, 1:409.

[116] Bock, *Luke*, 1:408 n. 29.

[117] So also Green, *Luke*, 211–12, citing Luke's use of the terms ἄφεσις (*aphesis*)
(Lk 1:77; 3:3; 24:47; Acts 2:38; 5:31; 10:43; 13:38; 26:18) and ἀφίημι (*aphiēmi*)
(Lk 5:20, 21, 23, 24; 7:47[twice], 48, 49; 11:4[twice]; 12:10; 17:3, 4; 23:34; Acts
8:22).

[118] κηρύξαι ἐνιαυτὸν κυρίου δεκτόν (*kēryxai eniauton kyriou dekton*).

[119] MT here reads: לִקְרֹא שְׁנַת־רָצוֹן לַיהוה (*liqrōʾ šěnat-rāṣôn layhwh*). MS 118 renders the dative κυρίῳ (*kyriō*) rather than the genitive κυρίου (*kyriou*). And MSS
579 and 1071 continue the MT's version of the Isaianic quotation καὶ ἡμέραν
ἀνταποδόσεως τῷ θεῷ ἡμῶν (*kai hēmeran antapodoseōs tō theō hēmōn*).

[120] The only exception (LXX MSS 534) influenced by Luke's reading of κηρύξαι
(*kēryxai*).

[121] France, *Jesus and the Old Testament*, 243.

[122] Marshall, *Luke*, 183.

[123] Nolland, *Luke*, 193; also Bock, *Luke*, 1:403.

[124] Throughout the Greek Bible, things said to be favorable (δεκτός; *dektos*)
with respect to the Lord (κύριος; *kyrios*) include Aaron's vestments (Ex 28:38),
particular offerings (Lv 1:3, 4; 17:4; 19:5; 22:19, 20, 21, 29; 23:11; cf. Phil 4:18),

favorable time in which God himself is the active agent in the restoration
of his people (Is 49:8–9; 60:7). In the NT, such favor (δεκτός; *dektos*) connotes the disclosure of God's end-time salvation (cf. Lk 4:24; Acts 10:35;
2 Cor 6:2; Phil 4:18), taken by some to also reference Jubilee legislation
(Lv 25).[125]

Here the Isaianic context continues ("and the day of vengeance of
our God," Is 61:2),[126] yet Luke's citation ends. Surely its omission accords
appropriately with Luke's eschatological outlook of present salvation and
future judgment.[127] The time of the Isaianic eschatological judgment of
God is not a primary facet of the present ministry of Jesus (9:51–56;
17:22–37; 21:5–37).[128]

Following Context (Luke 4:20–30)

Having completed the reading, Jesus next (v. 20) rolls up the scroll,
hands it to the attendant, and assumes the common teaching posture of
sitting (Lk 5:3; Mt 5:1; 23:2; 26:55; Mk 4:1).[129] Jesus now has the congregation's attention[130] and speaks (v. 21). Luke's ἤρξατο . . . λέγειν (*ērxato
. . . legein*) construction may suggest the beginning of Jesus' teaching
as a whole[131] but more likely suggests there is more to what Jesus says
than what is recorded, yet what is cited encapsulates its main point.[132]
Jesus' exposition, or what is recorded of it, is strikingly concise: "Today
this Scripture has been fulfilled (πεπλήρωται; *peplērōtai*) in your hearing" (4:21b). The location of Luke's σήμερον (*sēmeron*) may be emphatic,

---

just weights (Prv 11:1), truthful dealings (Prv 14:9), prayers of the upright (Prv
15:8, cf. 15:28; 16:7; 22:11; Jb 33:26).

[125] See Bock, *Luke*, 1:410; Similarly, Bovon, *Luke*, 154. It may function syn-
onomously with the "good news of the kingdom of God" seen in Lk 4:43 as a
declarative statement of the arrival of the kingdom of God. So Stein, *Luke*, 157.

[126] MT reads: וְיוֹם נָקָם לֵאלֹהֵינוּ לְנַחֵם כָּל־אֲבֵלִים (*wĕyôm nāqām lēʾlōhênû lĕnaḥēm
kol-ʾăbēlîm*). LXX has καὶ ἡμέραν ἀνταποδόσεως, παρακαλέσαι πάντας τοὺς
πενθοῦντας (*kai hēmeran antapodoseōs, parakalesai pantas tous penthountas*).

[127] Nolland, *Luke*, 198, citing E. Earle Ellis, "Present and Future Eschatology in
Luke," *NTS* 12 (1965–1966): 27–41. Similarly Fitzmyer, *Luke*, 532.

[128] Cf. Bock, *Luke*, 1:410. Jeremias, *Jesus' Promise*, 45, suggests its omission
is the basis for the ensuing hostilities, though judgment lies in the future. So also
Nolland, *Luke*, 198. See also E. Earle Ellis, "Eschatology in Luke," *NTS* 12 (1965–
1966): 27–41. Marshall's suggestion (*Luke*, 183) that the omission is done to stress
the grace of God overlooks the prevalent theme of judgment seen throughout the
Lukan corpus (11:29–32; 11:37–54; 12:46; 12:49–53; 12:57–59; 13:1–9).

[129] Schürer, *History of the Jewish People*, 1:453.

[130] Luke's ἀτενίζοντες (*atenizontes*) is an imperfect periphrastic form designating the continuous nature of their gaze upon Jesus (GGBB, 648) in anticipation
of his exposition. The term is one of amazement and anticipation (cf. Acts 1:10;
7:55; 13:9; 23:1).

[131] Marshall, *Luke*, 184–85.

[132] Nolland, *Luke*, 198.

congruent with the Evangelist's concern elsewhere for the immediate opportunity for salvation (2:11; 5:26; 12:28; 13:32–33; 19:5, 9; 22:34, 61; 23:43). The perfect passive verb from πληρόω (*pleroō*) occurs sixteen times in Luke-Acts, nine times in Luke alone.[133] Here it connotes the final accomplishment of an action or event predicted by an OT prophet. The accomplishment of this prediction is seen in either the personal identity or actions of Jesus (Lk 4:21; 24:44; Acts 3:18; 13:27). The perfect tense, though it denotes a completed sense to the fulfillment, also brings forth the concept that the effects of that fulfillment carry on into the present. The object of fulfillment is "this scripture" (ἡ γραφὴ αὕτη; *hē graphē hautē*), that is, this passage of Scripture. This fulfillment occurs quite literally in the presence of the congregation assembled there (ἐν τοῖς ὠσὶν ὑμῶν; *en tois ōsin hymōn*).[134] Jesus receives a generally positive (4:22) or at least curious (cf. Lk 11:38; see also Acts 4:13; 6:15) response.

The scene changes to one of hostility (vv. 23–29) with Jesus' confrontational proverb (v. 23) and an anticipated rejection (v. 24), directing his listeners' attention to an OT context of covenant infidelity (1 Kgs 17–18) where Gentiles—not Jews—receive God's blessings (see also Lk 2:30–32; 3:6). Elsewhere when Gentiles are included as benefactors of Jesus' messianic blessings, a similar response of rage ensues (Lk 20:15; Acts 6:9; 7:58). Yet their intent to do Jesus harm comes to nothing. Readers are left with a cryptic statement about Jesus passing through the angry mob (4:30). Presumably Jesus' role as the Isaianic herald and agent of God's salvation had not yet been completed (cf. Lk 22:53).

Synthesis and Conclusion

Luke's citation of Isaiah seems simple and concise at first sight. Yet upon careful examination it becomes clear that he provides readers with a masterfully crafted tapestry of carefully selected terminology to make his point at the outset of Jesus' public ministry in Luke's Gospel. The quotation contains the inclusion of Is 61:1–2, while excluding mention of binding up the broken-hearted and the day of vengeance. Included instead is proclamation of eschatological blessings for the people of God while pressing into service its particular affinities with the Jubilee Year. Yet where a function is omitted from Is 61, one is inserted from Is 58, where there is release of the captives (not merely the announcement of

---

[133] It can refer to the completion of an action (Lk 7:1; Acts 12:25; 13:25; 14:26), the passage of either a specified or unspecified period of time (Acts 7:23; 7:30; 9:23), to influence a person or persons with an idea (Acts 5:3, 38), a quality or feeling that indwells or fills up someone coupled with the filling of the Holy Spirit (Lk 2:40; Acts 2:28; 13:52) or the completion of an event predicted by Jesus (Lk 9:31).

[134] So Marshall, *Luke*, 185.

it). In this respect, Luke's selective appropriation of these texts depicts Jesus as both the herald (Is 61) and the one who releases captives (Is 58). In its Lukan context, its placement at the head of Jesus' public ministry provides a "programatic description of Jesus' task"[135] or "a manifesto setting out his programme."[136]

What brings the respective Isaianic texts together in Luke is their shared term ἄφεσις (*aphesis*) and their affinities with Jubilee legislation from Lv 25. The importance of this observation lies in its role in identifying the content that the proclaimer of Is 61 came to proclaim and the deliverer of Is 58 came to deliver. While Luke does not offer an extended Jubilaic theology,[137] his conflation of key Isaianic texts drawing collectively upon its imagery suggests that the eschatological restoration it entails begins at the inception of Jesus' ministry.[138] Later in Luke's Gospel, when John the Baptist is imprisoned and sends his disciples to Jesus, they ask if Jesus is the one whom they expected (Lk 7:20). In response Jesus does not offer an overt verbal answer but points to evidence from which the answer can be derived. This includes work of release ("the blind receive sight, the lame walk, the lepers are cleansed, and the deaf hear, the dead are raised up") and proclamation ("the poor have the gospel preached to them," Lk 7:22). The clear echo to the citation in Lk 4:18–19 and the citations therein place Jesus at the center of what Nolland calls Luke's "Isaianic collage."[139]

---

[135] Klyne Snodgrass, "The Use of the Old Testament in the New," in *The Right Doctrine from the Wrong Texts? Essays on the Use of the Old Testament in the New* (ed. G. K. Beale; Grand Rapids: Baker, 1994), 47.

[136] France, *Jesus and the Old Testament*, 134. Cf. C. H. Dodd, *According to the Scriptures: The Sub-Structure of New Testament Theology* (London: Nisbet, 1952), 52–53, 94.

[137] D. P. O'Brien, "A Comparison between Early Jewish and Early Christian Interpretations of the Jubilee Year," in *Historica, Biblica, Theologica et Philosophica*. vol. 1 of *Papers Presented at the Thirteenth International Conference on Patristic Studies Held in Oxford, 1999* (ed. M. F. Wiles, E. Yarnold, and P. M. Parvis; StPatr 24; Leuven: Peeters, 2001), 436–42 (438–39).

[138] See Beale, New *Testament Biblical Theology*, 431.

[139] Nolland, *Luke*, 193.

CHAPTER 8

GENESIS 15:6 IN THE NEW TESTAMENT

Douglas J. Moo

Introduction

Greg Beale's work on the use of the OT in the NT has had an enormous influence on an entire generation of students and scholars. His careful attention to methodology, his determination to work in both OT and NT at the highest exegetical levels, and his creativity in detecting subtle relationships between the Testaments have set a high standard for all who work in this area. I have learned a lot from his writings on this issue and especially through our personal interaction during the decade we were colleagues on the faculty at Wheaton College. I write this essay in gratefulness for his scholarly example and for the fellowship we have enjoyed in Christ.

The use of Gn 15:6 in the NT offers a particularly interesting test case in the way the NT authors use the OT. It is a theologically significant text in its own right. It is cited in three different NT passages: Gal 3, Rom 4, and Jas 2. It is applied in these passages to prove different and, at first sight, even conflicting points: righteousness by faith apart from works in Paul and righteousness by faith plus works in James. Scholars are very far from agreeing about the way the NT writers appropriate the verse. In this essay, I briefly look at the meaning of Gn 15:6 in its original context and then offer some comments on the way it functions in the three NT passages where it is cited.[1]

Before I turn to these matters, it will be good to set before us the textual situation:

MT: וְהֶאֱמִן בַּיהוָה וַיַּחְשְׁבֶהָ לּוֹ צְדָקָה (wĕheʾĕmin bayhwā wayyaḥšĕḇehā lô ṣĕḏāqā)

LXX: καὶ ἐπίστευσεν Αβραμ τῷ θεῷ καὶ ἐλογίσθη αὐτῷ εἰς δικαιοσύνην (kai episteusen Abram tō theō kai elogisthē autō eis dikaiosynēn)

---

[1] A certain precursor to this essay is an article by one of my former teachers, Richard N. Longenecker: "The 'Faith of Abraham' Theme in Paul, James, and Hebrews: A Study in the Circumstantial Nature of New Testament Teaching," *JETS* 20 (1977): 203–12.

Gal 3:6: [Ἀβραὰμ] ἐπίστευσεν τῷ θεῷ, καὶ ἐλογίσθη αὐτῷ εἰς δικαιοσύνην
([*Abraam*] *episteusen tō theō, kai elogisthē autō eis dikaiosynēn*)

Rom 4:3: ἐπίστευσεν δὲ Ἀβραὰμ τῷ θεῷ καὶ ἐλογίσθη αὐτῷ εἰς δικαιοσύνην
(*episteusen de Abraam tō theō kai elogisthē autō eis dikaiosynēn*)

Jas 2:23: ἐπίστευσεν δὲ Ἀβραὰμ τῷ θεῷ, καὶ ἐλογίσθη αὐτῷ εἰς δικαιοσύνην
(*episteusen de Abraam tō theō, kai elogisthē autō eis dikaiosynēn*)

As is his habit, Paul appears to quote from the LXX. James, at least in this case (his letter provides far less material for making textual comparisons), follows suit. The differences between the NT wording and the LXX are minor: Ἀβραάμ (*Abraam*) in place of Ἀβραμ (*Abram*); in Galatians and James, δέ (*de*) in place of καί (*kai*); and, if Paul intends it to be part of the quotation,[2] the placement of Ἀβραάμ (*Abraam*) in Galatians. Differences between the LXX and the MT are more significant: the subject of the first verb, specified only as third masculine singular by the Hebrew verbal form, is explicit in the LXX; and the active formulation of the second part of the verse in the MT—וַיַּחְשְׁבֶהָ (*wayyaḥšĕḇehā*), "he credited"—becomes a passive in the LXX: ἐλογίσθη (*elogisthē*), "it was reckoned." The importance of these changes will receive attention in the next section.

Genesis 15:6

Genesis 15:6 describes the reaction of Abram to the renewal of God's promise in vv. 1–5—a promise that restates and renews the initial promise in Gn 12:1–3.[3] Following v. 6 is a covenant ceremony, notable for its emphasis on the divine initative. Verse 6 is set out from its context by its verbal forms. The typical narrative *wayyiqtol* verbal forms in vv. 1–5 and vv. 7ff. are interrupted in v. 6 with a shift to the *weqatal*, thereby drawing attention to this verse.[4] The *hipʿil* of אמן (*ʾmn*) means "to regard something as trustworthy," "to have trust in," or "believe in" (*HALOT*, 1:63). Other places in the OT where this verb in the *hipʿil* is followed (as here) by ב (*b*)

---

[2] Ἀβραάμ (*Abraam*) may be Paul's identification of the subject that follows rather than part of the quotation; Christopher D. Stanley, *Paul and the Language of Scripture: Citation Techniques in the Pauline Epistles and Contemporary Literature* (SNTSMS 69; Cambridge: Cambridge University Press, 1992), 235; note the placement of the opening quotation marks in NIV, NRSV, and ESV (following NA²⁷).

[3] See, e.g., John Calvin, *Commentaries on the First Book of Moses, called Genesis* (Grand Rapids: Eerdmans, n.d.), 406; H. C. Leupold, *Exposition of Genesis* (Grand Rapids: Baker, 1942), 478. On the importance of the Abrahamic promise, see esp. Walter C. Kaiser Jr., *Toward an Old Testament Theology* (Grand Rapids: Zondervan, 1978), 91–92.

[4] See Robert B. Chisholm, *From Exegesis to Exposition* (Grand Rapids: Baker, 1999), 129. I was directed to Chisholm's work by an unpublished paper by Gordon Johnston ("A New Look at an Old Text: Genesis 15:6. Contextual and Canonical Readings"), which has been very helpful in forming my own views.

+ a divine name confirm that the idea is trust, reliance, or confidence in the Lord, especially in light of the revelation of his deeds and words (Ex 14:31; Nm 14:11; 20:12; Dt 1:32; 2 Kgs 17:14; 2 Chr 20:20; Ps 78:22, 32; Jon 3:5). Moreover, the faith in these texts often denotes people's fundamental stance vis-à-vis God, with consequences involving inclusion or exclusion from God's promises. Genesis 15:6, then, while following directly on the renewal of God's promise to Abraham, expresses a fundamental and characteristic feature of Abraham's response to God. This is not the first time that Abraham has trusted God: his response to God's call in Gn 12 expresses faith in some sense, and, indeed, some interpret הֶאֱמִן (*he'ĕmin*) in 15:6 to mean "he went on believing."[5] Nevertheless, it may be significant that this verb occurs here for the first time in the OT. It is commonplace to claim that the OT idea of "faith" includes what, from the NT perspective, might be labeled a combination of "faith" and "faithfulness." Without quarreling with this claim, I would stress that the key texts in which "faith" for God is expressed in the OT certainly include a disposition that would necessarily lead to a life of obedience, but that obedience in itself is not clearly included in the "faith" spoken of in these texts.

Particular debate surrounds the meaning of the second clause in the verse. First, the subject of the verb וַיַּחְשְׁבֶהָ (*wayyaḥšĕbehā*) is unclear. A few interpreters argue that "Abram" must be the subject, since the subject of the first clause should be extended into the second clause. In this case, the verse would mean something like, "he [Abraham] believed the Lord, and he [Abraham] reckoned it [the promise of seed] as justice before him [the Lord]."[6] However, while this reading of the syntax is possible, it must give a strained interpretation to some of the key words.[7]

---

[5] GKC §112e. Max Rogland ("Abram's Persistent Faith: Hebrew Verb Semantics in Genesis 15:6," *WTJ* 70 [2008]: 239–44) argues that the verb has an iterative/continuous force, as do other *waw*-consecutive perfects in the OT: Abraham "continued" to believe; "kept believing." See also J. J. Scullion, "Righteousness," *ABD* 5:727; and the discussion in Brian Vickers, *Jesus' Blood and Righteousness: Paul's Theology of Imputation* (Wheaton, IL: Crossway, 2006), 78 n. 12.

[6] This interpretation appears as early as the medieval interpreter Ramban; and see esp. M. Oeming, "Ist Genesis 15 ein Beleg für die Anrechnung des Glaubens zur Gerechtigkeit?" *ZAW* 95 (1983): 182–97; also Scullion, "Righteousness," *ADB* 5:727; Rudolf Mosis, " 'Glauben' und 'Gerechtigkeit': Zu Gen. 15:6," in *Gesammelte Aufsätze zum Alten Testament* (FzB 93; Würzburg: Echter, 1999), 78–89. For a survey of ancient and modern translations of Gn 15:6, see Joseph A. Fitzmyer, "The Interpretation of Genesis 15:6: Abraham's Faith and Righteousness in a Qumran Text," in *Emanuel: Studies in Hebrew Bible, Septuagint, and Dead Sea Scrolls in Honor of Emanuel Tov* (ed. Shalom M. Paul et al.; Leiden: Brill, 2003), 258–64. A brief overview of the interpretation history is provided by Sascha Flüchter (with Lars Schnor), *Die Anrechnung des Glaubens zur Gerechtigkeit: Auf dem Weg zu einer sozialhistorisch orientertierten Rezeptionsgeschichte von Gen 15,6 in der neutestamentlichen Literatur* (TANZ 51; Tübingen: Franke, 2010), 15–23.

[7] See esp. Benjamin Schliesser, *Abraham's Faith in Romans 4: Paul's Concept of Faith in Light of the History of Reception of Genesis 15:6* (WUNT 2/224; Tübingen:

Second, the nature of the "reckoning" described in v. 6b is not clear. The relevant Hebrew is (1) the verb חשׁב (ḥšb); with (2) a suffix referring to an impersonal object; followed by (3) the preposition ל (l); + (4) an object denoting a person; followed by (5) an adverbial accusative. Thus, in Gn 15:6: he (1) "reckoned" (2) it [faith?] (3) to (4) him [Abraham] (5) righteousness. No text in the HB exactly duplicates this sequence, but several come close. One set of texts uses the חשׁב + ל (ḥšb + l) combination followed by a personal pronoun but without a concluding impersonal object (i.e., these texts include elements 1, 3, and 4). See, for example, Lv 7:18: לֹא יֵחָשֵׁב לוֹ (lōʾ yēḥāšēḇ lô)—"it [the meat of the fellowship offering] will not be reckoned to him [i.e., his credit]"; 2 Sm 19:20(19): אַל־יַחֲשָׁב־לִי אֲדֹנִי (ʾal-yaḥăšāḇ-lî ʾăḏōnî)—"do not reckon me as guilty [i.e., on the basis of his wrongdoing]." Probably to be put in this category is Ps 32:2, which adds an impersonal object at the end (i.e., elements 1, 3, 4, and 5): אַשְׁרֵי אָדָם לֹא יַחְשֹׁב יהוה לוֹ עָוֹן (ʾašrê ʾāḏām lōʾ yaḥšōḇ yhwh lô ʿāwōn)—"Blessed is the man whose sin the Lord does not reckon against him." A second set of texts includes an object after the verb plus an impersonal object (i.e., all five elements are found, although the verb is sometimes in the passive rather than the active). See Jb 13:24: וְתַחְשְׁבֵנִי לְאוֹיֵב לָךְ (wĕṭaḥšĕḇēnî lĕʾōyēḇ lāḵ)—"you reckon me to be in the category of your enemy," that is, "consider me your enemy" (NIV) (also Jb 33:10; see also Jb 19:11 [with כ (k) in place of ל (l) on the word for "enemy"]); Nm 18:30: וְנֶחְשַׁב לַלְוִיִם כִּתְבוּאַת גֹּרֶן (wĕneḥšaḇ lalwiyim kiṯḇûʾaṯ gōren)—"and it will be reckoned to the sons of Levi as the product of the threshing floor" (see also Prv 27:14; Lam 4:2). Particularly significant, because it also uses ל חשׁב (ḥšb l) with צְדָקָה (ṣĕḏāqā), is Ps 106:31: וַתֵּחָשֵׁב לוֹ לִצְדָקָה (wattēḥāšeḇ lô liṣdāqā)—"And it [Phinehas's intervention to prevent Israelite unfaithfulness] was reckoned to him for righteousness." In the first set of texts, the reckoning involves a creative act whereby something is credited in such a way as to produce something else: for example, David blesses the man whose sin is not credited against him in such a way as to rescue him from judgment. In the second set of texts, by contrast, the reckoning involves equivalence: something is considered equivalent to something else. If one focuses on the first set of passages, Gn 15:6 might mean that Abraham's faith led God to consider him to be righteous, that is, to have the status of righteousness or be in right relation with God.[8] The second set of texts suggests that Gn

---

Mohr Siebeck, 2007), 115–50; and Bo Johnson, "Who Reckoned Righteousness to Whom?" SEAug 51 (1986): 108–15; Achim Behrens, "Gen 15,6 und das Vorverständnis des Paulus," ZAW 109 (1997): 329–34.

[8] See esp. O. Palmer Robertson, "Genesis 15:6: New Covenant Exposition of an Old Covenant Text," WTJ 42 (1980): 259–89 (who understands the object of "reckon" to be "righteousness"); Walter Brueggemann, Genesis (Atlanta: John Knox, 1982), 144–46; Brevard Childs, Old Testament Theology in a Canonical Context (Philadelphia: Fortress, 1985), 219–20; Schliesser, Abraham's Faith; Victor P. Hamilton, The Book of Genesis: Chapters 1–17 (NICOT; Grand Rapids: Eerd-

15:6 might mean that God considered Abraham's faith to be equivalent to "righteousness."[9] This latter option should probably be favored, since these texts are semantically closest to Gn 15:6 (in the sense that one thing is counted as something else). This, then, leads to the third issue: what does צְדָקָה (*ṣĕdāqā*) mean in Gn 15:6?

Interpreters who see in Gn 15:6 a creative act often suggest that צְדָקָה (*ṣĕdāqā*) refers to "relationship," and this view, in turn, is often tied to the broader understanding of צדק (*ṣdq*) terminology in the OT as having to do fundamentally with relationship. However, there is some reason to doubt this general approach to צדק (*ṣdq*) language in the HB. "Righteousness" in the OT is oriented more to the idea of standard, to the "right order" that God has built into his creation.[10] "Righteousness" in Gn 15:6, then, could refer to faith as a particular manifestation of this right order: Abraham's belief in God would be a right act, an instance of righteous behavior. But we have seen that "righteousness" in the OT frequently refers more broadly to the total right response to God that he demands of his people, a response that involves, as C. F. Keil and Franz Delitzsch put it, "correspondence to the will of God both in character and conduct."[11] I think this definition best explains Gn 15:6. God considers Abraham's faith to be equivalent to his having met God's standard of rightness.

---

mans, 1990), 425–26; Ferdinand Hahn, "Genesis 15:6 im Neuen Testament," in *Probleme biblischer Theologie: Gerhard von Rad zum 70. Geburtstag* (ed. Hans Walter Wolff; Munich: Kaiser, 1971), 90–107; Vickers, *Jesus' Blood and Righteousness,* 83–89. Gerhard von Rad set forth an influential interpretation along these lines that viewed Gn 15:6 as a pronouncement related to the cult ("Die Anrechnung des Glaubens zur Gerechtigkeit," *TLZ* 76 [1951]: 129–32); von Rad's view has also been widely criticized; see, e.g., Oeming, "Genesis 15."

[9] See, e.g., Bruce Waltke, *Genesis: A Commentary* (Grand Rapids: Zondervan, 2001), 242; J. A. Ziesler, *The Meaning of Righteousness in Paul: A Linguistic and Theological Enquiry* (SNTSMS 20; Cambridge: Cambridge University Press, 1974), 43, 181–85.

[10] The issue is large and contentious. The view I lean toward has been put forth in greatest detail by H. H. Schmid, *Gerechtigkeit als Weltordnung: Hintergrund und Geschichte der alttestamentlichen Gerechtigkeitsbegriffes* (BHT 40; Tübingen: Mohr Siebeck, 1968); see also Mark A. Seifrid, "Righteousness Language in the Hebrew Scriptures and Early Judaism," in *Justification and Variegated Nomism,* vol. 1: *The Complexities of Second Temple Judaism* (ed. D. A. Carson, P. T. O'Brien, and M. A. Seifrid; WUNT 2/140; Tübingen: Mohr Siebeck, 2001), 415–42; Stephen Westerholm, *Perspectives Old and New on Paul: The "Lutheran" Paul and His Critics* (Grand Rapids: Eerdmans, 2004), 267–78. I develop my views on this issue in a bit more detail in "Justification in Galatians," in *Understanding the Times: New Testament Studies in the Twenty-first Century. Essays in Honor of D. A. Carson on the Occasion of His Sixty-fifth Birthday* (ed. Andreas Köstenberger and Robert Yarbrough; Wheaton, IL: Crossway, 2011), 160–95.

[11] C. F. Keil and Franz Delitzsch, *Commentary on the Old Testament: The Pentateuch* (Grand Rapids: Eerdmans, 1969), 213. See also Behrens, "Gen 15,6," 331–32.

Galatians 3:6

Paul cites Gn 15:6 in both Galatians and Romans to underscore his insistence that righteousness, right standing with God, comes via faith and not "works" or "works of the law."[12] In Galatians—in contrast to Romans—Paul addresses a specific threat to the gospel, in the form of a Jewish insistence that ultimate vindication, the right standing recognized by God on the last day, would be granted only to those who added to their faith in Christ obedience to the law of Moses (see especially 5:4–6). Paul's argument against the "agitators" (cf. 5:12) is developed in the great central section of the letter (3:1–5:12), but its main lines are announced in 2:16 in the contrast between "works of the law" and "Christ faith." This contrast lies at the heart of the exhortation of 3:1–6 (see vv. 2, 5). Paul introduces Abraham into his argument by means of the quotation of Gn 15:6 in v. 6, and Abraham is a thread that runs through the argument of 3:7–4:7 (see also 4:21–31).[13]

Abraham, of course, plays a foundational role in the unfolding drama of redemption in the OT, so it would not be unexpected for Paul to make significant reference to him in his attempt to persuade the Galatians to accept his view of redemptive history. However, most scholars, rightly, think that Paul's extended references to Abraham are also, or mainly, polemical, directed against the teaching of the agitators. Jews in Paul's day traced their spiritual status to their biological relationship to Abraham, the "father of the nation." The Jewish traditions emphasize especially his true piety, as evidenced in his obedience and even in his conformity to the law. "Abraham was perfect in all his deeds with the Lord, and well-pleasing in righteousness all the days of his life" (*Jub.* 23:10); Abraham "did not sin against thee" (Pr Man 8); "no one has been found like him in glory" (Sir 44:19). Abraham's faithfulness in the midst of his trials (preeminently his "sacrifice" of Isaac [Gn 22]) was especially important: Jewish tradition tends to locate Abraham's "justification" after and in response to trials.[14] On the basis of Gn 26:5—"Abraham obeyed me and did everything I required of him, keeping my commands, my decrees and my instructions"—it was sometimes taught that Abraham had obeyed the law before it was given (*m. Qidd.* 4:14; Sir 44:19–21; *2 Bar.* 57:2).[15] Paul

---

[12] While unimportant for the argument of this essay, I think Galatians was probably written just before the Apostolic Council (Acts 15) and thereby predates Romans by around eight years; see Douglas J. Moo, *Galatians* (BECNT; Grand Rapids: Baker, forthcoming).

[13] Abraham occurs in vv. 7, 8, 9, 14, 16, 18, 29; and reference to the promise(s), closely connected with Abraham, in vv. 8, 14, 16, 17, 18, 19, 21, 22, 29.

[14] Simon J. Gathercole, *Where Is Boasting? Early Jewish Soteriology and Paul's Response in Romans 1–5* (Grand Rapids: Eerdmans, 2002), 236–38.

[15] For surveys of Abraham in Jewish literature, see Nancy Calvert-Koyzis, *Paul, Monotheism, and the People of God: The Significance of Abraham Traditions for*

reflects this tradition by introducing the language of "sons of Abraham" in v. 7—and at the same time strongly suggests that the issue was already a matter of contention in Galatia by introducing the concept without explanation. As we noted above, Jewish appropriation of the Abraham story highlighted his own virtues as an explanation of his foundational role in salvation history, focusing especially on his obedience and even at times claiming that he obeyed the law before it had been given. The agitators were probably citing the Abraham story in just these terms, arguing that the Galatian Christians could secure their righteous status before God by becoming "sons of Abraham" through the time-honored means of submission to the Torah.

Paul responds to this argument in two ways in 3:7–4:7, insisting that God's promise to Abraham was all along intended to include Gentiles and that it was Abraham's faith, in distinction from his obedience, that led to his righteousness. This last point is especially critical to Paul's argument—simply because we have no evidence that the agitators were disputing the fact that Gentiles could be included in Abraham's family. The issue, rather, was the means by which they could be included.

Galatians 3:6, where we find Paul's quotation of Gn 15:6, is a janus, connected to vv. 1–5 by means of καθώς (*kathōs*) and the theme of faith (vv. 2, 5) and connected to what follows with its focus on the experience of Abraham.[16] Paul clearly expects his rhetorical question in v. 5 to be answered with the response "not works of the law but hearing accompanied by faith." The καθώς (*kathōs*) builds on this: "Surely it is by 'hearing accompanied by faith' [v. 5b], even as it was in the case of Abraham, who . . . ."[17]

Early Judaism and Christianity (JSNTSup 273; London: T&T Clark, 2004), 6–84; Roy A. Harrisville, *The Figure of Abraham in the Epistles of St. Paul* (San Francisco: Mellen University Research Press, 1992), 47–135; Maureen W. Yeung, *Faith in Jesus and Paul: A Comparison with Special Reference to 'Faith That Can Remove Mountains' and 'Your Faith Has Healed/Saved You'* (WUNT 2/147; Tübingen: Mohr Siebeck, 2002), 232–64.

[16] The decision about whether to view the verse as the conclusion to vv. 1–5 (NIV; ESV; F. F. Bruce, *The Epistle to the Galatians: A Commentary on the Greek Text* [NIGTC; Grand Rapids, Eerdmans, 1982], 152; Moisés Silva, *Interpreting Galatians: Explorations in Exegetical Method* [2nd ed.; Grand Rapids: Baker, 2001], 253; Andrew H. Wakefield, *Where to Live: The Hermeneutical Significance of Paul's Citations from Scripture in Galatians 3:1–14* [SBLABib 14; Atlanta: Society of Biblical Literature, 2003], 136) or as the introduction to vv. 7–9 (e.g., NRSV; NLT; Ernest de W. Burton, *A Critical and Exegetical Commentary on the Epistle to the Galatians* [ICC; Edinburgh: T&T Clark, 1921], 153; Richard N. Longenecker, *Galatians* [WBC 41; Dallas: Word, 1990], 112) is a difficult one. But the introductory καθώς (*kathōs*) finally inclines me to attach v. 6, from a literary standpoint, to vv. 1–5.

[17] Sam K. Williams, "Justification and the Spirit in Galatians," *JSNT* 29 (1987): 92–95; Silva, *Interpreting Galatians*, 253; Stanley, *Paul and the Language of Scripture*, 235; similarly, George Howard, *Paul: Crisis in Galatia: A Study in Early Christian Theology* (SNTSMS 35; Cambridge: Cambridge University Press, 1979), 55; and see BDAG.

Paul's appeal to Gn 15:6 brings together two of the words critical for his argument: πιστεύω (*pisteuō*; cf. πίστις [*pistis*]) and δικαιοσύνη (*dikaiosynē*; cf. δικαιόω [*dikaioō*]). As I noted above, Gn 15:6 affirms that God graciously viewed Abraham's faith as having in itself fulfilled all that God expected of Abraham in order to be in the right before him. Just as, then, it was Abraham's faith that led to his being considered "in the right" before God, so it was the faith of the Galatians that led them to be "declared right" (vv. 16, 21).[18] It is more difficult to decide whether Abraham's attaining righteousness is to be compared with the Galatians' initial experience ("after beginning," v. 3) or to their continuing experience ("are you now trying to finish?"). Perhaps this is not a fair question. As often in Galatians, Paul appears to view righteousness as right standing without particular focus on its initiation. His concern is to make clear to the Galatians that, in contrast to the views of the agitators, righteousness is always, at every stage, manifested through faith.[19]

Romans 4

In contrast to Galatians, Paul's deployment of Abraham in Romans does not appear to be directed to any particular false teaching. In Romans, Paul exposits his gospel, with particular respect to its salvation-historical context and implications. This focus serves the several purposes Paul has in writing to the Roman Christians: to defend his view of the gospel in order to pave the way for his meeting with them (15:23–25); to address the debate in the community over certain Torah-related practices (14:1–15:13); and to request prayer for the success of the collection during his upcoming journey to Jerusalem (15:30–33).[20] In Rom 4, Paul provides an extended discussion of Abraham in order to buttress and develop the basic points he has made in 3:27–31. As the focus of both this paragraph and Rom 4 reveals, Paul's concern is to draw out the implications of his emphasis on the sufficiency of faith, apart from "works of the law" (3:28) / "works" (4:2, 4–5, 6), circumcision (3:29–30; 4:9–12), or the law (3:27, 28; 4:13–17). Genesis 15:6 occcupies center stage in this argument. Paul cites this text in v. 3 as the scriptural verdict on whether Abraham was "justified by works" (v. 2). Paul elaborates this fundamental contrast between faith and works in vv. 4–5 by aligning works with wages and reward, and faith with grace. In typical Jewish fashion, Paul then supports the witness of the Pentateuch with a confirmatory text from the

---

[18] Hans-Joachim Eckstein, *Verheissung und Gesetz: Eine Exegetische Untersuchung zu Galater 2,15–4,7* (WUNT 2/86; Tübingen: Mohr Siebeck, 1996), 98–99.

[19] See Moo, "Justification in Galatians," 160–95.

[20] See Douglas J. Moo, *The Epistle to the Romans* (NICNT; Grand Rapids: Eerdmans, 1996), 16–22.

Writings, Ps 32:1–2, a text connected with Gn 15:6 via the common word λογίζομαι (*logizomai*, "reckon" or "credit"). Paul reveals his key concern again by claiming that the text shows that God "credits righteousness apart from works." Paul continues to weave the language of Gn 15:6 into the rest of his argument in Rom 4 (λογίζομαι [*logizomai*] in vv. 9, 10, 11; δικαιοσύνη [*dikaiosynē*] in vv. 9, 11, 13 [cf. δικαιόω (*dikaioō*) in v. 5] and πιστεύω [*pisteuō*] in vv. 11, 17, 18, 24 [along with πίστις (*pistis*) in vv. 11, 12, 13, 14, 16, 19, and 20]). He then circles back to where he began, citing Gn 15:6 once again (v. 22) and claiming explicitly that the text was "written not for him alone, but also for us, to whom God will credit righteousness" (vv. 23b–24a).

As in Galatians, then, Paul focuses on Abraham's believing, arguing that the verse grounds his insistence that it is faith "apart from works" that is the sufficient human response to God as the means of securing righteousness. A matter of some significance in accurately estimating Paul's appropriation of Gn 15:6 and the relationship between his interpretation and that of James is the relationship between the simple "works" (which Paul uses in Rom 4) and the phrase "works of the law" (3:20, 28). In what is heralded as an interpretation that does justice to Paul's Jewish context and rightly isolates the key issue in that context, many interpreters insist that "works" is an abbreviation for "works of the law," interpreted in terms of "boundary-marking" Torah adherence. In Rom 4, then, Paul's claim that Abraham was granted righteousness "apart from works" has a specific and limited significance. It does not mean that he, or believers generally, are justified apart from anything they do; it means only that they are justified apart from those particular works demanded by the Jewish law.[21] I do not have the space to engage in adequate discussion of this claim, but I am not convinced that Paul's "works" can be confined to "Torah works." The evidence for the particular nuance of the phrase is not compelling, for Paul elsewhere appears to define "works" very broadly (see especially Rom 9:11–12), and the nature of his argument about works (especially in Gal 3:10; 5:3; Rom 4:4–5) confirms this broad anthropological reading. "Works of the law," then, are a subset of "works": what humans do in response to the Torah, as a particular form of human "doing" in general.

What, then, are we to make of Paul's appeal to Gn 15:6? In his commentary on Genesis, John Walton claims that "Abram's belief has nothing to do with salvation and nothing to do with a faith system"; Gn 15:6 is not "a reflection of soteriology proper" but "an *analogy* to salvation."[22] It

---

[21] See esp. James D. G. Dunn, *Romans 1–8* (WBC 38A; Dallas: Word, 1989), 200; Dunn, "The New Perspective on Paul: Whence, What, and Whither?" in *The New Perspective on Paul* (rev. ed.; Grand Rapids: Eerdmans, 2008), 47–48; N. T. Wright, "Romans," in *The New Interpreter's Bible*, 10:490.

[22] John H. Walton, *Genesis* (NIVAC; Grand Rapids: Zondervan, 2001), 423, 432.

must be noted that Walton defines "soteriology" quite specifically in this context: "being saved from sin by the blood of Christ." Yet, with all due respect to a very competent OT interpreter and valued colleague, I must question the strength of Walton's assertion. For one thing, I am not sure that Paul's citation of Gn 15:6 can be limited to an "analogy": the foundational nature of his appeal to this text, the way he weaves its language into his whole argument in Rom 4, and his use of the language of that text to refer to believers (especially in Rom 4:22–24) suggest that his use of Gn 15:6 works only if there is significant overlap between believers' (salvific) righteousness and Abraham's rightness before God. To be sure, if I am right about the meaning of Gn 15:6, the text does not directly refer to what Paul would call "justification by faith." Justification, for Paul, is forensic status, and this is not what Gn 15:6 is saying. However, if Gn 15:6 is referring to the full conformity to the rightness that God expects of his people, then Paul's use of the text is a quite legitimate application. It was Abraham's faith that God regarded as having met the standard that God expected of his people. And it is an obvious inference, justified by the close relationship in the OT between a person's righteousness and his acceptance before God, that Abraham, having, by his faith, met God's standard of rightness, would be then presumed to be in the right with God.

While a bit more daring, it might even be possible to find some ground in the OT itself for Paul's claim that Abraham's believing counted for his righteousness apart from works or the law. In Dt 6:25 righteousness is attached to doing the law: "And if we are careful to obey all this law before the LORD our God, as he has commanded us, that will be our righteousness" (צְדָקָה [ṣĕdāqā]; LXX ἐλεημοσύνη [eleēmosynē]). As Daniel Block comments, "In both Gen 15:6 and Deut 6:25 sdqh designates the loyalty of the human vassal before his divine Suzerain demonstrated in response acceptable to the Suzerain: trust in YHWH's promises in the first instance and scrupulous obedience to YHWH's commands in the second."[23] The salvation-history argument of Gal 3 and Rom 4 (though, to be sure, this focus is more muted in Romans) suggests that Paul is especially concerned to draw a line from Abraham to Christ, and Christians, that, as it were, bypasses the law. Righteousness in the new era is to be defined in terms of Gn 15:6, not Dt 6:25. What the agitators in Galatia were keeping together—faith (Gn 15:6) + obedience to the law (Dt 6:25) justifies—Paul separates—faith "alone" justifies.[24] The rightness that God demands

---

[23] Daniel I. Block, *How I Love Your Torah, O Lord! Studies in the Book of Deuteronomy* (Eugene, OR: Cascade, 2011), 17.

[24] As John Sailhammer has argued, then, Gn 15:6 might suggest that God counted Abraham's faith as "the keeping of the law" (*The Meaning of the Pentateuch: Revelation, Composition, and Interpretation* [Downers Grove, IL: InterVarsity Press, 2009], 244; see also Gordon J. Wenham, *Genesis 1–15* [WBC 1; Waco, TX: Word, 1987], 330). Francis Watson (*Paul and the Hermeneutics of Faith* [London: T&T Clark, 2004], 174–93) argues that Paul's focus on this text is in keeping with

of his people, later encoded in the law, has been fully met by Abraham in his simple yet profound act of faith. And so Paul uses this central OT statement about Abraham to say to believers, in effect: just as Abraham's full and complete rightness before God came by virtue of his faith—and so he was accepted on that basis before God—so your full and complete rightness before God (in a distinctively forensic sense) comes by virtue of your faith—"alone."

James 2

If Paul legitimately quotes Gn 15:6 as attesting to his teaching about justification by faith apart from the law—indeed, apart from works of any sort—it is at first sight very difficult to think that we could also claim legitimacy for an interpretation of this same text in terms of a righteousness based on faith *and* works. Yet it is with just this sense that James appears to quote the text in his famous insistence on a "working faith" (2:14–26).

This paragraph is the capstone on James' presentation of "true religion," begun in 1:21. Obedience to the word, James has insisted, is a necessary mark of authentic Christianity. But such obedience is more than external conformity to the demands of Scripture. And so James stresses in 2:14–26 that "true religion" begins with faith—but a faith that works. The "true religion" of 1:26 is nothing more than the genuine faith of 2:14–26, and the faith vs. works antithesis of this paragraph corresponds almost exactly to the "hearing the word" / "doing the word" antithesis of 1:22.[25] The polemical style of this paragraph, with quotations of and rebukes directed against an imaginary interlocutor (vv. 18, 20), suggests that James is combatting false views circulating among his readers. Moreover, these false views may have some relationship to the teaching of Paul, as the language of "faith only" in v. 24 suggests.[26] This is not the place to explore this relationship. In brief, I think the way in which Paul and James frame their discussions strongly suggests that the two are not directly confronting one another. The evidence suggests, rather, an indirect connection, which may be explained if James is writing in the middle to late forties, when garbled accounts of Paul's teaching of "justification by faith alone"

Genesis: Gn 15:6, he claims, is the "hermeneutical key" to the Abraham story, underlining the centrality of promise and the divine initiative.

[25] Luke Timothy Johnson, *The Letter of James* (AB 37A; Garden City, NY: Doubleday, 1995), 238; see also Donald J. Verseput, "Rewording the Puzzle of Faith and Deeds in James 2:14–26," *NTS* 43 (1997): 100–101.

[26] To be sure, a connection is not altogether clear, for this kind of view might well have been circulating in Jewish circles independent of Paul and early Christianity. See esp. Peter Davids, *The Epistle of James* (NIGTC; Grand Rapids: Eerdmans, 1982), 131–32; Richard J. Bauckham, *James: Wisdom of James, Disciple of Jesus the Sage* (London: Routledge, 1999), 127–31.

are beginning to circulate but before James and Paul have actually met to "compare notes."[27]

After insisting on the inseperability of faith and works in vv. 14–19, James confronts his readers with evidence that "faith without works is useless" (v. 20). This evidence consists of two OT examples of people who combined faith with works: Abraham (vv. 21–23) and Rahab (vv. 25–26). Both were "justified by works" (ἐξ ἔργων ἐδικαιώθη [ex ergōn edikaiōthē]; vv. 21, 25), leading to James' theological summary in v. 24: "a person is justified by works and not by faith alone" (ἐξ ἔργων δικαιοῦται ἄνθρωπος καὶ οὐκ ἐκ πίστεως μόνον; ex ergōn dikaioutai anthrōpos kai ouk ek pisteōs monon). James illustrates Abraham's works with reference to the famous incident of the "offering of Isaac" (Gn 22). In doing so, James stands solidly within the Jewish tradition of his day, which often focused on this incident, the greatest of Abraham's "works" (Philo *Abr.* 167); see especially 1 Mc 2:51–52: "Remember the deeds of the fathers, which they did in their generations; and receive great honor and an everlasting name. Was not Abraham our father found faithful when tested, and it was reckoned to him as righteousness?" Verse 22 states an inference from v. 21: "you see that his faith and his works [τοῖς ἔργοις αὐτοῦ; tois ergois autou] were working together [συνήργει; synērgei], and his faith was made complete [ἐτελειώθη; eteleiōthē] by his works." This cooperation of Abraham's faith and works in his justification signals that "the Scripture was fulfilled" (ἐπληρώθη ἡ γραφή; eplērōthē hē graphē, v. 23). In the singular, γραφή (graphē) can denote the whole OT canon (e.g., Gal 3:22) but more often refers to a specific text from the OT (see, e.g., Mk 12:10; Lk 4:21; Jn 19:24)—in this case, Gn 15:6, which James immediately quotes. Granted the Jewish tradition that James depends on in these verses, it is likely that Gn 15:6 has been in his mind from the beginning of his discussion of Abraham.

The significance that James attributes to his quotation of Gn 15:6 depends on three issues.

First, what is the relationship, in James's view, between Abraham's "believing" in Gn 15:6 and the works of Abraham that he has emphasized in vv. 21–22? In v. 22, as we have seen, James claims that Abraham's faith and works were "working together" (συνήργει; synērgei). A few commentators suggest that the verb means "assist" or "help," the idea being that Abraham's faith sustained his works by enabling him to produce them.[28]

---

[27] See Douglas J. Moo, *The Letter of James* (PNTC; Grand Rapids: Eerdmans, 2000), 23–27; see also Ralph P. Martin, *James* (WBC 48; Waco, TX: Word, 1988), 95–96, though he puts the letter at a later date; Craig L. Blomberg and Mariam Kamell, *James* (ZECNT; Grand Rapids: Zondervan, 2008), 30. This understanding of the historical context apparently goes back as far as Augustine (*Enarrat. Ps.* 31/ II, 3, 6); see P. Bergauer, *Der Jakobusbrief bei Augustinus und die damit verbundenen Probleme der Rechtfertigungslehre* (Vienna: Herder, 1962), 51–52.

[28] R. V. G. Tasker, *The General Epistle of James* (TNTC; Grand Rapids: Eerdmans, 1956), 69; C. E. B. Cranfield, "The Message of James," *SJT* 18 (1965): 341.

But the verb usually has the meaning "work with" in the NT (1 Cor 6:16; 2 Cor 6:1; [Mk 16:20]; Rom 8:28 is debated; see also one of the two occurrences in the LXX [1 Esd 7:2]). So the usual translation should probably be accepted. James is not saying that Abraham's faith produced his works but that his faith and works cooperated. This cooperation was a continuing feature of Abraham's life (the implication of the imperfect form συνήργει [*synērgei*]). Abraham's faith, James is pointing out, was not confined to a mental reorientation at the time of his "conversion"[29] or to an occasional verbal profession; it was an active force, constantly at work along with his deeds.

In chiastic relationship to this first assertion in v. 22 is the second: "works complete faith" as "faith cooperates with works."[30] Is James here saying that faith is incomplete until actions follow from it? To avoid this conclusion, John Calvin suggested that the idea might be that works revealed Abraham's faith to be perfect. But this would be an unlikely meaning for τελειόω (*teleioō*), which means "complete [a task or mission]" (e.g., Jn 17:4; 19:28; Acts 20:24) or to "bring to perfection or maturity" (Phil 3:10; Heb 2:10). Perhaps the closest parallel is 1 Jn 4:12: "if we love one another, God lives in us and his love is made complete in us" (ἡ ἀγάπη αὐτοῦ ἐν ἡμῖν τετελειωμένη ἐστίν; *hē agapē autou en hēmin teteleiōmenē estin*).[31] Clearly our love does not complete God's love in the sense that the love of God is inadequate or faulty without our response. It is rather that God's love comes to expression, reaches its intended goal, when we respond to his grace with love toward others. So also, Abraham's faith, James suggests, reached its intended goal when the patriarch did what God was asking him to do.

Particularly important is the way in which James perceives Abraham's faith and works to have "fulfilled" Gn 15:6. Some view James as claiming that Gn 15:6 is a prophecy that was "fulfilled" when Abraham offered Isaac.[32] But the word πληρόω (*plēroō*), signifying a general "filling up" of the meaning of the OT in the NT, denotes a variety of specific relationships between the two. Granted the lack of any "forward-look-

---

[29] Although most Jewish interpretations of Abraham stressed his works, some Jews interpreted his faith in an intellectual sense, as his turning from idolatry "to the worship of the one god" (see, e.g., Philo *Virt.* 216; Josephus *A.J.* 1.7.1 [§§154–57]; *Jub.* 11–12). See Davids, *James,* 128–29.

[30] See, e.g., J. C. Lodge, "James and Paul at Cross-Purposes," *Bib* 62 (1981): 201.

[31] The closest verbal parallels may be in Philo, who uses the combination τελειόω + ἐκ (*teleioō + ek*) at least twice, each time describing Jacob: he "was perfected as the result of discipline" (*Agr.* 42); "was made perfect through practice" (*Conf.* 181; see also *Congr.* 35 [with διά (*dia*)]). Jacob, these texts suggest, grew in maturity as a result of the challenges he faced in life. Nevertheless, the text in 1 Jn, because of the inanimate subject, might be the more relevant parallel.

[32] James Hardy Ropes, *A Critical and Exegetical Commentary on the Epistle of St. James* (ICC; Edinburgh: T&T Clark, 1916), 221.

ing" meaning in Gn 15:6, it makes sense to think that James is using the word in a broader sense to indicate that Abraham's "faith for righteousness" found its ultimate significance in Abraham's life of obedience. This need not mean that the claim of Gn 15:6 became true only when Abraham later produced works of obedience.[33] Rather, granted James's concern with the relationship of faith and works throughout this passage, a concern explicit in the immediately preceding v. 22, the "fulfillment" of Gn 15:6 may relate especially to Abraham's faith.[34] The faith that God considered sufficient to meet all his expectations of Abraham found its fulfillment in the works that he did in confirmation of that faith. But the faith of Abraham and God's verdict of acquittal were "filled up," given their ultimate significance, when Abraham "perfected" his faith with works. It is after the greatest of those works, cited by James in v. 21, that the angel of the Lord reasserted God's verdict: "now I know that you fear God" (Gn 22:12).

Even if James's main focus is on the way Abraham's faith was fulfilled in his later works, some concern with the righteousness credited to Abraham because of his faith is probably also present. Assessing the way James understands this righteousness has the danger of plunging into a bottomless hole of historical and contemporary debate about the means of justification.[35] So I can comment only briefly. I continue to doubt that δικαιόω (dikaioō, "justify") has the sense "demonstrate to be right" that so many adopt for the verb here.[36] This interpretation appears to me especially unlikely in light of James's appeal to Gn 15:6. In my commentary, I argued that James is "claiming that the ultimate vindication of the believer in the judgment is based on, or at least takes into account, the things that person has done."[37] I used "ultimate vindication" because I was emphasizing a temporal difference between James and Paul with respect to justification: Paul, in contrast to James, uses δικαιόω (dikaioō) to refer to the "initial declaration" of a sinner's new status before God. My work on Galatians, however, has led me to think

---

[33] As, e.g., Scot McKnight suggests ("Abraham was not justified until he laid Isaac on the altar"; see The Letter of James [NICNT; Grand Rapids: Eerdmans, 2011], 251).

[34] The four clauses in vv. 22–23 follow closely on one another, being joined to one another by καί (kai).

[35] Most scholars would continue to resist the sort of biblical-theological reconciliation that I attempt here and which is, in my view, inherent in the kind of robust view of biblical authority that I maintain and of which Greg Beale has been so notable a champion. For a contrary view, see, e.g., Andrew Chester (with Ralph P. Martin), The Theology of the Letters of James, Peter, and Jude (New Testament Theology; Cambridge: Cambridge University Press, 1994), who concludes his discussion of James and Paul by saying "[w]e may have to choose in the end between James and Paul, rather than simply hold both together" (p. 53).

[36] See Moo, James, 135.

[37] Moo, James, 134–35.

that in that letter (and perhaps rarely in Romans) a future aspect of justification is part of Paul's teaching. In Paul justification is an "already/not yet" pronouncement of right status before God. I can no longer argue for a reconciliation between Paul and James that rests on a temporal difference in justification. Moreover, in any case, the temporal distinction never really solved the basic issue, for I have always been convinced, with the Reformers, that Paul teaches that justification is "by faith alone"—whenever it might occur. A temporal distinction could never, in itself, harmonize Paul and James.

So Paul and James are using δικαιόω (*dikaioō*) with the same basic meaning; no clear temporal difference exists between them on this point; nor, as I have argued earlier, do Paul's "works of the law" mean something basically different from James' "works." The critical issue for bringing the two together must rest in a theologically sophisticated interpretation of the preposition ἐκ (*ek*), which Paul uses to assert justification "by" faith and James also uses to insist on justification "by" faith + works.[38] In my view, a persuasive although by no means watertight argument can be made that while Paul uses this preposition in these justification texts to indicate "instrument," James uses it to indicate a more "evidential" idea.[39] I would, therefore, want to revise the quotation from my commentary cited above to read "the ultimate vindication of the believer in the judgment *takes into account* the things that person has done."

---

[38] It is the failure of N. T. Wright to be clear about just what this preposition indicates about the relationship between works and ultimate justification that has generated criticism of his views. His most recent contribution continues to resist neat categorization, but he appears to stress a definitive initial justification and a final justification "in accordance with" works (see "Justification: Yesterday, Today, and Forever," *JETS* 54 [2011]: 60–62).

[39] See my comments on the biblical-theological issue in *James*, 37–43; I quote here my conclusion (p. 42): "The answer to the problem, we would suggest, lies in reading James' teaching about 'works' in light of Paul's teaching that Christian works are themselves the product of God's work of grace through the indwelling Holy Spirit. What appears on the surface to be synergism in James can without contradiction with anything James says, be read in light of the monergism of Paul. While not explicitly taught by James, a monergistic interpretation fits well into the emphasis in chap. 2 on true faith. James, it will be remembered, is not arguing that a Christian must 'add' works to faith; he insists that true saving faith *will* 'work.' It is but a short step from this insight to attributing the motive power of faith to the work of God. And, as T. Laato has shown, James gives evidence of a monergistic view of salvation in his emphasis on the creative power of the new birth in 1:18 ("Justification according to James: A Comparison with Paul," *TJ* 18 [1997]: 47–61). At the theological level, then, we think that Paul and James are complementary rather than contradictory. Faith alone brings one into relationship with God in Christ—but true faith inevitably generates the works that God will take into account in his final decision about the fate of men and women." Timo Laato has developed his argument in a slim volume: *Rechtfertigung bei Jakobus: Ein Vergleich met Paulus* (Saarijärvi: Gummerus, 2003).

Conclusion

But I run the risk here of making the mistake that so many make: spending so much time harmonizing Paul and James that we fail to hear their distinctive voices. These distinctive voices are no doubt heard in the way they cite Gn 15:6. To borrow a metaphor from the world of photography, Paul uses a telephoto lens to isolate the inherent meaning of the verse whereas James looks at the verse through a wide-angle lens, viewing it in the larger landscape of the Abraham narrative.[40] Paul cites the verse to highlight the adequacy of faith, in and of itself, to justify a person before God. The faith Abraham exercises here comes before his circumcision (Gn 17) and before his famous "work" of obedience (Gn 22). As so often, Paul gives a fuller meaning to the terms of the original text, especially in his strongly forensic interpretation of righteousness. But his application of the text, I have argued, is legitimate, since Gn 15:6 teaches that Abraham's faith was considered by God as meeting the entirety of his obligation before God. James gives us no reason to think that he ignores or changes the meaning of the text. But he insists that the faith of which Gn 15:6 speaks is, in the larger story of Genesis, a faith that expresses itself in works of obedience and that these works are also to be included in the "entirety of the obligation" that Abraham owes to God.

---

[40] Hahn, "Genesis 15:6 im Neuen Testament," 90–107, comes to similar though not identical conclusions.

CHAPTER 9

THE TEMPLE, A DAVIDIC MESSIAH, AND A CASE OF MISTAKEN PRIESTLY IDENTITY (MARK 2:26)

Nicholas Perrin

Introduction

One autumn afternoon, when Greg Beale and I were visiting in the study of his home, we spent a few moments puzzling over what has become known among Gospels scholars as the "Abiathar problem." The "problem" occurs in Mark's account of Jesus and his disciples plucking grain on the Sabbath (Mk 2:23–28); it falls at v. 26: "He entered the house of God, when Abiathar was high priest, and ate the bread of the Presence, which it is not lawful for any but the priests to eat, and he gave some to his companions."[1] The difficulty surfaces on the Evangelist's claim (through the mouth of Jesus) that Abiathar was high priest at the time (ἐπὶ Ἀβιαθὰρ ἀρχιερέως; *epi Abiathar archiereōs*) when, according to the relevant passage of 1 Sm 21:1–9, Ahimelech was the high priest (v. 1). Well noted down through the centuries, even attracting the attention of such patristic lights as Jerome and Chrysostom, the exegetical problem has been met with a small number of explanations.[2]

One approach has been to surmise some tampering with the text at an early stage in its transmission, whereby a misinformed scribe inserted the phrase "when Abiathar was high priest" or failed to preserve, on account of haplography, the original and accurate (Aramaic?) text that supposedly read: "when the father (*abba*) of Abiathar (*Abiathar*) was high priest." As for the latter hypothesis, this remains no more than speculation—remote at best. As for the former possibility, while this has some substantiation in the premier Western text that omits the phrase (ἐπὶ Ἀβιαθὰρ ἀρχιερέως;

---

[1] This and all subsequent references are taken from the NRSV.
[2] Craig A. Evans, "Patristic Interpretation of Mark 2:26: 'When Abiathar Was High Priest,'" *VC* 40 (1986): 183–86.

epi Abiathar archiereōs), the reading's slender witness forbids this as a strong option.[3] Maurice Casey assigns the problem to the other side of Mark, as it were, by envisioning a pre-Markan Aramaic substratum that in turn precipitated a misleading Greek translation in Mark's text.[4] In an earlier day of scholarship, J. W. Wenham understood ἐπί (*epi*) in v. 26 in the same sense as it is found in Mk 12:26, where the preposition is used to indicate not a time period but a text of Scripture. Thus, the phrase should properly be translated "in the passage concerning Abiathar the high priest."[5] Despite the ingenuity of this solution, which goes back at least to the eighteenth century, most commentators remain unconvinced, largely because Abiathar's name does not appear until the next chapter (1 Sm 22:20). Still one more possibility is that the event at Nob (1 Sm 21:1–9) was "associated in popular memory with the high priesthood of Abiathar" and thus the Evangelist's word is simply in accordance with convention.[6] This is not impossible, but it amounts to little more than a guess. All of these solutions to the Abiathar problem share the common feature of exculpating Mark; none of them appears very compelling prima facie.

This is perhaps why most commentators on this passage are content to conclude that the Evangelist failed to get his facts straight.[7] On one level, this approach has the virtue of presenting itself as a simple solu-

---

[3] The phrase is lacking in D W 217 *a b e ff i* and OS[s] but is retained in the weightiest witnesses. Moreover, the omission in D et al. could also be explained by the influence of Matthew (12:4) and Luke (6:4), which also drop the phrase. It is commonly thought that Matthew and Luke independently omitted the words to avoid reproducing an embarrassing error. Still other MSS (A C Q l F) insert a definite article after ἐπί (*epi*) (ἐπὶ τοῦ Ἀβιαθὰρ ἀρχιερέως; *epi tou Abiathar archiereōs*), presumably to achieve a meaning like "in the time of the one who named Abiathar who would be priest."

[4] M. Casey (*Aramaic Sources of Mark's Gospel* [SNTSMS 10; Cambridge: Cambridge University Press, 1998], 151) suggests that the original read: "In the days of Abiathar—a great/chief priest!"

[5] J. W. Wenham "Mark 2,26," *JTS* 1 (1950): 156. Followed with caution by William L. Lane, *The Gospel of Mark* (NICNT; Grand Rapids: Eerdmans, 1974), 116; also Craig Blomberg, *The Historical Reliability of the Gospels* (Downers Grove, IL: InterVarsity Press, 1987), 193; Damia Roure, *Jesús y la Figura de David en Mc 2,23–26: Trasfondo bíblico, intertestamentario y rabínico* (AnBib 124; Rome: Editrice Pontificio Istituto Biblico, 1990), 14.

[6] Alan D. Rogers, "Mark 2,26," *JTS* 2 (1951): 44–45; James R. Edwards, *The Gospel according to Mark* (PNTC; Grand Rapids: Eerdmans, 2002), 95; similarly K. Whitelam, "Abiathar," *ABD* 1:13–14, Joel Marcus, *Mark 1–8: A New Translation with Introduction and Commentary* (AB 27; New York: Doubleday, 2000), 241.

[7] So, e.g., Eduard Schweizer, *The Good News According to Mark* (trans. D. H. Madvig; Louisville: Westminster John Knox, 1970), 72; Robert A. Guehlich, *Mark 1–8:26* (WBC 34A; Nashville: Thomas Nelson, 1989), 122; Morna D. Hooker, *The Gospel According to Saint Mark* (BNTC; London: A&C Black, 1991), 103; R. T. France, *The Gospel of Mark* (NIGTC; Grand Rapids: Eerdmans, 2002), 146; Elizabeth Struthers Malbon, *Mark's Jesus: Characterization as Narrative Christology*

tion. Yet even so, as a summation of the situation, this explanation has its own problems, not least the fact—repeatedly confirmed by recent decades of research on Markan intertextuality—that the Evangelist had an extremely detailed knowledge of the Hebrew Scriptures. How plausible is it that an author who has elsewhere so carefully woven his Gospel from selected threads of Scripture should be so blatantly careless in retrieving the name of "Ahimelech" from 1 Sm 21:1–9? Add to this the fact that Mark must have been fully aware that he was authoritatively citing the words of Jesus at 2:26. If the Evangelist was intent on presenting Jesus as the true messianic teacher (a nearly indisputable point that I will touch on below), would he have not also made every effort to present a Jesus whose handling of the Torah was accurate and well-informed? How ironic it would be—and how shamefully sloppy on the Evangelist's part—if the same Jesus who charged his opponents with being ignorant of the Scriptures (Mk 12:24) was himself found (thanks to Mark) to be so ignorant on a rather obvious point! While redactional error of this magnitude is possible, it is not inherently probable.[8] Therefore, we must agree with Robert Stein's judgment that when it comes to this alleged case of mistaken priestly identity, one "must acknowledge that no satisfactory solution has come forward that resolves this problem."[9] We are best served considering alternative explanations as they present themselves.

Having devoted further thought and study to the issue since the day Greg Beale and I broached the matter, I wish in the remainder of the essay to set forth a fresh solution to the Abiathar problem. There are two stages to my argument. First, as has already been suggested by several scholars, the problem involving Mark's alleged confounding of Abiathar with his father Ahimelech is mitigated by the fact that ancient Judaism, at least during the Roman period, seems to have applied the term "high priest" not only to the unique officeholder but also to certain individuals, whether male relatives or colleagues, who were closely associated with him.[10] Therefore, however historically inaccurate Mark's insertion of "Abiathar" for "Abimelech" may appear to the modern reader, his original readers would not have necessarily considered it as such. Second, I shall go on to argue that Jesus' choice of names was intentionally preserved by Mark as a means of invoking a particular OT storyline. This storyline was a component piece

---

(Waco, TX: Baylor University Press, 2009), 166; Mary Ann Beavis, *Mark* (Paideia: Commentaries on the New Testament; Grand Rapids: Baker, 2011), 63.

[8] If the error originated with the historical Jesus and Mark preserves the error unwittingly, we have to imagine that both Jesus and Mark (and Peter who is said to have been behind Mark?) all overlooked the same mistake.

[9] Robert H. Stein, *Mark* (BECNT; Grand Rapids: Baker, 2008), 146–47.

[10] So Craig S. Keener, *The IVP Bible Background Commentary* (Downers Grove, IL: InterVarsity Press, 1993), 142; echoed with approval by Hans F. Bayer, *Das Evangelium des Markus* (Historisch Theologische Auslegung; Giessen: SCM Press, 2008), 161.

within the Evangelist's twofold agenda: negatively, sustaining a polemic against the regnant priesthood and, positively, offering an apologetic for a newly emerging priesthood made possible by the resurrection of Jesus the Messiah. In other words, when properly understood within the context of the Evangelist's broader narrative goals, the very mention of the "high priest Abiathar" can be seen as integral to Mark's theological program, a program which envisions the church—not the official cult at Jerusalem—as the continuation of the true temple into the future.

The Title of High Priest in Ancient Judaism

The history of modern biblical interpretation reminds us that, more often than we care to admit, biblical criticism identifies problems in the text that would not be problems were it not for our own mistaken assumptions. I believe that the Abiathar problem is one such case. The operative assumptions for most readings of this passage can be reduced to a syllogism that goes something like this: (a) there was in ancient Judaism one and only one high priest at any given time; (b) Ahimelech was high priest during the incident at Nob; (c) therefore, the incident at Nob did *not* take place when Abiathar was high priest (contra Mark's Jesus). However, when we take a closer look at the historical data, we realize that premise (a) stands in need of qualification. The term "high priest" is more elastic than most commentators are willing to grant.

In part, this elasticity is a function of the practice of co-regency in the ANE. In antiquity, as the titular ruler anticipated circumstances in which he would be unable to carry out the responsibilities of his office, it would be a matter of practicality and political expediency to have a stand-in readily available.[11] Since the postexilic high priesthood was as much a political office as it was a religious one, it would only make sense for the practice of royal surrogacy to extend to the cultic sphere. One would further expect that in the event that a high priest was absent or incapacitated, the temple administration would naturally look to the next of kin to serve as a kind of understudy.

Such situations almost certainly obtained in the postexilic priesthood. For example, we have to assume that even before Jason secured the priesthood in 175 B.C., he was already serving as a substitute high priest on occasions when his brother Onias was not in Jerusalem. The same practice must also have obtained for Lysimachus in the absence of his brother Menelaus (2 Mc 4:29).[12] To be sure, one brother standing in

---

[11] Edwin R. Thiele, "Corregencies and Overlapping Reigns Among the Hebrew Kings," *JBL* 93 (1974): 192.

[12] See James C. VanderKam, *From Joshua to Caiaphas: High Priests after the Exile* (Minneapolis: Fortress, 2004), 198.

for another does not mean the second brother shared the office in the fullness of its privileges and responsibilities. It did mean, however, that the function of the high priest could at times be extended beyond the normal office holder. That Judas Maccabaeus also seems to have performed the role of high priest during the *intersacerdotium* between the death of Alcimus (162 B.C.) and the ascension of Jonathan (152 B.C.) (*A.J.* 12.10.6 [§414]), despite his non-Zadokite lineage, also reminds us that by the second century the high priest could (and would necessarily) be granted a *de facto* authority.[13] Perhaps this dynamic had something to do with the term "high priest" moving beyond its narrow, technical sense.[14]

In any case, while it is uncertain whether the term "high priest" was already being used in an expanded sense in the Persian and Hellenistic periods, certainly by the time of the first century it was applied to personnel outside the official lineage of high priests. For example, in recounting the governance of the exilic returnees under Zerubbabel, Josephus writes:

> So these men offered the largest sacrifices on these accounts, and used great magnificence in the worship of God, and dwelt in Jerusalem, and made use of a form of government that was aristocratic, but mixed with an oligarchy, for the high priests were at the head of their affairs, until the posterity of the Asamoneans set up kingly government. (*A.J.* 11.5.8. [§111])

In this context, "high priests" refer not to a successive line of priestly rule but an oligarchy involving a plurality of high priests. Obviously, for this to make any sense, Josephus must be imagining a situation in which a set number of individuals were all considered "high priests" at the same time in a nontechnical sense. Later in *Antiquities*, in his account of the actions of Cuspius Fadus following Agrippa I's death (A.D. 44), Josephus brings together this nontechnical sense of "high priest" with the more specialized technical sense:

> He also at this time sent for *the high priests* [τοὺς ἀρχιερεῖς; *tous archiereis*] and the principal citizens of Jerusalem, and this at the command of the emperor, and admonished them, that they should lay up the long garment and the sacred vestment, which it is customary for no one but *the high priest* [ὁ ἀρχιερεὺς; *ho archiereus*] to wear, in the tower of Antonia, that it might be under the power of the Romans, as it had been formerly. (*A.J.* 20.1.1 [§6])

Given the two occurrences of "high priest" in this passage, there is a fluidity of usage that Josephus employs without feeling compelled to define just what he means by the former use of the term, although it is clear that

---

[13] VanderKam, *Joshua to Caiaphas*, 241–44.

[14] On the transition of the term, see Menahem Stern, *Greek and Latin Authors on Jews and Judaism: From Herodotus to Plutarch* (3 vols.; Jerusalem: Israel Academy of Sciences and Humanities, 1974), 1:40–41; Carl L. Holladay, *Fragments from Hellenistic Jewish Authors* (Chico, CA: Scholars Press, 1983), 326; VanderKam, *Joshua to Caiaphas*, 117.

it refers to a high-ranking official within the temple. Instances of the same can be multiplied in the writings of Josephus (e.g., *B.J.* 2.20.4 [§566]; *Vita* 1.1 [§3]). This is no surprise, for the NT itself often uses the term in just this way (Mt 2:4, 21:15, 23; Mk 11:18, 14:1; Lk 19:47; Jn 7:32; 11:47).

The NT writings also provide several well-known examples whereby the title of high priest extends through the family line. Setting the stage for his narrative of John the Baptizer, Luke famously locates the beginning of the prophet's ministry in "the fifteenth year of the reign of Emperor Tiberius [i.e., A.D. 28/29] . . . during the high priesthood of Annas and Caiaphas" ([ἐπὶ ἀρχιερέως Ἄννα καὶ Καϊάφα; *epi archiereōs Hanna kai Kaiapha*, Lk 3:1–2). Luke's assigning the fifteenth year of Tiberius to Annas's (Ananus) priesthood is problematic, since Annas was technically deposed by the Roman powers in A.D. 15, fourteen years earlier. The only way to make sense of this dating is to suppose either that Luke had made a mistake or that the Evangelist knew full well that Annas's son-in-law Caiaphas was the active priest but that convention allowed for Annas to retain the title *ad mortem* (cf. *m. Hor.* 3:1–4). The latter seems far more likely.[15] That would explain how in the Fourth Gospel Jesus can appear both before Annas *qua* high priest (Jn 18:19, 24) and then Caiaphas also *qua* high priest (Jn 18:24). (If Luke had mistakenly assigned the priesthood to Annas in 3:1–2, it would be an amazing coincidence that John has made the same mistake.) This dynamic is further confirmed in another Lukan passage focusing on a certain Sceva, who is called "high priest" (Acts 19:14), even though he quite evidently is not attached to the Jerusalem apparatus. Although different explanations have been set forth, it is likely that Sceva was a "high priest" simply by virtue of being descended from the high priest.[16] Thus, the NT itself affords instances when the title "high priest" is extended to the next of male kin, either up (Caiaphas) or down (Sceva) the family tree without further explanation.

Taking this observation on board, we are closer to shedding light on the Abiathar problem. If the term "high priest" was not necessarily restricted to one living person at one time but was indeed shared with the high priest's living children (among others), then it is not inconsistent for Mark's Jesus to describe David's entrance into the tabernacle taking place "when Abiathar was high priest." By first-century usage, Abiathar truly was a high priest during the event at Nob, and Mark is, technically speaking, quite correct despite the scholarly charge to the contrary. Clearly, the Abiathar problem has been overstated.

Yet, we must confess, it is still a problem. Why would Mark's Jesus associate this event with Abiathar as opposed to Ahimelech, when the lat-

---

[15] So, e.g., Joseph A. Fitzmyer, *The Gospel According to Luke I—IX* (AB 28; New York: Doubleday, 1981), 455.

[16] So, e.g., B. A. Mastin, "Scaeva the Chief Priest," *JTS* 27 (1976): 405–12; Alfons Weiser, *Die Apostelgeschichte* (ÖTK 5; Gütersloh: Mohn, 1985), 529.

ter was more properly the high priest and the text of 1 Sm 21:1–9 says as much? To resolve *this* problem, we must turn to the larger narrative and theological goals of Mark.

The Strategic Inclusion of Abiathar in Mark 2:26

As I intend to argue, the presence of Abiathar at 2:26 is explicable on a narrative reading of Mark that takes seriously both the Evangelist's thematic interests and his disposition to develop these interests by drawing on various storylines available to him in the Hebrew Scriptures. That Mark mined the Scriptures for the raw materials of his narrative is a point that has been sufficiently addressed, especially in the past generation of research, and requires no new substantiation.[17] Mark's thematic interests and Abiathar's connection with those interests, however, is another matter. This requires further elaboration.

On even a cursory reading of the Second Gospel, the reader is struck not only by the emphasis on Jesus' messianic identity but also by the way in which this identity is worked out within the context of a political struggle. The competing parties in this struggle are, on the one side, Jesus and his followers and, on the other side, the religious establishment ultimately embodied by the high priest. Given Mark's obvious interest in Jesus' messianic identity, it is not hard to see why the Evangelist also has a particular interest in the temple. After all, any claim to be the messiah would have had certain entailments regarding the temple, since in Second Temple Judaism messiah and temple were closely related. The eschatological expectation of Judaism, for all its diversity, held forth a consistent hope of a restored temple where YHWH could finally receive the worship he was due, and this would come through the agency of the messiah. It fell to the messiah to erect the temple at the culmination of redemptive history and thereby signal that Israel was finally, decisively, and enduringly poised to fulfill its vocation before YHWH.[18] Thus, in the first century, anyone claiming to be messiah would certainly be implying the introduction of a new temple order. Conversely, anyone hinting toward a new temple order was also raising the prospect of the great messianic unveiling. Quite clearly, the Evangelist's pronounced interest in both messianic themes and temple themes is no accident: the two concepts are intrinsically correlated within the Jewish mindset.

---

[17] See the bibliographical survey in Rikk E. Watts, *Isaiah's New Exodus in Mark* (WUNT 2/88; Tübingen: Mohr Siebeck, 1997; Grand Rapids: Baker Books, 2000), 9–27.

[18] 2 Sm 7:12–13; 2 Chr 36:22–23; Is 44:28–45:1a; Zec 6:12–13a; Sir 50:1–2, 5–6; *1 En.* 53:6, 90:29; *Pss. Sol.* 17:21–23a, 30; *Sib. Or.* 5:414–27, 432–33; *Tg. Is* 53:5.

In the Gospel of Mark, it hardly needs demonstrating that Jesus' messiahship takes front and center stage. This becomes clear from the beginning when the incipit announces "the gospel of Jesus *Christ*," that is, "the gospel of Jesus the Messiah" (1:1). When John the Baptizer appears five verses later in the guise of Elijah (Mk 1:6; 2 Kgs 1:8), the reader wonders, especially following the quotation of Mal 3:1 in Mk 1:2, whether this is the anticipated Elijahan forerunner of the messiah.[19] Mark's action begins with Jesus driving out demons (1:21–28), an activity that prompts the crowds to ask "What is this? A new teaching—with authority!" (1:27). Later, we find the disciples sitting in awed silence following the stilling of the storm; they ask one another, "Who is this?" (4:41). Eventually, both questions (the first dealing with the nature of Jesus' authority and the second with the nature of his identity) are answered through the words of Peter's confession of Jesus' messiahship (8:29). Eventually, too, the reader's musings regarding the Baptizer are confirmed when Jesus states that "Elijah has come, and they did to him whatever they pleased, as it is written about him" (9:13). By this midpoint in the narrative, it becomes clear that the whole narrative has been building up to this one climactic moment: the announcement of Jesus' messiahship.

However, the remainder of the Gospel will go on to reveal that this messiah is a rather upside-down messiah, one who must suffer, just as his disciples would also have to suffer (8:31–32). This surprising element of suffering helps makes sense of the resistance Jesus had been facing earlier in the narrative, especially from the religious establishment. Strangely, when Jesus comes preaching the kingdom, the demons recognize who he is (1:23–24, 34; 5:7), but the temple leadership does not (2:1–3:6). If one of messiah's appointed tasks was to drive out Satan, these same authorities accuse Jesus of colluding with Satan (3:20–30). Ironically, while Israel's expected messiah was supposed to have been gladly received, Jesus is scorned (5:40; 6:1–6). In Mark's theology, Jesus is not messiah despite his rejection and suffering but is marked out as messiah precisely through such things. The disciples anticipate a coronation fitting for the Son of David (10:37); little do they know that the coronation will take place, although not on their terms.

As Jesus enters Jerusalem, the expected stage of the messiah's self-revelation, it is only blind Bartimaeus who glimpses the truth, calling out "Jesus, Son of David, have mercy on me!" (10:47). This would not be the first time Mark's hearers would have associated Jesus with the Son of David. By virtue of his teaching and exorcisms, activities notably predicated of Solomon, Jesus has already proven himself to be a Son of David by his deeds. But now, by entering Jerusalem on a colt, he is re-enacting the coronation of Solomon (1 Kgs 1:33) and thereby symbolically laying

---

[19] But see Morris M. Faierstein, "Why Do the Scribes Say That Elijah Must Come First?" *JBL* 100 (1981): 75–86.

claim to the office of Davidic messiah in no uncertain terms. At the pitch of conflict with his temple opponents, Jesus speaks further to this Davidic ascension in his teaching on Ps 110 (Mk 12:35–37a), an enthronement psalm with obvious messianic and indeed Solomonic overtones (cf. 1 Kgs 1:36–37). When Jesus does finally take his royal seat, his enthronement is strange indeed; it takes place on a Roman cross—complete with all the elements of normal Roman coronation, including the enrobing, the crowning, and the homage (15:16–20). On Jesus' cross is nailed his messianic title: "the King of the Jews" (15:26), and as Jesus expires he calls out in words of the Davidic psalm (Ps 22:1; 15:34). As the Evangelist takes pains to show, Jesus enters Jerusalem as the true Son of David, teaches as the true Son of David, and dies as the true Son of David.

If Mark's eagerness to characterize Jesus as a Davidic messiah is commonly granted, perhaps less widely acknowledged is the Evangelist's equally strong determination to style Jesus as the rebuilder of the temple.[20] But in fact, if the Fourth Gospel can be fairly summarized with the phrase "Jesus *contra mundum*," the Second Gospel may with equal fairness be deemed by the phrase "Jesus *contra templum*." This surfaces early on in the narrative through Jesus' repeated implicit claim to lay the groundwork for a new temple. For example, when Jesus encounters the paralytic who had been lowered through the roof, he declares the man's sins to be forgiven (Mk 2:5), a bold pronouncement that forces onlookers to reflect: "Who can forgive sins but God alone?" (2:7). This question, together with the fact that Jesus has successfully backed his claim by healing the paralytic, serves as a springboard for Mark's readers to draw further inferences. While Jesus' declaration of forgiveness does not necessarily entail a claim to divine status, it does at least speak to Jesus' authority to provide forgiveness on God's behalf. The pronouncement of forgiveness was an activity that had traditionally been reserved for the priesthood.[21]

When Mark later recounts Jesus declaring that "nothing outside a man can make him unclean" (Mk 7:15), the Evangelist is not seeking, as so many interpreters want us to believe, to prioritize a warm, inner spirituality over cold, external rites. More to the point, Mark's intention is to recount a Jesus who, in revising the existent purity codes, is also redefining who may and who may not have legitimate access to the temple. Apparently possessing an authority that allows him either to circumvent or

---

[20] An early voice in contemporary discussion on this is Donald H. Juel, *Messiah and Temple: The Trial of Jesus in the Gospel of Mark* (SBLDS 31; Missoula, MT: Scholars Press, 1977).

[21] Similarly N. T. Wright, *Jesus and the Victory of God* (Christian Origins and the Question of God 2; London: SPCK; Minneapolis: Fortress, 1996), 406–21; G. K. Beale, *The Temple and the Church's Mission: A Biblical Theology of the Dwelling Place of God* (NSBT; Downers Grove, IL: InterVarsity Press, 2004), 177–78; Crispin Fletcher-Louis, "Jesus and the High Priestly Messiah, Part 2,"*JSHJ* 5 (2007): 71–74.

preempt standing temple regulations, Jesus is redefining temple membership along the lines of a new, more radical ethic (Mk 7:18–23). In doing so, he is also unavoidably redefining Israel itself. Because one's membership within Israel was constituted and predicated on one's membership within the temple community, the redefinition of the latter necessarily meant the redefinition of the former.

Understanding full well the radical nature of Jesus' program, the temple leaders remain firm in their resistance to it throughout the narrative. The result, Mark's Jesus promises, could only be judgment for both the priests and their temple. This could be inferred easily enough from his cleansing the temple (Mk 11:15–19), ensconced between two highly symbolic events of the cursing of the fig tree (v. 12–14) and the disciples' discovery that the same tree had shriveled (v. 20–25). Commentators on this passage regularly remark on the parallel between Jesus' condemnation of the fruitless fig tree and his stunning rebuke of the temple, which metaphorically has also failed to bear its appointed fruit. Unable to carry out the purposes for which it was created, the temple, much like the fig tree, will be destroyed through divine judgment.

Expanding on the significance of the withered fig tree, Jesus assures his disciples that through believing prayer they too can participate in the same power he himself had exercised in causing the fig tree to shrivel (v. 22–25). Jesus' exhortation to believing prayer following an intimation of the temple's destruction is no *non sequitur*. Rather, the encouragement follows on the disciples' newly acquired identity as those who would make up the temple. Perhaps in Mark's mind it was the temple functionaries' failure to pray, more precisely, their failure to employ the temple as a house of prayer (11:17), that constituted a crucial reason for its downfall. If so, then prayer would have to become the new order of the day for the disciples. That is why, as the proper owners of "the house," it fell to the disciples to "watch" and pray (Mk 13:32–37).

A separate but related aspect of new temple life offered in Jesus comes to the fore in 12:28–34. Here the Evangelist recounts a conversation in which a scribe approaches Jesus with the question "What is the first commandment of all?" (v. 28). Jesus responds by citing the *shema'* (Dt 6:4–5) and the Levitical command to "love your neighbor as yourself" (Lv 19:18b; see Mk 12:29–31), the fulfillment of which is said to be "much more important than all whole burnt offerings and sacrifices" (v. 33). The point is this: as the Jesus community sought to conduct itself appropriately in its horizontal and vertical relationships, it would be carrying out the essential functions of the temple, a temple, which, as the sacrificial language of the Last Supper makes clear (vv. 22–25), would be purified through the priestly atonement of Jesus himself.[22]

---

[22] So also John Paul Heil, "The Narrative Strategy and Pragmatics of the Temple Theme in Mark," *CBQ* 59 (1997): 84–85. For more on the double command-

Claims such as these—to the extent that they were comprehensible—would not go uncontested by the temple elite. In response the opponent's initial strategy is to discredit him through public debate, but this culminates in failure. For example, when Jesus is challenged by the chief priests, teachers of the law, and elders to identify the source of his authority, he turns the tables and asks them to settle the same question in regards to John the Baptist (11:27–33). Their refusal to do so and Jesus' rejoinder betoken, at least as the Evangelists portray it, a debating-match victory for Jesus. Jesus' success in outflanking his opponents in a bout of verbal fisticuffs is undoubtedly symbolic of a more fundamental victory over those who were entrusted with maintaining the temple on a day-to-day basis.

Hostilities are at their peak when Jesus gives his parable of the wicked tenants (12:1–10), where he identifies himself with the "stone the builders rejected . . . the cornerstone" (v. 10) and the tenants as the illegitimate temple leaders (vv. 9–12). As even Jesus' opponents knew, this parable was "against them" (v. 12). But Jesus is also conveying important truths about his own role and that of his disciples. As the "cornerstone" of Ps 118:22–23, he is, according to the contemporary interpretation of the text, the Davidic messiah.[23] Here too, among other places, the disciples are constituted as priests, for the text envisions their being established as the new temple servants (12:9).[24]

Matters come to a crossroads at the trial, where Jesus as the messianic high priest and the *soi-disant* high priest Caiaphas confront one another face to face (15:53–65). As one might expect, Jerusalem was big enough only for one great high priest (i.e., high priest in the narrow sense). On the pronouncement of the death sentence (14:64), following on the heels of a virtually explicit messianic claim (14:62), Jesus' fate is sealed and so too, in the mind of Mark's reader, is the final fate of the errant high priest and his temple. Thus, for Mark, the question of Jesus' messiahship was tightly bound up with another set of questions centered on Jesus' twin claim that he, precisely as the messiah, was the new temple builder and that his temple-based opponents were illegitimate tenants. Jesus' messianic identity and his conflict with the temple are intertwined themes centrally embedded in the fabric of Mark's narrative.

Even if largely awaiting development, these same twin themes of Davidic messianism and temple theology are operative both in the larger

---

ment as the basis for Jesus' temple ethics, see Nicholas Perrin, *Jesus the Priest* (London: SPCK; Grand Rapids: Baker, forthcoming).

[23] See Seyoon Kim, "Jesus—The Son of God, the Stone, the Son of Man, and the Servant: The Role of Zechariah in the Self-Identification of Jesus," in *Tradition and Interpretation in the New Testament: Essays in Honor of E. Earle Ellis for His Sixtieth Birthday* (ed. G. F. Hawthorne and O. Betz; Grand Rapids: Eerdmans; Tübingen: Mohr Siebeck, 1987), 134–48 (136).

[24] So too Heil, "Narrative Strategy," 82–83.

literary unit pertaining to Jesus' conflict with his enemies (2:1–3:6) and our pericope (2:23–28) within that. As Joanna Dewey has demonstrated, the five pericopae making up 2:1–3:6 are tightly structured in an overarching chiasm, whereby the healing of the paralytic (2:1–12) corresponds to the healing of the man with the shriveled hand (3:1–6), and the calling of Levi (2:13–17) matches up with the Lord of the Sabbath (2:23–27).[25] The middle section, Jesus questioned about fasting (2:18–22), binds the second and fourth pericopae together. Structurally the five pericopae are of a piece; across the five there is mounting criticism of Jesus, all leveled directly or indirectly by the temple-based leadership.[26] Intimations of messianic status are not far in the background (2:10, 28).

The scene in 2:23–28 focuses on a controversy involving Jesus and his disciples, not just Jesus himself. On this Sabbath day, the Pharisees find the disciples gleaning grain and accuse them of violating the Sabbath; Jesus responds to the challenge by citing the example of David (1 Sm 21:1–9). Just how Jesus intends to use David in his argument is an important and difficult question warranting its own discussion.[27] But for now it is enough to note the interesting repetition of the phrase "and those who were with him" in v. 25 (καὶ οἱ μετ' αὐτοῦ; *kai hoi met autou*) and in v. 26 (καὶ τοῖς σὺν αὐτῷ οὖσιν; *kai tois syn autō ousin*); in both instances they are in reference to David's men. The repetition, hardly necessary in the context, is all the more striking given that Mark later tells us that Jesus called his disciples that "they might be *with him*" (ὦσιν μετ' αὐτοῦ; *ōsin met autou*, 3:14). In other words, Mk 2:23–28 prepares us to surmise that Jesus' gathering of the Twelve is modeled on David's gathering of his movement. This also means that in our pericope the Evangelist intends a linkage not only between Jesus and David but also between Jesus' disciples and the men who were with David.

The Evangelist proceeds to attach a surprising significance to the disciples' unfolding role and status. He records Jesus pointing out (in v. 26) that David's men all ate the same bread that was not lawful for anyone but priests to eat. Given the obvious analogy between David's men and those "who are with" Jesus (i.e., the disciples), this raises the question as to whether Mark's Jesus intends to say that David's men (and by exten-

---

[25] Joanna Dewey, "The Literary Structure of the Controversy Stories in Mark 2:1–3:6," *JBL* 92 (1973): 394–401.

[26] Dewey, "Literary Structure," 398.

[27] Roure (*Jesús y la Figura de David*), who gives the fullest treatment of the question to date, argues that Jesus, in subordinating Torah to his own needs, is claiming a prophetic authority on par with David's (pp. 121–27). This may be true so far as this goes, but since the author does not fully consider the cultic elements of either 1 Sm 21:1–9 or the Markan passage, he is unable to speak to the possibility that Jesus' seeming usurpation of authority is modeled on David's rightful role as priestly king. For more on the priestly implications of Mk 2:23–28, see Fletcher-Louis, "Jesus and the High Priestly Messiah," 75–77.

sion his own disciples) were exceptions to the for-priestly-consumption-only rule or were, in fact, confirmation of it. In light of the way in which Mark shapes his narrative in the final six chapters, where Jesus implicitly confers the priesthood onto his disciples, the latter option seems much more attractive. Reading the pericope of the disciples' plucking grain in anticipation of the subsequent narrative, it becomes clear that Jesus permits the disciples to "desecrate the Sabbath" precisely because, like David's men, they had priestly prerogatives as part of a new temple regime. If as a rule the temple showbread was reserved for the priests, then David's men and the disciples were both exceptions that proved the rule. The scene contained in 2:23–28, then, is not to be understood as Jesus' attempt to engage in casuistic discussion over the scope of the Law (as it is so often taken) but rather an eschatological announcement that YHWH is about to transfer the priestly mantle from the official cult leadership, who in their resistance to the true Son of David were liable to judgment, to his very own disciples.

Once this reading of Mk 2:23–28 is in place, we are in excellent position to solve the mystery of Abiathar's appearance at v. 26. We recall that for most of David's reign there were not one but two high priests: Zadok and Ahimelech (2 Sm 8:17), the two sons of Ahitub (1 Chr 6:12; 1 Sm 22:11); Ahitub was of the line of Phinehas (1 Sm 14:3), who in turn was the son of Eli (1 Sm 1:3). Derelict in his duties as a priestly father to Hophni and Phineas (1 Sm 1–2), Eli had been informed through a word of the Lord that his priestly lineage would one day be terminated in divine judgment (1 Sm 2:30–36). That judgment begins to be actualized when in the course of Adonijah's rebellion against the heir apparent Solomon, the high priest Abiathar throws in his lot with the upstart pretender to the throne (1 Kgs 1:7). In short order, the rebellion collapses and Solomon is forced—all in fulfillment of the curse issued generations earlier against Eli (1 Kgs 2:26–27)—to depose the rebel priest Abiathar and transfer all priestly authority to the true priest Zadok, who had remained faithful throughout (1 Kgs 1:8).[28]

Employing Abiathar as an emblem of a rebellious and therefore failed priesthood, Mark's Jesus is in effect speaking a parable that draws upon a well-known story from history in order to explain the present. Drawing up lines of opposition between himself on the one side (represented by David) and the high priestly order on the other side (represented by Abiathar), Jesus anticipates the Solomonic enthronement of his final week (Mk 10:46–15:47), where despite accumulated markers of Solomonic identity (the invocation of blind Bartimaeus, a triumphal entry on a colt, and teaching from Ps 110), the wayward priests rise up in revolt in order

---

[28] Abiathar's fall from grace was no obscure moment in the eyes of first-century Judaism, for in his recounting of Jewish history Josephus takes pains to refer to it (*A.J.* 8.1.3 [§§11–12]).

to deprive him of his throne. Although the Abiathar-like opponents of Jesus seem successful, Mark promises that it is only for a time. In due course, Jesus and his followers will be confirmed as the true parallel to David and his band, and proleptically so, when Jesus took the bread "and gave it to them" (καὶ ἔδωκεν αὐτοῖς; *kai edōken autois*) at the Last Supper (Mk 14:22), just as David "gave it to them" (ἔδωκεν καὶ τοῖς; *edōken kai tois*) at Nob (2:26). Finally, despite the recalcitrance of the Abiatharesque priesthood, Jesus will secure his throne much like the first Son of David, but he will do it in a most unconventional way: through his own death and resurrection.[29] In due course, too, Caiaphas and his subordinates will go into exile, much as Abiathar was deposed and forced into exile.

By staging the temple leaders' resistance to Jesus against the scenery of Abiathar's participation in the failed rebellion against Solomon, Mark is not only anticipating the extended Solomonic enthronement in Mk 10:46–15:47, which again like Solomon's enthronement will not go unchallenged by the priestly ranks, but also reframing the question asked earlier regarding Jesus' authority (1:27). Even now, long before the invocative shouts of blind Bartimaeus, the words of Jesus force Mark's readers to decide whether Jesus is indeed the true Son of David and whether Jesus' detractors are indeed a kind of Abiathar *redivivus*, a priest who may have started well but in the end proved illegitimate. Of course, none of these rich nuances would be possible had Mark's Jesus simply said, "When Ahimelech was high priest."

Conclusion

In this essay, I have offered a twofold explanation for the so-called Abiathar problem. First, I have sought to confirm the suggestion already made by several scholars that Abiathar was indeed a bona fide high priest on account of his filial relationship to Ahimelech, even while the latter was alive, well, and fully functional in his office. Second, I have sought to argue that the inclusion of Abiathar (rather than the expected Ahimelech) at Mk 2:26 is a calculated, if not intentionally surprising, move to invoke a prior narrative involving a well-known earlier priestly rebellion against the Son of David. This reading makes most sense when considered within the Gospel as a whole, particularly within the stream of its two major themes, Davidic messianism and temple.

If my reading is persuasive, then there is some irony to the fact that the explanation for which Greg Beale and I were seeking turned out to be buried in his favorite garden, the temple garden. While Dr. Beale and I naturally disagree on a number of points, I am sure, I am equally sure

---

[29] See Stephen P. Ahearne-Kroll, *The Psalms of Lament in Mark's Passion: Jesus' Davidic Suffering* (SNTSMS, 142; Cambridge: Cambridge University Press, 2007).

that he and I are in consonant agreement on the central significance of the temple. As a result of this study, I for one am personally all the more convinced that Timothy C. Gray is correct when he writes that "[t]he temple plays a vital role in the plot of Mark's gospel and is deeply connected to the story of Jesus."[30] Thanks in good measure to Beale, we see more and more signs that the temple is beginning to be recognized as a crucial component in the thinking and theology of many NT writers. This alleged instance of mistaken priestly identity is, I believe, a case in point.

---

[30] Timothy C. Gray, *The Temple in the Gospel of Mark: A Study in its Narrative Role* (WUNT 2/242; Tübingen: Mohr Siebeck, 2008; Grand Rapids: Baker, 2010), 198.

CHAPTER 10

THE 144,000 IN REVELATION 7 AND 14: OLD TESTAMENT AND INTRATEXTUAL CLUES TO THEIR IDENTITY[1]

Joel R. White

Introduction

Greg Beale agrees with the majority opinion on the identity of the 144,000 from the twelve tribes of the Israel in Rv 7:1–8: This group's real-world referent is the same as that of the countless and ethnically diverse multitude described in Rv 7:9–17.[2] According to this interpretive tradition, the two groups described in these respective visions (cf. μετὰ τοῦτο εἶδον [meta touto eidon] in Rv 7:1 with μετὰ ταῦτα εἶδον [meta tauta eidon] in Rv 7:9) are both symbolic depictions of the church. The first vision stresses its identity as the "new" or "true" Israel; the second, its multi-ethnic universality. In spite of its popularity, however, this reading is by

---

[1] This article expands on arguments first put forward in my dissertation. See Joel White, *Die Erstlingsgabe im Neuen Testament* (TANZ 45; Tübingen: Francke, 2007), 260–84.

[2] G. K. Beale, *The Book of Revelation: A Commentary on the Greek Text* (NIGTC; Grand Rapids: Eerdmans, 1999), 424: "[t]here is only one group viewed from different perspectives." The following commentaries also take this position: George E. Ladd, *A Commentary on the Revelation of John* (Grand Rapids: Eerdmans, 1972), 115–16; G. R. Beasley-Murray, *The Book of Revelation* (NCB; London: Oliphants, 1974), 140–41; Robert H. Mounce, *The Book of Revelation* (NICNT; Grand Rapids: Eerdmans, 1977), 168; M. Eugene Boring, *Revelation* (Interpretation; Louisville: Westminster John Knox, 1989), 131; John P. M. Sweet, *Revelation* (TPINTC; London: SCM Press, 1990), 150–51; Grant R. Osborne, *Revelation* (BECNT; Grand Rapids: Baker, 2002), 311–12; Steven S. Smalley, *The Revelation to John: A Commentary on the Greek Text of the Apocalypse* (Downers Grove, IL: InterVarsity Press, 2005), 184–88. See also Christopher R. Smith, "The Portrayal of the Church as the New Israel in the Names and Order of the Tribes in Revelation 7:5–8," *JSNT* 39 (1990): 111–18; Philip L. Mayo, *"Those Who Call Themselves Jews": The Church and Judaism in the Apocalypse of John* (PTMS 60; Eugene, OR: Wipf & Stock, 2006), 77.

no means self-evident. Indeed, earlier generations of scholars were much less inclined to equate the two groups.[3] They generally followed an older interpretation going back at least as far as Victorinus of Petovium (d. ca. 304) who viewed the 144,000 as a group of Jews—their exact nature is debated—in contrast to the largely Gentile church.[4]

An assessment of the semantic phenomena of the visions themselves makes it clear that John[5] intends his hearers—he is not envisioning readers as the original recipients of his work[6]—to imagine two different groups. The first is manifestly Jewish, and their number is precisely delimited. The second group, by contrast, is so large that no one is able to count it, and it is drawn from "every nation and tribe and people and language group" (Rv 7:9).[7] Despite a clear contrast on the visionary level, however, the scholarly majority transmogrifies Israel into the church on the referential level with the alacrity of firm conviction.[8] While it is not impossible that these distinct groups could denote the same real-world entity, such an interpretive move would hardly be the first impulse of

---

[3] See, e.g., Wilhelm Bousset, *Die Offenbarung Johannis* (KEK 16; 1906; repr., Göttingen: Vandenhoeck & Ruprecht, 1996), 287; Theodor Zahn, *Die Offenbarung des Johannes* (KNT 18; Leipzig: Deichertsche Verlagsbuchhandlung, 1926), 68; T. F. Glasson, *The Revelation of John* (CBC; Cambridge: Cambridge University Press, 1965), 52–53.

[4] Victorinus, *Commentary on the Apocalypse*. More recent adherents of this position include Josephine M. Ford, *Revelation: Introduction, Translation, and Commentary* (AB 38; Garden City, NY: Doubleday, 1965), 120–26; André Feuillet, "Les 144,000 Israélites marqués d'un sceau," *NovT* 9 (1967): 191–224; J. A. Draper, "The Heavenly Feast of Tabernacles: Revelation 7,1–17," *JSNT* 19 (1983): 136.

[5] The identity of the author of Revelation is not crucial to the interpretation of this passage, but I accept the traditional ascription of the work to John the apostle and date the book with the majority to the mid-90s of the first cent. A.D.

[6] Careful consideration of the "oral-auricular setting" of Revelation (so Felise Tavo, "The Structure of the Apocalypse: Re-examining a Perennial Problem," *NovT* 47 [2005]: 56–57) is crucial to its interpretation both here and elsewhere. Cf. Gilbert Desrosiers, *An Introduction to Revelation: A Pathway to Interpretation* (Continuum Biblical Studies Series; London: Continuum, 2000), 57: "[t]he one very important point to remember . . . is the fact that the book [of Revelation] was read aloud to a congregation, not being studied as if it were a textbook."

[7] On the clear distinctions between the two groups, see esp. Feuillet, "144,000," 197–98.

[8] A crucial hermeneutical imperative that is too often overlooked in the interpretation of apocalyptic literature in general and the book of Revelation in particular is the need to distinguish between two levels of discourse: the symbolic or visionary level and the referential level. Thus, when we ask the question "Does John identify the 144,000 with Israel?" there are two different kinds of answers. On the visionary level, there is no doubt that he does so. What this refers to in the real world is the only matter of contention.

first-century hearers.[9] If John was hoping they would draw this conclusion, he did little to facilitate it.[10]

What, then, accounts for the strong support for the majority position? Historically, its acceptance has no doubt been expedited by a non-Jewish—and sometimes blatantly anti-Jewish—approach to the book of Revelation as a whole. Recent decades, however, have witnessed a growing appreciation for the Jewish flavor of the NT, including Revelation.[11] In particular, the facile assumption that the parting of the ways between Judaism and Christianity was more or less complete and irreversible by the time of the destruction of Jerusalem in A.D. 70 has given way to a more complex picture of the interactions between Jews and Christians, and indeed, between Jewish and Gentile believers in Jesus, that extended well into the second century.[12] This has opened up the possibility of reading Revelation not as the record of a schism long decided in favor of the Gentile church, with hostile Jews subsequently looking in from the outside, but as an attempt by John to preserve the nascent movement's Jewish heritage at a time when it still represented a viable, if clearly threatened (and for some, threatening), tradition within the church.[13] I will argue in what follows that this is precisely the impetus behind John's inclusion of his visions of the 144,000 in his narrative. They represent the Jewish Christian core of the church that in his thinking deserved the ongoing respect and admiration of its Gentile brothers and sisters.

---

[9] Cf. Peter Hirschberg, "Jewish Believers in Asia Minor according to the Book of Revelation and the Gospel of John," in *Jewish Believers in Jesus: The Early Centuries* (ed. Oskar Skarsaune and Reidar Hvalvik; Peabody, MA: Hendrickson, 2007), 224: "The Jewish particularity of the sealed 144,000 . . . makes it difficult to read [Rv 7:1–8] as a simple metaphorization of 'the church.'"

[10] Another interpretive tradition views the 144,000 as early Christian martyrs. See Robert W. Wall, *Revelation* (NIBC 18; Peabody, MA: Hendrickson, 1991); David E. Aune, *Revelation 6–16* (WBC 52B; Nashville: Thomas Nelson, 1998), 440, 480; Stephen Pattemore, *The People of God in the Apocalypse: Discourse, Structure, and Exegesis* (SNTSMS 128; Cambridge: Cambridge University Press, 2004), 140. While this theory respects the distinction drawn between the two groups, it shares the majority opinion's weakness of giving too little credence to the Jewishness of the 144,000.

[11] Cf. Hirschberg, "Jewish Believers," 218–19.

[12] Cf. James Carleton Paget, "Judenchristen: II. Alte Kirche," *RGG* 4:603–5; Hubert Frankemölle, *Frühjudentum und Urchristentum: Vorgeschichte—Verlauf—Auswirkungen (4. Jahrhundert v. Chr. bis 4. Jahrhundert n. Chr.)* (Studienbücher Theologie 5; Stuttgart: Kohlhammer, 2006), 330–33; Oskar Skarsaune, "The History of Jewish Believers in the Early Centuries—Perspectives and Framework," in *Jewish Believers in Jesus: The Early Centuries* (ed. O. Skarsaune and R. Hvalvik; Peabody, MA: Hendrickson, 2007), 749–53, 760–67.

[13] Cf. Hirschberg, "Jewish Believers," 218–30.

The Tale of the 144,000 and Its Place
in the Structure of Revelation

The importance of the 144,000 in John's thinking becomes clear when we note that their story interrupts the overarching septenary structure of the main story. The importance of cycles of seven for the book is not a matter of serious dispute. In particular, it is generally accepted that these cycles build the overarching structural framework in the section stretching from 4:1–16:21, as the graph on the page opposite makes clear.

This section is introduced by an inaugural vision of heaven that initiates the judgments described in the following three series of sevens: the seals, the trumpets, and the bowls. The seventh seal contains the seven trumpets, and the seventh trumpet contains the seven bowls. John interrupts this simple septenary structure at three points to introduce intercalations. These are positioned after the sixth seal and the sixth trumpet, respectively, and before the contents of the seven bowls are described. The second intercalation contains some of the most intriguing material in John's Apocalypse and may contain crucial hermeneutical keys for understanding the work as a whole.[14] More relevant for our present purposes is the fact that the 144,000 make appearances in the first intercalation (Rv 7:1–8) and the third, major intercalation (Rv 14:1–5). There are, to be sure, other narrative elements that come into focus in the major intercalation, but one function of these digressions from the overarching narrative structure is to highlight the crucial *heilsgeschichtliche* role John assigns this group.

It is important to note, as well, that the description of the 144,000 in Rv 7:1–8 and 14:1–5 is tied to the inaugural vision of heaven (Rv 5:6–10) by a series of interlocking motifs, as the graph on page 184 makes clear.

By means of this multifaceted common imagery John creates a unified story line that stretches across this section of Revelation, one it would seem legitimate to call the "tale of the 144,000." For our purposes this implies a hermeneutical expectation that we interpret each passage in light of information gained from all three (Rv 5:6–10; 7:1–10; 14:1–6). In particular, it seems beyond doubt that the 144,000 in Rv 7:1–4 are to be identified with the 144,000 in Rv 14:1–5.[15] In addition to perfect

---

[14] Cf. Richard J. Bauckham, "The Conversion of the Nations," in *The Climax of Prophecy: Studies on the Book of Revelation* (London: T&T Clark, 1993), 243–83.

[15] *Pace* Bousset, *Offenbarung*, 320, and David E. Aune, "Following the Lamb: Discipleship in the Apocalypse," in *Patterns of Discipleship in the New Testament* (ed. R. N. Longenecker; Grand Rapids: Eerdmans, 1969), 271, who argue that the groups cannot be identical since ἑκατὸν κτλ (*hekaton*, etc.) is anarthrous in Rv 14:1. But Revelation often dispenses with the anaphoric article where one would normally expect it (Beale, *Revelation*, 733–34). More importantly, in light of the book's oral-auricular setting (see n. 6) such grammatical nuances should

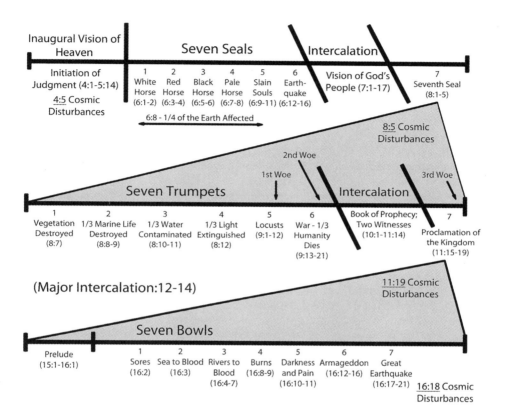

Inaugural Vision of Heaven	Seven Seals						Intercalation	
Initiation of Judgment (4:1–5:14)	1 White Horse (6:1-2)	2 Red Horse (6:3-4)	3 Black Horse (6:5-6)	4 Pale Horse (6:7-8)	5 Slain Souls (6:9-11)	6 Earth-quake (6:12-16)	Vision of God's People (7:1-17)	7 Seventh Seal (8:1-5)
4:5 Cosmic Disturbances								

6:8 - 1/4 of the Earth Affected

8:5 Cosmic Disturbances

2nd Woe

1st Woe

3rd Woe

	Seven Trumpets					Intercalation	
1 Vegetation Destroyed (8:7)	2 1/3 Marine Life Destroyed (8:8-9)	3 1/3 Water Contaminated (8:10-11)	4 1/3 Light Extinguished (8:12)	5 Locusts (9:1-12)	6 War - 1/3 Humanity Dies (9:13-21)	Book of Prophecy; Two Witnesses (10:1-11:14)	7 Proclamation of the Kingdom (11:15-19)

(Major Intercalation:12-14)

11:19 Cosmic Disturbances

	Seven Bowls						
Prelude (15:1-16:1)	1 Sores (16:2)	2 Sea to Blood (16:3)	3 Rivers to Blood (16:4-7)	4 Burns (16:8-9)	5 Darkness and Pain (16:10-11)	6 Armageddon (16:12-16)	7 Great Earthquake (16:17-21)

16:18 Cosmic Disturbances

not be accorded undue weight. It is unlikely that the hearers would have considered the latter 144,000 to be a new group based on the absence of an article, assuming they noticed it at all. Like a play that cues its audience to expect the return of a particular character by rebuilding the same stage scenery, the common imagery evoked by the visions of Rv 7 and 14 is a strong indication that the 144,000 are the same group in both scenes (similarly Peter Hirschberg, *Das eschatologische Israel: Untersuchungen zum Gottesverständnis der Johannesoffenbarung* [WMANT 51; Neukirchen-Vluyn: Neukirchener, 1999], 195). It should be noted that Aune later revised his view, conceding the fact that the groups are identical in the canonical form of Revelation but arguing that this was the work of the final redactor, who combined two independent pieces of tradition into one narrative (see *Revelation 6–16*, 440, 796). The fact that Bousset arrives at precisely the opposite conclusion—according to him the final redactor separated an initially unified tradition to create two distinct groups (Bousset, *Offenbarung*, 380)—points up the limits of a source/redaction-critical approach to the perceived problems here.

Common Motifs	Rev 5:6–10	Rev 7:1–10	Rev 14:1–6
the Lamb	√	√	√
"every tribe, tongue, people, and nation"	√	√	√
144,000		√	√
mark on the forehead		√	√
4 living beings and 24 elders	√		√
harps	√		√
a new song	√		√
redemption	√		√

agreement with respect to the number, both texts take note of the fact that the 144,000 bear a mark on their foreheads. Revelation 14:1 tells us that this mark was the name of the Lamb and his father. Both texts also set the story of the 144,000 within the larger context of the reception of the gospel by representatives of every "nation, tribe, people, and language group."[16]

The Identity of the 144,000

What, then, do we learn about the 144,000 in these two texts? The perspective of Rv 7:1–8 is grandiose and cosmic in its scope. Four angels hold back the winds at the four corners of the world. A fifth angel comes from the east with the seal of God in his hand. He commands the other angels not to inflict judgment on the world until the servants of the Lord have received the seal of God on their foreheads. This description evokes, according to general consensus, the visionary account of Ez 9:1–11. In Ezekiel's vision six angelic beings are held back from their work of judgment in Jerusalem until a man clothed in linen is able to pass through the city and put marks on the foreheads of those who have been faithful to YHWH.[17]

John, like Ezekiel, does not see the process of sealing itself—this often overlooked fact will prove important to a correct understanding of the vision—but rather hears the angel call out the number of those who are

---

[16] The terms, but not their order, are the same in both texts as well as in Rv 5:6–10.

[17] For a thorough analysis, see Hirschberg, *Israel*, 140–48.

sealed from the nation of Israel (Rv 7:4). The total of 144,000 has aesthetically pleasing associations with the numbers 12 and 1,000 (144,000 = 12 x 12 x 1,000) as well as symbolic value. In all likelihood it is designed to convey a sense of vast size and completeness.[18] This total is subsequently broken down according to the individual tribes of Israel, and John hears that 12,000 from each tribe are among the sealed. The Nestle-Aland text indents the listing of the tribes, giving the impression, probably correct, that John is recounting a herald-like announcement by the angel who reads these figures from an official document.

The list itself has been the subject of much discussion dating back to the earliest commentary on Revelation due to several peculiar features. To begin with, the order in which the tribes are listed is unprecedented when compared with the standard practice of early Judaism, according to which preference was given either to absolute birth order or to the sons of Jacob's wives over against those of his concubines.[19] Additionally, the probable substitution of Joseph for Ephraim and its listing as a separate tribe with no attempt to emphasize its relation to Manasseh—the two half-tribes occupy, respectively, the eleventh and sixth position in the list—remain enigmatic. Their de facto advancement to the status of full tribes is necessitated by the removal of the tribe of Dan, a mystery for which, to date, no satisfactory explanation has been offered.[20]

Whatever finally accounts for the idiosyncrasies of the list of tribes, there can be no doubt that it evokes the pervasive early Jewish tradition that expected and yearned for the reconstitution of the twelve tribes as an integral part of the return of Israel from exile. Despite the protestations of some,[21] the historical memory of the ten tribes of the Northern Kingdom had not been extinguished (Lk 2:36; Josephus *A.J.* 10.8.1 [§133]). These

---

[18] Cf. Alfred Wikenhauser, *Die Offenbarung des Johannes* (RNT 9; Regenburg: Friedrich Pustet, 1959), 67, followed by Ulrich B. Müller, *Die Offenbarung des Johannes* (ÖTK 19; Gütersloh: Gerd Mohn; Würzburg: Echter, 1984), 178.

[19] Richard J. Bauckham, "The List of the Tribes of Israel in Revelation 7 Again," *JSNT* 42 (1991): 111.

[20] Sometimes attention is directed to an early tradition, mentioned both by Irenaeus (*Haer.* 5.30.2) and Hippolytus (*Antichr.* 14), that the Antichrist was expected to come from the tribe of Dan, but this is "very unlikely to be pre-Christian" (Bauckham, "List," 100) and may well have been influenced, if not entirely generated, by Rv 7:1–8. Others note the stong association of Dan with idolatry and apostasy in some Jewish sources (Bousset, *Offenbarung*, 330; Müller, *Offenbarung*, 179; Hirschberg, *Israel*, 181). The Boharic textual tradition substitutes Dan for Manasseh, and many scholars have toyed with the idea of amending the text in this way (see, e.g., G. V. Sanderson, "In Defence of Dan," *Scr* 3 [1948]: 114–15; Bauckham, "List," 111), but apart from the perplexity it engenders among baffled readers, there are no good grounds for doing so: the text makes perfect sense as it stands.

[21] George B. Caird, *A Commentary on the Revelation of St. John the Divine* (HNTC; New York: Harper & Row, 1966), 95: Mounce, *Revelation*, 168; Boring, *Revelation*, 129; Beale, *Revelation*, 419.

were not "lost tribes" in the opinion of Jews during the Second Temple period—that assessment reflects later developments in Judaism (see, e.g., b. Sanh. 110b)—but, as it were, "distant tribes," and the hope that they, too, would one day be gathered back to Israel was very much alive in the first century.[22] That expectation was, after all, an indispensable part of the remnant theology of the OT (Ez 48:30–35; Is 11:11–16; 49:5–6; 63:17) and consequently the eschatological expectations of early Judaism (Sir 36:10–13; 48:10; Pss. Sol. 17:26–31; T. Benj. 9:2; T. Naph. 5:8; 4 Ezra 13:39–47; 2 Bar. 78:1–7; 1QM 2:2–3; 3:12–13), including the messianic movement that formed around the person of Jesus of Nazareth (Mt 19:28; Lk 22:30; Acts 26:7; Jas 1:1). Throughout the entire Second Temple period, in other words, Jewish hopes for the restoration of Israel envisioned not simply the return of an undifferentiated mass of Israelites from the Diaspora but, as the above texts make incontrovertibly clear, of representatives from all the tribes.

If, therefore, we wish to avoid a historically desensitized reading of a text such as Rv 7:1–8, which plainly evokes this hope, we must interpret it against the background of OT and early Jewish remnant theology and its concrete expectations. Otherwise we will end up with an eschatological vision of Israel that no Jew or Jewish Christian in the first century would have recognized: essentially the inchoate "tribeless" Israel of later Christian theology. To his credit, Richard Bauckham has avoided that pitfall and proposed a reading that respects the tribal structure of John's vision. In his view, the 144,000 represent "the Israelite army of the military Messiah of David."[23] He demonstrates on the basis of several Jewish texts, especially the War Scroll at Qumran (1QM 2–3), that the reconstituted tribal union was expected to play a military role in the Messiah's war against the rebellious nations. The designation of 12,000 from each tribe reflects, in his opinion, the census lists of the OT (see especially Nm 1), which always function to determine the military strength of the nation.[24] It should be noted, however, that the mustering of the Israelite tribes for messianic conflict is by no means a major motif in OT remnant theology or in the restoration traditions of early Judaism. Further, Bauckham and those who follow this reading[25] overlook a crucial difference between the

---

[22] E. P. Sanders, Jesus and Judaism (London: SCM Press, 1985), 95–98; William Horbury, "The Twelve and the Phylarchs," NTS 32 (1986): 509–13; John P. Meier, A Marginal Jew: Rethinking the Historical Jesus, vol. 3: Companions and Competitors (4 vols.; ABRL; New York: Doubleday, 2001), 3:148–54; Brant Pitre, Jesus, the Tribulation, and the End of Exile: Restoration Eschatology and the Origin of the Atonement (Tübingen: Mohr Siebeck; Grand Rapids: Baker, 2005), 38–39.

[23] Richard Bauckham, "The Apocalypse as a Christian War Scroll," in The Climax of Prophecy: Studies on the Book of Revelation (London: T&T Clark, 1993; repr., from NeoT 22 (1988): 17–40), 216.

[24] Bauckham, "Apocalypse," 217–18.

[25] Cf. Boring, Revelation, 131; Sweet, Revelation, 222; Beasley-Murray, Revelation 223; Beale, Revelation, 422–23.

census lists and Rv 7:1–8: the language of sealing in the latter.[26] This, as we saw, is a clear allusion to Ez 9, and thus it is much more likely that the primary thrust of Rv 7:1–8 is to emphasize the preservation of the faithful remnant of Israel through a period of intense tribulation, as is clearly the case in Ezekiel's vision.[27]

The further description of the 144,000 in Rv 14:1–5 serves to confirm this impression. To begin with, they are standing with the Lamb on Mount Zion. This is a transparent allusion to the messianic tradition preserved in Ps 2:6, where YHWH announces "I have installed my king on Zion, my holy mountain." Psalm 2 is generally regarded as one of the oldest psalms, dating from the tenth century B.C.[28] In all likelihood, it evokes the memory of David's victory over the Jebusites and his conquest of Mount Zion (2 Sm 5:7) and transposes that seminal event into a hymn celebrating the eschatological triumph of God over the rebellious nations.[29] Psalm 2 taps into the very root of "Zion theology," which held out the hope, in the face of and during the darkest days of exile, of a future Davidic kingdom to which a remnant of Israel (clearly including the tribes of the Northern Kingdom; cf. Is 10:20–21 with Is 11:11–16) would return. Within this context "Zion" became a potent symbol of God's promise to preserve and restore that remnant to its inheritance, for it was on Mount Zion that the remnant would be gathered (cf. 2 Kgs 19:31 = Is 37:32; Is 4:2–5; 10:12; Jl 2:32; Ob 17, 21; Mi 4:5–8).[30] In John's vision, then, "Mount Zion" functions as a literary trope, specifically metalepsis,[31] that alerts his hearers to interpret what he is about to recount against the background of OT Zion theology.[32]

Revelation 14:4–5 describes the 144,000 in further detail. These verses are set apart from John's account of the vision, as the Nestle-Aland

---

[26] On the function of seals and sealing with respect to persons in the OT and early Judaism, cf. Hirschberg, *Israel*, 148–66.

[27] Cf. Smalley, *Revelation*, 182.

[28] Cf. M. Dahood, *Psalms 1–50: A New Translation with Introduction and Commentary* (AB 16; New York: Doubleday, 1965), 7.

[29] Cf. Pattemore, *People*, 180.

[30] Cf. Beale, *Revelation*, 735, who notes that when *Mount* Zion is mentioned in the OT, "emphasis is placed on the deliverance of a remnant."

[31] Cf. Pattemore, *People*, 180. On the concept of metalepsis and its importance for the interpretation of allusions in the NT, cf. Richard Hays, *Echoes of Scripture in the Letters of Paul* (New Haven: Yale University Press, 1989), 14–21.

[32] Once that is recognized, the sometimes laborious discussion in the commentaries as to what Mount Zion refers to in the real world becomes much less urgent. Any referential value it has—whether the literal mountain in Jerusalem (cf. Bousset, *Offenbarung*, 380; Wikenhauser, *Offenbarung*, 111; Aune, *Revelation 6–16*, 803–4; Osborne, *Revelation*, 525) or heaven (Mounce, *Revelation*, 267) or the experience of heavenly existence in the present (cf. E. Lohmeyer, *Die Offenbarung des Johannes* [HNT 16; Tübingen: Mohr Siebeck, 1970], 121–22; Ladd, *Revelation*, 189–90; Müller, *Offenbarung*, 262; Beale, *Revelation*, 732–33)—is secondary to its metaleptic function.

text makes clear by indenting them. Since they are not the words of an *angelus interpres* or some other heavenly being, it seems best to understand them as John's own understanding of the identity of the 144,000. He makes four intriguing statements about them that we will examine in reverse order, since the connotations of the first two become clearer in light of the more transparent allusions in the latter two.

The fourth statement, "in their mouths no lie was found, for they are blameless" (Rv 14:5: καὶ ἐν τῷ στόματι αὐτῶν οὐχ εὑρέθη ψεῦδος, ἄμωμοί εἰσιν; *kai en tō stomati autōn ouch heurethē pseudos, amōmoi eisin*), is an overt allusion to Zep 3:13 (καὶ οὐ μὴ εὑρεθῇ ἐν τῷ στόματι αὐτῶν γλῶσσα δολία; *kai ou mē heurethē en tō stomati autōn glōssa dolia*). Here we have, as it were, another guy wire that anchors this vision in remnant theology in general and more particularly the Zion tradition of the OT. For in the context of Zep 3:13 YHWH is proclaiming his intention to gather the dispersed remnant of his people to his holy mountain (cf. Zep 3:9–11). The resulting moral purity of the remnant is emphasized, and this emphasis is carried over to John's vision.

The third statement made by John about the 144,000 is that "these have been redeemed from humanity as a firstfruits offering for God and the Lamb" (Rv 14:4c: οὗτοι ἠγοράσθησαν ἀπὸ τῶν ἀνθρώπων ἀπαρχὴ τῷ θεῷ καὶ τῷ ἀρνίῳ; *houtoi ēgorasthēsan apo tōn anthrōpōn aparchē tō theō kai tō arniō*). Commentators have seldom considered whether this is an allusion to a specific OT text, but in fact this seems quite likely, particularly when we discover that only one text in the OT metaphorically portrays a group of faithful Israelites as a firstfruits offering: Jer 2:3. Since this allusion will prove important for our overall argument, we will examine it in some detail in an excursus.

Excursus: Faithful Israel as a Firstfruits Offering in Jeremiah 2:3

Jeremiah 2:1–3 is a clearly demarcated, self-contained literary unit[33] containing a brief poem (Jer 2:2b–3) that serves in its present context as the introduction to the covenant lawsuit that follows (Jer 2:4–4:4). The first verse of the poem (Jer 2:2b) consists of two lines, each of which contains two cola characterized by *parallelismus membrorum*. The following representation is designed to bring out these relationships.

---

[33] Both the detailed introductory formula in Jer 2:1–2a and the familiar phrases כֹּה אָמַר יְהוָה (*kō ʾāmar yhwh*) and נְאֻם־יְהוָה (*nĕʾum-yhwh*), which serve, respectively, to introduce and conclude divine oracles, make that clear enough. Cf. Willy Schottroff, "Jeremia 2,1–3: Erwägungen zur Methode der Prophetenexegese," *ZTK* 67 (1970): 269.

I remember* you	זָכַרְתִּי לָךְ (zākartî lāk)	A
the devotion of your youth	חֶסֶד נְעוּרַיִךְ (ḥesed nĕ'ûrayik)	a
the love of your betrothals	אַהֲבַת כְּלוּלֹתָיִךְ ('ahăbat kĕlûlōtāyik)	a'
your following after me	לֶכְתֵּךְ אַחֲרַי (lektēk 'ahăray)	B
in the desert	בַּמִּדְבָּר (bammidbār)	b
in a land not sown	בְּאֶרֶץ לֹא זְרוּעָה (bĕ'ereṣ lō' zĕrû'ā)	b'

*On the rendering of זָכַרְתִּי (zākartî) in the present tense see GKC §106g.

It should be noted that the phrase זכר + לְ (le + zkr) with which the poem begins is often found in close association with the concept of covenant loyalty (Ex 32:13; Lv 26:45; Dt 9:27; 1 Chr 16:15; Pss 105:8; 106:4; 111:5). This strengthens the overall impression that the poem embodies a wistful remembrance of the Israel's allegiance to the covenant during the desert wanderings, that is, immediately before the period of the conquest of Canaan.[34]

The second verse of the poem (Jer 2:3) is simpler still, consisting of two more or less balanced bicola, whose members, like those of the first verse, exhibit typical Semitic parallelism, as the following representation makes clear.

Israel was* a sacred object to YHWH,	קֹדֶשׁ יִשְׂרָאֵל לַיהוָה (qōdeš yiśrā'ēl layhwh)	A
The firstfruits of his harvest.	רֵאשִׁית תְּבוּאָתֹה (rē'šît tĕbû'ātō)	A'
All who ate of it** incurred guilt,	כָּל־אֹכְלָיו יֶאְשָׁמוּ (kol-'ōkĕlāyw ye'šāmû)	B
Evil came upon them.	רָעָה תָּבֹא אֲלֵיהֶם (rā'ā tābō' 'ălêhem)	B'

*Along with most commentators (according to Schottroff, "Jeremia 2,1–3," 266, though he himself is not among them), I take Jer 2:3 to refer to the past throughout. Consequently, the imperfect forms יֶאְשָׁמוּ (ye'šāmû) and תָּבֹא (tābō') should be read as iteratives (cf. William L. Holladay, *Jeremiah I: A Commentary on the Book of the Prophet Jeremiah, Chapters 1–25* [Hermeneia; Philadelphia: Fortress, 1986], 85).

**The third masculine singular object suffix attached to אכל ('kl) makes the reference to קֹדֶשׁ (qōdeš) unmistakable.

The metaphorical description of Israel in terms associated with cultic offerings is by no means frequent in the OT,[35] and their accumulation

---

[34] *Pace* Michael Fox, "Jeremiah 2:2 and the 'Desert Ideal'," *CBQ* (1973): 441–50. In my opinion, Michael DeRoche proves beyond dispute that from Jeremiah's perspective "[t]here was an early period (the wilderness) when Israel loved Yahweh and followed his ways. . . ." See "Jeremiah 2:2–3 and Israel's Love for God during the Wilderness Wanderings," *CBQ* 45 (1983): 374.

[35] Holladay, *Jeremiah I*, 84.

in this poem is striking. In the first line of this verse, Israel is described as YHWH's קֹדֶשׁ (qōḏeš).[36] This is a general term for any object that may no longer be used for mundane purposes because it has been devoted to God. It is further specified in the second line: Israel is "the firstfruits of his harvest." The term translated "firstfruits" here (רֵאשִׁית; rēʾšîṯ) can refer to any number of firstfruits offerings, but the third line clearly alludes to the priestly ordinance according to which unauthorized persons who partook of the offerings incurred guilt. This provides a decisive clue for determining which of these firstfruits offerings Jeremiah has in mind.

Two OT texts in particular illuminate the cultic background evoked by the poem. The first is Nm 18:29–32, which allows for the consumption of offerings by the Levites and their families outside the sanctuary. The Levites must be sure, however, to offer a tithe of all the offerings they receive. Failing to do so brings guilt upon them and their families. The second text is Dt 26:1–11, which describes the ritual by means of which the Levites came into possession these offering. The historical setting the text lays claim to is the time immediately before Israel's conquest of Canaan. Moses is portrayed as instructing the Israelites about the proper procedure for presenting firstfruits offerings, beginning with the first harvest after the settlement of the land. The Israelites are commanded to put their offerings in a basket, bring them to the priest at the place that YHWH will choose as his habitation, and confess that the entire harvest is a gift from YHWH. Significantly, this passage is followed by one regulating the giving of tithes (Dt 26:12–15). It constrains the worshiper to affirm, among other things, that he has indeed transferred a tenth of his harvest (תְּבוּאָתֶךָ; tĕḇûʾāṯĕḵā) as a sacred offering (קֹדֶשׁ; qōḏeš) to the Levites (cf. Nm 18:21–24) and that the offering is ritually pure.

The link between Jeremiah's poem and the situation described in Dt 26:1–11 is confirmed by the sequence in which the metaphors occur in Jer 2:2–3 and the implied relationship between them. For by adding to the familiar picture of Israel as YHWH's bride in the first verse of the poem the unusual figure of Israel as a firstfruits offering in the second verse, Jeremiah is evoking the same historical situation as Dt 26:1–11. Whereas the first verse alludes to the desert wanderings, the second verse implies that the next event in Israel's *Heilsgeschichte* has occurred, namely, the conquest and settlement of the land,[37] and further that YHWH has, so to speak, brought in the first harvest and presented Israel as a sacred firstfruits offering.[38] In other words, Jeremiah figura-

---

[36] The fact that the term stands parallel to רֵאשִׁית (rēʾšîṯ) supports the MT's rendering of קֹדֶשׁ (qōḏeš) as a substantive.

[37] Jack R. Lundbom, *Jeremiah 1–20* (AB 21; New York: Doubleday), 254, concurs: "The shift to an agricultural metaphor corresponds to Israel's settlement in the land."

[38] Dieter Böhler, "Geschlechterdifferenz und Landbesitz: Strukturuntersuchungen zu Jer 2,2–4,2," in *Jeremia und die "deuteronomistische Bewegung,"*

tively applies the idealized scenario of Dt 26:1–11 to the relationship between YHWH and Israel.

To summarize: The brief poem in Jer 2:2–3 introduces a covenant lawsuit in which YHWH remembers his past relationship with Israel. He recalls that Israel maintained covenant faithfulness during the period of the desert wanderings.[39] YHWH rewarded Israel's faithfulness by leading her into the land of Canaan and establishing her there. After the conquest and settlement there was even a first "harvest." In other words, Jeremiah regards the generation that initially conquered and settled Canaan as faithful to the covenant, a viewpoint very much in the Deuteronomic tradition (see Jo 24:31).[40] During this period, YHWH treated Israel as a sacred firstfruits offering, an attitude that comes to concrete expression in his protection of Israel from its enemies. Every attempt by hostile forces to "devour" (i.e., conquer)[41] Israel was turned back.

(ed. Walter Gross; Weinheim: Beltz Athenäum, 1995), 108–9, maintains that the enigmatic and much-discussed variation between feminine and masculine pronouns with reference to Israel that characterizes Jer 2–3 throughout represents a conscious and carefully designed rhetorical strategy: it serves to differentiate between Israel before and after the conquest, respectively. Agreeably for our thesis, precisely this variation in the gender of the pronouns referring to Israel occurs between Jer 2:2b and Jer 2:3.

[39] I am not assuming the existence of an independent "Wüstentradition" that idealizes the nomadic period before the conquest. It seems more likely that Jeremiah is selecting certain motifs from the biblical traditions of Israel as a whole, some of which view Israel's origins and early development positively, others negatively. See Mark E. Biddle, *A Redaction History of Jeremiah 2:1–4:2* (AThANT 77; Zurich: Theologischer Verlag, 1990), 174–78.

[40] *Pace* DeRoche, "Jeremiah 2:2–3," 370, who maintains that Jeremiah believed "(1) that Israel is guilty of changing her early faithful attitude towards Yahweh to an unfaithful attitude, and (2) that the change occurs at the time when Israel leaves the wilderness and enters the promised land." If my thesis is correct, De Roche's second conclusion must be revised. In Jeremiah's view the disastrous change took place with the dying out of the generation that conquered the land. Jeremiah is probably tapping into a tradition that held that Israel maintained covenant faithfulness to YHWH at least through the time of the covenant renewal at Shechem (see Jo 24). This conforms to Jeremiah's general appraisal of Israel's history, for his interest does not lie in reprimanding Israel for its conduct since the conquest, as his positive attitude toward the Davidic monarchy (see Jer 17:25; 22:2–4; 23:5; 30:9) and toward the period of Samuel's judgeship (Jer 15:1) makes clear. Rather, his displeasure is aimed at the religious and moral decline characteristic of Israel and Judah since the division of the kingdom.

[41] On the use of אכל (ʾkl) as a metaphor for military conquest, see Holladay, *Jeremiah I*, 85. Jeremiah uses the same image in Jer 30:16, when he prophesies that the forces that devoured Israel will themselves be devoured upon Israel's return from exile. Jeremiah 30–31 has close thematic connections to Jer 2:2–3 (cf. Böhler, "Geschlechterdifferenz," 91; Taro Odashima, *Heilsworte im Jeremiabuch: Untersuchungen zu ihrer vordeuteronomistischen Bearbeitung* [BWANT 125; Stuttgart:

For the purpose of our analysis of Rv 14:1–5 it is especially important to note that Jer 2:3 makes metaphorical use of the concept of firstfruits to refer to the generation of Israelites that lived immediately before and after the conquest and settlement of the land of Canaan. From Jeremiah's perspective, they maintained covenant loyalty to YHWH, and he contrasts them with his own generation, which had largely turned away from YHWH. Jeremiah 2:2–3 is not a "remnant" text in the narrow sense, but its affinities to the remnant tradition are obvious enough. The "firstfruits" are a subset of the larger nation of Israel who have remained faithful to God and have been set apart for his purposes. This is the *tertium comparationis* that John activitates in his characterization of the 144,000 as the "firstfruits to God and the Lamb."

The identification of the firstfruits metaphor in Rv 14:4c as an allusion to Jer 2:3 facilitates the interpretation of the first two descriptive statements of the 144,000 in Rv 14:4, since both of these correspond to motifs found in the immediate context of Jer 2:3. The second statement in Rv 14:4b, "these are the ones who followed the Lamb wherever he went" (οὗτοι οἱ ἀκολουθοῦντες τῷ ἀρνίῳ ὅπου ἂν ὑπάγῃ; *houtoi hoi akolouthountes tō arniō hopou an hypagē*), recalls YHWH's utterance in Jer 2:2, the first verse of the poem, that Israel "followed after him in the desert." This is elaborated upon in Jer 2:6: God led Israel through a dangerous wilderness, but the faithful Israelites of that generation trusted God to lead them into the promised land. Revelation 14:4b alludes to this example of courageous loyalty and applies it, with characteristic christological aplomb, to those who were faithful to the Lamb despite the grave tribulation they were enduring.

It should be noted at this juncture that if Rv 14:4b does, in fact, contain an allusion to Jer 2:2, then it offers a viable solution to the motive behind John's replacement of Dan in the listing of the tribes in Rv 7:1–8. For, as any Jew who was well-versed in the OT knew, Dan was the only tribe that refused to follow YHWH where he intended to lead them. Judges 18 recounts that Dan was unwilling to conquer its assigned territory (cf. Jo 19:40–48) and chose instead to subjugate Laish, which lay outside the designated boundaries of the land. Thus, the Danites may have come to epitomize the faithless Israelites who failed to trust YHWH's promises and, as a consequence, to be viewed in John's community as a negative example of a group that refused to follow YHWH due to concern for their safety. Within the context of Revelation, this would serve to remind Jewish believers, particularly those in Smyrna and Philadelphia (Rv 2:9–10; 3:9) not to abandon their inheritance in the face of opposition from the non-believing Jews around them. They were called upon to follow the Lamb wherever he led them.

Kohlhammer, 1989], 288) and thus helps to illuminate the metaphorical use of אכל (*'kl*) in Jer 2:3.

The first descriptive statement of the 144,000 in Rv 14:4a, "these are the ones who have not defiled themselves with women, for they are virgins" (οὗτοί εἰσιν οἳ μετὰ γυναικῶν οὐκ ἐμολύνθησαν, παρθένοι γάρ εἰσιν; *houtoi eisin hoi meta gynaikōn ouk emolynthēsan, parthenoi gar eisin*), also has affinities with the larger context of Jer 2:2–3. As we noted above, this poem introduces the section that follows it in Jer 2:4–4:4, and one of the characteristic literary tropes in that section is the metaphor of adultery as applied to unfaithful Israel. Because of her continual idolatry, Israel is compared with a woman on the prowl (Jer 2:5) who commits adultery on every high place and under every tree (Jer 2:21; 3:2, 6, 12) with "stone and wood" (Jer 3:2; a metonomy for idols), who casts off her bridal attire (Jer 2:32), and who abandons her husband for other men (Jer 3:20). This is in stark contrast to Jeremiah's ideal conceptualization of Israel as a "virgin" (Jer 14:17; 18:13; 31:4, 21). Against this background the metaphorical description of the 144,000 as "those who have not defiled themselves with women" begins to make sense.[42] Their faithfulness to God is contrasted with the faithlessness of the majority of Jews.

Is John Distinguishing Between "Sealed" Jews and "Unsealed"Gentiles?

Our analysis of the tale of the 144,000 in Rv 7:1–8 and Rv 14:1–5 has pointed up its strong connections to what we might broadly term remnant traditions of the OT. Both texts evoke the pervasive conviction in early Judaism that throughout Israel's history, there was a core of faithful Israelites who maintained covenant loyalty to YHWH and could therefore reckon with his promise to one day gather them to his people. In applying these traditions to the 144,000, John goes out of his way to emphasize their Jewishness. Indeed, short of dressing them in tefillin and tallitot, it is difficult to imagine how he could have conveyed this impression with greater force. Yet, as we saw at the outset, most exegetes are reluctant to allow that these believers in Jesus are to be understood as Jews on

---

[42] This interpretation is at least as plausible as the view that the 144,000 represent a group of early Christian celibates (cf. C. H. Lindijer, "Die Jungfrauen in der Offenbarung des Johannes XIV 4," in *Studies in John Presented to J. N. Sevenster* [NovTSup 24; Leiden: Brill, 1970], 124–42) or that they take the place of the fallen angels who had sexual relations with women (cf. D. C. Olson, "'Those Who Have Not Defiled Themselves with Women': Revelation 14:4 and the Book of Enoch," *CBQ* [1997]: 492–510). If they represent a messianic army (a view I find ultimately unconvincing; see above), then this could be an allusion to the requirement that participants in holy war refrain from sexual activity (cf. Aune, "Following," 274).

the referential level. There are, perhaps, many reasons for this, but one in particular is frequently mentioned. In essence, it is this: Given the nature of the seal as a mark of possession by God and the Lamb (Rv 14:1), its protective function with regard to enduring end-time tribulation (Rv 9:4), and its obvious function as a symbolic contrast to the mark of the beast (Rv 13:16–17), John could not possibly have reserved this sealing for Jewish Christians.[43] It seems to function as a necessary badge of allegiance to Christ rather than (to make use of a well-worn term usually employed in another context) a "Jewish identity marker."

I agree. The seal is much more than that, and it is inconceivable that John would restrict its application to Jewish believers. I contend, however, that a careful reading of Rv 7:1–10 makes it clear that he does not do so. We begin with the most obvious of observations: John never states that the innumerable host of believers from the nations has not been sealed. In fact, as the account of the vision unfolds, it arouses the expectation that they will indeed be sealed, for the angel carrying the seal explains that further judgments must not begin until the "servants of God" (δοῦλοι τοῦ θεοῦ; *douloi tou theou*) receive a seal on their foreheads. This term is decidedly inclusive, denoting throughout the book of Revelation any and all worshipers of God or Jesus (Rv 1:1; 2:20; 10:7; 11:18; 15:3; 19:5; 22:3, 6).

We note further that John does not *see* the sealing of the 144,000 from the tribes of Israel. In fact, he does not see these people at all (in this vision; he does in Rv 14:1–5). He merely *hears* the angel recite the number of those designated to be sealed "from all the tribes of Israel" (cf. Rv 14:4). The next thing he sees, after hearing that the servants of God will be sealed and that 144,000 Jewish believers will be among them, is the vast multi-ethnic group that is assembled before the throne (cf. Rv 7:9). The clear implication is that this innumerable multitude is the company of the sealed ones, and that one of the nations represented among them is Israel. John's intention is to emphasize the place of Jews among the faithful servants of God. He is not, in other words, contrasting believing Jews with Gentile believers; on the contrary, he is including them among the believers from all other nations. The contrast he wishes to draw, one very much in line with an important concern of John's throughout the book of Revelation, especially in the letters to the seven churches, is between Jews who believe in Jesus as the Messiah and those who do not.

This appraisal of John's intentions in Rv 7:1–10 helps make sense of the enigmatic statement in Rv 14:3 that only the 144,000 were able to learn the song that they heard from heaven. Once again, when careful

---

[43] Cf. e.g., Beale, *Revelation*, 425; Smalley, *Revelation*, 188; Akira Satake, *Die Offenbarung des Johannes* (KEK 16; Göttingen: Vandenhoeck & Ruprecht, 2008), 227 n. 169.

attention is paid to the distinction John draws between what he has seen and he has heard, there is no inference in the text that the 144,000 were able to learn the new song but the innumerable multitude was not. In Rv 14:1 John sees the 144,000 and the Lamb on Mount Zion. He does not see anyone else. He hears the new song being sung from heaven. This is a transparent reference to the song that was sung before the throne in Rv 5:6–10, a text which, as we noted above, forms part of a continuous narrative with Rv 7:1–10 and Rv 14:1–5. The vast multitude from every nation, tribe, people, and language group is presumably still standing before the throne in heaven where John last saw them (cf. Rv 7:9), so they already know the song.[44] In fact, the song is about their redemption: it praises the Lamb because "you have redeemed people from every tribe, language group, people, and nation by your blood and have made them a kingdom and priests to God" (Rv 5:9–10). The point of contrast, then, in Rv 14:3 is once again not between the 144,000 and the multi-ethnic company of believers but between the 144,000 and the rest of the Jews. The point is that only these 144,000 *from tribes of Israel* were able to sing the song. In other words, only the faithful remnant of Israel recognized Jesus as the Messiah and was able to join in the song and affirm not only this christological truth but also the inclusion of the Gentiles in God's purposes for Israel.

There is no denying that by recounting the recitation of the names of the twelve tribes, John is highlighting the unique role that Jewish believers play. This, however, is in line with both Jesus' (Mt 10:6: "go first to the house of Israel") and Paul's (Rom 1:16: "to the Jew first also to the Greek") theologies of mission. If the emphasis seems rather one-sided, with excessive attention paid to the twelve tribes and much less to the rest of humanity, we should remember that it reflects precisely the math of Jesus' mission: twelve apostles for Israel, one for the nations.

Conclusion

If I have read John's intentions correctly, then the point of the tale of the 144,000 is straightforward: Jewish believers matter. They form a point of continuity with the OT remnant, and even though their influence was on the wane in the late first century, John is concerned to preserve the memory of their important *heilsgeschichtliche* role for an increasingly Gentile church. By following the Lamb wherever he went, even when the majority of their kinsmen rejected him, they proved themselves faithful to God.

---

[44] Beale, *Revelation*, 737, offers the intriguing suggestion that the multitude composed the song.

Thus, they demonstrated that they belong to God's "firstfruits offering" (cf. Jer 2:3), a metaphor that provides, as I have demonstrated
elsewhere, a particularly useful way of viewing the relationship between
Israel and the church.[45] Both Paul (Rom 11:16a) and James (Jas 1:18,
assuming that James is writing to Jewish believers, as the characterization of the addressees as "the twelve tribes in the diaspora" in Jas 1:1
suggests) employ it for that same purpose. Its utility stems from the fact
that a firstfruits offering is, in essence, a small portion of the harvest that
is dedicated to God for the purpose of establishing God's claim over the
entire harvest.[46] What better picture could there be of the relationship
between the Jewish core and the rest of the church?[47] It has the distinct
benefit, over against a classic dispensational approach, of emphasizing
the essential continuity between the remnant of Israel and the church.
It also militates against heavy-handed Reformed ecclesiological formula-
tions that imply a wholesale replacement of Israel by the church. It implies that the faithful remnant of Israel does not cease to exist as an entity
within the church. Jewish believers in Jesus will take their place of honor
at the messianic banquet (cf. Lk 22:30), and in the meantime they should,
in John's estimation, be held in high esteem by their Gentile brothers and
sisters, regardless of their relative numerical strength.

In his recent magnum opus Greg Beale generally affirms the continuity of the OT remnant of Israel with the NT church, noting that "gentiles,
who form the majority of the church, are viewed as part of the restoration
of latter-day faithful Israel."[48] Elsewhere, however, he claims that "the
church, composed of believing Jews and gentiles, is *the commencing fulfillment* of the prophecies of Israel's restoration."[49] The same tension surfaces
when he speaks, on the same page, of the church as "the transformed and
restored eschatological Israel," on the one hand, and as the "true Israel,"
on the other.[50] The latter term should, in my estimation, be avoided, for
it gives the impression that what came before was somehow false, and
it is difficult to imagine that the apostles and prophets viewed the faithful remnant as a false expression of Israel. It was merely, as I think my
distinguished teacher will agree, not yet the complete eschatological expression of what Israel would one day be: Jews and Gentiles gathered in
worship before their common Messiah. "Transformed and restored Israel"
is, therefore, a felicitous choice. It captures the sense of continuity be-

---

[45] White, *Erstlingsgabe*, 292–98.
[46] White, *Erstlingsgabe*, 17–66.
[47] John develops the full picture of the relationship between the firstfruits
(Jewish believers) and the rest of the harvest (Gentile believers) in Rv 14 (cf. 14:4
with Rv 14:14–20). For a thorough discussion see White, *Erstlingsgabe*, 281–82.
[48] G. K. Beale, *A New Testament Biblical Theology: The Unfolding of the Old Testament in the New* (Grand Rapids: Baker, 2011), 651.
[49] Beale, *New Testament Biblical Theology*, 684 (italics added).
[50] Beale, *New Testament Biblical Theology*, 651.

tween the faithful remnant of Israel, extending back at least to Jeremiah's day, and believers in Jesus, whether Jews or Gentiles. This may seem like splitting hairs to some, but I live and work in Germany, where one is constantly reminded of what can happen when the Gentile church loses sight of its organic connection to the remnant of Israel. [51]

---

[51] It might seem unusual to those who do not know Greg Beale that I would choose to contribute an article to his *Festschrift* that takes a position opposed to his own. But my esteemed teacher and friend is a passionate and humble devotee to the hunt for the "right doctrine from the right text," and I know of no better way to honor his influence on my scholarship than to challenge him, as he often did me, to reconsider his position based on a deeper understanding of the OT and Jewish background of the text.

CHAPTER 11

HOW DO YOU READ? GOD'S FAITHFUL CHARACTER AS THE PRIMARY LENS FOR THE NEW TESTAMENT USE OF ISRAEL'S SCRIPTURES

Rikk E. Watts

Introduction

It is with great pleasure that I offer this essay as a small token of thanks to Greg Beale, both in recognition of his contribution to biblical studies and with genuine gratefulness first for his academic guidance when I was a graduate student at Gordon-Conwell (1984–1987) and subsequently for his friendship over the last quarter century. His class on the use of the OT in the NT exercised a major influence on the topic and direction of my doctoral thesis, forever shaping one of my primary research interests for the rest of my career. Since then I have continued to find him a ready and perceptive conversation partner.

It is difficult to overestimate both the centrality and the complexity of the NT's engagement with Israel's Scriptures. In terms of centrality, it is impossible to conceive of a truly Christian theology without taking fully into account the fundamental continuity, so obviously assumed by the authors of the NT, of the one with the other.[1] Perhaps because of our human propensity to assume the familiar while focusing on the "new" it is all too easy to concentrate on the NT's discontinuities with the Jewish milieu out of which it emerged. This is all the more so given the disruptive social and religious implications, for example, of believing Gentiles receiving the eschatological Spirit apart from Torah obedience for the make-up of God's people, and of the resurrection of a crucified Jesus for the nature of messiahship, and indeed the very character of YHWH himself.

---

[1] For C. H. Dodd this usage was central to illuminating the substructure of New Testament theology, *According to the Scriptures: The Sub-Structure of New Testament Theology* (London: Nisbet, 1952).

Even so, the language of fulfillment and the NT authors' repeated use of such expressions as "as it is written" or "according to the Scriptures" make it very clear that for them the gospel was in deep and fundamental continuity with Israel's Scriptures, and necessarily therefore entirely in keeping with the character of the God who revealed himself therein. In Rom 9–11, which contain both the most extended and intense appeal to those Scriptures in the NT, Paul is at pains to affirm at the outset that Israel's priority in the adoption, the glory, the covenants, the giving of the law, the worship, and the promises still stands (9:1–5). Not only would there be no salvation for anyone without the continuing integrity of those gifts (9:6; 11:29), but for that very reason Gentiles can know God's promised salvation only insofar as they are grafted into that faithful Israel among whom those promises have been realized (11:13–32). Further underlining this continuity, the NT's high Christology leaves no doubt as to its writers' conviction that, however mysterious and unexpected, Israel's God was uniquely present in Christ, who himself repeatedly exercised prerogatives that belonged only to YHWH.[2] That being so, how could God's actions in him be anything but consistent with God's previously revealed character?

It seems equally clear, moreover, that the content of the NT cannot be separated from either its modality—God is known primarily and fundamentally through his self-revelation in history[3] and climactically so in Jesus (and not through abstract human reason based on first or fundamental principles; see, e.g., Jn 1:14; 14:9; 1 Jn 1:1–3; 1 Cor 1:20; 2:5; Col 2:8)—or its hermeneutic, that is, its engagement with Israel's Scriptures. Now it is a truism that later Western Christianity cannot properly be understood without appreciating its "inner rapprochement between Biblical faith and Greek philosophical inquiry."[4] That Jesus or Paul would have felt the same about their message, at least on the evidence of the NT, seems unlikely.[5] Along similar lines, the recent revival of interest

---

[2] E.g., Richard Bauckham, *God Crucified: Monotheism & Christology in the New Testament* (Grand Rapids: Eerdmans, 1998); Larry W. Hurtado, *Lord Jesus Christ: Devotion to Jesus in Earliest Christianity* (Grand Rapids: Eerdmans, 2003); C. Kavin Rowe, *Early Narrative Christology: The Lord in the Gospel of Luke* (BZNW 139; Berlin/New York: de Gruyter, 2006); Gordon D. Fee, *Pauline Christology: An Exegetical-Theological Study* (Peabody, MA: Hendrickson, 2007); and especially now Sigurd Grindheim, *God's Equal : What Can We Know About Jesus' Self-Understanding* (LNTS 446; London: T&T Clark, 2011).

[3] Admittedly a highly problematic and loaded term, the debates concerning which would be inappropriate here, by history I mean the world of human experience, and its subsequent refraction and selection through all the vagaries and interests of memory and subsequent recording.

[4] Cf. Pope Benedict XVI's claim, "Three Stages in the Program of De-Hellenization" (lecture, University of Regensberg, Germany, 2006).

[5] It is somewhat surprising that although Benedict's speech makes much of John's early use of *logos*, nothing is said of his almost immediate abandonment of

in patristic exegesis, especially when presented as constituting a kind of hermeneutical norm, only serves to sharpen the question of whether or not, for instance, Origen was right in appealing to Paul's statement that the following Rock was Christ (1 Cor 10:4; *Adnot. Exod.* 5:1;[6] cf. ἀλληγορούμενα [*allēgoroumena*] in Gal 4:24) as grounds for employing the same allegorical methods that the philosophers had used to save Homer[7] (for an alternative understanding of Paul's assertion but based on the intrinsic meaning of Ex 17 itself, see below). What is clear, then, is the utterly central role of Israel's Scriptures and the narrative of the one true creator God's self-revelation enshrined therein in understanding God's eschatological act in Christ.

It is precisely at this point that the complexity emerges. For many inside and outside the church, and all the way back to the earliest post-apostolic period, the NT's engagement with Scripture has been problematic. This complexity, if anything, has grown rather than diminished. Questions on this subject now cover a range of topics including: what is meant by the "OT" both in canonical and in textual terms; the problematics of both terminology and practice in considering (in increasing order of difficulty), citations, allusions, and echoes (if the latter are indeed truly distinguishable from allusion); the nature and degree of the influence of the NT's Jewish context and of various Jewish interpretative methods on NT authors' hermeneutics; the hermeneutical implications of the NT authors' perceived use of the OT for modern readers; the place of audience understanding, its textual knowledge, and their effect on questions of authorial intention; the degree of innovation in NT hermeneutics, its origin and relationship to, for example, Christology; the terminological lack of clarity, if not confusion, in current debate, over terms such as "midrash," "pesher," and "intertextuality"; the role of preunderstandings of OT texts in informing NT usage; the influence of ancient rhetoric on NT usage; and finally of course, the nature of the relationship between the OT and NT:

---

the term to expound not on reason *per se* but on Jesus. This is not to deny human thoughtfulness. Moses and the prophets assume non-contradiction, coherence, and consistency, and Jesus and Paul are quite capable of solid argumentation. The question is whether the "Hellenic" philosophical project makes a unique and necessary contribution to a biblical knowledge of YHWH; see further e.g., C. Kavin Rowe, "The Grammar of Life: The Areopagus Speech and Pagan Tradition," *NTS* 57 (2010): 31–50.

[6] On the early Antiochean response, e.g., Frances M. Young, "Alexandrian and Antiochene Exegesis," in *The Ancient Period (vol. 1 of A History of Biblical Interpretation;* eds. Alan J. Hauser and Duane Frederick Watson; Grand Rapids: Eerdmans, 2003), 334–54.

[7] On the latter, see Robert Lamberton, *Homer the Theologian: Neoplatonist Allegorical Reading and the Growth of the Epic Tradition* (The Transformation of the Classical Heritage 9; Berkeley: University of California Press, 1986); Luc Brisson, *How Philosophers Saved Myths: Allegorical Interpretation and Classical Mythology* (trans. Catherine Tihanyi; 1996; repr., Chicago: University of Chicago Press, 2004).

for example, is there a single consistent intent, a form of *sensus plenior*, or are both ideas too rigid?[8]

In his slim but significant 1958 work on typology, Francis Foulkes stated:

> One of the deepest convictions that the prophets and historians of Israel had about the God in whom they trusted, and whose word they believed they were inspired to utter, was . . . that he had not left them in ignorance of his nature and purpose. Rather he had revealed himself to them, and had shown himself to be a God who acted according to principles, principles that would not change as long as sun and moon endured. They could assume, therefore, that as he had acted in the past, he could and would act in the future. By such an assumption the whole of the Old Testament is bound together and given unity.[9]

Following Foulkes' lead this paper further suggests that one way toward resolving some of these questions, particularly those related to exegesis, hermeneutics, and theology, lies in interpreting the NT's engagement with Israel's Scriptures in the light of what stands behind both collections of documents: the constancy of God's character. For the NT authors, what God had done in Christ was necessarily entirely consistent with his previously revealed character as expressed throughout his ongoing dealings in word and deed with his people, the nations, and his creation at large. It is proposed that a citation of or an allusion to Israel's Scriptures is best understood as invoking some principle concerning God's character, and thus his intention, in a situation that is deemed similar to an earlier one or, given the significance of Jesus, the fulfillment of an earlier promise. The rest of the essay will begin by discussing something of the basis for this view before examining a number of the classic problem texts from this angle.

Persons, Narrative, and the Character of God in Israel's Scriptures

We begin with the near banal, if not seemingly jejune, observation that in practice, the primary way we as persons get to know other per-

---

[8] See the useful recent surveys in Dennis L. Stamps, "The Use of the Old Testament in the New Testament as a Rhetorical Device: A Methodological Proposal," in *Hearing the Old Testament in the New Testament* (ed. Stanley E. Porter; McMaster New Testament Studies; Grand Rapids: Eerdmans, 2006), 9–37, and Christopher D. Stanley, "Paul and Scripture: Charting the Course," in *As It Is Written: Studying Paul's Use of Scripture* (ed. Stanley E. Porter and Christopher D. Stanley; SBLSymS 50; Atlanta: Society of Biblical Literature, 2008), 3–12; cf. Stanley E. Porter, "The Use of the Old Testament in the New Testament: A Brief Comment on Method and Terminology," in *Early Christian Interpretation of the Scriptures of Israel* (ed. Craig A. Evans and James A. Sanders; JSNTSup 148; Sheffield: Sheffield Academic Press, 1997), 79–96.

[9] Francis Foulkes, *The Acts of God* (London: Tyndale, 1958), 9.

sons is by attending to their words and deeds over a sufficiently lengthy period of time. It is when we see others' responses in a range of different situations that we can begin to form judgments about their character, motivation, intentions, and so on. So while it is true that what people do and say tells us something about their worldview,[10] it tells us even more about who he or she is as a person and especially when set within a larger coherent narrative.[11]

The predominately "historical" narrative quality of the bulk of the biblical material suggests that its primary concern is also with revealing the character and intentions of Israel's unique god, YHWH. This narrative quality is expressed in the specific narrative-historical frame of individual books, including the Prophets whose words relate God's response in a range of different situations, and in the larger narrative presumed not only by Israel's Scriptures *en toto* but also in the writings of the NT.[12] Given YHWH's profound commitment to self-revelation, and the centrality of narrative to the same, the current emphasis on "narrative theology" and even narrative epistemology (as opposed to some propositional version of Platonic *stasis*) seems entirely appropriate.[13] Key Jewish ideas such as those listed in Rom 9:4–5—adoption, glory, covenants, giving of the Law, worship, promises, patriarchs, Messiah[14]—cannot themselves be properly understood apart from the narrative of God's unfolding dealings with his people from (roughly summarized) the creation/fall/flood, through Abraham and the patriarchs, exodus and conquest, the Davidic kingship, exile, and concluding finally with the hopes of eschatological restoration.

James Dunn has recently criticized the idea of a shared coherent first-century Jewish narrative, citing the eclipse of grand narratives in postmodern historiography.[15] But this seems merely an anachronistic imposition of a late Western relativism upon a biblical view of history. The latter assumes a linear and purposeful progression, as Dunn himself recognizes, which seems necessarily to imply some kind of unifying core in order to

---

[10] N. T. Wright, *The New Testament and the People of God* (Minneapolis: Fortress, 1992), 41.

[11] On the centrality and primacy of narrative in human cognition, Kay Young and Jeffrey L. Saver, "The Neurology of Narrative," *SubStance* 94/95 (2001): 72–84; cf. earlier, e.g., Stephen Crites, "The Narrative Quality of Experience," *JAAR* 39 (1971): 291–311.

[12] As discussed and summarized by Wright, *People of God*, 215–23.

[13] E.g., Ben Witherington III, *Paul's Narrative Thought World* (Louisville/Carlisle: Westminster/John Knox Press, 1994); Ian W. Scott, *Implicit Epistemology in the Letters of Paul: Story, Experience and the Spirit* (WUNT 205; Tübingen: Mohr Siebeck, 2006).

[14] Cf. Roy E. Ciampa, "Scriptural Language and Ideas," in *As it is Written: Studying Paul's Use of Scripture* (ed. Stanley E. Porter and Christopher D. Stanley; SBLSymS 50; Atlanta: Society of Biblical Literature, 2008), 41–57.

[15] James D. G. Dunn, *Jesus Remembered* (Grand Rapids: Eerdmans, 2003), 393–404.

give substantive expression to that linearity and purpose. Further, to the extent this eclipse relies on Jean-François Lyotard's critique of metanarrative[16] one needs to remember that his concern was not with large "first order" stories—stories about the world before our eyes—such as we find in the biblical material. On the contrary, he was concerned instead to unmask modernity's "second order" legitimating narratives—for example, that human liberation comes through politics (Marx), economics (Smith), education, science—which were designed to overthrow precisely those traditional first-order narratives such as we find in the Bible.[17] From this perspective the larger biblical narrative, being both first order—stories, for example, about what Moses, Israel, the prophets, Jesus, the Twelve, and Paul saw and experienced in history—and traditional, is not, as far as I can see, a Lyotardian metanarrative at all. The influence of Israel's historical memory on its feasts, and, as increasingly recognized, of the exodus narrative on Israel's Scriptures—pre-eminently the prophets[18]— and the NT writings suggests that Israel's "theology" was fundamentally coherent and historical/narrative in character and that they construed themselves as still living within this unfolding narrative.

Steven DiMattei's recent questioning of the ubiquitous use of "typology" to describe Paul's hermeneutic in, for example, 1 Cor 10:1–11 and Rom 5:14, seems also to confirm this approach.[19] He argues that present usage not only differs from the early visual iconography of Barnabas and Justin but is more characteristic of the later attempts of Irenaeus to demonstrate a "unified history" while also depending heavily on the subsequent Antiochean critique of Origen. None of them, he goes on to argue, owes much to Paul. His suggestion, that Paul's use of τύπος (*tupos*) in 1 Cor 10:6, not of the "rock" but of Israel's behavior, instead reflects the practice of providing historical *exemplae* (παράδειγμα; *paradeigma*), coheres well with the emphasis proposed herein on the priority of God's revealed character and consequent expectation that his people "be holy as he is holy" (Lv 19:2; Dt 26:19). In this respect one might say that these events bear the stamp or imprint of God's character, preserved for the edification of Israel and *tout force* of the eschatological Israel of God (cf. Gal 6:16).

---

[16] Jean-François Lyotard, *The Postmodern Condition: A Report on Knowledge* (Minneapolis: University of Minnesota Press, 1984).

[17] See the useful summary in Merold Westphal, *Overcoming Onto-theology: Toward a Postmodern Christian Faith* (1st ed.; New York: Fordham University Press, 2001), xii–xv.

[18] Considerably more than has been generally recognized, see Rikk E. Watts, "Exodus Imagery," in *Dictionary of the Old Testament Prophets* (ed. Mark J. Boda and J. Gordon McConville; Downers Grove, IL/Nottingham: InterVarsity Press, 2012), 205–14.

[19] Steven DiMattei, "Biblical Narratives," in *As it is Written: Studying Paul's Use of Scripture* (ed. Stanley E. Porter and Christopher D. Stanley; SBLSymS 50; Atlanta: Society of Biblical Literature, 2008), 59–93.

That being said, DiMattei's further suggestion that the NT's eschato-logical setting puts it outside Israel's scriptural narrative is less persua-sive.[20] He is, of course, in one sense correct in that the NT events happened after the writing of Israel's Scriptures. Nevertheless, from the perspective of God's ongoing acts, that the larger narrative of those Scriptures in-cludes both promises and descriptions of the coming eschatological and messianic day means that the NT authors can justifiably see themselves as lying within the ambit of the Scriptures' narrative arc. The only difference is that what the prophets described in the future tense, the NT authors describe also in the past and present (cf. Paul's "to us upon whom the ends of the ages have come," 1 Cor 10:11). It is all part of the one ongoing story of YHWH's consistent action.

It is to be expected then, as prophets, Qumran sectarians, rabbis, and modern scholars have noted, that given God's unchanging and consistent character his acts in the past necessarily reveal something about his acts in the future.[21] As David Instone Brewer's insufficiently appreciated volume shows, the same assumption concerning YHWH's unchanging character lies behind pre-A.D. 70 rabbinic exegesis as they sought legal precedent in the Scriptures as a basis for guidance in the present;[22] unsurprisingly the principles of equivalence and coherence significantly inform the seven rules attributed to Hillel.

The impression is only strengthened in the light of contemporary ma-terials: we lack anything comparable for the various deities of the ancient world. For example, Hesiod's *Theogony*, while a narrative of the history of the gods, reflects more the impetus to a universalizing synthesis than any particular interest in their character. This is perhaps not unexpected given the gods' relative disinterest in humanity and the conviction on the human side that the primary characteristic of a god being power the inequality in that respect rendered impossible any sense of relational recipricosity.[23] In contrast, Israel's God, especially as seen in Christ, is remarkable in the depth of intimacy and the extent of the relationship he seeks with not only his people but, especially now in the gospel, with humanity at large.

It seems too then that one of the reasons for this emphasis on char-acter-revealing narrative is that YHWH insists that he is a god unlike any other. From this perspective, Wittgenstein's advice that we begin by looking, instead of thinking, is entirely in keeping with coming to know

---

[20] DiMattei, "Biblical Narratives," 81–82.

[21] E.g., again Watts, "Exodus"; Otto Betz, "Past Events and Last Events in the Qumran Interpretation of History," *Proceedings of the World Congress of Jewish Studies* 6 (1977): 27–34; and Foulkes, *Acts of God*, 9–21.

[22] David Instone Brewer, *Techniques and Assumptions in Jewish Exegesis before 70 CE* (TSAJ 30; Tübingen: Mohr Siebeck, 1992).

[23] Paul Cartledge, *The Greeks: A Portrait of Self and Others,* 2nd ed. (Oxford/New York: Oxford University Press, 2002), 180, citing Aristotle *[Mag. mor.]* 1208[b] 27–31; *Eth. nic.* 1122[b] 20–22.

persons and hence with YHWH's "first order" self-revelation in the exodus. In answer to Moses' question, "Whom shall I say sent me?" (Ex 3:13), God's "I am who I am" is less an encouragement to meditate on questions concerning the nature of being or eternal essences—not least because such concerns seem wildly anachronistic to the concerns of Exodus—than a statement about *who* he is. He is indeed the God of the fathers, but his self-revelation to them had been limited; a significantly new development is about to begin (Ex 6:3). The implicit message is: Israel does not yet know, in the fully biblical sense of experiencing first hand, who "I Am" is, with the further implication that they should not guess based on their current experience of deities. It is in one important respect a negation of human supposition.

Exodus then proceeds to relate the story of YHWH's self-revelation. At the outset he is revealed as the one who hears the cry of his people in their distress (3:7–9). Not only a faithful God and just, his intervention on their behalf demonstrates that he is much more than a local deity. He is the all-powerful creator to whom Egypt's gods, the nations, and creation itself must submit. But even here Israel's experience of his power over creation and Pharaoh, the image of Amon-Re upon the earth, is less a new category than the transferal of what was claimed for Egypt's deities to YHWH.

The critical moment appears after the incident of the golden calf (Ex 32). It is not unreasonable that, finding themselves alone in a hostile space, Israel's attempts to invoke this YHWH's presence should reflect the standard means learned in their Egyptian sojourn. A matter of debate, it nevertheless seems to me that the calf reflects the revitalized Apis bull cult whereby Israel's construction of a "hypostatic" bull image serves to invoke the presence of the creator deity, now understood to be YHWH whose creatorly bona fides were so strongly attested by the plagues unleashed through his authoritative word. Hence Aaron's subsequent declaration that the morrow would be a חַג (ḥag, festival) to YHWH (Ex 32:5). In their minds, this was no apostasy but the conventional means of summoning and mediating the presence of the creator deity who was conceived as standing upon the back of the image.

But as careful readers of Ex 17 know, YHWH had already taken a hypostatic stance on something (the fundamental question at issue being God's presence, Ex 17:7), and that not made with human hands. It was YHWH's prerogative alone to choose to be present in whatsoever form he chose, and in doing so he identified with a very different conception of deity: the smitten rock at Horeb—the previously mentioned site of the inaugurating burning bush—upon which he stood facing Moses in a posture of judicial self-sentence (Ex 17:5–6). Whereas Moses had in an act of judgment struck the divine Nile causing its water to turn to blood, in commanding Moses to carry out a similar sentence on himself before elders and people, the smitten YHWH, here accused of attempted genocide, instead "bleeds" life-giving water for his people. That same God was present in Christ, as both John (7:37–39; 19:34) and Paul (1 Cor 10:4) recognized. This all-powerful YHWH, Israel now learns, is not primarily about power but self-giving life. His deep offense is at Israel's disobedient assumption that he was merely a more powerful version of Egypt's deities.

This brings us again to the critical texts of Ex 33–34 where, as indicated by the repetition of the *idem per idem* formula, the full and glorious character behind the "I am who I am" name is now revealed to be "I [am the one who] will be gracious (חָנַן; *ḥānan*) to whom I will be gracious and will show mercy on whom I will show mercy" (Ex 33:17–19; cf. 34:6–7). It is little wonder that Moses subsequently prays, "If I have gained Your favor [חֵן; *ḥēn*], O Lord, pray, let the Lord go in our midst, because this is a stiff-necked people, and pardon our iniquity and our sin, and take us for Your own!" (Ex 34:9). It is precisely *because* of YHWH's unexpectedly compassionate character, forgiving those who do not deserve it, that a headstrong Israel needs his presence with them. It is again hardly surprising that precisely this moment informs so much of the prophets' future hope, in spite of Israel's constant rebellion.[24]

The narrative shape of Israel's Scriptures seems then to be the necessary correlate of YHWH's overriding concern to reveal himself, that is, his character and his intentions, to his people and through them to the world. From this perspective, the rationale behind the narrative shape of the Gospels comes into clearer view. Of course the story of someone's life necessarily takes the shape of a narrative, in the case of the canonical Gospels, a form of Greco-Roman *bios*. But if the *Gospel of Thomas* is any indication, not everyone felt that impulse; likewise, apparently, the putative "Q" community: collections of sayings were deemed to suffice. The pervasive presence of Israel's Scriptures throughout the canonical Gospels suggests that their authors too were fundamentally concerned with presenting the character of Jesus and that in terms of God's historic self-revelation in their Scriptures.[25]

Examples

The proof of the pudding is, as they say, in the eating. In this section we will examine, albeit in each instance somewhat briefly, a range of generally acknowledged problem texts to test the utility of the proposed approach. Given the limits of this essay it is not possible, and given its aims—namely, to illustrate a specific proposal (as opposed to mediating a range of scholarly proposals)—perhaps not even desirable, to engage at length with the secondary literature. More obviously, the following

---

[24] Watts, "Exodus."

[25] See further, e.g., Meredith G. Kline, "The Old Testament Origins of the Gospel Genre," *WTJ* 38 (1975): 1–27.

are necessarily only a selection of some of the more consistently cited "problem" texts. But they should suffice to illustrate how this narrative-character reading might work.

At the outset, we face a critical question. Do we begin with the NT (con)text[26] or the Scripture to which it appeals? Based on the above discussion, the obvious fact that Jesus and his message were originally heard against the backdrop of Jewish scriptural expectations, and that the NT writers themselves most likely sought initially to comprehend Jesus within the larger and prior authoritative framework of Israel's Scriptures, we will begin with those texts.[27] The point to be noted though is that in many instances the NT author is not concerned with exegeting the scriptural text itself but with using it to exegete the situation under discussion. The question, on the view proposed here, then becomes whether a given use is consistent with what that Scripture reveals about God's faithful dealings with his people.

As Matthew opens the NT canon and has come in for his fair share of criticism over his handling of Israel's Scriptures, we can perhaps begin with him.

Isaiah 7:14 in Matthew 1:23

Matthew 1:23's appeal to Is 7:14 as a messianic text and apparent prediction of Mary's virginal conception is often criticized as an idiosyncratic attempt to legitimize Jesus' dubious origins or cited as an example of *sensus plenior*, with "Immanuel" signifying God's presence in him. But as I have argued elsewhere,[28] it need not be so understood especially if we take God's unchanging character as expressed in Is 7 as our starting point.

---

[26] As urged on the basis of narrative theory by, e.g., Thomas R. Hatina, *In Search of a Context: the Function of Scripture in Mark's Narrative* (SSEJC 8 / JSNTSup 232; London: Sheffield Academic Press, 2002).

[27] Hatina's proposal, *Search*, although it aims to be "Narrative-Historical," in practice denies that history by effectively disallowing the Scriptural texts and ideas to which Mark appeals any pre-understanding, i.e. "history," in the mind of Mark or his readers. Furthermore, in order to function, language presupposes a prior shared matrix of meaning. This must surely include the range of Jewish expectations and understandings of its Scriptures, as e.g., implied by notions of prophet and fulfilment (Mk 1:15), which had necessarily to be in place prior to Mark's writing. A similar confusion results when the modern shift in meaning of "gay" is invoked to downplay the importance of attending to what a given Scripture might have meant in other earlier contexts; Steve Moyise, *Evoking Scripture: Seeing the Old Testament in the New* (London/New York: T&T Clark, 2008), 3. The obvious problem is that Mark's thematic remark concerning "fulfilment" (1:15; cf. 14:49) suggests on the contrary a strong note of continuity, not radical discontinuity.

[28] Rikk E. Watts, "Immanuel: Virgin Birth Proof Text or Programmatic Warning of Things to Come (Isa 7:14 in Matt 1:23)?," in *From Prophecy to Testament* (ed. Craig A. Evans; Peabody, MA: Hendrickson: 2004), 92–113.

In Is 7 the child's name captures, as do the other two (7:3; 8:1), a key aspect of what God's people can expect from him. In the case of the first, שְׁאָר יָשׁוּב (*šĕʾār yāšûḇ*; "a remnant will return"), God encourages Ahaz to trust (7:4) that in spite of how things look in the present, in the end only a shattered "remnant" of the opposing forces will be left (7:3, 8). This promise of security is also accompanied by a warning—if Ahaz does not believe he will not stand at all—with God then offering a confirmatory sign even in the heavens if Ahaz requires (7:11). The cloaking of Ahaz's real intent with a pious demurral (7:12) is unmasked for what it is: an implicit rejection of God's faithfulness and commitment to keep his promises (7:13). But God is indeed faithful, including his commitment not to leave the guilty unpunished (cf. Ex 34:7). Consequently his presence (Immanuel) among his people can only mean, as it always has when confronted by rebellion, judgment (7:17; cf. 1:24–25; 5:1–30; 6:1–13; 8:6–8).

This is precisely what we find in Matthew: the rejection, by a faithless king, of God's offer of salvation through a named child, Jesus (1:21; cf. Isaiah's offered salvation in Mt 3:3; 4:15–16), and that in spite of a sign in the heavens being given (2:2), resulting in judgment. Matthew's unusual elucidation of both names (1:21, 23) similarly recalls Isaiah's emphasis. Because Jesus is himself God's presence with us, Israel's unbelieving response necessarily results, as it did in Isaiah's day, in the desolation of its house (Mt 23:38; cf. 8:11–12; 10:32–36; 12:20–24; 13:14–15; 21:43; see also e.g., Is 6:11), this time at the hands of the idolatrous Romans (Mt 24). Matthew's "fulfillment" simply recognizes that the birth of Jesus to the virginal Mary constituted the beginning of the climactic eschatological expression of that aspect of YHWH's character previously enunciated in Is 7. He would save those who believed and judge those who in spite of his mighty signs rejected his offer of salvation. As God had acted before, so he acts again.

Hosea 11:1 in Matthew 2:15

Hosea 11:1 expresses God's disappointment at Israel's failure to live up to his exodus intentions for them, not least in the light of his warnings concerning the mortal dangers of idolatry (1:2; 4:1–3; cf. Ex 23:24, 32–33; Dt 4:1–4). Consequently, in a restatement of his self-revelation on Sinai, he will no longer let the guilty go unpunished (Ex 33:19). Refusing to show compassion, they will no longer be his people, and he will no longer be their God (Hos 1:6, 9). But given God's unchanging character, the prophet knows that this punishment is only temporary and the time will come when under YHWH's patient persuasion his people will experience a new exodus (2:14–15; cf. 11:10–11). Matthew is not here suggesting that Hosea had some hidden additional meaning to "son" only now revealed in

Christ. He is declaring that Hosea's hope of God's accomplishing his initial purposes in Israel is now eschatologically fulfilled in Jesus, his truly obedient Son (cf. Mt 3:17–4:17), whom he also brought up from Egypt, and through and in whom he will patiently persuade his people (cf. Mt 11:25–30).[29]

Isaiah 14:13–15 in Matthew 11:23 (cf. Psalm 2:1–2 in Acts 4:26–27)

The principle here, repeated over and again in Israel's Scriptures, seems clear enough: when Israel becomes like the unbelieving nations, they will experience the same judgment. As in similar such texts (e.g., Is 13:10 and 34:4 applied to Jerusalem in Mk 13:24–25), Matthew's Jesus is not exegeting Isaiah but Capernaum. Jesus announces that Capernaum's rejection of his message, in spite of the mighty deeds worked among them (11:23), is tantamount to Babylon's exalting itself over against God's authority, a wickedness that surpasses even Sodom's legendary sin. The magnitude of this rejection is highlighted by the fact that Jesus is no mere prophet but, as the preceding citation of Mal 3:1 concerning John implies, none other than YHWH's own long-awaited personal presence come to his people. Consequently, God being no respecter of persons, a Babylon-imitating Capernaum will likewise experience Babylon's devastating downfall.

The appeal to Ps 2 in Acts 4 reflects a similar understanding. Although the psalm envisages only the nations rising in rebellion against God's anointed (as Acts 4:25 clearly appreciates), Israel's leaders' alignment with Rome against his holy servant Jesus (4:27) necessarily means that the psalmist's words apply equally to them (cf. Paul's application of David's imprecatory words against his enemies, Ps 69:22–23, to a rebellious Israel under God's judgment in Rom 11:9–10).

Turning now to Paul . . .

"The Following Rock" in 1 Corinthians 10:1–4

Although this text is often regarded as an a-contextual "midrashic" or allegorical reading of Israel's exodus experience, these assessments in my view fail to attend closely enough to the original text and its context and hence miss the deep symbolism already inherent in the original account. The brevity of Paul's rapid-fire identifications suggests that he sees nothing controversial about any of them. And in any case his main point is to draw out the implications of God's unchanging character for the Corinthians in this new exodus with whose relevance and pattern he apparently expects them to be familiar (cf. 1 Cor 5:7). That he easily asserts

---

[29] On a personal note, the temptation to see Matthew's application as a tad "cute" might be tempered by a moment's reflection on just how serious it was, and is, to be a refugee fleeing for one's life.

their shared ancestry (10:1a) reflects his fundamentally historical mode of thought and further strengthens the supposition that this was hardly a new way of thinking for them.

If the fiery-cloudy pillar was already associated with God's promised delivering presence (Gn 15:12–17), then Paul's identification of that cloud with God's presence among the Corinthians through his Spirit is surely no great step (cf. Is 63:9–10). Similarly Paul's description of the exodus as a baptism into Moses merely picks up on what it already was: a passing through the waters of death (cf. Ex 14:30), the dwelling place of the sundered chaos serpent (Ps 89:10; Is 51:9; cf. Jb 26:12; Is 30:7), under the aegis of God's "cloudy-fiery" presence, into a new creational life (note the several parallels with Gn 1: darkness, light, wind, the deep, and the emerging dry land) according to the terms of the Mosaic Torah (Dt 4, 30; Lv 18:5; Ps 119). The Corinthians' baptism into Christ (1 Cor 1:13) is the eschatological new exodus equivalent of passing from death to life (cf. Rom 6:4) to which the prophets themselves pointed. Both groups also ate of the food and drank of the drink God provided (hence "spiritual"). According to John, Jesus had already described himself as the true bread from heaven (cf. 6:31–58) and according to Moses (as discussed above) YHWH had already identified with the smitten rock—itself the source of Israel's drink—which, given Paul's high Christology, finds its obvious eschatological counterpart in the crucified yet resurrected Jesus (see also Jn 7:37–38; 19:34).

For Paul, these apparently noncontentious parallels rest on the fundamental assumption of YHWH's constant character—as he had acted in the past so he would act again—which leads as Paul had intended all along to his warning to the Corinthians not to participate in idol festivals. If their ancestors, for all their participation in God's presence, salvation, and provision under Moses, were liable to judgment for idolatry, then the same surely applied to their Corinthian descendants who were enjoying similarly divine benefits in Christ.

Deuteronomy 25:4 in 1 Corinthians 9:9

If Jesus himself affirmed the rescue of animals on the Sabbath (Mt 12:11) it is unlikely that Paul believes God has no concern for them. His rhetorical point seems instead that it is absurd to think that a God who cares about the treatment of laboring oxen is unconcerned about the treatment of human workers—Deuteronomy's command, as is often recognized, belongs to a series of instructions concerning preserving human dignity in various civil and domestic matters (22:10–25:19). The issue is one of principle. If laboring animals have a divine right to their share in the harvest, surely it is obvious (hence πάντως [*pantōs*]) how much more we ("us," 1 Cor 9:10) who, made in God's image, are laboring in his fields in his service (cf. 1 Cor 3:5–9)?

Isaiah 28:11–12 in 1 Corinthians 14:21

In Isaiah the unintelligibility of the alien Assyrians' speech was a sign to unbelieving Israel of God's *lex talionis* judgment on their stubborn refusal to respond to the clear words of his prophet. For Paul, this is precisely the problem with uninterpreted tongues in public worship. Although the Corinthian believers themselves understood what was going on, the unintelligibility to the uninitiated of uninterpreted tongues only alienated them. What was meant to be an expression of God's life-giving Spirit became for the unbelievers a sign that by causing their rejection of the gospel, effectively cut them off from any further hearing from God and so functioned as judgment. By contrast, prophecy, being intelligible, signified that God was still communicating with the hearers in order to encourage and sustain faith in himself. For Paul, the fundamental scriptural principle obtains. In terms of one's relationship with God, intelligible prophecy was the sign associated with belief; unintelligible tongues signified judgment on the unbelieving.

The "Seed" of Genesis 12:7 and 22:17–18 in Galatians 3:16

Paul's emphasis on the singular nature of Abraham's seed is often described as an atomistic exegesis that survives only if "seed" is examined in isolation. I suggest on the contrary that it reflects a solid awareness of the larger narrative. Paul is very much aware, as one would expect, that it was Isaac alone of all of Abraham's offspring, including his children from Keturah (Gn 25:1–4; 1 Chr 1:32–33), who was the child of promise (cf. Gal 4:21–31; Rom 9:6–13). Paul's claim is that the promise given to the one, Isaac, has likewise been fulfilled through the one, Jesus. God's well-known promissory act in Genesis—Jewish identity is based on it (as per the subsequent discussion in Gal 4:21–31)—is repeated in his eschatological act of realizing the promise. What matters now is not whether one is a descendant of Abraham through his one son Isaac but an heir of God's promises to him through his one true offspring Jesus.

Hagar and Sarah in Galatians 4:22–26

The same question concerning the true heirs of God's promises arises here. Much—indeed probably far too much—has been made of Paul's (and indeed the NT's) solitary use of the word group allegory/to allegorize. But, if we can avoid stumbling over that highly problematic stone for a moment, here too his thinking is quite straightforward.

Whereas Paul's interlocutors apparently began in the past with Isaac as the true son of promise (cf. seed in Gal 3:16; Rom 9:6), he starts in the present with those who have received the promise, namely, the Spirit (Gal

3:1–5), through God's one Son, Jesus (2:20). Whereas they argue from bloodline, Paul argues from the present eschatological reality. If we allow Abraham's two women to represent two covenants and two communities, then it is those Jews who seek to be justified by Torah (2:15–21) and are thus constitutive of present-day Jerusalem who, without Spirit, are in bondage, and hence, to add "insult" to irony, the effective descendants of the slave woman Hagar. Gentiles, however, having received the promised Spirit through faith in Christ are irrefutably the divinely attested heirs of Abraham and therefore the eschatological children of restored Daughter Zion of whom Isaiah spoke (Is 54:1; cf. 51:1–3; 44:3; 61:1–3).

Paul adds nothing to the grammar of Israel's storyline; the prophets had already made the critical move in realizing that the key ingredient to Israel's eschatological relationship with God was his out-poured Spirit (Is 44:3; Ez 11:16–20; 36:26–38; Jl 2:28). Simply put, once one allows that the Spirit was at the heart of God's promised blessing, then—God being unchanging—the true descendants of free Sarah's son must necessarily be those who have entered, through faith in God's Son, into the realization of that promise.

Hosea 2:23 and 1:10 in Romans 9:24–25

The obvious problem here is that having just spoken of not only Jews but also Gentiles as recipients of God's merciful call (Rom 9:24), Paul cites a text that speaks only to Israel. How can he justify including Gentiles? But if we think of his argument in terms of God's constant character the difficulty evaporates. As already noted in the preceding discussion of Hosea, God responded to Israel's rebellion by announcing that they were no longer his people (Hos 1:9). Paul's logic in citing the reversal of that judgment (Hos 2:23; 1:10) seems to be that if God, in the promised second exodus, could show mercy to a remnant of "not my people" Jews—with the result that they will be "called sons of God" (Hos 1:10; 2:23)—then surely he can show the same mercy to another "not my people," namely Gentiles whom he has also "called" (v. 24b).

Leviticus 18:5 and Deuteronomy 9:4 and 30:12–14 in Romans 10:4–10

In one of his more compressed passages, Paul here outlines, based on God's consistent ways, the character of the new exodus salvation in Christ over against the righteousness of Torah. In citing Lv 18:5 Paul begins by affirming that Israel had indeed experienced Torah's gift of life, based as it was on Torah righteousness with its demand for obedient "doing" of its statutes and ordinances. Even so the subsequent "do not say in your heart" (v. 6a; Dt 9:4) recalls Moses' later reminder to an Israel on the threshold of the promised land that it was not their own righteousness that earned them entrance, enjoining them therefore to love God by keeping Torah (Dt 10:12–13). In evoking Dt 30:12–14 (vv.6b–8) Paul then skips forward to Moses' prophetic word to an Israel in future exile, reminding them that God had made Torah both accessible and clear. The problem was not with Torah but with them, as Paul had earlier affirmed (Rom 7:7–20). With classic rabbinic brevity, Paul lays out the character and history of Israel under Torah, from its opening promise of life (Lv 18:5), through a warning not to think they earned it (Dt 9:4), and finally to the sad reality of failure and exile, due not to God's good gift but Israel's sin (Dt 30:12–14).

At the same time, Paul's interjection of "But the righteousness that comes by faith" (v. 6a) begins, midstream as it were, to overlay the narrative of Torah with the parallel eschatological narrative of God's promised saving response in Christ. As with Torah righteousness, Christ-faith righteousness also warns against "saying in one's heart"—he too is an underserved gift to failed Israel—but the focus quickly moves to a christological equivalent of Dt 30:12–14. Just as God had earlier brought Torah near and clear to his people, now that same God has done even more in his surpassing gift of an equally and more accessible and clear Christ to his now exiled people.

In the light of this eschatological gift, whereas Moses summoned postexilic Israel to Torah fidelity, Paul, knowing on the basis of his Damascus Road experience that God's eschatological answer is not Torah but Christ (Rom 7:24b–8:2), transfers the language of that climactic summary of Dt 30:11–14 to Jesus (vv. 6b–8). The resurrected, Spirit-gifting Christ is after all the *telos* of the Law and, as the one who truly inaugurated that release from exile of which Moses' spoke, the climax of Israel's history. Henceforth, to attempt to find life through Torah righteousness amounts in the face of what God has now done, to a disobedient establishing of one's own justification (v. 3). It becomes the kind of "saying in one's heart" that one ought not do. What God requires is no longer the Mosaic command "to do" Torah, but the speaking of a faith-filled confession of Christ (vv. 9–10). Once again the basic premise, given that for Paul Christ has supplanted Torah as the path to righteousness, is the consistency of God's actions and our expected response. Being given life (Lv 18:5), irrespective of our own efforts (Dt 9:4), we should seek to be obedient to what God has clearly revealed, which means no longer "doing Torah" but confessing Christ (Dt 30:4–10).

Concluding Comments

One of the strengths of this view is that it takes seriously what I would suggest is a properly contextual reading of the Scriptures. Just as the Law could be searched for precedent, so too the Prophets, both reflecting expressions of God's character in given situations. If I might be permitted, an analogy drawn from the late medieval debates over planetary motion and the question of helio- or geo-centrism might help.

It was long ago recognized by Hipparchus of Nicea (190–120 B.C.) that two mutually exclusive explanations could "save the appearances," that is, describe and predict celestial movements as seen from earth. What Galileo's critics—Osiander, Bellarmine, and Urban VIII—recognized and he and his fellow heliocentrists failed to address was why his explanation, his "saving of the appearances," should have any precedence over a Ptolemaic view when both explained the data. What was not fully grasped, though Galileo and Kepler had intuited it, was that a true explanation had to "save the appearances" not just on earth but in the heavens as well. This could not be addressed until the medieval distinction between two kinds of physics—sublunary or terrestrial and celestial—was overcome. Already implicit in Nicolas of Cusa's assertion that the stars were also made of the four elements, Brahe's observation (cf. Wittgenstein's "look first") of the 1572 supernova, and Galileo's of sunspots and mountains on the moon was the unity of both realms in the one physics. In the end, that realization in combination with Newtonian mechanics showed that only a heliocentric view saved the appearances in the one newly unified realm.[30]

Similarly, there are currently a range of ways of "saving the appearances" when it comes to explaining the NT use of the OT, for example, contextual awareness, *sensus plenior*, a-contextual-rhetorical, and so on. I want to suggest that the principle of universal physical laws applied to the inanimate universe both on earth and in the celestial sphere has, *mutatis mutandis*, a correlate in the realm of the personal. It is expressed, however, not in terms of mathematical laws but God's constant character, a constancy that unites at a more fundamental level both Israel's Scriptures and the NT writings.

Before pursuing this further, it is worthwhile noting that not unlike the medieval debates advocates of particular views do not always attend carefully enough to each others' arguments. As several of these are quite significant for our discussion, they warrant some attention. It is true that proponents of strict contextual adherence do not always fully address the problems raised by their view.[31] On the other hand, arguments against contextual awareness are sometimes insufficiently careful of that context. For example, Steve Moyise thinks a contextual christological reading of Mal 3:1 (in Mk 1:2–3) entails the improbable idea that Jesus aimed to purify the Levites (cf. Mal 3:3).[32] I suggest that a more careful reading

---

[30] Pierre Duhem, *To Save the Phenomena, an Essay on the Idea of Physical Theory from Plato to Galileo,* trans. Edmund Doland and Chaninah Maschler, with an Introductory Essay by Stanley L. Jaki (Chicago: University of Chicago Press, 1969).

[31] E.g., Darrell Bock's, "Response to Kaiser," in *Three Views on the New Testament Use of the Old Testament* (eds. Kenneth Berding and Jonathan Lunde; Grand Rapids: Zondervan, 2007), 90–95.

[32] *Evoking,* 14–15.

attributes that task to the Elijah messenger ("he" throughout 3:1b–4; cf. 4:5 ET) in preparation for YHWH's coming in judgment ("I" in 3:5–12; cf. 4:6b ET). It is precisely the priestly authorities' failure to respond to John's Elijah that Jesus cites in justifying his prophetic judgment on the temple (Mk 11:27–33; cf. v.17; 13:1–2).[33]

Along similar lines, sometimes reconstructions of the first century environment, in the interests of making a particular case, consider only one side of the story. In terms of access to Israel's Scriptures, for example, while it is true that conflict with the synagogue might have made it difficult to obtain exemplars to copy,[34] it is also possible that not every synagogue was in tension with Paul. And in any case he might have had some important scrolls of his own from his time as a "rabbi" or had received them as a gift from sending churches or from wealthy patrons, including those who themselves may once have been part of synagogues and have had their own select books.[35]

Likewise, the common claim that scrolls were too cumbersome seems not to have considered the then current trend toward portability—books that fitted the hand—for ease of reading, often while traveling.[36] In spite of the general perception that they were far too expensive, based on the evidence for a sizeable book culture[37] and on the only extant actual figures of which I know, Martial, *Epigr.* 1:117 and 13:3,[38] a portable book or two of Isaiah could have been available for as little as fifteen or up to thirty denarii.[39] This is hardly beyond the means of those who according to Rodney Stark must have had sufficient resources to take part in the kind of movement Christianity represented[40] and about whom Luke's account of their destroying fifty thousand silver denarii of magical materials, while

---

[33] Rikk E. Watts, "Mark," in *Commentary on the New Testament use of the Old Testament* (eds. G. K. Beale and D. A. Carson; Grand Rapids, Mich; Nottingham, England: Baker/Apollos, 2007), 117, 119–20.

[34] Stanley followed by Stanley E. Porter, "Paul and His Bible: His Education and Access to the Scriptures of Israel," in *As it is Written: Studying Paul's Use of Scripture* (ed. Stanley E. Porter and Christopher D. Stanley; SBLSymS 50; Atlanta: Society of Biblical Literature, 2008), 97–124.

[35] As briefly noted by Stanley, *Paul and the Language of Scripture: Citation Technique in the Pauline Epistles and Contemporary Literature* (SNTSMS 74; Cambridge: Cambridge University, 1992), 73 n. 27.

[36] Cf. E. Tov, "The Dimensions of the Qumran Scrolls," *DSD* 5 (1998): 69–81.

[37] Porter, "Paul," 106–15.

[38] William V. Harris, *Ancient Literacy* (Cambridge, Mass.: Harvard University Press, 1989), 225 n. 254.

[39] This is based on Martial's reference to the availability in Rome of a nice edition of 700 lines at five denarii *(Epigr.* 1:117), and a modest volume of 274 lines for just one *(Epigr.* 13:3). If we assume say an average of 32 characters per line, as per P[46], then a book of Greek Isaiah would take some 4165 lines, resulting in the above approximate figures.

[40] Rodney Stark, "The Class Basis of Early Christianity," in *The Rise of Christianity: How the Obscure, Marginal Jesus Movement Became the Dominant Religious*

remarkable, was apparently not considered unrealistic (Acts 19:19). Accordingly, Luke's comment on those who searched the Scriptures to see if "these things were so" is directed not at their either having the books or the ability to read them in depth, but at their nobility in being open to something so new (Acts 17:11; cf. 4 Mc 18:10–19).

Then there is the question of the ethics of citation. The recent interest in rhetoric as persuasion being integral to Christian proclamation and teaching is to be welcomed—as George A. Kennedy observed, the NT language of "being persuaded" is much more a rhetorical term than one of philosophical certainty via demonstration.[41] However, given both Quintilian's assertion that the critical qualification of a rhetor is that he be "good" (*Inst.* 12.1.3) and Paul's repeated defense of his own integrity, it seems odd that some recent proponents of a rhetorical approach suggest that Paul was, apparently knowingly, less than straightforward with his use of Scripture. Further, as Morna Hooker observed, the claim that Paul nevertheless had a "deep respect for Scripture" seems quite to miss the point that for him Scripture was the very embodiment of the Jewish faith;[42] and we might add, of the very oracles of God.

Based on the foregoing it seems likely that not only Paul but also some of the more well-to-do in his wealthier churches had access to various scriptural books and took them seriously as the very words of God. While it is highly unlikely that anyone, then as now, got everything Paul intended on the first reading, it seems likely too that he had in mind a range of hearers, not least the better educated "teaching elders" with whom rested the responsibility of instructing the community and whom he may have expected to search not just Scripture but his letters, aided if need be by the letter carrier.[43] It seems reasonable then to suppose that Paul himself envisaged in-depth and detailed consideration, at least by some, of his engagement with Scripture having both letter and said Scriptures to hand (cf. Acts 17:11).

With these considerations in view we can return to an examination of the various attempts to "save the appearances." I suggest that the approach proposed here offers a neater, deeper, and more consistent explanation in that it illuminates underlying causes. In spite of the much emphasized distinction between the spiritual and fleshly, the temporal

---

Force in the Western World in a Few Centuries (Princeton: Princeton University Press, 1996), 29–47.

[41] George A. Kennedy, *Classical Rhetoric and its Christian and Secular Tradition From Ancient to Modern Times* (Chapel Hill: University of North Carolina Press, 1980).

[42] Morna Hooker, "review of Christopher D. Stanley, *Arguing with Scripture: The Rhetoric of Quotations in the Letters of Paul,*" *JTS* 57 (2006): 270.

[43] See Peter Head, "Letter Carriers in the Ancient Jewish Epistolary Material," in *Jewish and Christian Scripture as Artifact and Canon* (ed. C. A. Evans and H. D. Zacharias; SSEJC 13 / LSTS 70; London: T&T Clark, 2009), 203–19.

and the eternal, especially in the later church, the one abiding and unifying constant throughout the Scriptures themselves and across the realms of the eternal, temporal, "spiritual," and "fleshly" is the unchanging character of God.[44] In implicit agreement with Quintilian's dictum, Paul's engagement with Scripture gives primacy both to YHWH's character and ways as revealed therein and, since he is this God's servant, to his own in handling these holy things and in the broader realm of his daily manner of life. Granted that absence of evidence is not evidence of absence, it is nevertheless noteworthy that while Paul frequently addresses a range of charges made against him, nowhere do we find any hint that he abuses the mind of Scripture. One obvious counter—that no one complained because this is what all ancient exegetes did anyway—might need to consider the not-so-much-later debates over the mind of Scripture,[45] as well as the several pagan accusations of "acontextual" readings of Scripture leveled against the Christians.[46] At the same time, if the NT authors in order to build a coherent argument were as intentional in structuring their own materials as they seem to be, it is difficult to believe that they would not have thought similarly about the Scriptures they consulted. Indeed, this is only to be expected when those Scriptures themselves, as is increasingly recognized, exhibit signs of careful literary art and larger contextual awareness, even when collating what appear to have been originally independent oracles.

It also helps explain a somewhat curious phenomenon that when it comes to debates about Torah, both Jesus and Paul seem, generally speaking, contextually aware. It is with the prophets that the real hermeneutical questions begin. But on the approach suggested here, both can be explained by the same basic principle. Both express, in word and deed, YHWH's consistent character, and it is to various particular expressions of his character that explanatory recourse by way of comparison is regularly made. From this angle then, it is not so much that the NT authors discerned "extra" meaning in certain OT texts but rather that they saw the various particulars of both the OT and NT contexts as expressions of the one unifying aspect of God's revealed character.

---

[44] That this same God describes his physical and temporal creation as his Temple in which earth his presence will eternally dwell (as opposed to us going to a spiritual heaven, e.g., Rv 21:3–4; Mt 6:10) should strongly caution against the ever-present danger of dichotomizing the material/historical and the spiritual; cf. Watts, "The New Exodus/New Creational Restoration of the Image of God," in *What Does it Mean to be Saved?* (ed. John J. Stackhouse, Jr.; Grand Rapids: Baker, 2002), 15–41.

[45] Frances M. Young, *Biblical Exegesis and the Formation of Christian Culture* (Cambridge/New York: Cambridge University Press, 1997), 24–45.

[46] See the various comments on the criticisms by Porphyry and Julian the Apostate in Robert Louis Wilken, *The Christians as the Romans Saw Them,* 2nd ed. (New Haven, CT/London: Yale University Press, 2003).

If so, then this might go some way to obviating the need for a *sensus plenior* approach. As I see it, the critical weakness of this view is its essentially ad hoc nature, a "hypothesis" invoked on an as-needed basis to "save the appearances." Not surprisingly, it does not really explain as much as, to borrow Newton's gloss on his fourth law,[47] it explains away; it does not give an adequate account of causality. That is, not only does its ad hoc nature seem at odds both with the idea of fulfillment and the constant character of the God we meet in Israel's Scriptures, but also it seems unable to make any larger contribution by means of, for example, articulating more fundamental causes and/or principles, to the question of why the NT authors invoke the texts they do in the way they do. If the core of biblical understanding is that God's character does not change, then just as the laws of nature do not change, we should, whether in foresight or hindsight, be able to see such constancy in all his works. This, it seems to me, is precisely what the NT authors seek to do in their appeals to Israel's Scriptures. Moreover, the "literal" sense, when seen—and I would say as it properly ought to be—as a particular reflection of a personal God's overriding concern to reveal his consistent character and purposes for his creation, no longer needs the hypothesis of an additional "spiritual" meaning to save it. If so, then perhaps the real problem lies in playing off the historical against the spiritual. It may well be a failure to appreciate that the fundamental division in Israel's "ontology" is not between the natural and the supernatural, flesh and spirit, temporal and eternal, but between the creator and the created. Which is why, if one will, Israel's Genesis long ago pre-emptively rejected the two-physics ontology the medievals inherited from the classical world. Because YHWH had made and continued to act in his creation, Israel's inscripturated history *is* its spiritual theology, provided we realize that we are intended to see in his words and deeds the revelation of the "I am who I am."

This might also help bring some clarity in the debate over whether typology, so-called, is fundamentally analogical based on patterns noticed by the later NT authors, or reflects an (intentional?) element of prophetic adumbration.[48] Aside from the ambiguities of the term due to its divergent uses in later Christian tradition—we might do well, in the interests of hearing the biblical authors themselves, to limit "type" to a meaning

---

[47] Cf. Barry Gower, *Scientific Method: An Historical and Philosophical Introduction,* (London: Routledge, 1997), 70.

[48] See the discussion in e.g., Walther Eichrodt, "Is Typological Exegesis an Appropriate Method?," in *Essays on Old Testament interpretation* (ed. Claus Westermann; trans. James Luther Mays; London: SCM Press, 1963), 224–45; R. T. France, *Jesus and the Old Testament: His application of Old Testament passages to Himself and His mission* (London: Tyndale Press, 1971), 39–40; David L. Baker, "Typology and the Christian Use of the Old Testament," *SJT* 29 (1976): 137–57; Leonhard Goppelt, *Typos: the Typological Interpretation of the Old Testament in the New* (Grand Rapids: Eerdmans, 1982).

that is more consistent with Paul's usage (1 Cor 10:6, 11; Rom 5:14)[49]—reading Israel's Scriptures as a reflection of God's character might suggest a both-and. From the human perspective, it may well be that traditional expectations blinded readers to the meaning and/or implication of various texts, only to be seen once the impact of Christ had shaken them free of their earlier assumptions and prejudices. At the same time, since God acts consistently, events in the past necessarily say something about his future actions. The rabbis expressed just this assumption in their hope that as Israel's first deliverance had come on Passover so, too, its second. And according to several NT writers, this is precisely what God had done, even to providing his own lamb.

---

[49] DiMattei, "Biblical Narratives," 61–75, 79–81.

Part 3

Biblical Theology

CHAPTER 12

THE TRIPARTITE DIVISION OF
THE LAW: A REVIEW OF PHILIP
ROSS, *THE FINGER OF GOD*

D. A. Carson

During the past few decades, few have devoted more thought and energy to the ways in which the NT quotes the OT than Greg Beale. Even when large-scale hermeneutical and theological issues are at stake, much of this work demands painstaking attention to detail, and Dr. Beale has amply and repeatedly demonstrated the relevant competencies.[1] The one volume we worked on together provides ample evidence of his competencies. Nevertheless it would be a mistake, while focusing on the minutiae related to OT quotations in the NT, to overlook the large synthetic categories that theological reflection has cast up across substantial swaths of the church's history. For this and other reasons we can be thankful for the recent book by Philip S. Ross, *From the Finger of God: The Biblical and Theological Basis for the Threefold Division of the Law*.[2] Elegantly and coherently written, the book demands more of an evaluation than what can be provided in one brief essay. This essay is no more than a start. It is gratefully offered to Greg Beale in gratitude to God for his friendship and scholarship across the decades.

What I shall attempt to do is summarize the argument of each chapter of Ross's book, offering a brief evaluation as we proceed, reserving some integrative evaluation for the end.

The first chapter, "A Catholic Doctrine" (pp. 1–50), begins by asserting that Ross's book

> is about a doctrine that has united Christians in every century and across denominations. Not uniquely Eastern or Western; Roman Catholic or Protestant;

---

[1] G. K. Beale and D. A. Carson, ed., *Commentary on the New Testament Use of the Old Testament* (Grand Rapids: Baker, 2007).

[2] Philip S. Ross, *From the Finger of God: The Biblical and Theological Basis for the Threefold Division of the Law* (Fearn, Ross-shire, Scotland: Christian Focus, 2010). Page references cited throughout the body of the essay refer to this volume.

conservative or liberal; Patristic or Puritan; Thomist, Calvinist, or anything else; the threefold division of the law is catholic doctrine. Through history, the church's most prominent theologians expounded, maintained, and defended its teaching. (p. 1)

The ensuing nineteen pages briefly summarize the views of a number of contemporary writers who distance themselves, in quite different ways and to different degrees, from this ostensibly catholic doctrine: Tom Wells, Jason Meyer, John Barton, Maurice Wiles, Samuel Balentine, Douglas Moo, Oliver O'Donovan, Norman Geisler, Christopher Wright, Gordon Wenham, Greg Bahnsen, Knox Chamblin, Vern Poythress, Walt Kaiser, and me. The next pages are devoted to demonstrating that "the threefold division of the law"—moral, civil, ceremonial—is well attested through a spread of (mostly early) patristic writers.

To Ross's credit, however, his handling of the Fathers is sufficiently careful and evenhanded that he undermines his own thesis. He shows, for example, that Irenaeus (second–third cent.) defended a twofold division of the law (pp. 20–21), not a threefold division. Clement of Alexandria (second–third cent.) divides "the Mosaic philosophy" into four parts and then argues that there is a threefold division of "the sense of the law": it is found to be "exhibiting a symbol, or laying down a precept for right conduct, or as uttering a prophecy"[3]—a long way removed from the later and better known tripartite division. Ross asserts that Ptolemy's *Letter to Flora* "includes what may be the first unambiguous example of a threefold division in the Patristic period" (p. 23), and he quotes Richard Bauckham to the effect that Ptolemy's three parts "correspond to the now traditional division into moral, judicial, and ceremonial law."[4] But Ross notes that *Letter to Flora* belongs to the Gnostic Valentinian tradition. He has no difficulty demonstrating that "Ptolemy's threefold division carries the same outward form as the division found in later centuries, but the correspondence is inexact. Even assuming his categories prove identical to those of later writers, his hermeneutic is different" (p. 24). For example, Ptolemy asserts that the civil law was "entangled with the inferior and with injustice" so that "the Savior abolished it because it was incongruous with his nature."[5] The Ten Words (the Decalogue) "needed completion by the Savior since they did not possess perfection"[6]—a stance rejected by most writers in the Reformed tradition. Some of the precepts of the law were ordained by mere human beings and included elements of unrighteous-

---

[3] *ANF* II.xxviii.341.

[4] "Sabbath and Sunday in the Post-Apostolic Church," in *From Sabbath to Lord's Day: A Biblical, Historical, and Theological Investigation* (ed., D. A. Carson; Grand Rapids: Zondervan, 1982), 268.

[5] Ptolemy, *Letter to Flora*, in *Biblical Interpretation in the Early Church* (ed. Karl Froehlich; Philadelphia: Fortress, 1984), 40.

[6] Ptolemy, *Letter to Flora*, 40.

ness.[7] Ross then goes on to show that Ptolemy's divisions are very confusing, since one of them is then divided into three further parts (pp. 25–26).

Scholars do not agree on the way Justin Martyr analyzes the law, but even if one accepts that he held to a threefold division, "their content was not identical" (p. 27) to the later tripartite division. Ross (p. 28) quotes the judgment of the historian Jaroslav Pelikan to the effect that whatever threefold division Justin Martyr had "proved difficult to maintain with any consistency and the fathers could not make it stick."[8] Similarly, Oliver O'Donovan says that the "hint of a threefold distinction was ignored by Justin's successors, who made a simple two-fold distinction between the moral commands, valid for all time, and those which prophesied the coming of Christ."[9] The best that Ross can do with these data is forge an argument from the silence:

> Even where the division appears to be only two-fold, however, it is unsafe to assume that patristic writers would not have expounded what would have been a threefold division had they felt the need to expand. An example of the risk of making such assumptions might be found in the 1559 *French Confession of Faith*, which presents no more than a straightforward two-fold division, yet this does not reflect the whole view of the Reformed church of that confession's probable authors: Calvin, Bizet, and Viret. (pp. 28–29)

This argument is very weak. By the sixteenth century, the tripartite division of the law was well established, so a twofold division might well be interpreted as a briefer summary of the larger threefold division. But one must not apply the same logic to the patristic period during which it is the very existence of the tripartite division that is in dispute.

Turning to the fifth century, Ross (pp. 29–30) rightly observes that Augustine, in common with several other Fathers, viewed the Decalogue as the natural law or the unwritten law originally given to humankind. Certainly Augustine distinguishes between moral precepts and symbolical precepts:

> [t]he moral precepts of the law are observed by Christians; the symbolical precepts were properly observed during the time that the things now revealed were prefigured. Accordingly, those observances, which I regard as no longer binding, I still look upon as a testimony, as I do also the carnal promises from which the Old Testament derives its name.[10]

---

[7] Cf. Maurice Wiles, *The Divine Apostle* (Cambridge: Cambridge University Press, 1967), 69.

[8] *The Christian Tradition: A History of the Development of Doctrine.* Vol. 1: *The Emergence of the Catholic Tradition (100–600)* (Chicago: University of Chicago Press, 1971), 16–17.

[9] Oliver O'Donovan, "Towards an Interpretation of Biblical Ethics," *TynBul* 27 (1976): 58–61.

[10] Augustine, *Reply to Faustus the Manichaean* X.ii, cited by Ross (p. 30) from www.newadvent.org/fathers/140610.htm (accessed 1 Feb 2003).

Note, however, that Ross does not cite Augustine as someone who supported that later tripartite division.

A number of writers, including me, have asserted that the unambiguous tripartite division of the law—moral, civil, ceremonial—as a fundamental ordering principle for establishing patterns of continuity and discontinuity between the Testaments is nowhere clearly delineated before Thomas Aquinas. Despite his best effort to insist that the tripartite division is "catholic doctrine" from the beginning, even Ross is forced to concede, "[t]he popular conception that the threefold division of the law can be traced back to Thomas Aquinas is not entirely baseless" (p. 30). His method for establishing his own thesis, it appears, is to uncover writers across the patristic period who insist on *some* kind of differentiation in OT law and presuppose that these are all indirect witnesses to the tripartite division. The fact of the matter is that he has not provided a single witness to a recognizable form of the tripartite division until Aquinas. It begins to appear that the appeal to "catholic doctrine" is achieved rather more by mere assertion than by responsible inferences from the evidence that Ross himself responsibly handles.

The second chapter, "What Would Moses Think?" (pp. 51–119), sets out an important argument:[11]

> If the Pentateuch represents what Moses thought, then the basic categories of the threefold division would not have left him in severe shock. The view that the laws of Moses are "one indivisible whole" finds no support in the Pentateuch. (p. 119)[12]

Much of this long chapter is devoted to defending two propositions: (1) that the Decalogue reflects the demands of God from creation itself and that they were given to the first humans, explicitly or implicitly (if the latter, "written on the heart" in some way); and (2) that the Pentateuch itself is aware that the laws it propounds are of very different kinds—some without prescribed punishments, for example; some bound up with the cult; statutes and ordinances that are tied to living in the promised land; and so forth.

I am inclined to offer three reflections on this chapter. First, in some ways, the central argument of the chapter is surely right: the laws of the Pentateuch are not all of a piece. Ross mounts a fine defense against the proposition that the laws of Moses are "one indivisible whole." In fairness to his opponents, however, most who make such an affirmation are not saying that *no* distinctions can be made among the Mosaic laws. Rather, they are saying something slightly different: for those who are under the

---

[11] In the rest of chap. 1, Ross makes some evaluative comments about exegesis, biblical theology, systematic theology, and theological interpretation. The coverage is responsible, but too brief to be of significant use in the development of his argument.

[12] The quoted words are drawn from Richard N. Longenecker, *Paul, Apostle of Liberty* (Grand Rapids: Baker, 1980), 119.

Mosaic covenant, the obligation to obey the entire array of stipulations under that covenant is sweeping and comprehensive. In some ways, it was a "take it or leave it" package: the Israelite bound by the Mosaic covenant was bound to observe the whole thing, one indivisible whole. In other words, those who defend the use of such terminology are themselves trying to emphasize the wholeness of the law-covenant, affirming that the tripartite distinction does not surface within the covenant itself to establish one part as somehow more binding than another part (even though all acknowledge that greater or lesser punishments are connected with different parts of the law). In other words, for those who go over the top in their use of "one indivisible whole" terminology, Philip Ross provides a fine rebuttal, even if his condemnation of all who use such terminology knocks down something of a straw man.

Second, Ross seems to think that because he can show that the laws of the Pentateuch are *not* all of a piece, they do not constitute "one indivisible whole," his preferred alternative—namely, the tripartite division of the law—is thereby established. But that does not follow. To show that something is not-X does not prove that it is Y. That is why the strongest conclusion he can muster is not that the Pentateuch reflects the threefold division but that if it reflects Moses' thought, then "the basic categories of the threefold division would not have left him in severe shock."

Third, Ross consistently tends to draw the strongest possible inferences from negligible or at best mixed evidence. In the effort to demonstrate that the Decalogue is largely reflected in the lives of the prelapsarian humans—part of the drive to show that, as moral law, the Decalogue has always been in place—Ross argues, persuasively, that if the laws of the Decalogue are cast in positive terms one can see that they were in fact lived out.

> The first couple had no God but the Lord, they worshipped no idol, hallowed God's name, and it is unlikely that Adam worked the garden nonstop (Gn 2:3, 15). Had they been fruitful and multiplied before the fall, their children would have honoured them. In a death-free world there would have been no murder. Where nakedness brought not shame a man would hold fast to his wife. In a world where all was good and pleasant, who would steal? Who would lie? Who would covet? (p. 79)

Ross acknowledges that the "Decalogue does include the concepts of punishment ('visiting the iniquity of the fathers on the children') and guilt ('the LORD will not hold him guiltless')" but argues that "stated positively the ten words could be the charter of a sin-free creation" (pp. 79–80). So far so good. But then he argues:

> On the other hand, it is impossible to think of the Mosaic Laws outside the Decalogue in the same terms. The law codes of Leviticus or Deuteronomy only make sense in a postlapsarian creation. The laws of Exodus 21–23 would be incomprehensible in a world free of slavery, murder, kidnapping, cattle-rustling, arson, burglary, usury, lies, and lawsuits. (p. 80)

What I do not understand in this assertion is the opening phrase, "on the other hand." For the fact of the matter is that most of the Ten Words presuppose, equally, that the postlapsarian world is in view. It was no more necessary to tell the prelapsarian couple not to have idols, murder, tell lies, and covet than it will be necessary to tell the resurrected redeemed in the new heaven and the new earth not to have idols, murder, tell lies, and covet. True, Ross acknowledges that the Ten Words could well depict the ideal world if spun positively, but not only does he not apply the same inversion to the non-Decalogue moral laws to which he refers, he does not reflect on why the Ten Words are cast in the form in which we have them. Even if I am happy to accept Ross's general conclusion at this juncture, the argument itself sounds like special pleading. I fear that this chapter throws up several such arguments.

The third chapter, much briefer (pp. 121–44), is titled "Law in Acton?" Ross devotes the chapter to a survey of the rest of the OT, examining juridical process and interpretation of the law to demonstrate that it is in continuity with the vision of the law that he finds in the Pentateuch. Some of this argument trails into the Gospels (more fully treated in the following chapter), since "Reformed interpreters have viewed the first part of the New Testament as being in close continuity with the Old Testament regarding the status of the law, since the hermeneutical turning point is the death and resurrection of Christ, not a blank page found between the testaments" (p. 121). Perhaps the most convincing part of this chapter is Ross's treatment of the "two opposing sentiments" found in various prophetic "mercy and not sacrifice" passages: for example, Am 5:21 ("I hate, I despise your feasts, and I take no delight in your solemn assemblies") compared with Am 6:6 ("I desire mercy"). "At a practical level, those statements are no more than further cases where 'not rite but right is demanded: devotion not devotions'" (p. 130).[13] At another level, however, the polarity discloses a "deliberate priority and ranking"[14] of these laws "in that there is certain obedience (mercy) the Lord consistently desires and can never hate, while there is other obedience (sacrifice) he does not always desire and may sometimes hate" (p. 130). Ross adds, "Nowhere does Scripture suggest that God ever hates obedience to any part of the Decalogue" (p. 130).

That is certainly true. Once again Ross is careful to note, however, that when the prophets apparently apply the Decalogue,[15] many of these

[13] Citing J. Alberto Soggin, *The Prophet Amos* (trans. John Bowden; London: SCM, 1987).

[14] The expression is from Walter C. Kaiser, "God's Promise Plan and His Gracious Law," *JETS* 33 (1990): 291.

[15] Ross (p. 137) lists examples drawn from O. Palmer Robertson, *The Christ of the Prophets* (P&R: Phillipsburg, NJ, 2008), including Jer 2:11–13; Hos 8:4–6; 9:10; Am 5:21–24; Is 48:1; Zep 1:12; Jer 5:12; Am 8:5; Jer 17:19–27; Ez 23:7; Mi 7:5–6; Hb 1:2–4; Mi 6:12; Jer 5:7–8; Am 2:7.

prophetic condemnations "could equally have been based on laws in the 'statutes and ordinances' of Deuteronomy" (p. 137)—though of course Ross views these as derived from the Decalogue. Ross acknowledges that "any expectations that references to juridical process in the Old Testament would lend support to the threefold division are not met" (p. 126). The best he can do is observe, "[a]t the same time, nothing undermines the idea or its basis in the Pentateuch" (p. 126).

Ross concludes the chapter by asserting that

> none of these things stand [sic] as single comprehensive arguments for the threefold division of the law, although they do suggest a clear division between ceremonial and non-ceremonial laws. Viewed together, in light of the Pentatuech's [sic] presentation of the Decalogue as distinct from other non-ceremonial laws, it is plausible that they fit within an interpretative structure which views the Decalogue, the statutes derived from it, and the cultic laws as distinct categories. An embryonic form of the threefold division therefore has a basis in the Old Testament. (p. 144)

In other words, the merely "plausible" morphs into the argument that "the threefold division therefore has a basis in the Old Testament." Once again it is necessary to make clear that the fundamental dispute is not whether there are distinctions regarding law in the OT (I do not know anyone who would disagree with that point) but whether the tripartite division of law that Ross defends is clearly presented or defended there. Ross does an admirable job of demonstrating the former, which is not much at issue, but then argues by assertion that he has established the latter.

The fourth chapter, "What Did Jesus Do?" (pp. 145–91), continues in similar vein to analyze Jesus' obedience to the law during the days of his flesh, as opposed to his teaching regarding the law—teaching that would be taken up by his followers after his cross and resurrection (the subject of the ensuing chapter). In the first part of the chapter Ross mounts evidence to support the position that Christ perfectly obeys the Decalogue and in various ways affirms it—even, he argues, in John's Gospel, which many commentators think is pretty bereft of most moral concerns. To those (myself included) who have argued that Jesus nowhere treats the Decalogue as the perfect sum of moral law, Ross falls back on the argument that in the pericope where Jesus answers the question about the greatest law (Mk 12:28–34 par.), the first commandment ("Love the Lord your God") is essentially a summary of the first table of the Decalogue, while the second ("Love your neighbor as yourself") is essentially a summary of the second table of the Decalogue (pp. 154–60). Here he relies very heavily on the work of George Keerankeri,[16] some of whose crucial arguments, even if one accepts them, work only in Mark's Gospel and not in Matthew or Luke. More importantly, even if the link between, on the one hand, the

---

[16] *The Love Commandment in Mark: An Exegetico-Theological Study of Mk 12,28–34* (Roma: Editrice Pontificio Istituto Biblico, 2003).

first and second greatest commandments, and, on the other, the two tables of the Ten Words, is theologically convincing (as I think it is), it does
not follow that his entire argument for the tripartite division of the law is
thereby established. For (1) that argument is not established by any OT
writer, and certainly not in the contexts from which Jesus quotes what he
calls the greatest two commandments (Dt 6 and Lv 19, respectively); and
(2) neither is that argument explicitly constructed by Jesus himself—that
is, it is at best a plausible inference rather than something demonstrated
by the exegesis of specific texts. Moreover, (3) while virtually all sides
agree that by both his practice and his teaching Jesus is able to distinguish more important laws and less important laws (note the "lighter"
and "weightier" distinction of Mt 23:23), it still does not follow that the
*three*fold division that Ross commends is entailed, or that this division is
the ground upon which patterns of continuity and discontinuity between
the Testaments are established.

The next section of the chapter is largely devoted to the Sabbath pericopae of the Gospels (pp. 160–73). All sides recognize that these biblical
passages are sometimes difficult to interpret. Ross himself asserts that
arguments in favor of the view that the Sabbath "belongs to the old order
that must change in the light of the new are . . . hampered by ambiguity"
(p. 190)—which sounds like a slightly less climactic argument than he
might have preferred.

The final section of the chapter focuses on Jesus' relation to the purity laws (pp. 173–90). Mark's explicit conclusion that Jesus declared all
foods clean (7:19), and his willingness in several Gospels to touch unclean
people such as lepers, are taken by some scholars to demonstrate Jesus'
independence from the ceremonial laws. Others argue that the phrase
εἰς μαρτύριον αὐτοῖς (*eis martyrion autois*; Mk 1:44 // Mt 8:4) means
"a testimony against Israel" and therefore does not substantiate Jesus'
faithfulness to the Mosaic law. In these and numerous other cases, Ross's
responses are basically convincing; indeed, I am bound to say so since
they often parallel my own arguments in my commentary on Matthew. (I
mention this in passing because Ross does not satisfactorily disclose how
his theological opponents are not all in the same camp. Many of them are
much closer to his thought than he admits.) The concluding lines to this
chapter are worth quoting in full:

> Jesus' statement that nothing going into a man could defile him was in har-
> mony with the law and reflected the impossibility of acquiring moral impurity
> from mere contact with food. The gospel writers came to believe that with the
> rending of the veil, the realities to which the pattern laws pointed had arrived.
> Jesus' death accomplished atonement ending all cultic separation. Thus Jesus
> made laws concerning clean and unclean foods bind no longer, not by the
> words recorded in Mark, but by the totality of his life and finished work. For
> those reasons, the confessional claim that 'ceremonial laws are now abrogated
> under the new testament' represents fairly the teaching of the Gospels. (p. 191)

By and large this is well said. My only caveat—I hesitate to use it because Ross more than once inveighs against it—is that it is just a shade too neat. Compare the way one answers the question, "When did the messianic kingdom begin?" It is not wrong to say that it began with Jesus' cross, resurrection, ascension, and session at the Father's right hand, taken together as one determinative theological event. That is where the preponderance of the evidence lies. Yet Jesus was born a king (Mt 2); his status is particularly acknowledged at the onset of his public ministry (Mt 3); he sees Satan fall from heaven in connection with the public ministry in which both he and his disciples engage (Lk 10). Sometimes this kingdom is portrayed as reigning over the wheat and the tares (Mt 13); sometimes it is portrayed as that subset of the reign of God under which there is life (Jn 3). Surely, then, it is fair to point out that, while it is true that Christ's kingdom dawns with his cross/resurrection/ascension/session, if that affirmation is understood as the *exclusive* NT witness, it is (How else shall we put it?) too neat. In the same way, I heartily concur with Ross that the bulk of the evidence in the Gospels affirms that the decisive theological end of ceremonies that pointed to Christ came with his cross/resurrection/ascension/session. Nevertheless, in the light of Jesus' handling of a number of situations during his ministry, I continue to wonder if the affirmation, understood too exclusively, is (Here we go again!) a tad too neat.

The fifth chapter, "Jesus Preaches on the Law" (pp. 193–238), focuses less on Jesus' practice and more on his teaching about the Law. Much of the space is devoted to Mt 5, especially what Jesus means by saying that he did not come to abolish the Law or the Prophets but to fulfill them (5:17). Even a hundred-page review essay would be inadequate to interact fully with Ross's chapter and with his second appendix (pp. 357–70) that treats the verb πληρόω (*plēroō*). In brief, Ross interprets the fulfillment language in terms of Jeremiah's promise of a new covenant: God will write his laws on their hearts and will forgive their sins (Jer 31:33). So the law itself is not in *any* sense abrogated but brought to its fulfillment in the lives of the people for whom that law is written on their hearts. For the same reason, the following so-called antitheses (5:21–48) are not genuine antitheses at all: rightly understood, these antitheses (if we may continue to call them that) do not portray Jesus in any sense modifying the substance of the laws in question but merely insisting on seeing them at work in what Paul would call "the inner man." "Matthew shows us what fulfillment looks like; he does not demolish, abolish, advance, or reconstruct the Law of Moses" (p. 237). Ross concludes his chapter by asserting:

> Yet again, viewed in isolation, none of the observations in the last two chapters force the conclusion that the "moral law doth for ever bind all." Taken together, however, the evangelists' attitudes to the law—implicit and explicit—along with Jesus' teaching confirm the categories described in chapters two and three. None of the arguments put forward by critics of the threefold division land [*sic*] a mortal blow to the ancient framework or

compel us to accept that Jesus and the evangelists [*sic*] broke away from the Old Testament view that some laws were a "pattern," others were to be obeyed "in the land," while the Decalogue was the controlling influence. . . . [I]t is possible to say that the premise of an embryonic threefold division in the Old Testament helps to make sense of Matthew 5 and other law-related parts of the Gospels in a way that is impossible if readers assume the law was an "indivisible whole." (pp. 237–38)

To which at least four things must be said.

First, Ross is again wise enough to admit that the Gospel texts do not establish the tripartite view he defends. Rather, he says that they "confirm the categories described in chapters two and three," where we have already noted that those OT texts do not themselves establish the tripartite construction. The form of the argument reminds me a bit of the argumentation of some classic Dispensationalists: passage after passage is acknowledged not to be determinative for the position, but it is said to be in line with the position that is established in a lot of other passages—except that when one turns to those passages, again the position is not determined by the passage but is said to confirm what is established by yet other passages.

Second, perhaps the weakest part of Ross's argument is his treatment of the "jot and tittle" (as he renders the famous expression in Mt 5:18). Once again Ross is shrewd enough to avoid the argument that the "law" in 5:17–20 and especially 5:19 really refers to the moral law or to the Decalogue (on this point, Ross distances himself from Calvin [p. 217]). But his own solution to 5:18–19 is wonderfully unconvincing. He argues that in 5:19 the law in view really must be the entire Mosaic law but asserts that embedded within that law are many individual laws that "are of temporary jurisdiction" (p. 218). As illustration, he mentions the regulations for gathering manna (Ex 16).

> Thus when Jesus says "not an iota, not a dot, will pass from the law until all is accomplished" he includes laws that no longer have jurisdiction. Though abrogated in so far as they regulated specific actions, they remain embedded in a *corpus juris* that will stand until the end of time. Their ongoing relevance is by way of memorial and foretoken. In the end, there is no incompatibility between Matthew 5:18 and the confessional language of abrogation, so long as abrogation is defined by the "built-in obsolescence" and temporal jurisdiction written into parts of the Mosaic Law. (p. 219)

So there is some "abrogation" of the Law and the Prophets after all! Ross has managed to make the nonabrogated part of the Law turn out to be moral law after all, a view that he nominally rejects. Moreover, he does not much reflect on the fact that Mt 5:17 speaks of both Law and Prophets, that is, *Tanakh*, the Hebrew canon. The entire issue, for him, turns on the meaning of "law" in vv. 18–19, even though the passage begins by referring to both Law and Prophets, and even though there is another passage in Matthew that speaks of all the Prophets and the Law prophesying until John the Baptist (11:13).

Third, nowhere does Ross carefully probe what strikes me as the most probable way in which "to fulfill" and "to accomplish" (5:17, 18) should be taken: *Tanakh*, the OT, is being taken in its anticipatory and predictive functions (on which more below). It is not abolished; rather, *its valid authority continues precisely in that to which it points, in that which fulfills it.* The result is that the structure of Scripture is strangely flattened. Law has many functions in Scripture, including straightforward *lex*, the multiplication of transgression, and other things yet to be named, but one of these functions is prediction. We know this to be so in the case of what is called ceremonial law; Jesus, I hold, insists that it is so for all the Law and the Prophets. I remain convinced that this stance, carefully worked out, handles more exegetical details in Mt 5:17–20 and elsewhere than any other. Better yet, it elevates the teleological thrust of Scripture, driving toward Christ and the gospel more believably than those approaches that seem to assert that *lex* is *rex*.

Fourth, in the light of these criticisms, the final rhetorical question of this chapter shuts us up to options that are too exclusive: "Did the apostles' attitudes to the law as recorded in the narrative of Acts and in the epistles terminate its progress or rather establish it as a fully developed Christian framework?" Are those the only alternatives? Why not throw in another possibility? Did the apostles' attitudes to the law as recorded in Acts and the epistles demonstrate a variety of perceptions about the law's significance, one important one being its prophetic role, which established the law's continuity in that to which it pointed?

Chapter 6, then, focuses on "The Law in Acts" (pp. 239–64). Ross is at pains to show that the Decalogue is largely reflected in various narratives in Acts. For example, the principled submission of Christians to rulers (Acts 23:5; 25:6–12) is said to reflect the principle of submission to authority found in the fifth commandment. That may be theologically correct, but it cannot be said that Luke in Acts expends much effort in tying the ethics of the early Christians to the Decalogue per se. Ross offers various comments on the ostensible use of Ex 22:27 in Acts 23:5, of Dt 10:17 in Acts 10:34, of Dt 23:21 in Acts 5:4, of Dt 18:10–14 in Acts 19:19, and of Dt 28:29 in Acts 22:11—most of them shrewd. The rest of his chapter (pp. 254–63) is devoted to the Jerusalem Council (Acts 15) and the so-called apostolic decree, which is often said to reflect Lv 17–18. If that were correct, it might suggest that Acts disagrees with the proposition that ceremonial laws are now abrogated. Moreover, the ruling on sexual immorality might be taken as support for the seventh commandment and thus for the Decalogue and moral law. Ross's view runs in another direction:

> The point of the apostolic decree, however, was not to uphold the Decalogue or any other part of the law. Compassion, shaped by an understanding of the

principle of the second-greatest commandment means the apostles call upon Gentile converts to respect three laws that no longer bind and one law that will always bind, yet the decree and other accounts of cultic obedience in Acts are legally neutral. They neither undermine nor explicitly support the threefold division of the law. (p. 264)

The treatment of Ben Witherington,[17] which ties all four elements of the apostolic decree to idolatry, is, I think, more convincing, but in any case his arguments, too, "neither undermine nor explicitly support the three-fold division of the law."

That brings us to the final substantive chapter of Ross's book, the seventh: "The Apostles and Their Epistles" (pp. 265–350). Ross rightly recognizes that contemporary discussion of the relationship between Paul and the law is extraordinarily complex, and of course he cannot be expected to interact with much of it. So he sets himself the task of considering "whether key passages from the epistles that impinge on the threefold division show continuity or discontinuity with ideas that have already appeared in the Old Testament and the Gospels" (p. 266). Ross begins with ceremonial laws (pp. 266–95), appealing especially to Paul and to Hebrews. Much of the treatment is competent and unexceptional. For whatever reasons, "Christians almost universally agree that the ceremonial laws of the Mosaic Law are no longer binding" (p. 295). He rightly draws attention to bits of evidence that suggest these laws were anticipatory, in that sense genuinely predictive, finding their fulfillment in Christ. Somewhat less convincing, though entirely predictable granted the direction of his book, is Ross's argument that the flexible way Paul treats the Sabbath in Colossians cannot be a reference to the seventh day.

Ross then turns to "judicial laws" (pp. 295–308), roughly Mosaic civil law. "Apart from a vociferous troop of theonomists who argue that Mosaic civil law is applicable in all ages, most Christians accept that the judicial laws are no longer binding" (p. 295). Theonomists argue that all "standing laws" (by which they mean laws enshrined in the law of Moses as opposed to commands given for one particular occasion) remain in force under the new covenant unless they are specifically modified or abrogated. Ross says that most Christians across the ages would have agreed with that formula but identified "standing laws" with the Decalogue. As for the judicial (civil) laws themselves, Ross holds that the "apostolic demand that Christians obey the laws of their land cannot coexist with the idea that the judicial laws of Israel remain binding" (p. 308). Apostolic treatment of these laws "sometimes meant literal application of a judicial law, but not always" (p. 308).

In the rest of the chapter Ross explores whether the moral law is "a perfect rule of righteousness" or something the epistles variously affirm,

---

[17] Ben Witherington III, *The Acts of the Apostles: A Socio-Rhetorical Commentary* (Grand Rapids: Eerdmans, 1998), 460–70.

develop, or undermine. In other words: "Do they overturn the view that it is perpetually binding?" He begins by probing various passages that express negativity toward the law (pp. 308–18), taking some swipes at Heikki Räisänen and others along the way, then turns to Rom 2:13–16 regarding the law written on human hearts (pp. 318–24), where he rightly (in my view) argues that Gentiles are in view, not Gentile Christians. The next section highlights passages where sin is the breaking of law (1 Jn 3:4; Jas 2:8–12), though there is no exploration how idolatry and sin relate to each other along a *temporal* axis in Rom 5. Ross briefly expounds a variety of other passages, and much of his exposition is insightful, even though he occasionally allows a *non sequitur* to slip by him, such as his insistence that the fact that the law is holy and good (Rom 7:12; 1 Tm 1:8) means it remains a rule of life for all (p. 348; the conclusion may or may not be valid, but it does not follow from the premise). Ultimately he concludes that those who disagree with his views on the moral law are profoundly mistaken in their understanding of the atonement: "the theology of substitutionary atonement is only coherent on the basis of such a view of moral law" (p. 348).

Perhaps what is most striking is the passage he does not treat. The apostle makes it clear that he himself is not under the law, even if he is prepared to flex in this regard in order to win those who are under the law. He can also flex to act like a Gentile, but of course there are limits on his flexibility: he is not "lawless" but is under the law to Christ (1 Cor 9:19–23). It is unlikely that he means he does not see himself under ceremonial law but rather under the Decalogue: he could easily have mentioned the Ten Words. Rather, he does not see himself as under the law-covenant, but ἔννομος Χριστοῦ (*ennomos Christou*), which suggests he sees himself under the new covenant. That raises important questions about the relationship between the content of the old and new covenants respectively. Transparently, the apostle would never say, "To the adulterers I became an adulterer, that I might win the adulterers." Remarkably, however, he does not complete his antithesis by appealing to the Decalogue but to Christ.

Ross's brief eighth chapter (pp. 351–53) is less a summary than a final exhortation in which he again ties his views of moral law to penal substitutionary atonement.

I conclude with four evaluations.

First, Ross regularly shuttles back and forth between defending the importance of moral law and defending the threefold division of the law into moral, civil, and ceremonial components. If by "moral law" he means something like "demands of God that are imposed on men and women everywhere, such that noncompliance is defiance of a holy God," and if he wants to add that not all the laws found in Scripture are "moral" in that sense, I for one cry "Amen!" and happily acknowledge the way this view is tied to our understanding of what sin is, and thus to our understanding of what the cross achieved. But it is quite possible to hold such views without being convinced that Ross is right in his defense of the threefold division of the law.

Second, Ross's careful handling of the early historical evidence, against his own stated conclusions, pretty convincingly demonstrates that the threefold division of the law as the fundamental explanation of patterns of continuity and discontinuity between the Testaments is not catholic doctrine but first surfaces with clarity in the medieval church.

Third, if Ross has not demonstrated that Scripture itself demonstrates that the threefold division of the law is the fundamental explanation of patterns of continuity and discontinuity between the Testaments, which would make this tripartite division an *a priori* assumption in such discussions, then there might be a place for supposing that the tripartite division is a useful heuristic device if we grant it *a posteriori* status: that is, as we proceed through redemptive history, the category of moral law (defined above) becomes clearer, as do the other two categories of law. In other words, we do not begin with a definition of moral law, civil law, and ceremonial law but observe (for example) what laws change least, across redemptive history, in the nature and details of their demands, and happily apply the category "moral" to them. This seems to me to reflect better exegesis and allows space to see the teleological, predictive, anticipatory nature of *Tanakh* as it points forward to the new covenant and beyond to the consummation.[18]

Finally, although Ross clearly feels strongly about the integrity and importance of his theological stance on the law, I think he would have been pastorally more convincing if he had tried to build a few more bridges. Of course, he is not the only contributor to these discussions who has adopted a polarized stance. I could name several "new covenant" theologians who so concentrate on where their opponents are wrong that they never try to see if some careful nuancing of arguments and of the position of at least some of their opponents might enrich all sides in the debate, rather than drive them away into defensive postures.

---

[18] I might add in passing that Ross is helpful in outlining some of the different ways the epistles talk of law. He might be helped by reading Brian S. Rosner, *Paul and the Law: Keeping the Commandments of God*, in the NSBT series (forthcoming).

CHAPTER 13

FROM CREATION TO NEW CREATION: THE BIBLICAL EPIC OF KING, HUMAN VICEGERENCY, AND KINGDOM

Christopher A. Beetham

The following essay offers a sketch of the entire biblical epic. It will develop the thesis that Christian Scripture presents a story that runs from creation to new creation.[1] Within the overall sketch, the essay will further argue that the theme of creation is inextricably interwoven with that of divine kingship and human vicegerency and that the divine program to renew creation is nothing less than the reassertion of rightful divine rule through restored human vicegerency over the usurped kingdom of the world.[2] Despite postmodern suspicion of metanarrative, Scripture narrates an ultimate epic that claims to make sense of all the smaller stories of the global community.[3] Christian Scripture is the story of the Creator-King fulfilling his original creation intentions to establish the earth as the kingdom

---

[1] This essay is dedicated with admiration to my doctoral supervisor, Dr. Greg Beale, whose own work on the theme of new creation has profoundly shaped my thought. I wish to thank colleagues Steve Bryan and Christopher Bernard for reading an initial draft of this essay and providing thoughtful and probing feedback.

[2] Vicegerency is the proper activity of a vicegerent, who is "a person exercising delegated power on behalf of a sovereign or ruler" (*OED*). Space constraints forbid tracing out the equally significant God-Priest-Temple theme that begins also in Genesis 1 and runs concurrently with the Creator-King-Vicegerent-Kingdom theme that this essay will attempt to highlight. Indeed, the two themes are ultimately inseparable. In the biblical worldview, which in this case mirrors its ANE context, the temple of a deity did not function merely as the locale of cultic duty but stood as the heavenly deity's governmental headquarters and royal residence on earth. For the temple theme, see G. K. Beale, *The Temple and the Church's Mission: A Biblical Theology of the Dwelling Place of God* (NSBT; Downers Grove, IL: InterVarsity Press, 2004). For a briefer treatment that touches consistently upon the priest and temple themes, see T. Desmond Alexander, *From Eden to the New Jerusalem: An Introduction to Biblical Theology* (Grand Rapids: Kregel Academic, 2009).

[3] Postmodernism does embrace story—especially narrative rich in local color that highlights diversity—and in actuality does not condemn communities for sharing their metanarratives with other communities. The disdain for

of God through flourishing human vicegerency. In sketching this cosmic drama, we start where most good stories do—at the beginning.

Creator-King, Human Vicegerency, Creation-Kingdom

"In the beginning, God created the heavens and the earth."[4] With majestic flourish, Gn 1 opens the epic with God's creation of the world in six days. Theologians rightly turn to it to formulate their doctrine of God as creator. What is often overlooked, however, is the explicit divine kingship motif that is communicated by the "image" and "ruling" language of vv. 26–28.

In the ANE context of Gn 1, the concept of a person as the image of a deity was tied to human kingship. Archaeological and epigraphic discoveries have revealed that at least some of the pharaohs of Egypt and rulers of Mesopotamia were understood to be the images of their respective deities. As the image, or physical representation, of their deity, they functioned as the human agent of their god's rule on earth. The deity's heavenly rule was thought to be implemented and his sovereign presence embodied on the earth through the pharaoh or king. Hans Wildberger offers two inscriptions and David Clines a third concerning various pharaohs that may suffice as examples (emphases added):

> Beloved, bodily son of Re, Lord of the foreign lands . . . the good god, the creation of Re, the ruler who has come out of the body already strong; **image** of Horus upon the throne of his father; great in strength. (Amada Stela)[5]

> My beloved, bodily Son . . . my living **image**, creation of my members, whom Mut, the mistress . . . gave birth to me, and who has been raised up as the only Lord of men. (Cairo 34025)[6]

> You are my beloved son, who came forth from my members, my **image**, whom I have put on earth. I have given to you to rule the earth in peace. (Stela of Amenophis III)[7]

These examples could be multiplied.[8] The inscriptions contain several descriptors for the pharaohs. For this essay's thesis, the most notable are

---

metanarrative, however, arises when its critics perceive that it has become a tool for grasping power.

[4] All biblical translations throughout the essay are mine unless otherwise noted.

[5] Hans Wildberger, "Das Abbild Gottes: Gen. 1, 26–30," *TZ* 21 (1965): 485.

[6] Wildberger, "Das Abbild Gottes," 485–86. The god Amon is speaking of pharaoh Amenophis III.

[7] David J. A. Clines, "The Image of God in Man," *TynBul* 19 (1968): 85.

[8] See J. Richard Middleton, *The Liberating Image: The Imago Dei in Genesis 1* (Grand Rapids: Brazos, 2005), 108–18

the statements that the pharaohs are the deity's "image," the "Lord of the foreign lands" and "Lord of men," who have been given authority "to rule the earth in peace." This ANE concept of a king functioning as the living image of his deity and therefore having authority to rule over the earth finds remarkable correspondence in the statement of Gn 1:26–28:

> Then God said, "Let us make man in our **image**, as our likeness, so they will **rule** over the fish of the sea and birds of the heavens, over the beasts, **over all the earth**. . . ." So God created man **in his own image, in the image of God** he created him; male and female he created them. And God blessed them and God said to them, "Be fruitful and multiply and fill the earth and **subdue** it; **rule** over the fish of the sea and the birds of the heavens and over every living creature that moves on the earth."

Genesis 1 thus reflects an ANE worldview but transforms it with the innovation of a democratization of the image to assert that God created not merely powerful kings but all humanity as the image of God. The upshot is that all humanity was created for vicegerency over the earth on behalf of God. The image and ruling language of vv. 26–28 signal that Gn 1 is not merely communicating that the biblical god is the world's creator; it is equally asserting that he is its king.

Before we move too far from the primary data, it is significant that the above ANE texts make much of the pharaohs as the sons of their deities. The pharaoh is described as the "bodily son of Re," begotten of his "father," and "creation of [his] members." The goddess "gave birth" to the pharaoh, who stands as the "beloved son" of his god. This language of sonship was doubtless familial, and Egyptian royal ideology developed it in an advantageous direction: the pharaohs became semi-divine sons of deity.

The biblical worldview abhors this distorted development of human sonship while affirming the primeval spring from which it flowed. In Gn 5:1–2, a genealogical account of Adam's family begins with a virtual quotation of Gn 1:26–27 that God created Adam/man "in his likeness," made them "male and female," and "called his name Adam/man." In v. 3, Adam fathers a son "in his likeness, as his image" and "called his name Seth." The narrative's intention is unmistakable. As Seth is the son of Adam, so Adam is the son of God.[9] As the royal son of the Creator-King, Adam's creation was his coronation. God appointed him to rule the earth.[10] We will trace the biblical development of this concept of a royal "son of God" throughout the essay, because the concept is connected tightly to our thesis concerning human vicegerency.

---

[9] Cf. Lk 3:38.

[10] Philo wrote that God "by express mandate appointed [Adam] king" over all creation and "charged him with the care of animals and plants, like a governor subordinate to the chief and great King" (*Opif.* 84, 88; *Philo* [trans. F. H. Colson and G. H. Whitaker; 10 vols.; LCL; Cambridge, MA: Harvard University Press, 1927–1962]); cf. *2 En.* 30:12; 31:3.

It is evident that the Gn 1 image-bearing humanity is to accomplish its task of ruling and subduing the earth by means of procreation. Humanity is to "be fruitful and multiply" and in this way "fill the earth" (v. 28). As humanity proliferated and spread abroad in expansion upon the earth, they would find greenery over the same as provision to fulfill the mandate (v. 29). We will also trace the biblical development of this creation mandate to "be fruitful and multiply" throughout the essay, because it is the means by which human vicegerency over the earth finds its realization.

Before we take leave of Gn 1, it is significant in light of the above mandate to note that in the ANE, a king erected statues or images of himself in outlying regions of his realm to signify that his sovereignty encompassed those conquered territories.[11] As the Gn 1 humanity spread abroad in expansion upon the earth, God as King would be laying claim to the area to which they had attained, because they served as his living statues, the physical representations and signposts of his dominion.

In summary, Gn 1 begins the epic by declaring that the biblical god is not merely the world's Creator but its rightful King. God created humanity as his living image, as his royal son, to fill the earth with his own rule through loyal human vicegerency. In this way, the created world would be established as the realm of the kingdom of God, wherein the will of God would be done on earth as it was in heaven.

The Rebellion

Genesis 3 narrates the account of the image's rebellion against its King. In disobedience to the one prohibition in the Garden of Eden, Adam and Eve chose to eat of the tree of the knowledge of good and evil (2:16–17; 3:1–7). The rebellion consisted in discontent with the role of vicegerency and resulted in a grasp for equality with God, their Father-King. The agent of temptation was a crafty "beast of the field," an animal over which Adam was to rule.[12] Instead of pronouncing a decree of condemnation against the serpent for its scheme of treason against their King, the lords of the world bowed the knee to the usurper and handed themselves and the creation-kingdom over to his malevolent designs. Satan was enthroned as ruler of the world.[13]

In his act of judgment against the rebels, God frustrates his own original creation mandate. His words of judgment toward the woman and man

---

[11] Hans Walter Wolff, *Anthropology of the Old Testament* (trans. M. Kohl; Philadelphia: Fortress, 1974), 160; see esp. Middleton, *Liberating Image*, 104–8.

[12] Cf. 3:1 with 1:28; 2:19–20.

[13] The NT understands that Satan is the ruler of the present fallen world (see Mt 4:8–9 // Lk 4:5–7; Jn 12:31; 2 Cor 4:4; Eph 2:2). Rv 12:9, 20:2 identifies the serpent as Satan.

target the mandate to "be fruitful and multiply" and thus thwart the program to fill the earth with image-bearers who rule the world for God. This is because Adam, now the image-in-rebellion, is incapacitated by sin to rule in the way he was created to rule (see below). Against the woman, God decrees that childbearing has become aggravated with intense affliction (3:16a). Against the man, the ground is cursed. Formerly providing an abundance of food to enable humanity to complete the mandate (1:29), the ground now only readily yields "thorns and thistles" (3:18a). The man must labor in anguish for the food he needs to survive. Moreover, against both the man and the woman, the sentence of mortality is decreed. Humanity will return to dust and die, as God had warned (2:17; 3:19). Adam is exiled from the life-giving presence of God, from the Garden of Eden, "lest he reach out his hand, and take also of the tree of life and eat, and live forever" (3:22b).

In the midst of judgment, however, there is mercy. God curses the serpent for his insubordination. Despite the fact that he has functionally become "the ruler of this world" (Jn 12:31), dethroning Adam as its lord, the serpent nevertheless remains a "beast of the field" (Gn 3:14). As such, he remains a creature subordinate to Adam's authority. The language of being forced to lie on one's stomach, of eating dust, and of having an enemy place his foot upon one's head or back is an OT idiom for what a conquering king does to a vanquished enemy after battle (3:14–15).[14] God ordains perpetual war between the seed of the woman and the seed of the serpent and intimates that humanity will once again rule the world, dethroning the usurper (3:15b).

In Gn 4, the degeneracy of human vicegerency takes further and darker turns. Adam's son Cain murders his brother, a fellow image, the living representation of the Creator-King. For his treason, Cain is exiled "away from the presence of the LORD . . . east of Eden" (4:16). Here he begets a lineage from which emerges Lamech, who distorts vicegerency further by injecting polygamy and vengeance killing into the downward spiraling drama (4:23–24).

While Gn 5 hammers home that death rules over the sons of Adam,[15] in Gn 6 sin goes viral as Adam's fallen race multiplies across the face of the earth (v. 1). Created to fill the earth with the rule of their Creator-Father-King, humanity instead "fills the earth with violence."[16] This is because "every inclination of the thoughts of his heart was only evil continually" (6:5). Degenerate human vicegerency manifests itself publicly in acts of violence but stems from the inward seat of volition and desire, now

---

[14] Cf. Jo 10:24–25; Ps 110:1.

[15] Note the repetition eight times of the refrain throughout the genealogy, "and he died."

[16] Gn 6:13 alludes to the original creation mandate of 1:28 with grievous irony.

rendered incapable of fidelity to its King because it is sick with the cancer of sin. In the hands of distorted vicegerency, God's original creation intentions have gone terribly awry. The Creator-King is grieved by his image-in-rebellion and determines to wipe them off the face of the earth in judgment (6:6–7).

Pattern of Renewal: Noah as Second Adam and the Postdiluvian New Creation

God decrees to destroy all his corrupt image-bearers in judgment by a flood. He further promises to destroy the earth with them (Gn 6:13c). Why, however, does God decree to devastate the earth? The allusion of Gn 6:12 to 1:31 provides the clue:

Gn 6:12: And God saw the earth, and behold, it was corrupt.[17]

Gn 1:31: And God saw all that he had made, and behold, it was very good.

The earth itself will be destroyed because the image-in-rebellion has ruined it. It is no longer "very good"; it no longer exists as a fit arena for the construction of the kingdom of the holy Creator-King. Trampled underfoot and stained with blood by its warmongering tyrants, the earth is consigned to perish together with and because of them.

The flood itself is de-creation. God de-creates the earth, reversing the creation process of Gn 1 by opening creation's floodgates above and below to deluge the earth and return it to its primordial chaos.[18] In this way the fiat that separated the waters and created an expanse of sky in day 2, as well as that which gathered the seas together so that dry land appeared in day 3, are undone.[19] The author also picks up language from Gn 1:20–26, used to describe the land animals and birds in their creation (days 5 and 6), and employs it in the account of their destruction to signal that the flood is de-creation.[20] Everything in whose nostrils was the "breath of life" dies.[21] The flood rises fifteen cubits above the highest mountains and prevails 150 days to ensure that nothing survives (7:20, 24).

Just as the destruction by flood is depicted as de-creation, so the postdiluvian renewal is depicted as re-creation, as new creation. While the text had reported God's intention to destroy the earth together with its renegade overlord (6:13b), the text clarifies that it was the surface of

---

[17] See the ESV or NASB; the NIV and NRSV translate freely and thus the allusion is obscured.

[18] Cf. 7:11 with 1:2.

[19] Cf. 7:17–20 with 1:6–8, 9–10.

[20] 6:7; 7:21–23.

[21] Cf. 6:17 and 7:22 with 2:7.

the earth that was to be destroyed and that humanity was to be "wiped" off—like unwanted filth—from it.[22] The waters have a dual function in that they simultaneously cleanse and destroy. They destroy humanity but cleanse the surface of the land and prepare it for the act of new creation. As in the original creation, a רוּחַ (*rûaḥ*; "spirit/wind") from God functions as agent of the (re)creating process.[23] The waters recede and land appears once more, as in the first creation.[24] The animals that entered the ark and then disembarked it alive to inhabit the new world are described in the language of their original creation account to indicate that the postdiluvian world is a new creation.[25] God commands that these animals "be fruitful and multiply," even as he commanded them in their original creation.[26]

Most significantly, Noah is depicted as a second Adam. This is demonstrated by a comparison of the relevant texts placed side by side.

Genesis 1:28–29	Genesis 9:1–3
And God blessed them and God said to them, "Be fruitful and multiply and fill the earth and subdue it and rule over the fish of the sea and over the birds of the heavens and over every living thing that moves upon the earth." And God said, "Behold, I have given to you every plant yielding seed that is upon the face of all the earth, and every tree in it, fruit trees yielding seed. To you it will be for food."	And God blessed Noah and his sons and he said to them, "Be fruitful and multiply and fill the earth. The fear of you and the dread of you will be upon every living thing of the earth and upon every bird of the heavens, upon everything that moves upon the ground and on all the fish of the sea. Into your hand they are given. Every moving thing that lives, to you it will be for food. As [I gave] the green plants, I now give to you everything."

Furthermore, the "image" language is repeated in this context and applied to Noah and his family (9:6), further strengthening the connection to the original vicegerency mandate.

The pattern for cosmic renewal is established, and by it God's original creation intentions are reaffirmed. By his righteousness, an Adam figure has delivered a remnant, whose purpose is to fulfill God's original intentions for creation. Noah's family is to fill the earth with image-bearers, who rule over the earth as the vicegerents of the Creator-King. In this way they will establish the earth as the realm of the kingdom of God. There remains, however, one significant problem.

---

[22] See 6:7; 7:4, 23.
[23] Cf. 8:1 with 1:2.
[24] Cf. 8:2–5, 11–14 with 1:9–10.
[25] Cf. 1:20–26 with 6:19–20; 7:2–3, 8–9, 14–15; 8:17, 19.
[26] Cf. 8:17 with 1:22.

Noah's family has inherited the prediluvian, Adamic evil heart.

Fallen Adam's Race before the Flood (Gn 6:5)	Noah's Family after the Flood (Gn 8:21)
The LORD saw that great was the wickedness of man on the earth, and every inclination of the thoughts of his heart was only evil all the day.	The LORD said in his heart, "I will not again curse the ground because of man, for the inclination of the heart of man is only evil from his youth."

What the chart shows is that the flood did not solve the problem of humanity's rebellion but rather unveiled its root cause. The human heart is a corrupt desire factory, churning out only evil continually. All the world's manifold expressions of rebellion against its Creator-King stem from the deeper, more fundamental issue of the fallen heart—the seat of the will and spring of every desire. The animating core of what makes the image of God human is defective. Humanity is enslaved to the power of sin.[27] In short, humanity despite the flood remains the image-in-rebellion.

Noah and his family unknowingly carried the hereditary spiritual disease within them upon the very ark delivering them from the flood. Unchecked by the judgment, the heart of sin spreads once more as Noah's family begins to proliferate upon the earth (Gn 9:19).[28]

The reason God sends the flood (Gn 6:5) becomes after it the basis for why he will not curse the ground or destroy all the living again by flood (8:21). Despite humanity's entrenched enmity, the theater of redemptive history is fixed. God will not again bring universal judgment until all is accomplished. Creation must await another who will give it relief from the curses of Gn 3 (cf. 5:29).

The Seed of Abraham as Bearer of the Program of the New Creation-Kingdom

The narrative wastes no time unfolding God's next step in the history of redemption. God chooses Abraham and his descendants, focusing the program of cosmic restoration on this one family. The purpose of the book of Genesis is to shape this family's self-understanding in order to prepare them for this vocation. The book accomplishes this purpose by telling Israel its story and its history. God had chosen its patriarchal head and his family to be the mediator of blessing to the world (Gn 12–50) as his solution to his image's rebellion and creation's ruination (Gn 1–11).

---

[27] Cf. Mt 7:11a; Rom 3:9–20; 6:15–22; 7:13–24.
[28] See also Noah's world genealogy in Gn 10.

Abraham is God's answer to the problem of the fall. Genesis 12:1–3 functions as the hinge between these two great sections—the primeval and the patriarchal—of the book. God promises to make Abraham a great nation whose function is to serve as a platform for divine blessing to the world. "Blessing" is mentioned five times here in just two verses (vv. 2–3). God promises to bless Abraham profusely in order that he might be a blessing. In this way, the narrative hints that the curses of Gn. 3–11 will be swallowed up by the divine blessing of Abraham. Not a single family of the earth will be excluded (12:3).

Themes begun in Gn 1 reappear in the patriarchal history, confirming that God has concentrated his program of new creation-kingdom in this one family. First, the theme of human vicegerency resurfaces. Abraham is recognized as a "prince of God" (23:6 ESV), and God promises him that "kings shall come from you" (17:6; cf. v. 16). God reiterates this promise to Abraham's son Isaac (35:11). Joseph, Isaac's grandson, becomes ruler over all Egypt, the superpower of the day. He is second to none save the Pharaoh, and thus virtually the ruler of the entire world (41:38–44). Most significantly, Jacob, father of the twelve sons that will become Israel, blesses his fourth son, Judah. He prophesies that the tribe of Judah shall reign over the nation, that his government shall endure forever, and that it will extend to encompass the peoples of the earth (49:10). The Gn 1 intention that envisioned human vicegerency over the earth is thus concentrated in Judah of Israel for its fulfillment.

Second, the Gn 1 mandate God gave his image to "be fruitful and multiply" extends beyond its reiteration to Noah in the primeval history to run throughout the patriarchal history. God promises Abraham, "I will make my covenant between me and you, and will multiply you exceedingly. . . . I will make you exceedingly fruitful" (17:2, 6).[29] Concerning Ishmael, Abraham's son from Hagar, God promises that he will "make him to be fruitful and to multiply exceedingly" (17:20). Isaac tells Jacob that "God Almighty will bless you and make you be fruitful and multiply, so that you become an assembly of peoples" (28:3). Later God himself declares to Jacob, "I am God Almighty, be fruitful and multiply; a nation and an assembly of nations will come from you" (35:11). Because of the famine, Jacob moves his family of seventy to Egypt. Here they "settled down in the land, and they became fruitful and multiplied greatly" (47:27). On his deathbed, Jacob informs Joseph that "God Almighty appeared to me at Luz in the land of Canaan. And he blessed me and he said to me, 'I am about to make you be fruitful and multiply, and I will make

---

[29] Jeremy Cohen, *"Be Fertile and Increase, Fill the Earth and Master It": The Ancient and Medieval Career of a Biblical Text* (Ithaca: Cornell University Press, 1989), 28, writes that here "as the narrative of Genesis emerges from its primeval history and focuses on Abraham and his Israelite descendants, the blessing of 'be fertile and increase' [from Gn 1:28] continues to reappear."

you an assembly of peoples' " (48:3–4). After the death of Jacob and then Joseph, the Hebrews continued their profuse growth in Egypt. "And the sons of Israel became fruitful and teemed and multiplied and became exceedingly numerous, so that the land was filled with them" (Ex 1:7). The intentional use of the language of the original Gn 1 vicegerency mandate and its application to the patriarchal family further demonstrates that God's original creation intentions have been concentrated in and are being accomplished through the seed of Abraham.

Israel: Typical Pattern of the New Creation-Kingdom

The seed of Abraham carries and advances the program of the new creation-kingdom forward toward its eschatological denouement. As Israel dwells in the land, Abraham's family functions within the Mosaic covenant stage of redemptive history as a microcosm of this ultimate global program of new creation. To gaze upon Israel within its Mosaic covenant structures and institutions is to catch a true—albeit partial—glimpse into how it was meant to be in Gn 1 and how it will be in the new creational kingdom envisioned in Rv 21–22.

First, the Creator-King of the world comes to dwell enthroned in the midst of his people at his temple-palace in Jerusalem. Jerusalem, or Zion, is "the city of the Great King" (Ps 48:2). The Creator-King's original intention was that he would dwell among his people in the world-Eden-kingdom.

Second, the Creator-King appoints Israel to be the son of God (Ex 4:22; Hos 11:1). Like Adam, the first son of God, Israel is created to serve as prince of the Creator-King. Therefore, Israel is to manifest God's rule upon the earth in loyal vicegerency. Israel functions to mediate the Creator-King's presence and rule to the rest of the world in fulfillment of its task to bear the Abrahamic blessing to all the families of the earth (Gn 12:3; Ex 19:6). Israel is the son of God and to be about the royal business of his Father, whose relentless goal is that of fulfilling his original kingdom intentions for creation. If the nation remains faithful to this vocation, God promises to make them to "be fruitful and multiply" in the land (Lv 26:9).

Third, Scripture depicts the promised land as an Eden. Genesis 13:10 and Jl 2:3 compare it with Eden, and Dt 8:7–10 describes it as an Edenic-like paradise:

> For the LORD your God is bringing you into a good land, a land of brooks of water, of fountains and springs, flowing out in the valleys and hills, a land of wheat and barley, of vines and fig trees and pomegranates, a land of olive trees and honey, a land in which you will eat bread without scarcity, in which you will lack nothing, a land whose stones are iron, and out of whose hills you can dig copper. And you shall eat and be full, and you shall bless the LORD your God for the good land he has given you. (ESV)

It is the land "for which the Lord cares" and which the "eyes of the Lord your God are always upon" (Dt 11:12). It drinks from "the rain of heaven" (Dt 11:11). Israel is the Eden-kingdom of God upon the earth.[30]

Under Solomon's rule, Israel attained to a fulfillment of its vocation to become an Eden-kingdom (1 Kgs 4:20–25). This microcosm, however, was only briefly realized, because the rest of Israel's history spiraled downward in rebellion against God and resulted in Babylonian destruction and exile. Despite this, God promises in its restoration from exile that Israel will again "be fruitful and multiply."[31] In its return, the land will once again become like the Garden of Eden (Is 51:3; Ez 36:35).

The Sons of David, Vicegerency, and the Abrahamic Program of New Creation

In the Mosaic covenant stage of redemptive history, the Creator-King appointed Israel to be the son of God. Consequently, Israel existed to implement the Creator-King's rule upon the earth in vicegerency. Nevertheless, God further concentrated this vocation and chose an individual Israelite from the tribe of Judah to rule over his people (recall Gn 49:8–10). The Mosaic legislation expected such a king but circumscribed his role clearly so that it was understood that the position was one of dependent vicegerency, not autonomous tyranny. The king's task was to implement the rule of God over the people of God. To ensure that he carried out this vocation, the king was to write for himself a copy of the scroll of the law of Moses before the priests (for accountability) and then read it "all the days of his life" (Dt 17:19). The divine prohibitions against amassing wealth, military resources, or wives reinforced who was Israel's true and ultimate king (Dt 17:16–17).

In 1 Sm 16, God anoints David of the town of Bethlehem of Judah as this king. He replaces Saul, who had rebelled as vicegerent of God (1 Sm 15). In 2 Sm 7, God promises that David's lineage will endure forever upon the throne over Israel (vv. 12–16). Here, the task of vicegerency is restated. As the appointed kings of Israel forever, the sons of David are the sons of God (v. 14a). As such, they will be divinely disciplined when they deviate from their task of implementing God's rule over God's people (v. 14b). In this way, an individual son of God leads the national son of God to ensure that the intention of God to establish the land as the kingdom of God is realized. His palace is built adjacent to God's temple-palace in Jerusalem, with similar building materials and construction, to convey

---

[30] Ex 19:6; 1 Chr 17:14; 28:5; 2 Chr 9:8a; 13:8. "Kingdom" here would be defined as "the chosen realm in which the rule of God is to be manifested through appointed human vicegerency."

[31] Jer 3:16; 23:3; Ez 36:11.

visually that the Davidic ruler was the vicegerent of the King of Israel (1 Kgs 6:1–7:12).

Because the deity of Israel sat enthroned as the Creator-King of the world, the son of David ruled not merely over Israel but over all the nations of the earth. Psalm 2, a royal psalm probably composed for the coronation of a Davidic king, understands the new king to have become the son of God upon his installment (v. 7). God promises to extend his subordinate's rule from Zion to the very ends of the earth, since that is the reach of his own reign (vv. 8–12). Psalm 89, another royal psalm, likewise describes the Davidic king as the son of God and recognizes that his rule encompasses the earth (vv. 23–27). The Davidic line will rule forever because the Creator-King rules forever (vv. 28–29). Divine discipline for any deviation from the task of implementing the rule of God over the people of God is reasserted (vv. 30–32). In Ps 110, another royal psalm, God commands his Davidic lieutenant to sit enthroned on the right side of his own throne until he subdues all his Gentile enemies for him.[32]

The Davidic king serves not only as vicegerent of God; he functions also as the royal representative of the nation. As the embodiment of Israel, he bears the Abrahamic program of new creation in his own person. Psalm 72 is a royal psalm and a prayer for the Davidic king. In the final, climactic verse of the psalm at v. 17,[33] the language of the Abrahamic promise in Genesis is taken up and applied to him.

The Abrahamic Promise in Genesis	Psalm 72:17
And in you all families of the earth will be blessed. (12:3, to Abraham) And in him all nations of the earth will be blessed. (18:18, Abraham) And in your seed all nations of the earth will be blessed. (22:18, to Abraham) And in your seed all nations of the earth will be blessed. (26:4, to Isaac) And in you, in your seed, all families of the earth will be blessed. (28:14, to Jacob)	And in him all nations will be blessed. LXX (71:17): And in him all the families of the earth will be blessed, all the nations pronounce him happy.

The implication of the five-word Hebrew allusion is to convey that the Davidic king, the individual representative and embodiment of Israel, takes up Israel's task as the bearer of the Abrahamic promise. The LXX makes

---

[32] "Sit at my right hand until I make your enemies a footstool for your feet" (v. 1). Cf. Mi 5:2–5; Zec 9:9–10.

[33] Vv. 18–20 are a later addition by an editor to serve as the concluding doxology to Book 2 of the Psalms.

the connection to the Abrahamic promise explicit. It adds the phrase "all the families of the earth" from Gn 12:3 and 28:14 and thus expands the reference into a nine-word quotation.[34] God has concentrated the Abrahamic program of new creation within Israel upon the royal Davidic line. It bears the divine solution to creation's ruination and the Adamic rebellion. Viewed in light of the allusion to this theme in Genesis and the primeval cause for its utterance, Ps 72 begins to read like an entreaty for an Edenic kingdom, secured by Davidic vicegerency, in fulfillment of God's original intentions for creation.

Prophetic Developments of the Hope of the New Creation-Kingdom

By intertextual connection, Is 11:1–9 and Is 65:17–25 mutually inform and interpret one another concerning the coming new creation-kingdom. Isaiah 11 stresses that the arrival of a Spirit-empowered, ultimate son of David ushers in the new creation by his faithful vicegerency. Isaiah 65 indicates in poetry that the entire new creation will be "Jerusalem," that is, the throne-city of the Creator-King, where God dwells among his people. Once again, then, the themes of divine kingship, human vicegerency, and creation are interwoven. Amos 9:11–15 likewise connects ultimate Davidic vicegerency with Edenic land and abundance, as does Ez 34.[35]

Wisdom Literature: Preparation for Vicegerency

It is increasingly recognized that the book of Proverbs was originally composed for young men preparing for royal positions within the government and court of Israel.[36] A similar argument could be made for Ecclesiastes and Song of Solomon, and all three books bear the stamp of King Solomon, the son of David, upon them.[37] The Wisdom literature provides training for royal administration in Judah. It is instruction for vicegerency. Young men in government in Israel must conduct their royal duties with the "fear of the LORD" as their foundation, lest they stray and become autonomous tyrants (Prv 1:7). Viewed biblical-theologically, the

---

[34] See *BHS* note c at Ps 72:17. For definitions of "allusion" and "quotation," see Christopher A. Beetham, *Echoes of Scripture in the Letter of Paul to the Colossians* (BIS 96; Leiden: Brill, 2008; repr., Atlanta: Society of Biblical Literature, 2010), 15–20.

[35] Cf. Hos 2:16–3:5; Jer 23:3–6; 30:9; 31:10–14; 33:14–26.

[36] See, e.g., Michael V. Fox, *Proverbs 1–9* (AB 18A; New York: Doubleday, 2000), 10; James L. Crenshaw, "Proverbs, Book of," *ABD* 5:518.

[37] See Prv 1:1, 10:1, 25:1; Eccl 1:1; Sg 1:1.

Wisdom literature is moral instruction acquired along the journey as Israel functions as the son of God upon the earth (Ex 4:22). It equips Israel in its vocation to manifest the Creator-King's rule before all the nations as the vicegerent of God (Ex 19:5–6).

Unlike Proverbs, the book of Psalms functioned as a sort of hymnbook for worship at the temple. Psalm 8 nevertheless stands out for comment because of its content. Psalm 8 is the psalmist's meditation upon Gn 1:26–28. He marvels that God has crowned otherwise insignificant humanity with "glory" and "majesty" and authorized him to rule over the earth (vv. 4–8). That this is a position of vicegerency is carefully reaffirmed by the literary artistry of the *inclusio* that encompasses the body of the psalm: "YHWH, our Lord, how magnificent is your name in all the earth!"

The Lord Jesus Christ, Human Vicegerency, and the New Creation-Kingdom

The NT presents Jesus Christ as the one through whom God restores human vicegerency on earth and in whom God reestablishes creation as the realm of the kingdom of God.[38] Jesus, the ultimate human, dethrones Satan, the usurper. The various NT documents, despite differences in authorship, audience, genre, and purpose, nevertheless converge in agreement on these points.

The Gospels and Acts

In light of the foregoing development that the OT is the story of the Creator-King fulfilling his original intentions to establish the earth as the kingdom of God through flourishing human vicegerency, Jesus' announcement of the kingdom makes perfect sense. Moreover, all of his healing miracles—the blind see, the lame walk, the deaf hear, the mute speak, the demon-oppressed are freed, the lepers are healed, the dead are raised—not only attest to the arrival of this kingdom but also function as signposts as to how this new creation-kingdom will be in its eschatological consummation.

Matthew's Gospel begins by identifying Jesus as "the son of David, the son of Abraham" (1:1). The immediately following genealogy in-

---

[38] For an article that focuses on this point and elaborates upon it in ways complementary to the present essay, see Dan G. McCartney, "*Ecce Homo*: The Coming of the Kingdom as the Restoration of Human Vicegerency," *WTJ* 56 (1994): 1–21. His thesis is that "the arrival of the reign of God [in Christ] is the reinstatement of the originally intended divine order for earth, with man properly situated as God's vicegerent" (p. 2).

structs that this is not merely one of many sons of David but the ultimate Son of David, the Messiah (v. 16). Jesus is not merely one of many sons of Abraham but his ultimate descendant, in whom creation's curses will be reversed.[39]

The Gospels also identify Jesus as the Son of God, the multivalency of which is, in some texts, probably exploited.[40] At other times, however, the narrator specifies how he understands Jesus to be the Son of God. In Luke 3:22–38, Jesus is understood to be the Son of God as the ultimate Adam.[41] In Matthew, Jesus is the fulfillment of Israel as the son of God (Mt 2:15). In Luke's second volume, Jesus is the fulfillment of Ps 2 and its ideal of an ultimate Davidic son of God.[42] With their descriptions of Jesus as the Son of God in these three ways, the Gospel authors announce that Jesus is the ultimate human vicegerent of God, succeeding in the task at which Adam, Israel, and the Davidic sons had failed. In the Gospel of John, the concept of Jesus as Son of God crests its highest summits, offering stunning unforeseen vistas, as the Son executes his vicegerency in perfect imitation of the Father.[43]

The Pauline Letters

Paul likewise understood Jesus to be the ultimate seed of Abraham, in whom the promised Genesis blessing is unleashed upon the world (Gal 3). He further affirms Jesus to be the ultimate Son of God, enthroned at his resurrection (Rom 1:3–4). More than any other NT author, however, Paul emphasizes that Jesus is the last Adam. Christ is the head of the new humanity of the new creation, whose righteousness reverses the first Adam's rebellion and delivers a remnant.[44] Christ is the prototypical and unique image of God.[45] By virtue of his obedience, even to execution upon a Roman cross, he holds the position of preeminent vicegerency over the cosmos.[46] He "sits at the right hand" of God in fulfillment of Ps 110.[47] Paul also understands Ps 8 to find its fulfillment in Christ; the perfect "son of man," the obedient "son of Adam," has reinstated true human

---

[39] Cf. Mt 8:11; 19:28.

[40] For the most recent discussion on the Roman background to the title, see Michael Peppard, *The Son of God in the Roman World: Divine Sonship in Its Social and Political Context* (Oxford: Oxford University Press, 2011).

[41] Cf. 3:22 with 3:38cd.

[42] Acts 13:33; cf. 2:23–36. See also Mk 12:35–37 // Mt 22:41–46 // Lk 22:41–44.

[43] See 5:19–20a, 30; 6:38; 8:26–29; 10:34–38; 12:49–50; 14:10, 24, 31; 15:15; 17:8; cf. 4:34; 7:16–18.

[44] Rom 5:12–21; 1 Cor 15:21–22, 42–49.

[45] Rom 8:29; 1 Cor 15:49; 2 Cor 4:4; Col 1:15.

[46] Col 1:15–20; Phil 2:5–11; Eph 1:10.

[47] 1 Cor 15:25; Rom 8:34; Col 3:1; Eph 1:20.

vicegerency over the world.[48] By his resurrection from the dead, Christ is the "beginning" of this new creation (Col 1:19; cf. Gn 1:1).

Hebrews through Revelation

In Hebrews, Jesus is the Son of God who fulfills the promises that God would install a Davidic vicegerent over the world forever.[49] Moreover, Christ is the fulfillment of Ps 8. By his obedience and solidarity with his people, he restores them to share in the glory of ruling the world (2:5–10).

First John states that the rightful human king of the world, Jesus, the Son of God, has "appeared to destroy the works of the devil," the usurper (3:8). The book of Revelation asserts that Christ is "the ruler of the kings of the earth" (1:5). He was born to "rule all the nations with a rod of iron."[50] He holds the keys to the gate of the new creation, granting the disciple who overcomes "to eat of the tree of life, which is in the paradise of God" (2:7). His name is "King of kings and Lord of lords" (Rv 19:16). Revelation 4–5 shows, however, that this name does not signify autonomous rule. God Almighty sits upon the throne of heaven, and "the Lion of Judah and Root of David" stands nearby to carry out the divine decrees contained in the scroll in faithful vicegerency.

The People of God in Christ, Vicegerency, and the New Creation-Kingdom

In Jesus Christ, a community is recreated and restored for flourishing human vicegerency. In union with Christ, the ultimate son of God, his people become royal sons of God (2 Cor 6:18; Rv 21:7). In Christ, the ultimate seed of Abraham, his people become sons of Abraham (Gal 3:29). This is the family that will inherit and rule the world (Rom 4:13). In Christ, the one true son of Adam, his people become true sons of Adam, who will rule the world in fulfillment of Ps 8 (Heb 2:5–10). In Christ, the ultimate image, no longer do his people remain the image-in-rebellion. They are being restored as the image of God, healed of the Adamic "evil heart."[51]

---

[48] 1 Cor 15:24–28; Eph 1:22. This is, after all is said and done, also the message of Dn 7, its vision of "one like a son of man," and its fulfillment in Jesus (e.g., Mt 26:64).

[49] See 1:2–13, quoting the Davidic catena of Ps 2:7, 2 Sm 7:14, Ps 45:6–7, and Ps 110:1.

[50] See 12:5, alluding to Ps 2; cf. 19:15.

[51] Rom 8:29; 2 Cor 3:18; Col 3:9–10; Eph 4:24. Biblical-theologically, Jer 31:31–34 / Ez 36:26–27 / Dt 30:6 should be viewed as the promise of God to recreate a renewed humanity able to function as his image. These OT promises are God's solution to the "evil heart" inherited from Adam and passed on, through Noah and his family, to Israel and to the rest of humanity.

Although overzealous in their expectation, the Corinthians understood well that they were destined to rule the world (1 Cor 4:8). Since Christ is Israel's messianic representative, those in him take up Israel's vocation and have become a "kingdom of priests." They shall rule over the earth forever.[52] The Gn 1 vicegerency motif also ultimately stands behind the "faithful saying" that "if we endure, we will also reign together with Christ" (2 Tm 2:12). Disciples who overcome will share in Christ's rule over the nations in fulfillment of Ps 2.[53] They are exhorted to "hold fast" so that no one may "seize your crown," that is, the right to rule in the new creation-kingdom of God (Rv 3:11–12).

By virtue of their union with the resurrected Christ, who is himself the beginning of the new creation, individual believers become partakers of the inaugurated new creation.[54] They wait in hope for the cosmic renewal of all things, for the creation itself to be "set free from its bondage to decay for the freedom of the glory of the children of God."[55] The royal gospel of God is "bearing fruit and multiplying across the world," recreating a people who will ultimately fulfill humanity's destiny to rule the world.[56]

Revelation 21–22: Creator-King, Restored Vicegerency, New Creation-Kingdom

The story of the Creator-King climaxes with the final battle, defeat, and destruction of the satanic usurper of Adam's throne (Rv 20:7–10). The dead are raised and judged. The image-bearers who refused to repent and cease from their rebellion, as evidenced by their deeds, are thrown into the lake of fire (20:11–15).

Judgment accomplished, God consummates his new creation. "Then I saw a new heaven and a new earth, for the first heaven and the first earth had passed away" (21:1). The New Jerusalem, the heavenly throne-city of the Creator-King, descends to the new earth (21:2–3). Heaven and earth intersect. The entire city of God is a magnificent Garden of Eden. The tree of life grows on each side of the river of life, unleashing healing and life to the world (22:2). The King has made all things new (21:5). The

---

[52] Rv 1:6; 5:10; 20:6; 22:5; cf. 3:21.

[53] Rv 2:26–27; cf. 3:21.

[54] 2 Cor 5:17; Gal 6:15. Individual regeneration of the heart/new creation is the first stage of cosmic new creation.

[55] Rom 8:21; cf. 2 Pt 3:13, alluding to Is 65:17.

[56] Acts 6:7; 12:24; Col 1:6. See David W. Pao, *Acts and the Isaianic New Exodus* (WUNT 2/130; Tübingen: Mohr Siebeck, 2000; repr., Grand Rapids: Baker, 2002), 147–80 (esp. 167–71); Beetham, *Echoes of Scripture in the Letter of Paul to the Colossians*, 41–59.

Gn 3 curses have been swallowed up (22:2). His kingdom has come (cf. Mt 5:10).

At the center of the new creation-kingdom sits the Creator-King enthroned, and the Lamb (22:1, 3). "The kingdom of the world has become the kingdom of our Lord and of his Christ, and he shall reign forever and ever" (Rv 11:15). In fulfillment of his original intentions for creation, however, God rules this kingdom through his image. The redeemed have become full sons of God (21:7). They will "reign forever and ever" (22:5). Human vicegerency has been fully restored upon the earth through the Son of God, the "one like a son of Adam," "the root and descendant of David," the Lord Jesus Christ.[57] Because of him, the exiled sons and daughters of Adam have returned home.

Conclusion

This essay has offered a sketch of the entire biblical epic. It has developed the thesis that Christian Scripture presents a story that runs from creation to new creation. Within the overall sketch, the essay has further argued that the theme of creation is inextricably interwoven with that of divine kingship and human vicegerency and that the divine program to renew creation is nothing less than the reassertion of rightful divine rule through restored human vicegerency over the usurped kingdom of the world. Christian Scripture is the story of the Creator-King fulfilling his original creation intentions to establish the earth as the kingdom of God through flourishing human vicegerency.

---

[57] Rv 1:13; 2:18; 22:16.

CHAPTER 14

DARE TO BE A DANIEL: AN EXPLORATION OF THE APOSTLE PAUL AS A DANIELIC FIGURE

Benjamin L. Gladd

Introduction

The past few decades have witnessed an increasing amount of attention to the use of the OT in Paul.[1] In this vein, scholars have recently begun to suggest that Paul views himself in light of prominent OT personas, such as the Isaianic Servant figure(s),[2] Moses,[3] apocalyptic visionaries,[4] and prophets in general.[5] Though much attention has been given to various

---

[1] Professor Beale, my *Doktorvater* and friend, has been a great scholarly and godly influence in my life furnishing me with an unabashed love of the Scriptures. His work has also stimulated me to grasp the use of the OT in the NT, particularly how the NT uses the book of Daniel.

[2] Rainer Riesner, *Paul's Early Period: Chronology, Mission Strategy, Theology* (Grand Rapids: Eerdmans, 1998), 236. Lucien Cerfaux, *The Christian in the Theology of St. Paul* (New York: Herder & Herder, 1967), 75–107. But see also the critiques of this view by J. Ross Wagner, "Heralds of Isaiah and the Mission of Paul," in *Jesus and the Suffering Servant: Isaiah 53 and Christian Origins* (ed. W. H. Bellinger Jr. and W. R. Farmer; Harrisburg, PA: Trinity Press International, 1998), 193–222. Note also the recent work of Mark S. Gignilliat, *Paul and Isaiah's Servants: Paul's Theological Reading of Isaiah 40–66 in 2 Corinthians 5:14–6:10* (LNTS 330; London: T&T Clark, 2007), who identifies Paul with the "servants" of the Isaianic Servant.

[3] Peter R. Jones, "The Apostle Paul: Second Moses to the New Covenant Community: A Study in Pauline Apostolic Authority," in *God's Inerrant Word: An International Symposium of the Trustworthiness of Scripture* (ed. J. W. Montgomery; Minneapolis: Bethany Fellowship, 1974), 219–41.

[4] Louis Martyn, *Theological Issues in the Letters of Paul* (Nashville: Abingdon, 1997); R. Barry Matlock, *Unveiling the Apocalyptic Paul: Paul's Interpreters and the Rhetoric of Criticism* (JSNTSup 127; Sheffield: Sheffield Academic Press, 1996).

[5] Karl Olav Sandnes, *Paul, One of the Prophets? A Contribution to the Apostle's Self-Understanding* (WUNT 2/43; Tübingen: Mohr Siebeck, 1991).

apocalyptic streams in Paul, a study has yet to emerge that examines Paul's relationship to the apocalyptic seer Daniel.[6]

Drawing a connection between the individual Daniel and the apostle Paul is a bit tricky, so I will proceed as follows: I will briefly set forth Daniel's popularity in Judaism and early Christianity and then survey two figures—the Teacher of Righteousness and Josephus—who appear to model particular aspects of their career after that of the character Daniel. If others have emulated Daniel, it increases the likelihood that Paul did as well. I will then argue for two thematic connections between Daniel and Paul, which will be followed up by a discussion of a few allusions in the Pauline corpus to the book of Daniel.

Examples of Daniel's Prominence in the OT, Second Temple Judaism, and Early Christianity

Obviously the figure Daniel plays a central role in the OT book that bears his name. In light of the constraints of this essay, I am unable to rehearse the book's depiction of its protagonist. I can, though, list some of the more prominent details of Daniel's ministry as described in the book. First, Daniel is the pietistic Jew par excellence. This theme is on display in his adherence to Torah in the face of grave political pressure (1:8–15; 6:1–28). Second, Daniel possesses an unparalleled ability to receive and interpret revelation. In the first half of the book, Daniel functions as the interpreter of dream reports and enigmatic writing (Dn 2, 4, 5), whereas the second half focuses on Daniel receiving the initial revelation and angels function as interpreters (Dn 7–12). Third, in light of the second point, Daniel possesses superior wisdom; his wisdom surpasses that of the Babylonian "wise men," who were unable to give the interpretation of the dreams and the writing on the wall (2:1–11; 4:4–18; 5:5–12).[7]

---

[6] In my previous work on the use of "mystery" in 1 Corinthians, I suggest that Paul may deem himself as analogous to Daniel but with reference to 1 Corinthians (Benjamin L. Gladd, *Revealing the Mysterion: The Use of Mystery in Daniel and Second Temple Judaism with Its Bearing on First Corinthians* [BZNW 160; Berlin: de Gruyter, 2008], 268). Here my aim is to develop this possibility even further, bringing to bear several texts that have gone relatively unnoticed in this regard.

[7] The only other place in the OT where Daniel *may* be mentioned is Ez 14:14, 20, and 28:3. It is not entirely clear which character is in view, and scholars continue to debate the issue. *Tg. Ez* 28:3 connects Daniel with receiving mysteries: "Behold, are you [king of Tyre] wiser than Daniel? Is no secret concealed from you?" (Translation from Samson H. Levey, *The Targum of Ezekiel* [ArBib 13; Edinburgh: T&T Clark, 1987]). Though some doubt that the Hebrew text of Ezekiel refers to the biblical character of Daniel, the targum suggests that the biblical Daniel is in mind through the use of the key Danielic word רז (*rāz*; "secret" or, better, "mystery"). This point is obvious: the targum of Ezekiel draws attention to Daniel's unparalleled ability to receive divine revelation.

Scholars have long noted the influence of the book of Daniel in Second Temple Judaism, especially, Qumran,[8] and the NT.[9] Detailing the prominence of the character Daniel is a related but distinct task. Given the restraints of this essay, I am unable to sketch this out in great detail. I will, however, provide several examples of Daniel's notoriety and discuss a few texts that recount the figure of Daniel.

The Greek additions to the book of Daniel underscore his remarkable wisdom. For example, Susanna (Dn 13) states, "the elders said to him [Daniel], 'Come, sit among us and inform us, for God has given you the standing of an elder'" (NRSV; v. 50; see vv. 46–64). In Bel and the Dragon (Dn 14), Daniel is again portrayed as a pietistic Jew who obeys God's law in the midst of grave danger. The stories of Daniel vanquishing the idol Bel (vv. 3–22) and the "great dragon" (vv. 23–27) illustrate the false Babylonian deities over against the one true God whom Daniel worships. Notably Daniel is once again cast into the lion's den, but this time Daniel survives under more extreme measures; he endures six days in the pit with seven lions (vv. 31–32).

Perhaps the longest commentary on the character Daniel stems from Josephus in his *Antiquitates judaicae*. Given the large and comprehensive scope of this work, a lengthy discussion of Daniel is hardly surprising. I will, though, observe some highlights from Josephus's retelling of the story. Near the end of the account, Josephus states the reason why he desires to promote Daniel: "It is fit to give an account of what this man did . . . for he was so happy as to have strange revelations made to him, and those as to one of the greatest of the prophets, insomuch, that while he was alive he had the esteem and applause both of the kings and of the multitude" (10.11.7 [§266]). Daniel's piety regarding the food laws is emphasized (10.10.2 [§§190–94]) and especially Daniel's ability to receive revelation as it pertained to Nebuchadnezzar's dreams (10.10.3–6 [§§195–218]). He was, according to Josephus, "sufficiently skilled in wisdom, [and] was very busy about the interpretation of dreams" (10.10.2 [§194]). Josephus also retells the writing on the wall and Daniel's success in decrypting it (10.11.2–4 [§§229–47]). Immediately following that account, the story of Daniel and the lions' den receives no small amount of attention (10.11.5–7 [§§250–63]). Josephus ends his retelling with Daniel's vision of the four beasts, which Josephus interprets as Babylon, Medo-Persia, Greece, and Rome (10.11.7 [§§269–77]).

---

[8] E.g., F. García-Martínez, "4QPseudo Daniel Aramaic and the Pseudo Daniel Literature," in *Qumran and Apocalyptic: Studies on the Aramaic Texts from Qumran* (STDJ 9; Leiden: Brill, 1992), 137–61; Otto Betz, *Offenbarung und Schriftforschung in der Qumransekte* (WUNT 6; Tübingen: Mohr Siebeck, 1960).

[9] E.g., G. K. Beale, *The Use of Daniel in Jewish Apocalyptic Literature and in the Revelation of St. John* (Lanham, MD: University Press of America, 1984); Beale, *John's Use of the Old Testament in Revelation* (JSNTSup 166; Sheffield: Sheffield Academic Press, 1998).

The Christian interpolation of *Sib. Or.* 2:246–48 lists Daniel alongside of many patriarchs, and the *Liv. Pro.* 4:1–21 pays special attention to Daniel's piety and ability to prophesy and understand "mysteries" (vv. 8, 13). The section describes Daniel as "chaste" (v. 2) and a man of prayer (vv. 4, 12), and that he "abstained from all desirable food" during fasts (v. 3). *Third Maccabees* 6:7 accentuates his character during the episode with the lions: "When, through the slanderous accusations brought against him out of envy, Daniel was thrown to the lions underground as food for beasts, you brought him up to the light unscathed" (see 1 Mc 2:51; 4 Mc 16:3, 21; 18:13). *First Clement* reiterates Daniel's blamelessness as he was cast into the lion's den: "Was Daniel cast into the lions' den by those who feared God? . . . Of course not! Who, then, were the people who did these things?" (46:6; cf. *2 Clem.* 6:8).

In light of this very brief review, three traits of Daniel surfaced: his strict observance of the law of Moses, unwavering faithfulness in the lions' den, and the ability to receive apocalyptic revelations. The first and third characteristics are hardly surprising, since they are often highlighted in the book of Daniel. The account of Daniel being thrown in the pit of lions, however, appears to have played a quite prominent role in later sources. This event in Daniel's life no doubt encouraged the Jewish people and early Christians to persevere in the midst of intense persecution.[10]

Teacher of Righteousness

Qumran's fascination with the character Daniel has received considerable attention, particularly in light of 4Q174 1 iii 3,[11] specifically, the mediatorial role of the Teacher of Righteousness. The purpose of the following survey is to highlight a few texts that illustrate the Teacher's prerogative to receive revelation.

The debate concerning the identification of the Teacher arises from the autobiographical nature of some portions of the Hodayot or *Lehrlieder*. Svend Holm-Nielsen emphatically denies the probability that the Teacher composed the Hodayot due to the lack of the text's internal unity.[12] Oth-

---

[10] Note also the prominence of Daniel in the Babylonian Talmud, particularly his piety (*b. Ber.* 31a; *'Abod. Zar.* 3a; 36a), participation in miraculous events (*b. Ber.* 57b), superior wisdom (*b. Yoma* 77a), ability to receive revelation (*b. Sanh.* 93b), and possession of messianic characteristics (*b. Sanh.* 98b). For further discussion of Daniel in Judaism, see Louis Ginzberg, *Legends of the Jews* (trans. Henrietta Szold and Paul Radin; 2 vols.; Philadelphia: JPS, 2003), 2:1095–1101.

[11] 4Q174 1 iii 3: "it is [. . . a]s is written in the book of Daniel, *the prophet*: '[The wicked] act wicked[ly . . .] and the just [. . . shall be whi]tened and refined and a people knowing God will remain strong.'" Here Daniel is labeled a "prophet" (חנביא; ḥnbʾ), thus most likely placing him in the category of prominent OT prophets.

[12] Svend Holm-Nielsen, *Hodayot: Psalms from Qumran* (ATD 2; Aarhus: Universitetsforlaget, 1960), 316–31.

ers, however, hold the more balanced view that the Teacher is responsible for certain portions.[13]

Several texts in the Hodayot envision the Teacher as the community's mediator of apocalyptic revelation. For example, 1QH^a 10 highlights his mediatorial role in the midst of persecution and rejection: "The wicked is roused against me; . . . when their waves beat they spew out slime and mud. But you have set me like a banner for the elect of justice, like a *knowledgeable mediator* [מליץ דעת; *mlyṣ dʿt*] *of secret wonders* [ברזי פלא; *brzy plʾ*]" (12–13).[14] In the midst of contentious barraging, God preserves the Teacher and steadies his faithful servant (27–36). He is commissioned as a "banner for the elect of justice" and a "knowledgeable mediator" (מליץ דעת; *mlyṣ dʿt*), or, more aptly, a "mediator of knowledge." John Collins, representing the majority of scholarship, labels the Teacher as "the official mediator of revelation for the community."[15] Several passages within the Hodayot and outside likewise affirm revelation and mediation of mysteries:

> Though you have enlightened the face of the Many, you have increased them, so that they are uncountable, for you have shown me [the Teacher] your wondrous mysteries. (1QH^a 12:27; see 1QH^a 13:25–26; 1QH^a 13:35–36)

> He [the Teacher] should lead them with knowledge and in this way teach them the mysteries of wonder and of truth in the midst of the men of the Community, so that they walk perfectly, one with another, in all that has been revealed to them. (1QS 9:18–19 = 4Q256 18:1–3; 4Q258 8:3–4; cf. 1QS 9:12–14, 20 = 4Q259 3:2–17)

In addition to these relevant texts, the role of the Teacher in 1QpHab 7:1–8 augments our analysis:

> And God told Habakkuk to write *what was going to happen* [את הבאות; *ʾt hbʾwt*] to the last generation, but he did not let him know *the consummation of the*

---

[13] J. Becker, *Das Heil Gottes: Heils—und Sündenbegriffe in den Qumrantexten und in Neuen Testament* (SUNT 3; Göttingen: Vandenhoeck & Ruprecht, 1964); G. Jeremias, *Der Lehrer der Gerechtigkeit* (SUNT 2; Göttingen: Vandenhoeck & Ruprecht, 1963); Michael C. Douglas, "Teacher Hymn Hypothesis Revisited: New Data for an Old Crux," *DSD* 6/3 (1999): 239–66.

[14] Unless otherwise noted, all translations from the DSS are taken from F. García-Martínez and Eibert J. C. Tigchelaar, *The Dead Sea Scrolls Study Edition* (2 vols.; Leiden: Brill, 1997–1998).

[15] John J. Collins, *The Apocalyptic Imagination: An Introduction to Jewish Apocalyptic Literature* (2nd ed.; Grand Rapids: Eerdmans, 1998), 151. See also James E. Bowley, "Prophets and Prophecy at Qumran," in *The Dead Sea Scrolls after Fifty Years* (ed. Peter W. Flint and James C. VanderKam; 2 vols.; Leiden: Brill, 1998), 2:371–76; John Yueh-Han Yieh, *One Teacher: Jesus' Teaching Role in Matthew's Gospel Report* (BZNW 124; Berlin: de Gruyter, 2004), 110–37; Markus Bockmuehl, *Revelation and Mystery in Ancient Judaism and Pauline Christianity* (WUNT 36; Tübingen: Mohr Siebeck, 1990; repr., Grand Rapids: Eerdmans, 1997), 49.

era [גמר הקץ; *gmr hqṣ*]. And as for what he says: "So that may run the one who reads it." Its interpretation concerns the Teacher of Righteousness, to whom God has made known all the mysteries of the words of his servants, the prophets. For the vision has an appointed time, it will have an end and not fail. Its interpretation: the final age will be extended and go beyond all that the prophets say, because the mysteries of God are wonderful. (1QpHab 7:1–8)

Even though God spoke to the prophet Habakkuk concerning *"what was going to happen"* (את הבאות; *'t hbʾwt*),[16] according to the *pešer*, he did not primarily divulge when this would take place:[17] "He [God] did not let him know the consummation of the era." In other words, the Teacher has received complete revelation previously given to the prophet Habakkuk. Not only has God revealed the timing and content of Habakkuk's prophecy to the Teacher but also prophecy *in toto*: "to whom God has made known all the mysteries of the words of his servants, the prophets." Despite revelation given to the OT prophets, there remained a time when God would issue a second and more complete disclosure. This final revelation is called appropriately "mysteries"—revelation that was previously veiled to the OT prophets but has now been revealed to the Teacher.[18]

The Teacher's description as one who receives and mediates mysteries recalls the character Daniel. The character Daniel is privy to apocalyptic wisdom, in contrast to Nebuchadnezzar and the Babylonian wise men. Since Nebuchadnezzar received only the dream and his "wise men" were unable to interpret the dream, Daniel pleads with God to reveal the dream and its interpretation (2:17–18). After receiving the revelation, Daniel relates to the king that only his God is capable of revealing "what will happen in the latter days" (2:28–29)[19] and that, unlike Nebuchadnezzar who was privy only to the initial revelation (2:1, 28–29), God revealed to Daniel both the dream and its interpretation ("as for me, this mystery has not been revealed to me [Daniel] . . . for the purpose of making the inter-

---

[16] It is probable that Qumran believed that the prophet Habakkuk did not fully grasp the content of what was revealed to him in addition to the timing of prophetic fulfillment. William H. Brownlee, *The Midrash Pesher of Habakkuk* (SBLMS 24; Missoula, MT: Scholars Press, 1979), 110, argues, "[i]t was not mere chronological knowledge which Habakkuk lacked, such as when the consummation would come or how long the period of the last days would last . . . but it was an understanding of the specific events. . . . The prophets did not know all that the messianic age would contain."

[17] See F. F. Bruce, *Biblical Exegesis in the Qumran Texts* (Grand Rapids: Eerdmans, 1959), 9; Gershon Brin, *The Concept of Time in the Bible and the Dead Sea Scrolls* (STDJ 39; Leiden, Brill, 2001) 271; Beale, *The Use of Daniel,* 37–38.

[18] See Alfred Mertens, *Das Buch Daniel im Lichte der Texte vom Toten Meer* (SBM 12; Echter: KBW Verlag, 1971) 122; Bruce, *Biblical Exegesis*, 9; Samuel I. Thomas, *The 'Mysteries' of Qumran: Mystery, Secrecy, and Esotericism in the Dead Sea Scrolls* (SBLEJL 25; Atlanta: Society of Biblical Literature, 2009), 204.

[19] Unless otherwise noted, all biblical translations are taken from NASB.

pretation known to the king"). The complete and full revelation, the dream *and* its interpretation, was given only to Daniel (2:19–24, 30, 36–45). In Dn 4:4–5 Nebuchadnezzar has another apocalyptic dream that only Daniel could interpret (4:6–27). Similarly, Daniel's interpretation of the enigmatic writing on the wall (5:5–29) again exemplifies God's revealing apocalyptic wisdom to him. In Dn 7–12, Daniel is now under pressure, while an *angelus intepres* emerges. Daniel receives revelation, but the revelation requires an interpretation that an angel provides (7:16; 8:17; 9:22–23; 10:1, 14). The book of Daniel certainly portrays the character Daniel as receiving apocalyptic revelations and dispensing them to others.

That the Teacher analogously functions as Daniel is not a radical deduction, since several scholars have advanced similar claims.[20] Both the Teacher and Daniel receive and mediate eschatological mysteries. God reveals to Daniel the content and interpretation of dreams and visions, whereas God makes known to the Teacher the interpretation of Scripture. Alex Jassen likewise comments, "In Pesher Habakkuk, the Teacher of Righteousness appears as a latter-day Daniel, applying the mechanics of dream (and vision) interpretation to the process of reading prophetic Scripture."[21]

Josephus

Many scholars have also compared Josephus to Daniel.[22] Josephus's descriptions of himself and his professed interest in the book of Daniel make him another prime candidate for further investigation.

Several passages suggest that Josephus had quite a penchant for the book of Daniel, intimating that Josephus considered himself to be a Danielic figure in some capacity.[23] According to *B.J.* 3.8.3 (§352), Josephus

---

[20] Others make similar claims that the Teacher analogously functions like the prophet Daniel (Bruce, *Biblical Exegesis*, 16–17; Beale, *Use of Daniel*, 36; Betz, *Offenbarung und Schriftforschung*, 86). David E. Orton comments, "Daniel is a type of the Teacher of Righteousness; indeed, in effect, in one sense the Teacher is a New Daniel, who instead of finally *not* understanding (cf. Dan. 12.8) *does* understand, as the eschatological Maskil *par excellence* of the prophecy (Dan. 12.10)" (italics original; *The Understanding Scribe: Matthew and the Apocalyptic Ideal* [JSNTSup 25; Sheffield: Sheffield Academic, 1989], 228 n. 32).

[21] Alex P. Jassen, *Mediating the Divine: Prophecy and Revelation in the Dead Sea Scrolls and Second Temple Judaism* (STDJ 68; Leiden: Brill, 2007), 352. Brownlee, *Habakkuk*, 112, agrees: "the Righteous Teacher is like Daniel, who in the interpretation of Nebuchadnezzar's dream was called upon to disclose its hidden meaning which constituted *rāz.*"

[22] E.g., David Daube, "Typology in Josephus," *JJS* 31 (1980): 18–36; Robert Karl Gnuse, *Dreams and Dream Reports in the Writings of Josephus: A Traditio-Historical Analysis* (AGJU 36; Leiden: Brill, 1996), 29–30.

[23] In a private conversation, David E. Garland initially demonstrated to me the connection between Josephus and Daniel.

interprets dreams and is familiar with "prophecies": "He [Josephus] was an *interpreter of dreams* [περὶ κρίσεις ὀνείρων; *peri kriseis oneirōn*][24] and skilled in *divining* [συμβαλεῖν; *symbalein*] the meaning of ambiguous utterances of the Deity; . . . he was not ignorant of the prophecies in the sacred books."[25] Probably not coincidentally, in *A.J.* 10.10.2 (§194) Josephus describes Daniel using the precise language: "Daniel, who had already acquired sufficient skill in wisdom, devoted himself *to the interpretation of dreams*" (περὶ κρίσεις ὀνείρων; *peri kriseis oneirōn*). In addition, the notion of "interpreting dreams" in conjunction with "prophecies contained in the sacred books" probably recalls Daniel's "prophecy" of the fourfold kingdom in Dn 2 and 7 (see *A.J.* 10.11.7 [§§269–77]). Also, Josephus is here functioning like Daniel by "interpreting dreams" and "giving shrewd conjectures" (cf. *B.J.* 2.7.3 [§§112–13]).

Not only did Josephus interpret dreams, he also experienced them. Again, in *B.J.* 3.8.3 (§353), Josephus recalls, "At that hour he [Josephus] was inspired to read their meaning, and, recalling the dreadful images of his recent dreams, he offered up a silent prayer to God." We find another account in *Vita* 208: "That night I beheld a marvelous vision in my dreams . . . I thought that there stood by me one who said: 'Cease, man, from thy sorrow of heart, let go all fear' " (cf. *Vita* 209–10; *B.J.* 3.8.9 [§406]).[26]

Josephus functioned like an apocalyptic seer by both interpreting and receiving dreams. Likewise, his understanding of Jewish history is also indebted to Daniel. In *A.J.* 10–11, Josephus conceives of Jewish history to mirror the fourfold kingdom schema of Dn 2 and 7:[27] "These misfortunes

---

[24] The notion of furnishing an "interpretation" of dreams is prevalent in the book of Daniel. The word κρίσις (*krisis*) is generally a technical word in the OG of Daniel (Dn 2:9, 36, 45; 4:25 [LXX 4:28]; 7:16).

[25] All quotations from Josephus are taken from the LCL editions.

[26] According to Bart J. Koet, "Trustworthy Dreams? About Dreams and References to Scripture in 2 Maccabees 14–15, Josephus' *Antquites Judaicae* 11.302–347, and in the New Testament," in *Persuasion and Dissuasion in Early Christianity, Ancient Judaism, and Hellenism* (ed. Pieter van der Horst et al.; CBET 33; Dudley, MA: Peeters, 2003), 95, we have evidence that Josephus received fifty dream reports and "experiences." Josephus, in *B.J.* 3.8.3. (§§352–54) and 3.8.9 (§§399–408), claims prophetic inspiration: "Josephus replied that he had *foretold* [προειτεῖν; *proeitein*] to the people of Jotapata that their city would be captured after forty-seven days and that he himself would be taken alive by the Romans" (*B.J.* 3.8.9 [§406]); "since thou hast made choice of my spirit to announce the things that are to come, I willingly surrender to the Romans and consent to live" (*B.J.* 3.8.3 [§354]). "Without saying it, the way in which he describes himself suggests that Josephus wants to present himself as a prophet" (Koet, "Dreams and References," 96). Gnuse also affirms this conclusion; "All [scholars] agree that Josephus attributes prophetic skills to himself and contemporaries" (*Dreams and Dream Reports*, 24; cf. David E. Aune, "The Use of προφήτης in Josephus," *JBL* 101 [1982]: 419–21).

[27] Louis H. Feldman, *Josephus's Interpretation of the Bible* (Los Angeles: University of California Press, 1998), 629–69; Paul Spilsbury, "Flavius Josephus on the Rise and Fall of the Roman Empire," *JTS* 54 (2003): 1–24.

our nation did in fact come to experience under Antiochus Epiphanes, just as Daniel many years before saw and wrote that they would happen . . . Daniel also wrote about the empire of the Romans" (*A.J.* 10.11.7 [§§275–76]; cf. 11.8.5 [§§336–39]).

In light of these observations, it is not surprising to come across Josephus acknowledging his indebtedness to the book of Daniel:

> Now it is fitting to relate certain things about this man [Daniel] which one may greatly wonder at hearing, namely that all things happened to him in a marvelously fortunate way as to one of the greatest prophets, . . . since his death, his memory lives on eternally. For the books which he wrote and left behind are still read by us even now, and we are convinced by them that Daniel spoke with God. (*A.J.* 10.11.7 [§§266–67])

According to this passage, Josephus and some of his contemporaries consider Daniel to be one of the "greatest prophets" and affirm that Daniel's prophecies are "still read by us even now" (cf. *A.J.* 10.10.4 [§210]; 10.11.7 [§§276–77]).

Since Josephus interprets and experiences dreams, prophesies, and gains his understanding of history from the book of Daniel, it should not surprise us that Josephus considered himself as analogous to Daniel. After drawing parallels between Josephus and Jeremiah and Ezekiel, Robert Karl Gnuse lists fifteen similarities between the figure Daniel and Josephus.[28] The more important comparisons are as follows: (1) both men were thrown into a "pit" or cave (*B.J.* 3.8.1 [§§341–42]; Dn 6:16–24); (2) both predicted that Rome would conquer Jerusalem (*A.J.* 10.11.7 [§§276–77]; *B.J.* 3.8.3 [§§351–54]; Dn 2:40–43; 7:23–25); (3) both could interpret dreams (*A.J.* 10.10.2 [§194]; Dn 1:17); (4) they predicted events before foreign kings (*B.J.* 3.8.9 [§§399–408]; Dn 2; 4). At the end of the comparisons, Gnuse concludes, "[t]he biblical figures of Daniel and Joseph probably fascinated Josephus tremendously, and the remarkable similarities between their experiences and his own led him to stress and augment these parallels in his autobiography and the narration of those biblical personages in the *Antiquities*."[29] In addition to Gnuse, C. T. Begg, in a brief

---

[28] Gnuse, *Dreams and Dream Reports*, 29–30.

[29] Gnuse, *Dreams and Dream Reports*, 31. Daube, "Typology in Josephus," 18–36, was one of the first to draw parallels between Josephus and Daniel. Daube suggests that Josephus is similar to Daniel in that both interpret dreams, they descend from a royal lineage, and both men went before the king with a "prophecy" (p. 28). For those who view Josephus as functioning in a similar capacity to Daniel, see also Joseph Blenkinsopp, "Prophecy and Priesthood in Josephus," *JJS* 25 (1974): 239–62 (esp. 245–46); Arnaldo Momigliano, *Essays on Ancient and Modern Judaism* (ed. Silvia Berti; trans. Maura Masella-Gayley; Chicago: University of Chicago Press, 1994), 76; Gary Lance Johnson, "Josephus: Heir Apparent to the Prophetic Tradition?" in *Society of Biblical Literature 1983 Seminar Papers* (ed. Kent Harold Richards; Chico, CA: Scholars Press, 1993), 346; Marianus de Jonge, "Josephus und die Zukunftserwartungen seines Volkes," in *Josephus—Studien: Untersuchungen zu Josephus, dem antiken Judentum und dem Neuen Testament* (ed. Otto

essay on the relationship between Josephus and Daniel, argues, "Josephus, . . . not only worked over Scripture's portrayal of Daniel with his own career in view, but also recounted the latter with an eye to the former."[30]

Therefore, in the light of the preceding discussion, it appears possible, even likely, that Josephus read the book of Daniel and identified with the figure of Daniel in various circumstances and events. He explicitly acknowledges the book of Daniel's importance and appears to model himself after certain aspects of Daniel's career.

Paul and Daniel: Mediating Apocalyptic Revelation

A few unique concepts in Paul evince a deep familiarity with the book of Daniel and its protagonist. Perhaps one of the clearest is Paul's use of the term μυστήριον (*mystērion*). From a linguistic perspective, the word μυστήριον (*mystērion*) occurs more often in the Pauline tradition than any other corpus. The term appears three times in the Synoptics (Mt 13:11; Mk 4:11; Lk 8:10), four times in Revelation (1:20; 10:7; 17:5, 7), and, depending on the variant in 1 Cor 2:1, twenty-one times in the Pauline corpus.[31] Moreover, scholars are in general agreement that the NT use of the term originates from apocalyptic Judaism, particularly Daniel.[32] In addition, the use of the term reflects not only a dependence upon the book of Daniel but also the apostle's relationship to mystery. In various contexts, Paul is seen performing Danielic tasks such as declaring and administrating revealed mysteries or eschatological revelations. The only OT figure who receives and mediates mysteries is Daniel. I mentioned above how throughout the book of Daniel the character Daniel is privy to eschatological revelations or mysteries and mediates them to others (e.g., 2:19–24, 30, 36–45; 4:6–27).

Perhaps more than any other book in the Pauline corpus, 1 Corinthians (especially chs. 1–2) appears to be indebted to the book of Daniel.[33] For example, 1 Cor 1:18–2:16 constitutes Paul's longest discourse

---

Betz, Klaus Haacker, and Martin Hengel; Göttingen: Vandenhoeck & Ruprecht, 1974), 207–10; Steve Mason, "Josephus, Daniel, and the Flavian House," in *Josephus and the History of the Greco-Roman Period* (ed. Fausto Parente and Joseph Sievers; StPB 41; Leiden: Brill, 1994), 176–77.

[30] C. T. Begg, "Daniel and Josephus: Tracing Connections," in *The Book of Daniel in the Light of New Findings* (ed. A. S. van der Woude; BETL 106; (Leuven: Leuven University Press, 1993), 540 (see also pp. 540–44).

[31] Rom 11:25; 16:25; 1 Cor 2:1, 7; 4:1; 13:2; 14:2; 15:51; Eph 1:9; 3:3, 9; 5:32; 6:19; Col 1:26; 2:2; 4:3; 2 Thes 2:7; 1 Tm 3:9, 16.

[32] E.g., Raymond E. Brown, *The Semitic Background of the Term 'Mystery' in the New Testament* (Philadelphia: Fortress, 1968); G. Bornkamm, "μυστήριον, μυέω," *TDNT* 4:802–28; David E. Aune, *Prophecy in Early Christianity and the Ancient Mediterranean World* (Grand Rapids: Eerdmans, 1983), 250–53, 333. For further discussion on the history of interpretation of this term, see Gladd, *Revealing the* Mysterion, 8–16.

[33] NA[27] (2:10 cf. Dn 2:22; 6:2 cf. Dn 7:22; 13:3 cf. Dn 3:19; 14:25 cf. Dn 2:47; 15:24 cf. Dn 2:44); A. E. Harvey, "The Use of Mystery Language in the Bible,"

on wisdom. Though this section has received much attention the last few decades, it appears that the emerging consensus is that the wisdom Paul boldly declares to his Corinthian audience is notably apocalyptic.[34] Central to his discussion is 2:7: "We declare God's wisdom, *a mystery* [μυστηρίῳ; *mystēriō*] that has been hidden and that God destined for our glory before time began" (TNIV). If the wisdom found in 2:6–16 is to be identified with 1:18–31, which seems likely, then the entirety of 1:18–2:16 should be considered a "revealed mystery" or apocalyptic revelation. Paul thus presents himself mediating apocalyptic wisdom to the Corinthians.

At his arrival at Corinth, Paul ministered to the Corinthians by delivering to them the mystery of the cross. This is evident from 2:1: "When I came to you, brothers and sisters, I did not come proclaiming *the mystery* [τὸ μυστήριον; *to mystērion*] of God to you in lofty words or wisdom" (NRSV).[35] A few chapters later, Paul explicitly claims in 4:1 that he ought to be considered a "steward of the mysteries of God." Other texts portray Paul in a similar light as dispensing mysteries: "Behold, I tell you a mystery" (1 Cor 15:51) and "I do not want you, brethren, to be uninformed of this mystery" (Rom 11:25; cf. Eph 6:19; Col 4:3).[36]

The most extended account of Paul receiving and mediating apocalyptic wisdom occurs in Eph 3:2–10, a text that is saturated with apocalyptic mystery language.[37] This passage is the clearest and most detailed account of Paul mediating apocalyptic revelation, so I will cite it at length:

> If indeed you have heard of the *stewardship of God's grace which was given to me for you; that by revelation there was made known to me the mystery*, as I wrote before in brief. By referring to this, when you read you can understand

JTS 31 (1980): 330–31; (2:1–10 cf. Dn 2, 4; 15:51 cf. Dn 2, 4); Hans Hübner, *Vetus Testamentum in Novo* (2 vols.; Göttingen: Vandenhoeck & Ruprecht, 1997), 2:228–33 (1:21 cf. Dn 2:20 [Theod.]; 1:24 cf. Dn 2:23; 1:28 cf. Dn 4:14; 2:1 cf. Dn 2:30; 3:12 cf. Dn 11:38 [Theod.]; 3:17 cf. Dn 9:27; 6:2 cf. Dn 7:22; 6:19 cf. Dn 4:5; 8:4 cf. Dn 3:17; 13:3 cf. Dn 3:28; 14:25 cf. Dn 2:47; 15:12 cf. Dn 12:2; 15:24 cf. Dn 2:44); Raymond H. Collins, *First Corinthians* (SP 7; Collegeville, MN: Liturgical Press, 1999), 119, 124–25, 477 (2:6–16 cf. Dn 2, 4, 5, 7, 8, 10–12; 13:3 cf. Dn 3); Brian S. Rosner and Roy E. Ciampa, "Use of the Old Testament in 1 Corinthians," in *A Commentary on the Use of the Old Testament in the New* (ed. G. K. Beale and D. A. Carson; Grand Rapids: Baker, 2007), 72 (2:6–12 cf. Dn 2:19–23).

[34] Jeffrey S. Lamp, *First Corinthians 1–4 in Light of Jewish Wisdom Traditions: Christ, Wisdom, and Spirituality* (SBEC 42; Lewiston, NY: Edwin Mellen Press, 2000), 177–79; Alexandra Brown, *Cross and Human Transformation: Paul's Apocalyptic Word in 1 Corinthians* (Minneapolis: Fortress, 1995), 23–25, 97–98, 107–8; Hans Hübner, *Biblische Theologie des Neuen Testaments* (2 vols.; Göttingen: Vandenhoeck & Ruprecht, 1993), 2:121.

[35] On reading μυστήριον (*mystērion*) and not μαρτύριον (*martyrion*), see Gladd, *Revealing the* Mysterion, 123–26.

[36] Cf. Eph 3:2–10; Col 1:25–29; 4:3.

[37] I am assuming Pauline authorship of Ephesians and 2 Timothy (see below), as I do not find the arguments against this position persuasive. Even if Paul did not write this epistle, the force of my argument would not be mitigated.

my insight into the mystery of Christ, which in other generations was not made known to the sons of men, *as it has now been revealed to His holy apostles and prophets in the Spirit; to be specific,* that the Gentiles are fellow heirs and fellow members of the body . . . To me, the very least of all saints, this grace was given, to preach to the Gentiles the unfathomable riches of Christ, *and to bring to light what is the administration of the mystery* which for ages has been hidden in God who created all things; so that the manifold wisdom of God might now be made known through the church to the rulers and the authorities in the heavenly *places.* (emphasis added)

Paul begins by mentioning how God "gave" him the "stewardship of God's grace" for the church (3:2). The next line further explains this notion: "that by revelation there was made known to me the mystery" (3:3).

Not only did Paul receive an eschatological revelation, but also he was charged with mediating it to the church.[38] Paul's role of proclamation comes to the fore in 3:8–10: "To me . . . this grace was given, . . . to bring to light what is the *administration of the mystery* [οἰκονομία τοῦ μυστηρίου; *oikonomia tou mystēriou*] which for ages has been hidden in God . . . in order that the manifold wisdom of God *might now be made known* [ἵνα γνωρισθῇ νῦν; *hina gnōristhē nyn*] through the church to the rulers and the authorities in the heavenly places." In Paul's estimation, the cosmic "rulers and authorities" perceive God's "manifold wisdom" through Paul's promulgation of the unveiled mystery to the church. In other words, the effect of the mystery to the church is the resounding wisdom of God to the cosmic forces.

To sum up,[39] Paul understands himself and "the apostles and prophets" as receiving the "mystery of Christ." Paul is an overseer of the "stewardship" of God's redemptive plan. This stewardship involves announcing the mystery to the church that, in effect, proclaims God's wisdom to the cosmic forces.

Consequently, Paul seems to conceive of himself as an apocalyptic figure by receiving and promulgating apocalyptic revelation. Much of what

---

[38] For those who link mystery with Paul's apostolic ministry, see K. Prümm, "Zur Phänomenologie des paulinischen Mysterion und dessen seelischer Aufnahme. Eine Übersicht," *Bib* 37 (1956): 142–43; John Reumann, "OIKONOMIA-Terms in Paul in Comparison with Lucan *Heilsgeschichte*," *NTS* 13 (1966–1967): 157–66; Romano Penna, *Il "Mysterion" Paolino* (SRB 10; Brescia: Paideia, 1978), 39–41); Bornkamm, "μυστήριον," *TDNT* 4:821; Chantal Reynier, *Évangile et Mystère: Les enjeux théologiques de l'épître aux Éphésiens* (Paris: Cerf, 1992), 89–104; Gene R. Smillie, "Ephesians 6:19–20: A Mystery for the Sake of Which the Apostle is an Ambassador in Chains," *TJ* 18 (1997): 199–222.

[39] Much of what I said regarding Eph 3 could be applied to Col 1:25–29, where Paul rehearses his stewardship of the mystery and its proclamation. It, along with Ephesians, mentions how Paul is a "minister according to the stewardship from God," he is to "proclaim" the unveiled mystery (see Col 4:3), and that the mystery has been revealed to the "saints." But this passage further emphasizes Paul and the other apostles' ministry of "admonishing every man and teaching every man with all wisdom" (1:28). That this admonishment and teaching dealt with the mystery in vv. 26 and 27 is likely.

we have seen in the preceding examples applies to Daniel who likewise receives and disseminates mysteries. In the book of Daniel, the figure Daniel acquires mysteries or eschatological revelations (2:17–18, 28–29) and procures great insight into the rise and fall of nations (2:36–45; 4:19–27; 5:13–28; 7:14–27).

The Polemical Use of Mystery in 1 Corinthians 1–2

In a community filled with factions, rivalry, and competition, Paul delivers his remedy—the *theologia crucis*. If the Corinthians embrace the wisdom of the cross and adopt a cruciform lifestyle, then their divisions will cease. In other words, God's apocalyptic wisdom, that is, the unveiled mystery, is the antidote. The mystery in 1 Cor 2 is the paradoxical event of the crucifixion: At the moment of his death and defeat, Christ was, nevertheless, the sovereign "Lord of glory." That Israel's long-awaited Messiah would be crucified and put under a curse was hidden in the OT. Not only is God's wisdom expressed through the event of the crucifixion, his wisdom, like other early instances, also defeats all forms of human sophistry. The divine wisdom is superior to and nullifies the wisdom of "this age." The mystery of the cross is polemically used against those in the Corinthian church who attempt to evaluate things according to the wisdom of the world (1:17–28; 2:1–7). The Corinthians must not identify with the way "the rulers of this world" exercise their purported wisdom, which, in reality, is foolishness according to the cross. The quotation of Is 64:4 in 2:9, though complex, supports the notion that the rulers were unable to perceive God's wisdom in the crucifixion of his Messiah. The quotation also resembles several Jewish texts that describe individuals having the capacity or incapacity to perceive revelation. Typically, terms such as eyes, ears, and heart are used. Paul thus weaves this well-known sensory language into his argument and, like other Jewish texts, associates it with apocalyptic wisdom, in order to counter the world's wisdom.

In 2:6–8, Paul discusses two groups: the mature and the rulers of this age. He then proceeds to explain why some understand the apocalyptic wisdom and others do not (2:9–16). "The rulers of this age," whoever they might be precisely, are identified with the old sinful and idolatrous age. The "rulers" are "passing away" (καταργουμένων; *katargoumenōn*) or better "perishing" and have come under eschatological judgment, because of their role in the crucifixion.[40]

We ought to likewise connect the "rulers of this age" with Paul's discussion in 1:18–31. If the "rulers of this age" are indeed part of the world's wisdom, which appears likely given the amount of shared vocabulary and

---

[40] Scott J. Hafemann, *Paul, Moses, and the History of Israel: The Letter/Spirit Contrast and the Argument from Scripture in 2 Corinthians 3* (WUNT 2/81; Tübingen: Mohr Siebeck, 1995), 307.

thematic correspondence, then the quotation of Is 29:14 may also refer to the rulers: "I will destroy the wisdom of the wise [i.e., "rulers of this age"], and the cleverness of the clever I will set aside."[41] The "rulers of this age" should also be identified with the "perishing" (1:18), "wise man," (1:20), "world," (1:21), "wisdom of the world," (1:20), "wise" (1:27), "strong" (1:27), and "things that are" (1:28). Therefore, when Paul sets forth the two groups in 2:6–16, he deliberately connects them with his preceding discussion regarding the superiority of God's wisdom. The rulers, who are the embodiment of the "wisdom of the world," have been defeated by God's wisdom through the cross.

Returning to the notion of the apocalyptic wisdom polemic, we are now in a position to compare 1 Cor 1–2 and the book of Daniel. The main thrust of the court narratives in Daniel is God's superior apocalyptic wisdom. Second, the opponents are leaders or professionals that are part of a world system (e.g., Babylon). Third, wisdom in each instance is apocalyptic. God's superior apocalyptic wisdom defeats the wise of "this age."

Furthermore, that 1 Corinthians is conscious of Daniel's narrative is strengthened by a number of Danielic allusions in 1 Cor 1–2.[42] Since Paul quotes Is 29 in 1:19, which is probably a part of the larger Isaianic wisdom polemic, it would seem natural for him to merge this into his discussion of apocalyptic wisdom, for the same Isaianic wisdom polemic is possibly behind, or at least related to, some parts of Daniel.

In conclusion, if we are correct in detecting allusions to Daniel, specifically, the court narrative, Paul's point could not be clearer: God's apocalyptic wisdom of the cross, a mystery and hidden to the opponents of God's people, utterly defeats the wisdom of the world and the representative "rulers of this age" who are analogous to the Babylonian wise men—sophistic professionals who embody the wisdom of the world.

A Danielic Praise: Daniel 2:20–23 and Romans 11:33

Now that we have examined two conceptual traits, let us now turn to Danielic textual connections between Paul and Daniel. One of the more prominent allusions to a key passage in the book of Daniel is Rom 11:33. After discussing the revealed mystery and its significance (11:26b–32), Paul punctuates Rom 11 with a doxology (vv. 33–36). The first line of the doxology is of particular interest to us: "Oh, the depth of the riches both of the wisdom and knowledge of God! How unsearchable are his judg-

---

[41] Notice a conceptual overlap between 1:19 and 2:6: ἀπολῶ τὴν σοφίαν τῶν σοφῶν καὶ τὴν σύνεσιν τῶν συνετῶν ἀθετήσω (apolō tēn sophian tōn sophōn kai tēn synesin tōn synetōn athetēsō); τῶν ἀρχόντων τοῦ αἰῶνος τούτου τῶν καταργουμένων (tōn archontōn tou aiōnos toutou tōn katargoumenōn).

[42] See Gladd, Revealing the Mysterion, 129–32.

ments and unfathomable his ways!" It may not be a matter of coincidence that very similar language occurs in the hymn of Dn 2:20–23.[43]

Daniel 2:20–23 (LXX-Brenton [Theod.])	Romans 11:33
"May the name of God be blessed from everlasting and to everlasting: for *wisdom* [ἡ σοφία; *hē sophia*] and understanding are his. And he changes times and seasons; he appoints kings, and removes them, giving *wisdom to the wise* [σοφίαν τοῖς σοφοῖς; *sophian tois sophois*], and prudence to them that have understanding; he reveals *deep* [βαθέα; *bathea*] and secret matters; *knowing* [γινώσκων; *ginōskōn*] what is in darkness, and the light is with him. I give thanks to thee, and praise thee, O God of my fathers, for thou has given me *wisdom* [σοφίαν; *sophian*] and power, and has made known to me the things which we asked of thee; and thou has made known to me the king's vision."	"Oh, *the depth* [βάθος; *bathos*] of the riches both *of the wisdom* [σοφίας; *sophias*] and *knowledge* [γνώσεως; *gnōseōs*] of God! How unsearchable are his judgments and unfathomable his ways!"

Linguistically, an allusion to Dn 2 seems warranted. The cluster of "depth"/"deep" (βάθος/βαθύς; *bathos/bathys*), "wisdom," (σοφία; *sophia*) and "know"/"knowledge" (γινώσκω/γνῶσις; *ginōskō/gnōsis*) is unique to Dn 2:20–23. Though three other passages in the LXX likewise employ this language (Prv 22:4–20; Eccl 7:4–23; Wis 10:4–21), none uses this language in a tight, literary unit. When examined in its original context, Dn 2:20–23 consists of a hymn that summarizes the entire book of Daniel *in nuce*. It would make sense, then, for Paul to allude to a distinct literary unit. Greatly increasing the likelihood of an allusion to Dn 2 is the pairing of μυστήριον (*mystērion*) in v. 25 and the cluster of these terms. When μυστήριον (*mystērion*) and these unique words are considered together, an allusion to Dn 2:20–23 becomes all the more reasonable.

On a conceptual level, this allusion to Dn 2:20–23 makes good sense. Daniel's hymn of praise to God is the result of the revelation of mystery: "Then the mystery was revealed to Daniel in a night vision. Then Daniel blessed the God of heaven" (2:19). Daniel and his friends pleaded with God, asking him to reveal Nebuchadnezzar's dream. Once Nebuchadnezzar's dream and its interpretation, that is, the mystery, were revealed to Daniel,

---

[43] For other OT and Second Temple Jewish texts that lie behind the doxology, see E. Elizabeth Johnson, *The Functions of Apocalyptic and Wisdom Traditions in Romans 9–11* (SBLDS 109; Atlanta: Scholars Press, 1989), 164–75.

he immediately offered praise to God. The first strophe (20a–22b) articulates God "removing" and "establishing" kings and giving wisdom to "wise men." In the second strophe (v. 23), God gave Daniel wisdom concerning the rise and fall of kings. In Rom 11, Paul's doxology resembles Daniel's hymn of praise on a few levels. First, immediately following the disclosure of mystery in 11:25–26, Paul—like Daniel—offers up praise to God in v. 33. Ernst Käsemann makes a similar observation of 11:33–36 when he states, "Paul is crowning his assurance of salvation with doxology like that in Dan 2:20ff."[44] In other words, Daniel's praise becomes Paul's. What is true of Daniel is true of Paul. Second, Daniel and Paul extol God for his unsurpassed knowledge. God's newly revealed plan for the salvation of Israel is so grand, so counterintuitive, that Paul alludes to the hymn of Dn 2 in order to underscore God's unparalleled wisdom and power in his dealings with Israel.

"Rescued from the Lion's Mouth": The Use of Daniel 6 in 2 Timothy 4:17

Perhaps one of the clearest instances of Paul resembling the figure Daniel occurs in 2 Tm 4:17: "But the Lord stood with me and strengthened me, so that through me the proclamation might be fully accomplished, and that all the Gentiles might hear; and *I was rescued out of the lion's mouth* [ἐρρύσθην ἐκ στόματος λέοντος; *errysthēn ek stomatos leontos*]." Once again, it appears that Paul is alluding to one of the most notable events of Daniel's career—Daniel and the lions' den.

2 Timothy 4:17	Daniel 6:20, 23, 28 (Theod.; NETS)
"I was rescued out of the lion's mouth" (ἐρρύσθην ἐκ στόματος λέοντος; *errysthēn ek stomatos leontos*)	"O Daniel, the slave of the living God, has your God whom you continually serve been able *to deliver you from the mouth of the lions*?" (ἐξελέσθαι σε ἐκ στόματος τῶν λεόντων; *exelesthai se ek stomatos tōn leontōn*) "My God sent his angel and *shut the lions' mouths*" (ἐνέφραξεν τὰ στόματα τῶν λεόντων; *enephraxen ta stomata tōn leontōn*) "He helps and *rescues* [ῥύεται; *rhyetai*], and he works signs and wonders in heaven and on earth; *he delivered Daniel from the power of the lions*" (ἐξείλατο τὸν Δανιηλ ἐκ χειρὸς τῶν λεόντων; *exeilato ton Daniēl ek cheiros tōn leontōn*)

[44] Ernst Käsemann, *Commentary on Romans* (trans. G. W. Bromiley; Grand Rapids: Eerdmans, 1980), 319.

Though some see an allusion to Ps 21:22 (LXX),[45] Dn 6 seems to be in mind for a variety of reasons. On a linguistic level, Dn 6 is the only passage in the OT that uses ῥύομαι (*rhyomai*) in conjunction with στόμα (*stoma*) and λέων (*leōn*). The Theodotion version of Dn 6:20 employs the synonym ἐξαιρέω (*exaireō*) instead of ῥύομαι (*rhyomai*), but the hymn of praise at the end of the chapter switches to the synonym ῥύομαι (*rhyomai*, v. 28). First Maccabees 2:60 confirms the allusion to Dn 6 when it uses the precise language found in 2 Tm 4:17, but it does so in the context of Daniel and the lions' den: "Daniel, because of his innocence, *was delivered from the mouth of the lions*" (ἐρρύσθη ἐκ στόματος λεόντων; *errysthē ek stomatos leontōn*).

The conceptual parallels between 2 Tm 4 and Dn 6 also affirm the legitimacy of the allusion. The most obvious parallel between the two texts is the deliverance from a dire situation in which both figures rely completely on God's mercy. Daniel trusted that God would rescue him from the lions, and Paul was delivered from the clutches of the Roman government, probably in the context of a formal trial (4:16). Second, Paul states in 4:17 that the "Lord stood with me and strengthened me." This is not a far cry from Dn 6:22, where Daniel claims that "God sent his angel." In both situations, God's presence offers safety and comfort. God's "kingdom" also plays prominently in both passages. Paul takes comfort in knowing that, upon his death, he will be ushered into God's "heavenly kingdom" (4:18). The hymn of Dn 6:26–27, like the other hymns in the book of Daniel (e.g., 2:20–23), highlights the permanence of God's kingdom: "his *kingdom* is one which will not be destroyed, and his *dominion* will be forever" (v. 26). Lastly, Paul's utterance "to him be the glory *forever and ever*," though a common expression, may reflect indebtedness to Dn 6:26: "He is the living God and he endures *forever*."

The result of our lexical and conceptual analyses leads us to the conclusion that Paul likely had Dn 6 in mind in 2 Tm 4. An allusion to Dn 6 fits marvelously with the immediate context of 2 Tm 4:16–18: Paul's (preliminary?) defense before the Roman court resembles Daniel's situation in the lions' den. Like Daniel in the den of lions, Paul stood before the Roman magistrates and their fatal punishment, the figurative "lion." With

---

[45] E.g., George W. Knight, *The Pastoral Epistles: A Commentary on the Greek Text* (NIGTC; Grand Rapids: Eerdmans, 1992), 471; Gordon D. Fee, *1 and 2 Timothy, Titus* (NIBC; Peabody, MA: Hendrickson, 1995), 298. Ps 21:22 (LXX) reads, "*Save me from the lion's mouth* [σῶσόν με ἐκ στόματος λέοντος; *sōson me ek stomatos leontos*]; from the horns of the wild oxen you answer me." Not unlike Daniel in the den of lions, in Ps 22 (MT) David recalls God's salvation in the midst of affliction and distress. Bulls, lions, and dogs were "surrounding" David (vv. 12–13, 16), but God "rescued" him (v. 21). This theme would fit Paul's purposes in 2 Tm 4, so this allusion should not be immediately discounted. Dn 6, however, is probably Paul's primary allusion, because of tighter linguistic and conceptual parallels between the two texts. It is even possible that Paul may have also combined Ps 22 with Dn 6. In any case, Dn 6 ought to be deemed the primary allusion.

the aid of Christ's presence (4:17a), Paul was rescued from their schemes and persecutions. We noted above that, according to Second Temple Judaism and early Christianity, Daniel and the lions' den is the most popular passage in the book of Daniel. Paul's allusion to Dn 6 is, therefore, hardly surprising.

Conclusion

As we have seen, both the Teacher of Righteousness and Josephus display unique traits that closely resemble the character Daniel. The correlation between the Teacher and Daniel concerns the acquiring and dispensing of eschatological mysteries. God primarily revealed mysteries to Daniel through dream reports, whereas the Teacher perceived mysteries through Scripture. In any case, both individuals function as mediators of apocalyptic wisdom. The figure of Daniel also resonates throughout Josephus's career. His ability to interpret and receive dreams certainly points in this direction. Josephus even fastidiously studied the book of Daniel and likely identified with the figure of Daniel in a variety of circumstances. It is possible, perhaps even probable, that both characters consciously consider themselves as analogously functioning like the figure Daniel.

These two precedents lend credibility to the suggestion that Paul functions analogously to the prophet Daniel.[46] Perhaps the clearest connection between the two characters lies in their prerogative to acquire and mediate eschatological mysteries. Like Daniel who receives the mystery and interprets Nebuchadnezzar's dream (Dn 2:18–47), Paul receives the mystery of the cross and delivers it to the Corinthians (1 Cor 2:1–5) and to the audience of Ephesians (3:2–10). One of the more striking features of Daniel's narrative is the protagonist's display of wisdom in contrast to the failure of the Babylonian "wise men." Paul's exchange with the Corinthians in 1 Cor 1–2 becomes all the more forceful in light of the Danielic wisdom polemic. The divinely revealed wisdom of the cross defeats all forms of human sophistry.

Two allusions to the book of Daniel further support Paul's conscious identification as a Danielic figure. The use of Dn 2:20–23 in Rom 11:33 aligns Paul's exuberant praise with Daniel's. Just as Daniel thanked God for disclosing Nebuchadnezzar's dream, a mystery (Dn 2:19), so too Paul

---

[46] Though only the Teacher of Righteousness is in mind, C. Marvin Pate surmises, "Paul, like the Teacher of Righteousness at Qumran, viewed himself to be the mediator of divine revelation, based on a charismatic/mystic interpretation of the OT" (*The Reverse of the Curse: Paul, Wisdom, and the Law* [WUNT 2/114; Tübingen: Mohr Siebeck, 2000], 189). Pate has in view Paul's exegesis of OT quotations in Galatians, but he rightly detects similarities between both figures.

praises God for disclosing his mysterious plan to "save" Israel. Likewise, in 2 Tm 4:17 Paul recalls Dn 6:20–27 and resonates with Daniel and the den of lions.

Aligning the apostle with Daniel not only explains the presence of Danielic allusions but also Paul's larger apostolic role. Whether or not Paul's ministry functions typologically or analogically to the figure Daniel is difficult to determine. At the least, the apostle appears to view himself as someone who wades in the stream of Danielic behavior.

When taken individually, these Danielic concepts and allusions are admittedly tenuous. But if they are considered cumulatively, then these Danielic links become all the more forceful. Such an understanding of Paul engenders further explorations into his *modus operandi* and the use of the apocalyptic term "mystery" (and similar apocalyptic words). By aligning these two notable figures, we can look afresh at a number of Pauline texts and determine to what extent Paul took up Daniel's mantle.

LIST OF G. K. BEALE'S PUBLICATIONS

Books

1. *The Use of Daniel in Jewish Apocalyptic Literature and in the Revelation of St. John.* Lanham, MD: University Press of America, 1984. Repr., Eugene, OR: Wipf & Stock, 2009.

2. Editor, *Right Doctrine from Wrong Texts? Essays on the Use of the Old Testament in the New Testament.* Grand Rapids: Baker, 1994.

3. *John's Use of the Old Testament in Revelation.* Journal for the Study of the New Testament Supplement Series 166. Sheffield: JSOT Press: 1998.

4. *The Book of Revelation.* New International Greek Testament Commentary Series. Edited by I. H. Marshall and D. Hagner. Grand Rapids: Eerdmans, 1999.

5. *1–2 Thessalonians.* InterVarsity Press New Testament Commentary Series. Downers Grove, IL: InterVarsity Press, 2003.

6. *The Temple and the Church's Mission: A Biblical Theology of the Dwelling Place of God.* New Studies in Biblical Theology 17. Downers Grove, IL: InterVarsity Press, 2004.

7. Co-Editor with D. A. Carson, *A Commentary on the New Testament Use of the Old Testament.* Grand Rapids: Baker, 2007.

8. *The Erosion of Inerrancy in Evangelicalism: Responding to New Challenges to Biblical Authority.* Wheaton, IL: Crossway, 2008.

9. *We Become Like What We Worship: A Biblical Theology of Idolatry.* Downers Grove, IL: InterVarsity Press, 2008.

10. *A New Testament Biblical Theology: The Unfolding of the Old Testament in the New.* Grand Rapids: Baker, 2011.

11. *Handbook on the New Testament Use of the Old Testament: Exegesis and Interpretation.* Grand Rapids: Baker, 2012.

Articles and Essays

1. "The Danielic Background for Revelation 13:18 and 17:9." *Tyndale Bulletin* 31 (1980): 163–70.

2. "The Problem of the Man from the Sea in *4 Ezra* 13 and Its Relation to the Messianic Concept in John's Apocalypse." *Novum Testamentum* 25/2 (1983): 182–88.

3. "An Exegetical and Theological Consideration of the Hardening of Pharaoh's Heart in Exodus 4–14 and Romans 9." *Trinity Journal* 5/2 (1984): 129–54.

4. "The Influence of Daniel upon the Structure and Theology of John's Apocalypse." *Journal of the Evangelical Theological Society* 27/4 (1984): 413–23.

5. "The Origin of the Title 'King of Kings and Lord of Lords' in Revelation 17:14." *New Testament Studies* 31/4 (1985): 618–20.

6. "The Use of Daniel in the Synoptic Eschatological Discourse and in the Book of Revelation." In *Gospel Perspectives*, vol. 5: *The Jesus Tradition Outside the Gospels*, 129–53. Edited by David Wenham. Sheffield: JSOT Press, 1985.

7. Co-authored with J. Bibza. "The New Testament: The Covenant of Redemption in Jesus Christ." In *Building a Christian World View*, vol. 1: *God, Man, and Knowledge*, 49–70. Edited by W. Andrew Hoffecker. Phillipsburg, NJ: P&R, 1986.

8. Co-authored with W. Andrew Hoffecker. "Biblical Epistemology." In *Building a Christian World View*, vol. 1: *Volume 1: God, Man, and Knowledge*, 193–216. Edited by W. Andrew Hoffecker. Phillipsburg, NJ: P&R, 1986.

9. "A Reconsideration of the Text of Daniel in the Apocalypse." *Biblica* 67/4 (1986): 539–43.

10. "Revelation." In *It Is Written: Scripture Citing Scripture. Essays in Honor of Barnabas Lindars*, 318–36. Edited by D. A. Carson and H. G. M. Williamson. Cambridge: Cambridge University Press, 1988.

- Reprinted as "The Use of the Old Testament in Revelation." In *Right Doctrine from Wrong Texts? Essays on the Use of the Old Testament in the New Testament*, 257–76. Edited by G. K. Beale. Grand Rapids: Baker, 1994.

- Reprinted, pages 60–129 in G. K. Beale, *John's Use of the Old Testament in Revelation*. Journal for the Study of the New Testament Supplement Series 166. Sheffield: JSOT Press: 1999.

11. "The Old Testament Background of Reconciliation in 2 Corinthians 5–7 and Its Bearing on the Literary Problem of 2 Cor. 6:14–7:1." *New Testament Studies* 35/4 (1989): 550–81.

- Reprinted as "The Old Testament Background of Reconciliation in 2 Corinthians 5–7 and Its Bearing on the Literary Problem of 2 Cor. 6:14–7:1." In *Right Doctrine from Wrong Texts? Essays on the Use of the Old Testament in the New Testament,* 217–47. Edited by G. K. Beale. Grand Rapids: Baker, 1994.

12. "Did Jesus and His Followers Preach the Right Doctrine From the Wrong Texts? An Examination of the Presuppositions of the Apostles' Exegetical Method." *Themelios* 14 (1989): 89–96.

- Reprinted as "Positive Answer to the Question Did Jesus and His Followers Preach the Right Doctrine from the Wrong Texts? An Examination of the Presuppositions of Jesus' and Apostles' Exegetical Method." In *Right Doctrine from Wrong Texts? Essays on the Use of the Old Testament in the New Testament,,* 387–404. Edited by G. K. Beale. Grand Rapids: Baker, 1994.

- Reprinted as "Did Jesus and His Followers Preach the Right Doctrine from the Wrong Texts?" In *Solid Ground: Twenty-five Years of Evangelical Theology*, 155–71. Edited by C. R. Trueman, T. J. Gray, and C. L. Blomberg. Leicester: Apollos, 2000.

13. "Isaiah 6:9–13: A Retributive Taunt Against Idolatry." *Vetus Testamentum* 41/3 (1991): 257–78.

14. "The Interpretative Problem of Rev. 1:19." *Novum Testamentum* 34/4 (1992): 360–87.

- Reprinted, pages 165–92 in G. K. Beale, *John's Use of the Old Testament in Revelation.* Journal for the Study of the New Testament Supplement Series 166. Sheffield: JSOT Press, 1999.

15. "The Self-Sufficiency of God and His Purpose in Creation." *Table Talk* 16 (1992): 8–10.

16. Review Article *After the Thousand Years: Resurrection and Judgment in Revelation 20*, by J. W. Mealy. Journal for the Study of the New Testament: Supplement Series 70. Sheffield: JSOT Press, 1992. *Evangelical Quarterly* 66 (1994): 229–49.

17. "The Old Testament Background of Rev 3.14." *New Testament Studies* 42/1 (1996): 133–52.

- Reprinted, pages 273–94 in G. K. Beale, *John's Use of the Old Testament in Revelation.* Journal for the Study of the New Testament Supplement Series 166. Sheffield: JSOT Press, 1999.

18. "Eschatology." In *Dictionary of the Later New Testament and Its De-velopments*, 330–45. Edited by R. P. Martin and P. H. Davids. Downers Grove, IL: InterVarsity Press, 1997.

- Reprinted, pages 129–65 in G. K. Beale, *John's Use of the Old Testament in Revelation.* Journal for the Study of the New Testament Supplement Series 166. Sheffield: JSOT Press, 1999.

19. "The Eschatological Conception of New Testament Theology." In *'The Reader Must Understand.' Eschatology in the Bible and Theology*, 11–52. Edited by K. E. Brower and M. W. Elliott. Downers Grove, IL: InterVarsity Press; Leicester: Apollos, 1997.

- Abbreviated, revised, and reprinted as "The New Testament and New Creation." In *Biblical Theology: Retrospect and Prospect*, 159–73. Edited by Scott J. Hafemann. Downers Grove, IL: InterVarsity Press, 2002.

20. "The Hearing Formula and the Visions of John in Revelation." In *A Vision for the Church. Studies in Early Christian Ecclesiology in Honour of J. P. M. Sweet*, 167–80. Edited by M. Bockmuehl and M. B. Thompson. Edinburgh: T&T Clark, 1997.

- Reprinted, pages 298–317 in G. K. Beale, *John's Use of the Old Testament in Revelation.* Journal for the Study of the New Testament Supplement Series 166. Sheffield: JSOT Press, 1999.

21. "Solecisms in the Apocalypse as Signals for the Presence of Old Testament Allusions: A Selective Analysis of Revelation 1–22." In *Early Christian Interpretation of the Scriptures of Israel*, 421–46. Edited by C. A. Evans and J. A. Sanders. Journal for the Study of the New Testament: Supplement Series 148. Studies in Scripture in Early Judaism and Christianity 5. Sheffield: Sheffield Academic Press, 1997.

- Reprinted, pages 318–55 in G. K. Beale, *John's Use of the Old Testament in Revelation.* Journal for the Study of the New Testament Supplement Series 166. Sheffield: JSOT Press, 1999.

22. "Peace and Mercy Upon the Israel of God: The Old Testament Background of Galatians 6, 16b." *Biblica* 80/2 (1999): 204–23.

23. "Questions of Authorial Intent, Epistemology, and Presuppositions and Their Bearing on the Study of the Old Testament in the New: A Rejoinder to Steve Moyise." *Irish Biblical Studies* 21/4 (1999): 152–80.

24. "The Structure and Plan of John's Apocalypse." In *Creator, Redeemer, Consummator, a Festschrift for Meredith G. Kline*, 117–52. Edited by H. Griffith and J. R. Meuther. Greenville, SC: Reformed Academic Press, 2000.

25. "The Theology of the Book of Revelation." In *New Dictionary of Biblical Theology*, 356–63. Edited by T. D. Alexander and Brian Rosner. Downers Grove, IL: InterVarsity Press, 2000.

26. "A Response to Jon Paulien on the Use of the Old Testament in Revelation." *Andrews University Seminary Studies* 39 (2001): 23–33.

27. "The Garden Temple." *Kerux* 18 (2003): 3–50.

28. "Biblical Faith and Other Religions in New Testament Theology." In *Evangelical Christianity and Other Religions,* 77–105. Edited by David Baker. Grand Rapids: Kregel, 2004.

29. "The Final Vision of the Apocalypse and Its Implications for a Biblical Theology of the Temple." In *Heaven on Earth. The Temple in Biblical Theology,* 191–209. Edited by S. Gathercole and T. D. Alexander. Carlisle: Paternoster Press, 2004.

30. "The Revelation on Hell." In *Hell Under Fire,* 111–34. Edited by Christopher W. Morgan and Robert A. Peterson. Grand Rapids: Zondervan, 2004.

31. "The Descent of the Eschatological Temple in the Form of the Spirit at Pentecost: Part I." *Tyndale Bulletin* 56/1 (2005): 73–102.

32. "The Descent of the Eschatological Temple in the Form of the Spirit at Pentecost: Part II." *Tyndale Bulletin* 56/2 (2005): 63–90.

33. "Eden, the Temple, and the Church's Mission in the New Creation." *Journal of the Evangelical Theological Society* 48/1 (2005): 5–31.

34. "The Old Testament Background of Paul's Reference to the 'Fruit of the Spirit' in Galatians 5:22." *Bulletin for Biblical Research* 15/1 (2005): 1–38.

35. "Did Jesus and the Apostles Preach the Right Doctrine from the Wrong Texts? Revisiting the Debate Seventeen Years Later in the Light of Peter Enns' Book, *Inspiration and Incarnation.*" *Themelios* 32/1 (2006): 18–43.

36. "Myth, History, and Inspiration: A Review Article of Peter Enns' *Inspiration and Incarnation.* Evangelicals and the Problem of the Old Testament." *Journal of the Evangelical Theological Society* 49/2 (2006): 287–312.

37. "The Purpose of Symbolism in the Book of Revelation." *Calvin Theological Journal* 41/1 (2006): 53–66.

38. "The Unseen Sources of Suffering." *Calvin Theological Journal* 41/1 (2006): 115–26.

39. "Colossians." In *A Commentary on the New Testament Use of the Old Testament,* 841–70. Edited by G. K. Beale and D. A. Carson. Grand Rapids: Baker, 2007.

40. "A Surrejoinder to Peter Enns." *Themelios* 32/3 (2007): 14–25.

41. "A Surrejoinder to Peter Enns's Response to G. K. Beale's JETS Review Article of His Book, *Inspiration and Incarnation*." *The Southern Baptist Journal of Theology* 11/1 (2007): 16–36.

42. Co-author with Sean McDonough. "Revelation." In *A Commentary the New Testament Use of the Old Testament*, 1081–1161. Edited by G. K. Beale and D. A. Carson. Grand Rapids: Baker, 2007.

43. "A Specific Problem Confronting the Authority of the Bible: Should the New Testament's Claim That the Prophet 'Isaiah' Wrote the Whole Book of Isaiah Be Taken at Face Value?" In *Resurrection and Eschatology: Theology in Service of the Church: Essays in Honor of Richard B. Gaffin*, 125–76. Edited by L. G. Tipton and Jeffrey C. Waddington. Philipsburg, NJ: P&R, 2008.

44. "Christ and the Church as the Emerging Eschatological Temple: James' Testimony in Acts 15." In *Christ, Salvation, and the Eschaton: Essays in Honor of Hans K. LaRondelle*, 349–66. Edited by Daniel Heinz and Jiří Moskala. Berrien Springs: Andrews University Press, 2009.

45. "The Overstated 'New' Perspective?" *Bulletin for Biblical Research* 19/1 (2009): 85–94.

46. "The Role of Resurrection in the Already-and-Not-Yet Phases of Justification." In *For the Fame of God's Name: Essays in Honor of John Piper*, 190–212. Edited by Sam Storms and Justin Taylor. Wheaton, IL: Crossway, 2010.

47. "Can the Bible Be Completely Inspired by God and Yet Still Contain Errors? A Response to Some Recent 'Evangelical' Proposals." *Westminster Theological Journal* 73/1 (2011): 1–22.

48. "The Eschatological Hour in 1 John 2:18 in the Light of Its Daniel Background." *Biblica* 92/2 (2011): 231–54.

49. "The Inaugurated End-Time Tribulation and Its Bearing on the Church Office of Elder and on Christian Living in General." *Midwestern Journal of Theology* 10 (2011): 32–57.

50. "The Inaugurated Eschatological Indicative and Imperative in Relation to Christian Living and Preaching." *Midwestern Journal of Theology* 10 (2011): 12–31.

51. "The Use of Hosea 11:1 in Matthew 2:15: One More Time." *Journal of the Evangelical Theological Society* 55 (2012), 697–715.

Bibliography

Alexander, T. Desmond. *From Eden to the New Jerusalem: An Introduction to Biblical Theology*. Grand Rapids: Kregel Academic, 2009.

Allen, Leslie C. "David as Exemplar of Spirituality: The Redactional Function of Psalm 19." *Biblica* 67/4 (1986): 544–46.

Alter, Robert. *The Art of Biblical Narrative*. New York: Basic Books, 1981.

———. *The David Story: A Translation with Commentary of 1 and 2 Samuel*. New York: W. W. Norton & Co., 1999.

Anderson, Bernhard W. *Understanding the Old Testament*. 3rd ed. Englewood Cliffs, NJ: Prentice Hall, 1975.

Aune, David E. "Following the Lamb: Discipleship in the Apocalypse." In *Patterns of Discipleship in the New Testament*, 269–84. Edited by R. N. Longenecker. Grand Rapids: Eerdmans, 1969.

———. *Prophecy in Early Christianity and the Ancient Mediterranean World*. Grand Rapids: Eerdmans, 1983.

———. *Revelation 6–16*. Word Biblical Commentary 52B. Nashville: Thomas Nelson, 1998.

Averbeck, Richard. "Ancient Near Eastern Mythography as It Relates to Historiography in the Hebrew Bible: Genesis 3 and the Cosmic Battle." In *The Future of Biblical Archaeology: Reassessing Methodologies and Assumptions*, 328–56. Edited by J. K. Hoffmeier and A. R. Millard. Grand Rapids: Eerdmans, 2004.

Baker, David L. "Typology and the Christian Use of the Old Testament." *Scottish Journal of Theology* 29 (1976): 137–57.

Bal, Mieke. *Death and Dissymmetry. The Politics of Coherence in the Book of Judges*. Chicago: University of Chicago Press, 1988.

Barber, Cyril J. *Judges: A Narrative of God's Power*. Neptune, NJ: Loizeaux, 1990.

Bar-Efrat, S. *Narrative Art in the Bible*. Sheffield: Almond Press, 1989.

Barnett, R. D. *Ancient Ivories in the Middle East and Adjacent Countries*. Qedem 14. Jerusalem: Institute of Archaeology, 1982.

———. "Ezekiel and Tyre." *Eretz Israel* 9 (1969): 6–13.

Bauckham, Richard J. "The Apocalypse as a Christian War Scroll." In *The Climax of Prophecy: Studies on the Book of Revelation*, 210–37. London: T&T Clark, 1993. Reprinted from *Neotestimentica* 22 (1988): 17–40.

——. "The Ascension of Isaiah: Genre, Unity, and Date." In *The Fate of the Dead: Studies on the Jewish and Christian Apocalypses*, 363–90. Novum Testamentum Supplements 93. Leiden: Brill, 1998.

——. "The Conversion of the Nations." In *The Climax of Prophecy: Studies on the Book of Revelation*, 243–83. London: T&T Clark, 1993.

——. *God Crucified: Monotheism and Christology in the New Testament*. Grand Rapids: Eerdmans, 1998.

——. *James: Wisdom of James, Disciple of Jesus the Sage*. London: Routledge, 1999.

——. *Jesus and the God of Israel: God Crucified and other Studies on the New Testament's Christology of Divine Identity*. Milton Keynes: Paternoster; Grand Rapids: Eerdmans, 2008.

——. "The List of the Tribes of Israel in Revelation 7 Again." *Journal for the Study of the New Testament* 42 (1991): 99–115.

——. "Sabbath and Sunday in the Post-Apostolic Church," in *From Sabbath to Lord's Day: A Biblical, Historical, and Theological Investigation*, 251–98. Edited by D. A. Carson. Grand Rapids: Zondervan, 1982.

Bayer, Hans F. *Das Evangelium des Markus*. Historisch Theologische Auslegung. Giessen: SCM Press, 2008.

Beale, G. K. *The Book of Revelation: A Commentary on the Greek Text*. New International Greek Testament Commentary. Grand Rapids: Eerdmans, 1999.

——. "Eden, the Temple, and the Church's Mission in the New Creation." *Journal of the Evangelical Theological Society* 48 (2005): 5–31.

——. *John's Use of the Old Testament in Revelation*. Journal for the Study of the New Testament: Supplement Series 166. Sheffield: Sheffield Academic, 1998.

——. *A New Testament Biblical Theology: The Unfolding of the Old Testament in the New*. Grand Rapids: Baker, 2011.

——. *The Temple and the Church's Mission: A Biblical Theology of the Dwelling Place of God*. New Studies in Biblical Theology 17. Downers Grove, IL: InterVarsity Press, 2004.

——. *The Use of Daniel in Jewish Apocalyptic Literature and in the Revelation of St. John*. Lanham, MD: University Press of America, 1984. Repr., Eugene, OR: Wipf & Stock, 2009.

Beale, G. K. and D. A. Carson, ed. *Commentary on the New Testament Use of the Old Testament*. Grand Rapids: Baker, 2007.

Beasley-Murray, G. R. *The Book of Revelation*. New Century Bible. London: Oliphants, 1974.

Beavis, Mary Ann. *Mark*. Paideia: Commentaries on the New Testament. Grand Rapids: Baker, 2011.

——. *Mark's Audience: The Literary and Social Setting of Mark 4.11–12*. Journal for the Study of the New Testament: Supplement Series 33. Sheffield: JSOT Press, 1989.

Beck, J. A. "Why Do Joshua's Readers Keep Crossing the River? The Narrative-Geographical Shaping of Joshua 3–4." *Journal of the Evangelical Theological Society* 48/4 (2005): 689–99.

Becker, J. *Das Heil Gottes: Heils—und Südenbegriffe in den Qumrantexten und in Neuen Testament.* Studien zur Umwelt des Neuen Testaments 3. Göttingen: Vandenhoeck & Ruprecht, 1964.

Beetham, Christopher A. *Echoes of Scripture in the Letter of Paul to the Colossians.* Biblical Interpretation Series 96. Leiden: Brill, 2008. Reprint, Atlanta: Society of Biblical Literature, 2010.

Begg, C. T. "Daniel and Josephus: Tracing Connections." In *The Book of Daniel in the Light of New Findings,* 539–45. Edited by A. S. van der Woude. Bibliotheca ephemeridum theologicarum lovaniensium 106. Leuven: University Press, 1993.

Behrens, Achim. "Gen 15,6 und das Vorverständnis des Paulus." *Zeitschrift für die Alttestamentliche Wissenschaft* 109 (1997): 329–34.

Benedict XVI. "Three Stages in the Program of De-Hellenization." Lecture, University of Regensberg, Germany, 2006.

Bergauer, P. *Der Jakobusbrief bei Augustinus und die damit verbundenen Probleme der Rechtfertigungslehre.* Vienna: Herder, 1962.

Bergen, R. D. *1, 2 Samuel.* New American Commentary. Nashville: Broadman & Holman, 1996.

Bergsma, John Sietze. *The Jubilee from Leviticus to Qumran.* Vetus Testamentum Supplements 115. Leiden: Brill, 2006.

Berlin, A. *Poetics and Interpretation of Biblical Narrative.* Sheffield: Almond Press, 1983.

Betz, Otto. *Offenbarung und Schriftforschung in der Qumransekte.* Wissenschaftliche Untersuchungen zum Neuen Testament 6. Tübingen: Mohr Siebeck, 1960.

———. "Past Events and Last Events in the Qumran Interpretation of History." *Proceedings of the World Congress of Jewish Studies* 6 (1977): 27–34.

Biddle, Mark E. *A Redaction History of Jeremiah 2:1–4:2.* Abhandlungen zur Theologie des Alten und Neuen Testaments 77. Zurich: Theologischer Verlag, 1990.

Billerbeck, P. "Ein Synagogengottesdienst in Iesu Tagen." *Zeitschrift für die neutestamentliche Wissenschaft und die Kunde der älteren Kirche* 55 (1964): 143–61.

Bird, Michael F. *Are You the One Who Is to Come? The Historical Jesus and the Messianic Question.* Grand Rapids: Baker, 2009.

Black, Matthew. *The Book of Enoch or I Enoch.* Studia in Veteris Testamenti pseudepigraphica 7. Leiden: Brill, 1985.

Blenkinsopp, Joseph. *Ezra—Nehemiah.* Old Testament Library. Philadelphia: Westminster Press, 1988.

———. "Prophecy and Priesthood in Josephus." *Journal of Jewish Studies* 25 (1974): 239–62.

———. *Isaiah 56–66.* Anchor Bible Commentary 19B. New York: Doubleday, 2003.

Bloch-Smith, Elizabeth. "Solomon's Temple: The Politics of Ritual Space." In *Sacred Time, Sacred Space: Archaeology and the Religion of Israel,* 83–94. Edited by B. M. Gittlen. Winona Lake, IN: Eisenbrauns, 2002.

——. "Who Is the King of Glory? Solomon's Temple and Its Symbolism." In *Scripture and Other Artifacts*, 18–31. Edited by M. Coogan, J. C. Exum, and L. E. Stager. Louisville: Westminster John Knox, 1994.

Block, Daniel I. *The Book of Ezekiel Chapters 25–48*. New International Commentary on the Old Testament. Grand Rapids: Eerdmans, 1998.

——. *How I Love Your Torah, O Lord! Studies in the Book of Deuteronomy*. Eugene, OR: Cascade, 2011.

——. "'In Spirit and in Truth': The Mosaic Vision of Worship." In *The Gospel according to Moses: Theological and Ethical Reflections on the Book of Deuteronomy*, 272–98. Edited by Daniel I. Block. Eugene, OR: Cascade, 2012.

——. "Reading the Decalogue Left to Right: The Ten Principles of Covenant Relationship in the Hebrew Bible." In *How I Love Your Torah, O Lord! Studies in the Book of Deuteronomy*, 21–55. Eugene, OR: Cascade, 2011.

Blomberg, Craig. *The Historical Reliability of the Gospels*. Downers Grove, IL: InterVarsity Press, 1987.

——. Review of *Introducing Romans: Critical Issues in Paul's Most Famous Letter* by Richard Longenecker. Accessed April 11, 2012. http://www.denverseminary.edu/article/introducing-romans-critical-issues-in-pauls-most-famous-letter/.

Blomberg, Craig L., and Mariam Kamell. *James*. Zondervan Exegetical Commentary on the New Testament. Grand Rapids: Zondervan, 2008.

Bock, Darrell L. *Blasphemy and Exaltation in Judaism: The Charge against Jesus in Mark 14:53–65*. Tübingen: Mohr Siebeck, 1998. Repr., Grand Rapids: Baker, 2000.

——. *Luke*. Baker Exegetical Commentary on the New Testament. 2 vols. Grand Rapids: Baker, 1994, 1996.

——. "Response to Kaiser." In *Three Views on the New Testament Use of the Old Testament*, 90–95. Edited by Kenneth Berding and Jonathan Lunde. Grand Rapids: Zondervan, 2007.

Bockmuehl, Markus. *Revelation and Mystery in Ancient Judaism and Pauline Christianity*. Wissenschaftliche Untersuchungen zum Neuen Testament 36. Tübingen: Mohr Siebeck, 1990. Reprint, Grand Rapids: Eerdmans, 1997.

Böhler, Dieter. "Geschlechterdifferenz und Landbesitz: Strukturuntersuchungen zu Jer 2,2–4,2." In *Jeremia und die "deuteronomistische Bewegung,"* 91–127. Edited by Walter Gross. Weinheim: Beltz Athenäum, 1995.

Boling, Robert G., and G. Ernest Wright. *Joshua. A New Translation with Notes and Commentary*. Anchor Bible 6. Garden City, NY: Doubleday, 1982.

Booth, Wayne C. *The Rhetoric of Fiction*. Chicago: University of Chicago Press, 1961.

Bordreuil, Pierre, and Dennis Pardee. *A Manual of Ugaritic*. Linguistic Studies in Ancient West Semitic 3. Winona Lake, IN: Eisenbrauns, 2009.

Boring, M. Eugene. *Revelation*. Interpretation. Louisville: Westminster John Knox, 1989.

Bouma-Prediger, Steven. *For the Beauty of the Earth: A Christian Vision for Creation Care*. Grand Rapids: Baker, 2001.

Bousset, Wilhelm. *Die Offenbarung Johannis*. Kritisch-exegetischer Kommentar über das Neue Testament (Meyer-Kommentar) 16. 1906. Reprint, Göttingen: Vandenhoeck & Ruprecht, 1996.

Bovon, François. *Luke 1: A Commentary on the Gospel of Luke 1:1–9:50*. Translated by Christine M. Thomas. Hermeneia. Minneapolis: Fortress, 2002.

Bowley, James E. "Prophets and Prophecy at Qumran." In *The Dead Sea Scrolls after Fifty Years*, 2:371–76. 2 vols. Edited by Peter W. Flint and James C. VanderKam. Leiden: Brill, 1998.

Bray, Gerald. *Romans*. Ancient Christian Commentary on Scripture: New Testament 6. Downers Grove, IL: InterVarsity Press, 1998.

Brin, Gershon. *The Concept of Time in the Bible and the Dead Sea Scrolls*. Studies on the Texts of the Desert of Judah 39. Leiden: Brill, 2001.

Brisson, Luc. *How Philosophers Saved Myths: Allegorical Interpretation and Classical Mythology*. Translated by Catherine Tihanyi. 1996. Reprint, Chicago: University of Chicago Press, 2004.

Brown, Alexandra. *Cross and Human Transformation: Paul's Apocalyptic Word in 1 Corinthians*. Minneapolis: Fortress, 1995.

Brown, Raymond E. *The Death of the Messiah*, vol. 1. New York: Doubleday, 1994.

———. *The Semitic Background of the Term 'Mystery' in the New Testament*. Philadelphia: Fortress, 1968.

Brownlee, William H. "Messianic Motifs of Qumran and the New Testament." *New Testament Studies* 3/3 (1957): 195–210.

———. *The Midrash Pesher of Habakkuk*. Society of Biblical Literature Monograph Series 24. Missoula, MT: Scholars Press, 1979.

Bruce, F. F. *Biblical Exegesis in the Qumran Texts*. Grand Rapids: Eerdmans, 1959.

———. *The Epistle to the Galatians: A Commentary on the Greek Text*. New International Greek Testament Commentary. Grand Rapids, Eerdmans, 1982.

Brueggemann, Walter. *Genesis*. Atlanta: John Knox, 1982.

Buber, M. "Leitwort Style in Pentateuch Narrative." In *Scripture and Translation*, 114–28. Edited by M. Buber and F. Rosenzweig. Translated by L. Rosenwald and E. Fox. Bloomington: Indiana University Press, 1994.

Budde, K. *Die Bucher Richter und Samuel, ihre Quellen und ihre Aufbau*. Giessen: Ricker, 1890.

Burton, Ernest de W. *A Critical and Exegetical Commentary on the Epistle to the Galatians*. International Critical Commentary. Edinburgh: T&T Clark, 1921.

Caird, George B. *A Commentary on the Revelation of St. John the Divine*. Harper's New Testament Commentaries. New York: Harper & Row, 1966.

Callender, Dexter E., Jr. *Adam in Myth and History: Ancient Israelite Perspectives on the Primal Human*. Harvard Semitic Studies 48. Winona Lake, IN: Eisenbrauns, 2000.

Calvert-Koyzis, Nancy. *Paul, Monotheism, and the People of God: The Significance of Abraham Traditions for Early Judaism and Christianity*. Journal for the Study of the New Testament: Supplement Series 273. London: T&T Clark, 2004.

Calvin, J. *Commentaries on the First Book of Moses, called Genesis*. Grand Rapids: Eerdmans, n.d.

Campbell, Douglas A. *The Deliverance of God: An Apocalyptic Rereading of Justification in Paul*. Grand Rapids: Eerdmans, 2009.

Carter, Warren. *The Roman Empire and the New Testament: An Essential Guide*. Nashville: Abingdon, 2006.

Cartledge, Paul. *The Greeks: A Portrait of Self and Others*. 2nd ed. Oxford: Oxford University Press, 2002.

Casey, Maurice. *Aramaic Sources of Mark's Gospel*. Society for New Testament Studies Monograph Series 10. Cambridge: Cambridge University Press, 1998.

Cassel, Paulus. "Judges." In *Commentary on the Holy Scriptures, Critical, Doctrinal, and Homiletical*, 3–261. 1865. Reprint. Edited by Johann Peter Lange. Translated by P. H. Steenstra. Edinburgh: T&T Clark, 1872.

Cerfaux, Lucien. *The Christian in the Theology of St. Paul*. New York: Herder & Herder, 1967.

Charlesworth, James H., ed. *Old Testament Pseudepigrapha*. 2 vols. New York: Doubleday, 1983.

Charette, B. " 'To Proclaim Liberty to the Captives': Matthew 11:28–30 in the Light of OT Prophetic Expectation." *New Testament Studies* 38/2 (1992): 290–97.

Chester, Andrew. *Divine Revelation and Divine Titles in the Pentateuchal Targumim*. Texte und Studien zum Antiken Judentum 14. Tübingen: Mohr Siebeck, 1986.

———. *Messiah and Exaltation: Jewish Messianic and Visionary Traditions and New Testament Christology*. Wissenschaftliche Untersuchungen zum Neuen Testament 207. Tübingen: Mohr Siebeck, 2007.

Chester, Andrew, and Ralph P. Martin. *The Theology of the Letters of James, Peter, and Jude*. With the assistance of Ralph P. Martin. New Testament Theology. Cambridge: Cambridge University Press, 1994.

Childs, Brevard. *Introduction to the Old Testament as Scripture*. Philadelphia: Fortress, 1979.

———. *Old Testament Theology in a Canonical Context*. Philadelphia: Fortress, 1985.

———. "Psalm Titles and Midrashic Exegesis." *Journal of Semitic Studies* (1971): 137–50.

Chilton, Bruce D. *Glory of Israel: The Theology and Provenience of the Isaiah Targum*. Journal for the Study of the Old Testament: Supplement Series 23. Sheffield: JSOT Press, 1982.

Chisholm, Robert B. *From Exegesis to Exposition*. Grand Rapids: Baker, 1999.

———. *Interpeting the Historical Books: An Exegetical Handbook*. Grand Rapids: Kregel, 2006.

Ciampa, Roy E. "Paul's Theology of the Gospel." In *Paul as Missionary: Identity, Activity, Theology, and Practice*, 180–91. Edited by Trevor J. Burke and Brian S. Rosner. Library of New Testament Studies 420. London: T&T Clark, 2011.

———. "Scriptural Language and Ideas." In *As It Is Written: Studying Paul's Use of Scripture*, 41–57. Edited by Stanley E. Porter and Christopher D. Stanley. Society of Biblical Literature Symposium Series 50. Atlanta: Society of Biblical Literature, 2008.

Clines, David J. A. "The Image of God in Man." *Tyndale Bulletin* 19 (1968): 53–103.

Cohen, Jeremy. *"Be Fertile and Increase, Fill the Earth and Master It": The Ancient and Medieval Career of a Biblical Text*. Ithaca: Cornell University Press, 1989.

Collins, John J. *The Apocalyptic Imagination: An Introduction to Jewish Apocalyptic Literature*. 2nd ed. Grand Rapids: Eerdmans, 1998.

———. *The Scepter and the Star: The Messiahs of the Dead Sea Scrolls and Other Ancient Literature*. Anchor Bible Reference Library. New York: Doubleday, 1995.

———. "The Works of the Messiah." *Dead Sea Discoveries* 1 (1994): 98–112.

Collins, Raymond H. *First Corinthians*. Sacra Pagina 7. Collegeville, MN: Liturgical Press, 1999.

Craigie, Peter C. *Psalms 1–50*. Word Biblical Commentary 19. Waco, TX: Word, 1983.

Cranfield, C. E. B. *Romans*. 2 vols. International Critical Commentary. London: T&T Clark, 1975.

Crenshaw, James L. "The Samson Saga: Filial Devotion or Erotic Attachment?" *Zeitschrift für die Alttestamentliche Wissenschaft* 86 (1974): 470–504.

Crites, Stephen. "The Narrative Quality of Experience." *Journal for the American Academy of Religion* 39 (1971): 291–311.

Cross, Frank Moore. *Canaanite Myth and Hebrew Epic: Essays in the History of the Religion of Israel*. Cambridge, MA: Harvard University Press, 1973.

Cundall, Arthur E. *Judges: An Introduction and Commentary*. Tyndale Old Testament Commentaries. Downers Grove, IL: InterVarsity Press, 1968.

Currid, J. *Strong and Courageous: Joshua Simply Explained*. Welwyn Commentary Series. Darlington, UK: Evangelical Press, 2011.

Dahood, M. *Psalms 1–50: A New Translation with Introduction and Commentary*. Anchor Bible 16. New York: Doubleday, 1965.

Dalman, Gustaf. *The Words of Jesus*. Translated by D. M. Kay. Edinburgh: T&T Clark, 1902.

Daube, David. "Typology in Josephus." *Journal of Semitic Studies* 31 (1980): 18–36.

Davids, Peter. *The Epistle of James*. New International Greek Testament Commentary. Grand Rapids: Eerdmans, 1982.

de Jonge, Marinus. "Josephus und die Zukunftserwartungen seines Volkes." In *Josephus—Studien: Untersuchungen zu Josephus, dem antiken Judentum und dem Neuen Testament*, 205–19. Edited by Otto Betz, Klaus Haacker, and Martin Hengel. Göttingen: Vandenhoeck & Ruprecht, 1974.

de Jonge, M., and A. S. van der Woude. "11QMelchizedek and the New Testament." *New Testament Studies* 12 (1965–1966): 301–26.

Delitzsch, Franz. *Psalms*. Translated by James Martin. 1888. Reprint, Grand Rapids: Eerdmans, 1982.

DeRoche, Michael. "Jeremiah 2:2–3 and Israel's Love for God during the Wilderness Wanderings." *Catholic Biblical Quarterly* 45 (1983): 364–76.

Desrosiers, Gilbert. *An Introduction to Revelation: A Pathway to Interpretation*. Continuum Biblical Studies Series. London: Continuum, 2000.

Dewey, Joanna. "The Literary Structure of the Controversy Stories in Mark 2:1–3:6." *Journal of Biblical Literature* 92 (1973): 394–401.

Dietrich, Manfried. "Das biblische Paradies und der babylonische Tempelgarten: Überlegungen zur Lage des Gartens Eden." In *Das biblische Weltbild und seine altorientalischen Kontexte*, 281–323. Edited by B. Janowski and B. Ego. Forschungen zum Alten Testament 32. Tübingen: Mohr Siebeck, 2004.

DiMattei, Steven. "Biblical Narratives." In *As It Is Written: Studying Paul's Use of Scripture*, 59–93. Edited by Stanley E. Porter and Christopher D. Stanley. Society of Biblical Literature Symposium Series 50. Atlanta: Society of Biblical Literature, 2008.

Dodd, C. H. *According to the Scriptures: The Sub-Structure of New Testament Theology*. London: Nisbet, 1952.

Douglas, Michael C. "Teacher Hymn Hypothesis Revisited: New Data for an Old Crux." *Dead Sea Discoveries* 6/3 (1999): 239–66.

Draper, J. A. "The Heavenly Feast of Tabernacles: Revelation 7,1–17." *Journal for the Study of the New Testament* 19 (1983): 133–47.

Driver, G. R., and John C. Miles. *The Babylonian Laws*. 2 vols. Oxford: Clarendon Press, 1955.

Duhem, Pierre. *To Save the Phenomena, an Essay on the Idea of Physical Theory from Plato to Galileo*. Translated by Edmund Doland and Chaninah Maschler. Introductory essay by Stanley L. Jaki. Chicago: University of Chicago Press, 1969.

Dunn, James D. G. *Jesus Remembered*. Grand Rapids: Eerdmans, 2003.

———. "Messianic Ideas and Their Influence on the Jesus of History." In *The Messiah: Developments in Earliest Judaism and Christianity*, 365–81. Edited by James H. Charlesworth. Minneapolis: Fortress, 1992.

———. "The New Perspective on Paul: Whence, What and Whither?" In *The New Perspective on Paul*, 1–88. Rev. ed. Grand Rapids: Eerdmans, 2008.

———. *Romans 1–8*. Word Biblical Commentary 38A. Dallas: Word, 1988.

Eckstein, Hans-Joachim. *Verheissung und Gesetz: Eine Exegetische Untersuchung zu Galater 2,15–4,7*. Wissenschaftliche Untersuchungen zum Neuen Testament 2/86. Tübingen: Mohr Siebeck, 1996.

Edwards, James R. *The Gospel according to Mark*. Pillar New Testament Commentary. Grand Rapids: Eerdmans, 2002.

Eichrodt, Walther. *Theology of the Old Testament*. Translated by J. A. Baker. 2 vols. London: SCM Press, 1967.

———. "Is Typological Exegesis an Appropriate Method?" In *Essays on Old Testament Interpretation*, 224–45. Edited by Claus Westermann. Translated by James Luther Mays. London: SCM Press, 1963.

Eliade, Mircea. *Patterns in Comparative Religion*. New York: Sheed & Ward, 1958.

———. *The Sacred and the Profane: The Nature of Religion*. Translated by W. R. Trask. New York: Harper & Brothers, 1959.

Elliott, Mark Adam. *The Survivors of Israel: A Reconsideration of the Theology of Pre-Christian Judaism*. Grand Rapids: Eerdmans, 2000.

Elliott, Neil. "'Blasphemed among the Nations': Pursuing an Anti-imperial 'Intertextuality' in Romans." In *As It Is Written: Studying Paul's Use of Scripture*, 213–33. Society of Biblical Literature Symposium Series 50. Edited by Stanley E. Porter and Christopher D. Stanley. Atlanta: Society of Biblical Literature, 2008.

Ellis, E. Earle. *Eschatology in Luke*. Edited by John Reumann. Biblical Series 30. Philadelphia: Fortress, 1972.

———. "Eschatology in Luke." *New Testament Studies* 12 (1965–1966): 27–41.

———. *The Gospel of Luke*. London: Nelson, 1966.

Eskola, Timo. *Messiah and the Throne: Jewish Merkabah Mysticism and Early Christian Exaltation Discourse*. Wissenschaftliche Untersuchungen zum Neuen Testament 2/142. Tübingen: Mohr Siebeck, 2001.

Evans, Craig A. *Mark 8:27–16:20*. Word Biblical Commentary 34B. Nashville: Thomas Nelson, 2001.

———. "Patristic Interpretation of Mark 2:26: 'When Abiathar Was High Priest.'" *Vigiliae christianae* 40 (1986): 183–86.

Exum, J. Cheryl. "Aspects of Symmetry and Balance in the Samson Saga." *Journal for the Study of the Old Testament* 19 (1981): 3–29.

Faierstein, Morris M. "Why Do the Scribes Say that Elijah Must Come First?" *Journal of Biblical Literature* 100 (1981): 75–86.

Farb, Peter. *Consuming Passions: The Anthropology of Eating.* New York: Washington Square Press, 1980.

Fee, Gordon D. *1 and 2 Timothy, Titus.* New International Bible Commentary. Peabody, MA: Hendrickson: 1995.

———. *Pauline Christology: An Exegetical-Theological Study.* Peabody, MA: Hendrickson, 2007.

Feldman, Louis H. *Josephus's Interpretation of the Bible.* Los Angeles: University of California Press, 1998.

Feuillet, André. "Les 144,000 Israélites marqués d'un sceau." *Novum Testamentum* 9 (1967): 191–224.

Fischer, Loren R. "Creation at Ugarit and in the Old Testament." *Vetus Testamentum* 15 (1965): 313–24.

Fishbane, Michael. "The 'Eden' Motif/The Landscape of Spiritual Renewal." In *Biblical Text and Texture: A Literary Reading of Selected Texts,* 110–20. Oxford: Oneworld, 1998.

Fitzmyer, Joseph A. "Further Light on Melchizedek from Qumran Cave 11." *Journal of Biblical Literature* 86 (1967): 25–41.

———. *The Gospel According to Luke I–IX: Introduction, Translation, and Notes.* Anchor Bible 28. New York: Doubleday, 1982.

———. "The Interpretation of Genesis 15:6: Abraham's Faith and Righteousness in a Qumran Text." In *Emanuel: Studies in Hebrew Bible, Septuagint and Dead Sea Scrolls in Honor of Emanuel Tov,* 258–64. Edited by Shalom M. Paul, Robert A. Kraft, Lawrence H. Schiffman, and Weston W. Fields. Leiden: Brill, 2003.

Flesher, Paul V. M., and Bruce Chilton. *The Targums: A Critical Introduction.* Studies in the Aramaic Interpretation of Scripture 12. Leiden: Brill, 2011.

Fletcher, Verne H. "The Fundamental Shape of Old Testament Ethics." *Scottish Journal of Theology* 24 (1971): 47–73.

Fletcher-Louis, Crispin. "Jesus and the High Priestly Messiah, Part 2."*Journal for the Study of the Historical Jesus* 5 (2007): 57–79.

Flüchter, Sascha. *Die Anrechnung des Glaubens zur Gerechtigkeit: Auf dem Weg zu einer sozialhistorisch orientierten Rezeptionsgeschichte von Gen 15,6 in der neutestamentlichen Literatur.* With the assistance of Lars Schnor. Texte und Arbeiten zum neutestamentlichen Zeitalter 51. Tübingen: Franke, 2010.

Ford, Josephine M. *Revelation: Introduction, Translation, and Commentary.* Anchor Bible 38. Garden City, NY: Doubleday, 1965.

Forman, Mark. *The Politics of Inheritance in Romans.* Cambridge: Cambridge University Press, 2011.

Fossum, Jarl E. *The Name of God and the Angel of the Lord: Samaritan and Jewish Concepts of Intermediation and the Origin of Gnosticism.* Wissenschaftliche Untersuchungen zum Neuen Testament 1/36. Tübingen: Mohr Siebeck, 1985.

Foulkes, Francis. *The Acts of God*. London: Tyndale, 1958.

Fox, Michael V. "Jeremiah 2:2 and the 'Desert Ideal.'" *Catholic Biblical Quarterly* (1973): 441–50.

——. *Proverbs 1–9*. Anchor Bible 18A. New York: Doubleday, 2000.

France, Richard T. *The Gospel of Mark*. New International Greek Testament Commentary. Carlisle: Paternoster; Grand Rapids: Eerdmans, 2002.

——. *The Gospel of Matthew*. New International Commentary on the New Testament. Grand Rapids: Eerdmans, 2007.

——. *Jesus and the Old Testament*. 1971. Reprint, Vancouver: Regent, 1998.

Frankemölle, Hubert. *Frühjudentum und Urchristentum: Vorgeschichte— Verlauf—Auswirkungen (4. Jahrhundert v. Chr. bis 4. Jahrhundert n. Chr.)*. Studienbücher Theologie 5. Stuttgart: Kohlhammer, 2006.

Freedman, D. N., ed. *Anchor Bible Dictionary*. 6 vols. New York: Doubleday, 1992.

Fretheim, Terence E. *God and World in the Old Testament: A Relational Theology of Creation*. Nashville: Abingdon, 2005.

Froehlich, Karl, ed. *Biblical Interpretation in the Early Church*. Philadelphia: Fortress, 1984.

García-Martínez, F. "4QPseudo Daniel Aramaic and the Pseudo Daniel Literature." In *Qumran and Apocalyptic: Studies on the Aramaic Texts from Qumran*, 137–61. Studies on the Texts of the Desert of Judah 9. Leiden: Brill, 1992.

García-Martínez, F., and Eibert J. C. Tigchelaar. *The Dead Sea Scrolls Study Edition*. 2 vols. Leiden: Brill, 1997–1998.

Gathercole, Simon J. *Where Is Boasting? Early Jewish Soteriology and Paul's Response in Romans 1–5*. Grand Rapids: Eerdmans, 2002.

George, Andrew. *The Epic of Gilgamesh: A New Translation*. London: Penguin, 1999.

Gesenius' Hebrew Grammar. Edited by E. Kautzsch. Translated by A. E. Cowley. 2nd ed. Oxford: Clarendon Press, 1910.

Gignilliat, Mark S. *Paul and Isaiah's Servants: Paul's Theological Reading of Isaiah 40–66 in 2 Corinthians 5:14–6:10*. Library of New Testament Studies 330. London: T&T Clark, 2007.

Ginzberg, Louis. *Legends of the Jews*. 2 vols. Translated by Henrietta Szold and Paul Radin. Philadelphia: JPS, 2003.

Gladd, Benjamin L. *Revealing the* Mysterion*: The Use of Mystery in Daniel and Second Temple Judaism with Its Bearing on First Corinthians*. Beihefte zur Zeitschrift für die neutestamentliche Wissenschaft 160. Berlin: de Gruyter, 2008.

Glasson, T. F. *The Revelation of John*. Cambridge Bible Commentary. Cambridge: Cambridge University Press, 1965.

Gnuse, Robert Karl. *Dreams and Dream Reports in the Writings of Josephus: A Traditio-Historical Analysis.* Arbeiten zur Geschichte des antiken Judentums und des Urchristentums 36. Leiden: Brill, 1996.

Goldberg, Arnold M. "Sitzend zur Rechten der Kraft: Zur Gottesbezeichnung Gebura in der frühen rabbinischen Literatur." *Biblische Zeitschrift* 8 (1964): 284–93.

———. *Untersuchungen über die Vorstellung von der Schekhinah in der frühen rabbinischen Literatur—Talmud und Midrasch.* Studia Judaica 5. Berlin: de Gruyter, 1969.

Goldin, Judah. *The Fathers according to Rabbi Nathan.* Yale Judaica Series 10. New Haven: Yale University Press, 1955.

Goodhead, Paul. "The Search for the Hanging Gardens: 170 Cuneiform and Biblical Evidence." In *Babylon: Myth and Reality*, 109–17. Edited by I. L. Finkel and M. J. Seymour. London: British Museum Press, 2008.

Goppelt, Leonhard. *Typos: the Typological Interpretation of the Old Testament in the New.* Grand Rapids: Eerdmans, 1982.

Gordon, R. P. "David's Rise and Saul's Demise; Narrative Analogy in 1 Samuel 24–26." *Tyndale Bulletin* 31 (1980): 37–64.

Görg, Manfred. "*Bdlh* ("Bdellium"): zur Etymologie." *Biblische Notizen* 48 (1989): 12–16.

Gosse, Bernard. "Ezéchiel 28,11–19 et les détournements de malédictions." *Biblische Notizen* 44 (1988): 30–38.

Gottwald, Norman K. *The Hebrew Bible: A Socio-Literary Introduction.* Philadelphia: Fortress, 1985.

Gourgues, Michel. *Á la Droite de Dieu: Résurrection de Jésus et Actualisation du Psaume 110:1 dans le Nouveau Testament.* Études bibliques. Paris: Gabalda, 1978.

Gower, Barry. *Scientific Method: An Historical and Philosophical Introduction.* London: Routledge, 1997.

Grant, Jamie A. *The King as Exemplar: The Function of Deuteronomy's Kingship Law in the Shaping of the Book of Psalms.* Atlanta: Society of Biblical Literature, 2004.

Gray, John. *Joshua, Judges, Ruth.* New Century Bible. Grand Rapids: Eerdmans, 1986.

Gray, Timothy C. *The Temple in the Gospel of Mark: A Study in its Narrative Role.* Wissenschaftliche Untersuchungen zum Neuen Testament 2/242. Tübingen: Mohr Siebeck, 2008. Repr., Grand Rapids: Baker, 2010.

Green, Joel B. *The Gospel of Luke.* New International Commentary on the New Testament. Grand Rapids: Eerdmans, 1997.

Greenberg, Moshe. *Ezekiel 21–37: A New Translation with Introduction and Commentary.* Anchor Bible 22. New York: Doubleday, 1997.

Grelot, P. "Sur Isaïe lxi: La Première Consécration D'un Grand-Prêtre." *Revue biblique* 97 (1990): 414–31.

Grindheim, Sigurd. *God's Equal: What Can We Know about Jesus' Self-understanding.* Library of New Testament Studies 446. London: T&T Clark, 2011.

Groenewoud, E. M. C. "Use of Water in Phoenician Sanctuaries." *Journal of the Ancient Near Eastern Society* 38 (2001): 139–59.

Grossfeld, Bernard. *Targum Neofiti 1: An Exegetical Commentary to Genesis, Including Full Rabbinic Parallels.* New York: Sepher-Hermon, 2000.

Gruenwald, Ithamar. *Apocalyptic and Merkavah Mysticism.* Arbeiten zur Geschichte des antiken Judentums und des Urchristentums 14. Leiden: Brill, 1980.

Guehlich, Robert A. *Mark 1–8:26.* Word Biblical Commentary 34A. Nashville: Thomas Nelson, 1989.

Guillaume, Philippe. *Waiting for Josiah: The Judges.* Journal for the Study of the Old Testament: Supplement Series 385. New York: T&T Clark, 2004.

Hafemann, Scott J. *Paul, Moses, and the History of Israel: The Letter/Spirit Contrast and the Argument from Scripture in 2 Corinthians 3.* Wissenschaftliche Untersuchungen zum Neuen Testament 81. Tübingen: Mohr Siebeck, 1995.

Hahn, Ferdinand. "Genesis 15:6 im Neuen Testament." In *Probleme biblischer Theologie: Gerhard von Rad zum 70. Geburtstag,* 90–107. Edited by Hans Walter Wolff. Munich: Kaiser, 1971.

Halperin, David J. *The Faces of the Chariot: Early Jewish Responses to Ezekiel's Vision.* Texte und Studien zum Antiken Judentum 16. Tübingen: Mohr Siebeck, 1988.

Hamilton, Victor. P. *The Book of Genesis: Chapters 1–17.* New International Commentary on the Old Testament. Grand Rapids: Eerdmans, 1990.

Harbin, Michael A. "The Manumission of Slaves in Jubilee and Sabbath Years." *Tyndale Bulletin* 63/1 (2012): 53–74.

Harris, William V. *Ancient Literacy.* Cambridge, MA: Harvard University Press, 1989.

Harrison, James R. *Paul and the Imperial Authorities at Thessalonica and Rome: A Study in the Conflict of Ideology.* Tübingen: Mohr Siebeck, 2010.

Harrisville, Roy A. *The Figure of Abraham in the Epistles of St. Paul.* San Francisco: Mellen University Research Press, 1992.

Harvey, A. E. "The Use of Mystery Language in the Bible." *Journal of Theological Studies* 31 (1980): 320–36.

Hatina, Thomas R. *In Search of a Context: the Function of Scripture in Mark's Narrative.* Studies in Early Judaism and Christianity 8/Journal for the Study of the New Testament: Supplement Series 232. London: Sheffield Academic Press, 2002.

Hay, David M. *Glory at the Right Hand: Psalm 110 in Early Christianity.* Nashville: Abingdon, 1973.

Hays, Richard. *Echoes of Scripture in the Letters of Paul.* New Haven: Yale University Press, 1989.

Head, Peter. "Letter Carriers in the Ancient Jewish Epistolary Material." In *Jewish and Christian Scripture as Artifact and Canon*, 203–19. Edited by C. A. Evans and H. D. Zacharias. Studies in Early Judaism and Christianity 13/Library of Second Temple Studies 70. London: T&T Clark, 2009.

Heil, John Paul. "The Narrative Strategy and Pragmatics of the Temple Theme in Mark." *Catholic Biblical Quarterly* 59 (1997): 76–100.

Hengel, Martin. "Sit at My Right Hand." In *Studies in Early Christology*, 119–225. Edinburgh: T&T Clark, 1995.

Heskett, Randall. *Messianism within the Scriptural Scrolls of Isaiah.* Library of Hebrew Bible/Old Testament Studies 456. New York: T&T Clark, 2007.

Hess, Richard S. "West Semitic Texts and the Book of Joshua." *Bulletin for Biblical Research* 7 (1997): 63–76.

Hilber, John W. "Psalms." Pages 316–463 in *Zondervan Illustrated Bible Backgrounds Commentary*, vol. 5. Edited by John H. Walton. 5 vols. Grand Rapids: Zondervan, 2009.

Hirschberg, Peter. *Das eschatologische Israel: Untersuchungen zum Gottesverständnis der Johannesoffenbarung.* Wissenschaftliche Monographien zum Alten und Neuen Testament 51. Neukirchen-Vluyn: Neukirchener, 1999.

———. "Jewish Believers in Asia Minor according to the Book of Revelation and the Gospel of John." In *Jewish Believers in Jesus: The Early Centuries*, 217–38. Edited by Oskar Skarsaune and Reidar Hvalvik. Peabody, MA: Hendrickson, 2007.

Holladay, Carl L. *Fragments from Hellenistic Jewish Authors.* Chico, CA: Scholars Press, 1983.

Holladay, William L. *Jeremiah I: A Commentary on the Book of the Prophet Jeremiah, Chapters 1–25.* Hermeneia. Philadelphia: Fortress, 1986.

Hollander, H. W., and M. de Jonge. *The Testaments of the Twelve Patriarchs: A Commentary.* Studia in Veteris Testamenti pseudepigraphica 8. Leiden: Brill, 1985.

Holmes, Michael W., ed. *The Greek New Testament: SBL Edition.* Atlanta: Society of Biblical Literature, 2010.

Holm-Nielsen, Svend. *Hodayot: Psalms from Qumran.* Das Alte Testament Deutsch 2. Aarhus: Universitetsforlaget, 1960.

Holtz, T. *Untersuchungen über die alttestamentliche Zitate bei Lukas.* Akademie: Berlin, 1968.

Hooker, Morna D. Review of Christopher D. Stanley, *Arguing with Scripture: The Rhetoric of Quotations in the Letters of Paul.* *Journal of Theological Studies* 57 (2006): 270.

———. *The Gospel According to Saint Mark.* Black's New Testament Commentaries. London: A&C Black, 1991.

Horbury, William. "The Twelve and the Phylarchs." *New Testament Studies* 32 (1986): 509–13.

Horsley, Richard A., ed. *Paul and Empire: Religion and Power in Roman Imperial Society*. Harrisburg, PA: Trinity Press International, 1997.

———. *Paul and the Roman Imperial Order*. Harrisburg, PA: Trinity Press International, 2004.

Howard, George. *Paul: Crisis in Galatia. A Study in Early Christian Theology*. Society for New Testament Studies Monograph Series 35. Cambridge: Cambridge University Press, 1979.

Hübner, Hans *Biblische Theologie des Neuen Testaments*. 2 vols. Göttingen: Vandenhoeck & Ruprecht, 1993.

Hugenberger, Gordon P. *Marriage as a Covenant*. Supplements to Vetus Testamentum 52. Leiden: Brill, 1994. Reprint, Grand Rapids: Baker, 1998.

———. "The Servant of the Lord in the 'Servant Songs' of Isaiah." Pages 105–39 in *The Lord's Anointed: Interpretation of Old Testament Messianic Texts*. Edited by Philip E. Satterthwaite, Richard S. Hess, and Gordon J. Wenham. Grand Rapids: Baker, 1995.

Hundley, Michael. "To Be or Not to Be: A Reexamination of Name Language in Deuteronomy and the Deuteronomistic History." *Vetus Testamentum* 59 (2009): 533–55.

Hurowitz, Victor Avigdor. *"I have built you an exalted house": Temple Building in the Bible in the Light of Mesopotamian and Northwest Semitic Writings*. Journal for the Study of the Old Testament: Supplement Series 115. Sheffield: Sheffield Academic Press, 1992.

———. "YHWH's Exalted House—Aspects of the Design and Symbolism of Solomon's Temple." In *Temple and Worship in Biblical Israel*, 63–110. Edited by John Day. Library of Hebrew Bible/Old Testament Studies 422. New York: T&T Clark, 2007.

Hurtado, Larry W. *Lord Jesus Christ: Devotion to Jesus in Earliest Christianity*. Grand Rapids: Eerdmans, 2003.

Hutter, Manfred. "Adam als Gärtner und König (Gen 2:8,15)." *Biblische Zeitschrift* 30 (1986): 258–62.

Instone-Brewer, David. *Techniques and Assumptions in Jewish Exegesis before 70 CE*. Texte und Studien zum antiken Judentum 30. Tübingen: Mohr Siebeck, 1992.

Jacobs, Louis. *The Jewish Mystics*. London: Kyle Cathie, 1990.

James, Carolyn Custis. "Disposable Girls?" Last modified April 15, 2012. http://www.whitbyforum.com/2012/04/disposable-girls.html.

Janowski, Bernd. "Der Himmel auf Erden: Zur kosmologischen Bedeutung des Tempels in der Umwelt Israels." In *Das biblische Weltbild und seine altorientalischen Kontexte*, 229–60. Edited by B. Janowski and B. Ego. Forschungen zum Alten Testament 32. Tübingen: Mohr Siebeck, 2004.

Janowitz, Naomi. *The Poetics of Ascent: Theories of Language in a Rabbinic Ascent Text*. Albany: State University of New York Press, 1989.

Jassen, Alex P. *Mediating the Divine: Prophecy and Revelation in the Dead Sea Scrolls and Second Temple Judaism*. Studies on the Texts of the Desert of Judah 68. Leiden: Brill, 2007.

Jeremias, Gert. *Der Lehrer der Gerechtigkeit.* Studien zur Umwelt des Neuen Testaments 2. Göttingen: Vandenhoeck & Ruprecht, 1963.

Jeremias, Joachim. *The Eucharistic Words of Jesus.* London: SCM Press, 1966.

———. *New Testament Theology.* Translated by John Bowden. New Testament Library. London: SCM Press, 1971.

Jervis, L. Ann. "Reading Romans 7 in Conversation with Postcolonial Theory: Paul's Struggle toward a Christian Identity of Hybridity." In *The Colonized Apostle: Paul Through Postcolonial Eyes,* 95–109. Edited by Christopher D. Stanley. Minneapolis: Fortress, 2011.

Jewett, Robert. *Romans: A Commentary.* Hermeneia. Minneapolis: Fortress, 2006.

Johnson, Benjamin J. M. "What Type of Son Is Samson? Reading Judges 13 as a Biblical Type-Scene." *Journal of the Evangelical Theological Society* 53/2 (2010): 269–86.

Johnson, Bo. "Who Reckoned Righteousness to Whom?" *Studia ephemeridis Augustinianum* 51 (1986): 108–15.

Johnson, E. Elizabeth. *The Functions of Apocalyptic and Wisdom Traditions in Romans 9–11.* Society of Biblical Literature Dissertation Series 109. Atlanta: Scholars Press, 1989.

Johnson, Gary Lance. "Josephus: Heir Apparent to the Prophetic Tradition?" In *Society of Biblical Literature 1983 Seminar Papers,* 337–46. Edited by Kent Harold Richards. Chico, CA: Scholars Press, 1993.

Johnson, Luke Timothy. *The Letter of James.* Anchor Bible 37A. Garden City, NY: Doubleday, 1995.

Johnston, Gordon. "A New Look at an Old Text: Genesis 15:6. Contextual and Canonical Readings." Unpublished paper.

Jones, Douglas. *Isaiah 56–66 and Joel.* London: SCM Press, 1964.

Jones, Peter R. "The Apostle Paul: Second Moses to the New Covenant Community: A Study in Pauline Apostolic Authority." In *God's Inerrant Word: An International Symposium of the Trustworthiness of Scripture,* 219–41. Edited by J. W. Montgomery. Minneapolis: Bethany Fellowship, 1974.

Josephus. Translated by H. St. J. Thackeray. 10 vols. Loeb Classical Library. Cambridge, MA: Harvard University Press, 1926–1965.

Juel, Donald H. *Messiah and Temple: The Trial of Jesus in the Gospel of Mark.* Society of Biblical Literature Dissertation Series 31. Missoula, MT: Scholars Press, 1977.

———. *Messianic Exegesis: Christological Interpretation of the Old Testament in Early Christianity.* Philadelphia: Fortress, 1988.

Kaiser, Walter C., Jr. "God's Promise Plan and His Gracious Law," *JETS* 33 (1990): 289–302.

———. *Toward an Old Testament Theology.* Grand Rapids: Zondervan, 1978.

Kalluveettil, Paul, C. M. I. *Declaration and Covenant: A Comprehensive Review of Covenant Formulae from the Old Testament and the Ancient Near East*. Analecta Biblica 88. Rome: Biblical Institute Press, 1982.

Käsemann, Ernst. *Commentary on Romans*. Translated by G. W. Bromiley. Grand Rapids: Eerdmans, 1980.

Kee, H. C. *Community of the New Age*. New Testament Library. London: SCM Press, 1977.

Keel, Othmar. *The Symbolism of the Biblical World: Ancient Near Eastern Iconography and the Book of Psalms*. Translated by T. J. Hallett. New York: Seabury, 1978.

Keener, Craig S. *The IVP Bible Background Commentary*. Downers Grove, IL: InterVarsity Press, 1993.

Keerankeri, George. *The Love Commandment in Mark: An Exegetico-Theological Study of Mk 12,28–34*. Rome: Editrice Pontificio Istituto Biblico, 2003.

Keil, C. F. *Joshua, Judges, Ruth*. Translated by J. Martin. 1863. Reprint, Grand Rapids: Eerdmans, 1982.

Keil, C. F., and F. Delitzsch. *Commentary on the Old Testament: The Pentateuch*. Translated by James Martin. Edingurgh: T&T Clark, 1866–1981. Grand Rapids: Eerdmans, 1969. Repr., Peabody, MA: Hendrickson, 1996.

Kennedy, George A. *Classical Rhetoric and its Christian and Secular Tradition from Ancient to Modern Times*. Chapel Hill: University of North Carolina Press, 1980.

Kim, Seyoon. *Christ and Caesar: The Gospel and the Roman Empire in the Writings of Paul and Luke*. Grand Rapids: Eerdmans, 2008.

———. "Jesus—The Son of God, the Stone, the Son of Man, and the Servant: The Role of Zechariah in the Self-Identification of Jesus." In *Tradition and Interpretation in the New Testament: Essays in Honor of E. Earle Ellis for His Sixtieth Birthday*, 134–48. Edited by G. F. Hawthorne and O. Betz. Grand Rapids: Eerdmans; Tübingen: Mohr Siebeck, 1987.

Kirk, J. R. Daniel. *Unlocking Romans: Resurrection and the Justification of God*. Grand Rapids: Eerdmans, 2008.

Kittel, G., and G. Friedrich. *Theological Dictionary of the New Testament*. Translated by G. W. Bromiley. 10 vols. Grand Rapids: Eerdmans, 1964–1976.

Klein, Lillian R. *The Triumph of Irony in the Book of Judges*. Sheffield: Almond Press, 1988.

Klein, Michael L. "The Preposition קדם ("Before"): A Pseudo-Anti-Anthropomorphism in the Targums." *Journal of Theological Studies* 30 (1979): 502–7.

———. "The Translation of Anthropomorphisms and Anthropopathisms in the Targumim." In *Congress Volume Vienna 1980*, 162–78. Edited by John A. Emerton. Vestus Testamentum Supplements 32. Leiden: Brill, 1981.

Klein, R. W. *1 Samuel*. Word Biblical Commentary 10. Waco, TX: Word, 1983.

Kline, Meredith G. "The Old Testament Origins of the Gospel Genre." *Westminster Theological Journal* 38 (1975): 1–27.

Knight, George W. *The Pastoral Epistles: A Commentary on the Greek Text*. New International Greek Testament Commentary. Grand Rapids: Eerdmans, 1992.

Koch, K. *The Growth of the Biblical Tradition: The Form-Critical Method*. New York: Charles Scribner's Sons, 1969.

Koet, Bart J. "'Today This Scripture Has Been Fulfilled in Your Ears': Jesus' Explanation of Scripture in Luke 4:16–30." *Bijdragen* 47 (1986): 368–94.

———. "Trustworthy Dreams? About Dreams and References to Scripture in 2 Maccabees 14–15, Josephus' *Antiquites Judaicae* 11.302–347, and in the New Testament." In *Persuasion and Dissuasion in Early Christianity, Ancient Judaism, and Hellenism*, 87–108. Edited by Pieter van der Horst, Maarten J. J. Menken, Joop F. M. Smit, and Geert van Oyen. Contributions to Biblical Exegesis and Theology 33. Dudley, MA: Peeters, 2003.

Kristof, Nicholas D., and Sheryl WuDunn. *Half the Sky: Turning Oppression into Opportunity for Women Worldwide*. New York: Alfred A. Knopf, 2009.

Laato, T. "Justification according to James: A Comparison with Paul." *Trinity Journal* 18 (1997): 47–61.

———. *Rechtfertigung bei Jakobus: Ein Vergleich met Paulus*. Saarijärvi: Gummerus, 2003.

Ladd, George E. *A Commentary on the Revelation of John*. Grand Rapids: Eerdmans, 1972.

Lamberton, Robert. *Homer the Theologian: Neoplatonist Allegorical Reading and the Growth of the Epic Tradition*. The Transformation of the Classical Heritage 9. Berkeley: University of California Press, 1986.

Lamp, Jeffrey S. *First Corinthians 1–4 in Light of Jewish Wisdom Traditions: Christ, Wisdom and Spirituality*. Studies in Bible and Early Christianity 42. Lewiston, NY: Edwin Mellen Press, 2000.

Lane, William L. *The Gospel of Mark*. New International Commentary on the New Testament. Grand Rapids: Eerdmans, 1974.

Lasine, Stuart. "Judicial Narratives and the Ethics of Reading: The Reader as Judge of the Dispute Between Mephibosheth and Ziba." *Hebrew Studies* 30 (1989): 49–69.

Le Déaut, Roger. *Targum du Pentateuque*, vol. 1. Sources chrétiennes 245. Paris: Cerf, 1978.

Légasse, Simon. *L'Évangile de Marc*, vol. 2. Lectio divina. Paris: Cerf, 1997.

León, Domingo Muñoz. "Soluciones de los Targumim del Pentateuco a los antromorfismos." *Estudios Bíblicos* 28 (1969): 263–81.

Leupold, H. C. *Exposition of Genesis*. Grand Rapids: Baker, 1942.

Levenson, Jon D. "1 Samuel 25 as Literature and History." *Catholic Biblical Quarterly* 40 (1978): 11–28.

——. "The Temple and the World." *Journal of Religion* 64 (1984): 275–98.

Levey, Samson H. *The Targum of Ezekiel.* Aramaic Bible 13. Edinburgh: T&T Clark, 1987.

Levin, M. Z. "A Protest Against Rape in the Story of Deborah [Hebrew]." *Beth Mikra* 25 (1979): 83–84.

Levine, Baruch A. *Leviticus.* Philadelphia: JPS, 1989.

Levison, John R. "Adam and Eve in Romans 1.18–25 and the Greek *Life of Adam and Eve.*" *New Testament Studies* 50 (2004): 519–34.

Lim, Timothy H. "11QMelch, Luke 4, and the Dying Messiah." *Journal of Jewish Studies* 43 (1992): 90–92.

Lindijer, C. H. "Die Jungfrauen in der Offenbarung des Johannes XIV 4." In *Studies in John Presented to J. N. Sevenster,* 124–42. Novum Testamentum Supplements 24. Leiden: Brill, 1970.

Lodge, J. C. "James and Paul at Cross-Purposes." *Biblica* 62 (1981): 195–213.

Lohmeyer, E. *Die Offenbarung des Johannes.* Handbuch zum Neuen Testament 16. Tübingen: Mohr Siebeck, 1970.

Longenecker, Richard N. "The 'Faith of Abraham' Theme in Paul, James, and Hebrews: A Study in the Circumstantial Nature of New Testament Teaching." *Journal of the Evangelical Theological Society* 20 (1977): 203–12.

——. *Galatians.* Word Biblical Commentary 41. Dallas: Word, 1990.

——. *Introducing Romans: Critical Issues in Paul's Most Famous Letter.* Grand Rapids: Eerdmans, 2011.

——. *Paul, Apostle of Liberty.* Grand Rapids: Baker, 1980.

Lundbom, Jack R. *Jeremiah 1–20.* Anchor Bible 21. New York: Doubleday.

Lundquist, John M. "What Is a Temple? A Preliminary Typology." In *The Quest for the Kingdom of God: Studies in Honor of George E. Mendenhall,* 205–20. Edited by A. B. Huffmon, F. A. Spina, and A. R. W. Green. Winona Lake, IN: Eisenbrauns, 1983.

Lyotard, Jean-François. *The Postmodern Condition: A Report on Knowledge.* Minneapolis: University of Minnesota Press, 1984.

Malbon, Elizabeth Struthers. *Mark's Jesus: Characterization as Narrative Christology.* Waco, TX: Baylor University Press, 2009.

Mallowan, M. E. L. *Nimrud and Its Remains.* London: Collins, 1966.

Malul, Meir. *Studies in Mesopotamian Legal Symbolism.* Alter Orient und Altes Testament 221. Kevelaer: Butzon & Bercker; Neukirchen-Vluyn: Neukirchener, 1988.

Marbecke, John. *The lyues of holy sainctes, prophets, patriarches, and others, contayned in Holye Scripture.* London, 1574.

Marcus, Joel. *Mark 1–8: A New Translation with Introduction and Commentary.* Anchor Bible 27. New York: Doubleday, 2000.

——. *The Way of the Lord: Christological Exegesis of the Old Testament in the Gospel of Mark.* Edinburgh: T&T Clark, 1992.

Marmorstein, Arthur. *The Old Rabbinic Doctrine of God: I: The Names and Attributes of God.* Jews' College Publications 10. London: Oxford University Press, 1927.

——. *The Old Rabbinic Doctrine of God: II: Essays in Anthropomorphism.* Jews' College Publications 14. London: Oxford University Press, 1937.

Marshall, I. Howard. *The Gospel of Luke.* New International Greek Testament Commentary. Grand Rapids: Eerdmans, 1978.

Martin, Ralph P. *James.* Word Biblical Commentary 48. Waco, TX: Word, 1988.

Martyn, Louis. *Theological Issues in the Letters of Paul.* Nashville: Abingdon, 1997.

Mastin, B. A. "Scaeva the Chief Priest." *Journal of Theological Studies* 27 (1976): 405–12.

Mason, Steve. "Josephus, Daniel, and the Flavian House." In *Josephus and the History of the Greco-Roman Period,* 161–91. Edited by Fausto Parente and Joseph Sievers. Studia post-biblica 41. Leiden: Brill, 1994.

Matlock, R. Barry. *Unveiling the Apocalyptic Paul: Paul's Interpreters and the Rhetoric of Criticism.* Journal for the Study of the New Testament: Supplement Series 127. Sheffield: Sheffield Academic, 1996.

Matthews, Victor H. *Judges and Ruth.* New Cambridge Bible Commentary. Cambridge: Cambridge University Press, 2004.

Mayo, Philip L. *"Those Who Call Themselves Jews": The Church and Judaism in the Apocalypse of John.* Pittsburgh Theological Monograph Series 60. Eugene, OR: Wipf & Stock, 2006.

Mays, James Luther. "The Place of the Torah-Psalms in the Psalter." *Journal of Biblical Literature* 106 (1987): 3–12.

McCarter, P. Kyle, Jr. *1 Samuel.* Anchor Bible 8. Garden City, NY: Doubleday, 1980.

McCarthy, Carmel. "The Treatment of Biblical Anthropomorphisms in Pentateuchal Targums." In *Back to the Sources: Biblical and Near Eastern Studies: In Honour of Dermot Ryan,* 45–66. Edited by Kevin J. Cathcart and John F. Healey. Dublin: Glendale Press, 1989.

McCarthy, Dennis J., S. J. *Treaty and Covenant: A Study in Form in the Ancient Oriental Documents and in the Old Testament.* Analecta Biblica 21a. Rome: Pontifical Biblical Institute, 1981.

McCartney, Dan G. *"Ecce Homo*: The Coming of the Kingdom as the Restoration of Human Vicegerency." *Westminster Theological Journal* 56 (1994): 1–21.

McCree, W. T. "The Covenant Meal in the Old Testament." *Journal of Biblical Literature* 45 (1926): 120–28.

McKnight, Scot. *The Letter of James.* New International Commentary on the New Testament. Grand Rapids: Eerdmans, 2011.

McNamara, Martin. *The New Testament and the Palestinian Targum to the Pentateuch.* Analecta biblica 27. Rome: Pontifical Biblical Institute, 1966.

——. *Targum and Testament.* Shannon: Irish University Press, 1972.

Meier, John P. *A Marginal Jew: Rethinking the Historical Jesus.* 4 vols. Anchor Bible Reference Library. New York: Doubleday, 1991–2009.

Mertens, Alfred. *Das Buch Daniel im Lichte der Texte vom Toten Meer.* Stuttgarter biblische Monographien 12. Echter: KBW Verlag, 1971.

Mettinger, Tryggve N. D. *The Eden Narrative: A Literary and Religio-historical Study of Genesis 2–3.* Winona Lake, IN: Eisenbrauns, 2007.

Meyers, Carol L. *The Tabernacle Menorah: A Synthetic Study of a Symbol from the Biblical Cult.* American Schools of Oriental Research Dissertation Series 2. Missoula, MT: Scholars Press, 1976.

Middleton, J. Richard. *The Liberating Image: the Imago Dei in Genesis 1.* Grand Rapids: Brazos, 2005.

Milgrom, J. *Leviticus 23–27.* Anchor Bible 3B. New York: Doubleday, 2001.

Millard, Alan R. "The Etymology of Eden." *Vetus Testamentum* 34 (1984): 103–6.

——. "King Solomon in His Ancient Context." In *The Age of Solomon: Scholarship at the Turn of the Millennium,* 30–53. Edited by L. K. Handy. Studies in the History and Culture of the Ancient Near East 11. Leiden: Brill, 1997.

——. "King Solomon's Gold: Biblical Records in the Light of Antiquity." *Society for Mesopotamian Studies Bulletin* 15 (1988): 5–18.

Miller, M. "The Function of Isa. 61:1–2 in 11Q Melchizedek." *Journal of Biblical Literature* 88 (1969): 467–69.

Miscall, Peter D. *The Workings of Old Testament Narrative.* Semeia Studies. Philadelphia: Fortress; Chico, CA: Scholars, 1983.

Momigliano, Arnaldo. *Essays on Ancient and Modern Judaism.* Edited by Silvia Berti. Translated by Maura Masella-Gayley. Chicago: University of Chicago Press, 1994.

Moo, Douglas J. *The Epistle to the Romans.* New International Commentary on the New Testament. Grand Rapids: Eerdmans, 1996.

——. *Galatians.* Baker Exegetical Commentary on the New Testament. Grand Rapids: Baker, 2013.

——. "Justification in Galatians." In *Understanding the Times: New Testament Studies in the 21st Century. Essays in Honor of D. A. Carson on the Occasion of His Sixty-fifth Birthday,* 160–95. Edited by Andreas Köstenberger and Robert Yarbrough. Wheaton, IL: Crossway, 2011.

——. *The Letter of James.* Pillar New Testament Commentary. Grand Rapids: Eerdmans, 2000.

Morgenstern, J. "Isaiah 61." *Hebrew Union College Annual* 40 (1969): 109–21.

Mosis, Rudolf. " 'Glauben' und 'Gerechtigkeit': Zu Gen. 15:6." In *Gesammelte Aufsätze zum Alten Testament,* 78–89. Forschung zur Bibel 93. Würzburg: Echter, 1999.

Mounce, Robert H. *The Book of Revelation.* New International Commentary on the New Testament. Grand Rapids: Eerdmans, 1977.

Moyise, Steve. *Evoking Scripture: Seeing the Old Testament in the New*. London: T&T Clark, 2008.

Müller, Ulrich B. *Die Offenbarung des Johannes*. Ökumenischer Taschenbuch-Kommentar 19. Gütersloh: Gerd Mohn; Würzburg: Echter, 1984.

Myers, Jacob M. "Judges, Introduction and Exegesis." In *The Interpreter's Bible*, 677–826. 12 vols. Edited by G. A. Buttrick, W. R. Bowie, and P. Scherer. Nashville: Abingdon, 1953.

Nelson, Richard D. *Joshua*. Old Testament Library. Louisville: Westminster John Knox, 1997.

Nestle, E. "Luc 4, 18:19." *Zeitschrift für die neutestamentliche Wissenschaft und die Kunde der älteren Kirche* 2 (1901): 153–57.

Neumann-Gorsolke, Ute. "Bedolachharz." *Das Bibellexikon* (2006). No pages. Online: http://www.bibelwissenschaft.de/nc/wibilex/das-bibellexikon/details/quelle/WIBI/zeichen/b/referenz/10445/cache/bd8dbd8e00030e0d2b6901000fbdae2a/.

Neusner, Jacob. *Mekhilta according to Rabbi Ishmael: An Analytical Translation*, vol. 1. Brown Judaic Studies 148. Atlanta: Scholars Press, 1988.

——. *Pesiqta deRab Kahana*, vol. 1. Brown Judaic Studies 122. Atlanta: Scholars Press, 1987.

——. *Sifré to Numbers: An American Translation and Explanation*, vol. 1. Brown Judaic Studies 118. Atlanta: Scholars Press, 1986.

——. *Sifré to Numbers: An American Translation and Explanation*, vol. 2. Brown Judaic Studies 119. Atlanta: Scholars Press, 1986.

——. *The Talmud of Babylonia: An American Translation*, vol. IIC: *Shabbat Chapters 7–10*. Brown Judaic Studies 273. Atlanta: Scholars Press, 1993.

——. *The Talmud of Babylonia: An American Translation*, vol. XVII: *Tractate Sotah*. Brown Judaic Studies 72. Chico, CA: Scholars Press, 1984.

——. *The Talmud of Babylonia: An American Translation*, vol. XXIB: *Tractate Bava Mesia Chapters 3–4*. Brown Judaic Studies 214. Atlanta: Scholars Press, 1990.

Newman, M. L. "Rahab and the Conquest." Pages 167–81 in *Understanding the Word: Essays in Honor of Bernhard W. Anderson*. Edited by J. T. Butler, E. W. Conrad, and B. C. Ollenburger. Journal for the Study of the Old Testament: Supplement Series 37. Sheffield: JSOT Press, 1985.

Nickelsburg, George W. E. *1 Enoch 1*. Hermeneia. Minneapolis: Fortress, 2001.

Nickelsburg, George W. E., and James C. VanderKam. *1 Enoch: A New Translation*. Minneapolis: Fortress, 2004.

Nolland, John. *Luke 1–9:20*. Word Biblical Commentary 35A. Dallas: Word, 1989.

Norelli, Enrico. *Ascensio Isaiae: Textus*. Edited by Paolo Bettiolo, Alda Giambelluca Kossova, Claudio Leonardi, Enrico Norelli and Lorenzo Perrone. Corpus Christianorum, Series Apocryphorum 7. Turnhout: Brepols, 1995.

Noth, M. *The Deuteronomistic History*. Sheffield: JSOT Press, 1981.

O'Brien, D. P. "A Comparison between Early Jewish and Early Christian Interpretations of the Jubilee Year." In *Historica, Biblica, Theologica et Philosophica*, 436–42. Vol. 1 of *Papers Presented at the Thirteenth International Conference on Patristic Studies Held in Oxford, 1999*. Edited by M. F. Wiles, E. Yarnold, and P. M. Parvis. StPatr 34. Leuven: Peeters, 2001.

O'Connor, M. "Judges." In *The New Jerome Bible Commentary*, 132–44. Edited by R. E. Brown, J. A. Fitzmyer, and R. E. Murphy. Upper Saddle River, NJ: Prentice Hall, 1990.

Odashima, Taro. *Heilsworte im Jeremiabuch: Untersuchungen zu ihrer vordeuteronomistischen Bearbeitung*. Beiträge zur Wissenschaft vom Alten (und Neuen) Testament 125. Stuttgart: Kohlhammer, 1989.

O'Donovan, Oliver. "Towards an Interpretation of Biblical Ethics," *Tyndale Bulletin* 27 (1976): 54–79.

Oeming, M. "Ist Genesis 15 ein Beleg für die Anrechnung des Glaubens zur Gerechtigkeit?" *Zeitschrift für die Alttestamentliche Wissenschaft* 95 (1983): 182–97.

Olson, D. C. "'Those Who Have Not Defiled Themselves with Women': Revelation 14:4 and the Book of Enoch." *Catholic Biblical Quarterly* 59 (1997): 492–510.

Orton, David E. *The Understanding Scribe: Matthew and the Apocalyptic Ideal*. Journal for the Study of the New Testament: Supplement Series 25. Sheffield: Sheffield Academic, 1989.

Osborne, Grant R. *Revelation*. Baker Exegetical Commentary on the New Testament. Grand Rapids: Baker, 2002.

Oswalt, J. N. *The Book of Isaiah*. 2 vols. New International Commentary on the Old Testament. Grand Rapids: Eerdmans, 1986, 1998.

Oxford Encyclopedia of Archaeology in the Near East. Edited by E. M. Meyers. New York: Oxford, 1997.

Pao, David W. *Acts and the Isaianic New Exodus*. Wissenschaftliche Untersuchungen zum Neuen Testament 2/130. Tübingen: Mohr Siebeck, 2000. Reprint, Grand Rapids: Baker Academic, 2002.

Pate, C. Marvin. *The Reverse of the Curse: Paul, Wisdom, and the Law*. Wissenschaftliche Untersuchungen zum Neuen Testament 2/114. Tübingen: Mohr Siebeck, 2000.

Pattemore, Stephen. *The People of God in the Apocalypse: Discourse, Structure, and Exegesis*. Society for New Testament Studies Monograph Series 128. Cambridge: Cambridge University Press, 2004.

Pelikan, Jaroslav. *The Christian Tradition: A History of the Development of Doctrine*. Vol. 1. *The Emergence of the Catholic Tradition (100–600)*. Chicago: University of Chicago Press, 1971.

Penna, Romano. *Il "Mysterion" Paolino*. Supplementi alla Rivista biblica 10. Brescia: Paideia, 1978.

Peppard, Michael. *The Son of God in the Roman World: Divine Sonship in Its Social and Political Context*. Oxford: Oxford University Press, 2011.

Petersen, David L. *Late Israelite Prophecy*. Philadelphia: Fortress, 1980.

Philo. Translated by F. H. Colson and G. H. Whitaker. 10 vols. Loeb Classical Library. Cambridge, MA: Harvard University Press, 1929–1962.

Pitkänen, Pekka M. A. *Joshua.* Apollos Old Testament Commentary. Downers Grove, IL: InterVarsity Press, 2010.

Pitre, Brant. *Jesus, the Tribulation, and the End of Exile: Restoration Eschatology and the Origin of the Atonement.* Tübingen: Mohr Siebeck. Repr., Grand Rapids: Baker, 2005.

Plummer, Alfred. *A Critical and Exegetical Commentary on the Gospel According to St. Luke.* International Critical Commentary. 5th ed. Edinburgh: T&T Clark, 1922.

Porter, Stanley E. "Paul and His Bible: His Education and Access to the Scriptures of Israel." In *As It Is Written: Studying Paul's Use of Scripture,* 97–124. Edited by Stanley E. Porter and Christopher D. Stanley. Society of Biblical Literature Symposium Series 50. Atlanta: Society of Biblical Literature, 2008.

———. "The Use of the Old Testament in the New Testament: A Brief Comment on Method and Terminology." In *Early Christian Interpretation of the Scriptures of Israel,* 79–96. Edited by Craig A. Evans and James A. Sanders. Journal for the Study of the New Testament: Supplement Series 148. Sheffield: Sheffield Academic Press, 1997.

Prümm, K. "Zur Phänomenologie des paulinischen Mysterion und dessen seelischer Aufnahme. Eine Übersicht." *Biblica* 37 (1956): 135–61.

Puech, É. "Notes sur le manuscrit de XIQMelkîsédeq." *Revue de Qumran* 12 (1985–1987): 483–84.

Rabinowitz, J. J. "'The Great Sin' in Ancient Egyptian Marriage Contracts." *Journal of Near Eastern Studies* 18 (1959): 73.

Rad, Gerhard von. "Die Anrechnung des Glaubens zur Gerechtigkeit." *Theologische Literaturzeitung* 76 (1951): 129–32.

Reicke, Bo. "Jesus in Nazareth—Lk 4,14–30." In *Das Wort und die Wörter: Festschrift Gerhard Friedrich,* 47–55. Edited by H. Balz and S. Schulz. Stuttgart: Kohlhammer, 1973.

Reumann, John. "OIKONOMIA-Terms in Paul in Comparison with Lucan *Heilsgeschichte.*" *New Testament Studies* 13 (1966–1967): 157–66.

Reynier, Chantal. *Évangile et Mystère: Les enjeux théologiques de l'épître aux Éphésiens.* Paris: Cerf, 1992.

Riesner, Rainer. *Paul's Early Period: Chronology, Mission Strategy, Theology.* Grand Rapids: Eerdmans, 1998.

Roberts, J. J. M. "Melchizedek (11Q13 = 11QMelchizedek = 11QMelch)." In *Pesharim, Other Commentaries, and Related Documents,* 264–73. Princeton Theological Seminary Dead Sea Scrolls 6B. Tübingen: Mohr Siebeck, 1994.

Robertson, O. Palmer. "Genesis 15:6: New Covenant Exposition of an Old Covenant Text." *Westminster Theological Journal* 42 (1980): 259–89.

———. *The Christ of the Prophets.* Phillipsburg, NJ: P&R, 2008.

Rogers, Alan D. "Mark 2,26." *Journal of Theological Studies* 2 (1951): 44–45.

Rogland, Max. "Abram's Persistent Faith: Hebrew Verb Semantics in Genesis 15:6." *Westminster Theological Journal* 70 (2008): 239–44.

Ropes, James Hardy. *A Critical and Exegetical Commentary on the Epistle of St. James*. International Critical Commentary. Edinburgh: T&T Clark, 1916.

Rosner, Brian S. *Paul and the Law: Keeping the Commandments of God*. New Studies in Biblical Theology. Downers Grove, IL: Intervarsity Press, 2013.

Rosner, Brian S., and Roy E. Ciampa. "Use of the Old Testament in 1 Corinthians." In *A Commentary on the Use of the Old Testament in the New*, 695–752. Edited by G. K. Beale and D. A. Carson. Grand Rapids: Baker, 2007.

Ross, Philip S. *From the Finger of God: The Biblical and Theological Basis for the Threefold Division of the Law*. Fearn, Ross-shire, Scotland: Christian Focus, 2010.

Roure, Damia. *Jesús y la Figura de David en Mc 2,23–26: Trasfondo bíblico, intertestamentario y rabínico*. Analecta biblica 124. Rome: Editrice Pontificio Istituto Biblico, 1990.

Rowe, C. Kavin. *Early Narrative Christology: The Lord in the Gospel of Luke*. Beihefte zur Zeitschrift für die neutestamentliche Wissenschaft 139. Berlin and New York: de Gruyter, 2006.

———. "The Grammar of Life: The Areopagus Speech and Pagan Tradition." *New Testament Studies* 57 (2010): 31–50.

Rowland, Christopher. *The Open Heaven: A Study of Apocalyptic in Judaism and Early Christianity*. London: SPCK, 1982.

Sailhammer, John. *The Meaning of the Pentateuch: Revelation, Composition, and Interpretation*. Downers Grove, IL: InterVarsity Press, 2009.

Sanders, E. P. *Jesus and Judaism*. London: SCM Press, 1985.

Sanderson, G. V. "In Defence of Dan." *Scripture* 3 (1948): 114–15.

Sandness, Karl Olav. *Paul, One of the Prophets? A Contribution to the Apostle's Self-Understanding*. Wissenschaftliche Untersuchungen zum Neuen Testament 2/43. Tübingen: Mohr Siebeck, 1991.

Sarna, N. M. *Genesis: The JPS Torah Commentary*. Philadelphia: The Jewish Publication Society, 1989.

Satake, Akira. *Die Offenbarung des Johannes*. Kritisch-exegetischer Kommentar über das Neue Testament (Meyer-Kommentar) 16. Göttingen: Vandenhoeck & Ruprecht, 2008.

Sauer, J. "The River Runs Dry." *Biblical Archaeology Review* 22/4 (1996): 52–57, 64.

Schäfer, Peter. *The Hidden and Manifest God: Some Major Themes in Early Jewish Mysticism*. Translated by Aubrey Pomerance. Albany: State University of New York Press, 1992.

———. *Übersetzung der Hekhalot-Literatur II §§81–334*. Texte und Studien zum Antiken Judentum 17. Tübingen: Mohr Siebeck, 1987.

———. *Übersetzung der Hekhalot-Literatur III §335–597*. Texte und Studien zum Antiken Judentum 22. Tübingen: Mohr Siebeck, 1989.

Schiffman, Lawrence H., and James C. VanderKam. *Encycolopedia of the Dead Sea Scrolls*. 2 vols. New York: Oxford University Press, 2000.

Schliesser, Benjamin. *Abraham's Faith in Romans 4: Paul's Concept of Faith in Light of the History of Reception of Genesis 15:6*. Wissenschaftliche Untersuchungen zum Neuen Testament 2/224. Tübingen: Mohr Siebeck, 2007.

Schlosser, Jacques. *Le Dieu de Jésus*. Lectio divina 129. Paris: Cerf, 1987.

Schmid, H. H. *Gerechtigkeit als Weltordnung: Hintergrund und Geschichte der alttestamentlichen Gerechtigkeitsbegriffes*. Beiträge zur historischen Theologie 40. Tübingen: Mohr Siebeck, 1968.

Schneck, R. *Isaiah in the Gospel of Mark, I–VII*. Bibal Dissertation Series 1. Vallejo, CA: BIBAL, 1994.

Scholem, Gershom G. *Jewish Gnosticism, Merkabah Mysticism, and Talmudic Tradition*. New York: Jewish Theological Seminary of America, 1960.

Schottroff, Willy. "Jeremia 2,1–3: Erwägungen zur Methode der Prophetenexegese." *Zeitschrift für Theologie und Kirche* 67 (1970): 263–94.

Schreiner, Thomas R. *Romans*. Baker Eexegetical Commentary on the New Testament. Grand Rapids: Baker, 1998.

Schultz, Richard L. "The King in the Book of Isaiah." In *The Lord's Anointed: Interpretation of Old Testament Messianic Texts*, 141–65. Edited by Philip E. Satterthwaite, Richard S. Hess, and Gordon J. Wenham. Grand Rapids: Baker, 1995.

———. *The Search for Quotation: Verbal Parallels in the Prophets*. Journal for the Study of the Old Testament: Supplement Series 180. Sheffield: Sheffield Academic Press, 1999.

Schürer, E. *History of the Jewish People in the Age of Jesus Christ*. Edited by M. Black, G. Vermes, F. Millar, and P. Vermes. 2 vols. Edinburgh: T&T Clark, 1984.

Schürmann, H. *Das Lukasevangelium*. Herders theologischer Kommentar zum Neuen Testament. 2 vols. Freiburg: Herder, 1969.

Schweizer, Eduard. *The Good News According to Mark*. Translated by D. H. Madvig. Louisville: Westminster John Knox, 1970.

Scott, Ian W. *Implicit Epistemology in the Letters of Paul: Story, Experience, and the Spirit*. Wissenschaftliche Monographien zum Alten und Neuen Testament. 2. Reihe. 205. Tübingen: Mohr Siebeck, 2006.

Scott, James C. *Domination and the Arts of Resistance: Hidden Transcripts*. New Haven: Yale University Press, 1990.

Seccombe, David. "Luke and Isaiah." In *Right Doctrine from the Wrong Texts? Essays on the Use of the Old Testament in the New*, 248–56. Edited by G. K. Beale. Grand Rapids: Baker, 1994.

———. "Luke and Isaiah," *New Testament Studies* 27 (1981): 252–59.

Segal, Alan F. *Two Powers in Heaven: Early Rabbinic Reports about Christianity and Gnosticism*, chap. 2. Leiden: Brill, 1977.

Seifrid, Mark A. "Righteousness Language in the Hebrew Scriptures and Early Judaism." In *Justification and Variegated Nomism*, vol. 1: *The Complexities of Second Temple Judaism*, 415–42. Edited by D. A. Carson, P. T. O'Brien, and M. A. Seifrid. Wissenschaftliche Untersuchungen zum Neuen Testament 2/140. Tübingen: Mohr Siebeck, 2001.

Shunary, Jonathan. "Avoidance of Anthropomorphism in the Targum of Psalms." *Textus* 5 (1966): 133–44.

Silva, Moisés. *Interpreting Galatians: Explorations in Exegetical Method*. 2nd ed. Grand Rapids: Baker, 2001.

Simon, Maurice. *Midrash Rabbah: Song of Songs*. London: Soncino Press, 1939.

Skarsaune, Oskar. "The History of Jewish Believers in the Early Centuries—Perspectives and Framework." In *Jewish Believers in Jesus: The Early Centuries*, 745–81. Edited by O. Skarsaune and R. Hvalvik. Peabody, MA: Hendrickson, 2007.

Skehan, Patrick W., and Alexander A. Di Lella. *The Wisdom of Ben Sira*. Anchor Bible 39. New York: Doubleday, 1987.

Smalley, Steven S. *The Revelation to John: A Commentary on the Greek Text of the Apocalypse*. Downers Grove, IL: InterVarsity Press, 2005.

Smillie, Gene R. "Ephesians 6:19–20: A Mystery for the Sake of Which the Apostle is an Ambassador in Chains." *Trinity Journal* 18 (1997): 199–222.

Smith, Christopher R. "The Portrayal of the Church as the New Israel in the Names and Order of the Tribes in Revelation 7:5–8." *Journal for the Study of the New Testament* 39 (1990): 111–18.

Smith, H. P. *A Critical and Exegetical Commentary on the Books of Samuel*. Edinburgh: T&T Clark, 1899.

Smith, Mark S. *The Ugaritic Baal Cycle*, vol. 1: *Introduction with Text, Translation, and Commentary of KTU 1.1–1.2*. Leiden: Brill, 1994.

Smith, Ralph L. *Micah-Malachi*. Word Biblical Commentary 32. Waco, TX: Word, 1984.

Snodgrass, Klyne. "The Use of the Old Testament in the New." In *The Right Doctrine from the Wrong Texts? Essays on the Use of the Old Testament in the New*, 29–51. Edited by G. K. Beale. Grand Rapids: Baker, 1994.

Soggin, J. Alberto. *Judges: A Commentary*. Old Testament Library. Philadelphia: Westminster Press, 1981.

———. *The Prophet Amos*. Trans. John Bowden. London: SCM, 1987.

Spilsbury, Paul. "Flavius Josephus on the Rise and Fall of the Roman Empire." *Journal of Theological Studies* 54 (2003): 1–24.

Spurgeon, C. H. *C. H. Spurgeon's Prayers*. New York: Fleming H. Revell Company, 1906.

Stager, Larry. "Jerusalem and the Garden of Eden." In *Eretz-Israel 26*, 183–94. Edited by B. A. Levine, P. J. King, J. Naveh, and E. Stern.

Jerusalem: Israel Exploration Society, Hebrew University, Union College-Jewish Institute of Religion, 1999.

——. "Jerusalem as Eden." *Biblical Archaeology Review* 26/3 (2000): 35–47.

Stamps, Dennis L. "The Use of the Old Testament in the New Testament as a Rhetorical Device: A Methodological Proposal." In *Hearing the Old Testament in the New Testament*, 9–37. Edited by Stanley E. Porter. McMaster New Testament Studies. Grand Rapids: Eerdmans, 2006.

Stanley, Christopher D. *Paul and the Language of Scripture: Citation Technique in the Pauline Epistles and Contemporary Literature.* Society of New Testament Studies Monograph Series 69. Cambridge: Cambridge University Press, 1992.

——. "Paul and Scripture: Charting the Course." In *As It Is Written: Studying Paul's Use of Scripture*, 3–12. Edited by Stanley E. Porter and Christopher D. Stanley. Society of Biblical Literature Symposium Series 50. Atlanta: Society of Biblical Literature, 2008.

Stark, Rodney. "The Class Basis of Early Christianity." In *The Rise of Christianity: How the Obscure, Marginal Jesus Movement Became the Dominant Religious Force in the Western World in a Few Centuries*, 29–47. Princeton: Princeton University Press, 1996.

Stearns, Richard. *The Hole in Our Gospel: What Does God Expect of Us?* Nashville: Thomas Nelson, 2009.

Stein, Robert H. *Luke.* New American Commentary 24. Nashville: B&H, 1992.

——. *Mark.* Baker Exegetical Commentary on the New Testament. Grand Rapids: Baker, 2008.

Stern, Menahem. *Greek and Latin Authors on Jews and Judaism: From Herodotus to Plutarch.* 3 vols. Jerusalem: Israel Academy of Sciences and Humanities, 1974.

Sternberg, M. *The Poetics of Biblical Narrative.* Bloomington: Indiana University Press, 1985.

Stone, Michael E. *Fourth Ezra.* Hermeneia. Minneapolis: Fortress, 1990.

Stordalen, T. *Echoes of Eden: Genesis 2–3 Symbolism and the Eden Garden in Biblical Hebrew Literature.* Contributions to Biblical Exegesis and Theology 25. Leuven: Peeters, 2000.

Strack, Hermann Leberecht, and Paul Billerbeck. *Kommentar zum Neuen Testament aus Talmud und Midrasch*, vol. 1. Munich: Beck, 1922.

Swanson, Reuben. *New Testament Greek Manuscripts: Luke.* Sheffield: Sheffield Academic Press, 1995.

Sweet, John P. M. *Revelation.* TPI New Testament Commentaries. London: SCM Press, 1990.

Tasker, R. V. G. *The General Epistle of James.* Tyndale New Testament Commentaries. Grand Rapids: Eerdmans, 1956.

Tavo, Felise. "The Structure of the Apocalypse: Re-examining a Perennial Problem." *Novum Testamentum* 47 (2005): 47–68.

Taylor, Edward. *Upon the Types of the Old Testament*, vol. 1. Edited by Charles W. Mignon. Lincoln: University of Nebraska Press, 1989.

Testuz, M. *Les Idées religieuses du livre des Jubilés*. Geneva: E. Droz, 1960.

Thiele, Edwin R. "Corregencies and Overlapping Reigns among the Hebrew Kings." *Journal of Biblical Literature* 93 (1974): 174–200.

Thomas, Samuel I. *The 'Mysteries' of Qumran: Mystery, Secrecy, and Esotericism in the Dead Sea Scrolls*. Society of Biblical Literature Early Judaism and Its Literature 25. Atlanta: Society of Biblical Literature, 2009.

Torrey, C. C. *Second Isaiah: A New Interpretation*. New York: Scribner, 1928.

Tov, E. "The Dimensions of the Qumran Scrolls." *Dead Sea Discoveries* 5 (1998): 69–81.

Tromp, Johannes. *The Assumption of Moses: A Critical Edition with Commentary*. Studia in Veteris Testamenti pseudepigraphica 10. Leiden: Brill, 1993.

Urbach, Ephraim E. "The Epithet *Gĕvûrā* and the Might of God." Pages 80–96 in *The Sages: Their Concepts and Belief*, chap. 5. Translated by Israel Abrahams. Jerusalem: Magnes Press, 1979.

VanderKam, James C. *From Joshua to Caiaphas: High Priests after the Exile*. Minneapolis: Fortress, 2004.

Verseput, Donald J. "Rewording the Puzzle of Faith and Deeds in James 2:14–26." *New Testament Studies* 43 (1997): 97–115.

Vickers, Brian. *Jesus' Blood and Righteousness: Paul's Theology of Imputation*. Wheaton, IL: Crossway, 2006.

Wagner, J. Ross. "Heralds of Isaiah and the Mission of Paul." In *Jesus and the Suffering Servant: Isaiah 53 and Christian Origins*, 193–222. Edited by W. H. Bellinger Jr. and W. R. Farmer. Harrisburg, PA: Trinity Press International, 1998.

Wakefield, Andrew H. *Where to Live: The Hermeneutical Significance of Paul's Citations from Scripture in Galatians 3:1–14*. Society of Biblical Literature Academia Biblica 14. Atlanta: Society of Biblical Literature, 2003.

Wall, Robert W. *Revelation*. New International Bible Commentary 18. Peabody, MA: Hendrickson, 1991.

Waltke, Bruce K. *Genesis: A Commentary*. Grand Rapids: Zondervan, 2001.

———. *An Old Testament Theology*. Grand Rapids: Zondervan, 2007.

Waltke, Bruce K., and M. O'Conner. *An Introduction to Biblical Hebrew Syntax*. Winona Lake, IN: Eisenbrauns, 1990.

Walton, John H. *Ancient Near Eastern Thought and the Old Testament: Introducing the Conceptual World of the Hebrew Bible*. Grand Rapids: Baker, 2006.

———. *Genesis*. New International Version Application Commentary. Grand Rapids: Zondervan, 2001.

———. *Genesis 1 as Ancient Cosmology*. Winona Lake, IN: Eisenbrauns, 2011.

Watson, Francis. *Paul and the Hermeneutics of Faith*. London: T&T Clark, 2004.

Watts, John D. W. *Isaiah 34–66*. Word Biblical Commentary 25. Rev. ed. Nashville: Thomas Nelson, 2005.

Watts, Rikk E. "Exodus Imagery." In *Dictionary of the Old Testament Prophets*, 205–14, Edited by Mark J. Boda and J. Gordon McConville. Downers Grove, IL: InterVarsity Press, 2012.

——. "Immanuel: Virgin Birth Proof Text or Programmatic Warning of Things to Come (Isa 7:14 in Matt 1:23)?" In *From Prophecy to Testament*, 92–113. Edited by Craig A. Evans. Peabody, MA: Hendrickson: 2004.

——. *Isaiah's New Exodus in Mark*. Wissenschaftliche Untersuchungen zum Neuen Testament 2/88. Tübingen: Mohr Siebeck, 1997. Reprint, Grand Rapids: Baker, 2000.

——. "The New Exodus/New Creational Restoration of the Image of God." In *What Does it Mean to Be Saved?* 15–41. Edited by John J. Stackhouse Jr. Grand Rapids: Baker, 2002.

Weinfeld, Moshe. "Sabbath, Temple, and the Enthronement of the Lord— The Problem of the Sitz im Leben of Genesis 1:1–2:3." In *Mélanges bibliques et orienteaux en l'honneur de M. Henri Cazelles*, 501–12. Edited by A. Caquot and M. Delcor. Alter Orient und Altes Testament 212. Neukirchen-Vluyn: Neukirchener Verlag/Butzon & Bercker Kevelaer, 1981.

Weiser, Alfons. *Die Apostelgeschichte*. Ökumenischer Taschenbuch-Kommentar 5. Gütersloh: Mohn, 1985.

Wellhausen, J. *Prolegomena to the History of Ancient Israel*. 1883. Reprint. Cleveland: World Publishing, 1957.

Wells, L. S. A. "The Books of Adam and Eve." Pages 123–54 in *The Apocrypha and Pseudepigrapha of the Old Testament in English*. 2 vols. Edited by R. H. Charles. Oxford: Clarendon Press, 1913.

Wenham, Gordon J. *Genesis 1–15*. Word Biblical Commentary 1. Waco, TX: Word, 1987.

——. *Leviticus*. New International Commentary on the Old Testament. Grand Rapids: Eerdmans, 1979.

——. "Sanctuary Symbolism in the Garden of Eden Story." In *I Studied Inscriptions before the Flood*, 399–404. Edited by R. S. Hess and D. T. Tsumura. Sources for Biblical and Theological Study 4. Winona Lake, IN: Eisenbrauns, 1994.

Wenham, J. W. "Mark 2,26." *Journal of Theological Studies* 1 (1950): 156.

Westerholm, Stephen. *Perspectives Old and New on Paul: The "Lutheran" Paul and His Critics*. Grand Rapids: Eerdmans, 2004.

Westermann, Claus. *Genesis 1–11: A Commentary*. Minneapolis: Augsburg, 1984.

——. *Prophetic Oracles of Salvation in the Old Testament*. Translated by Keith Crim. Louisville: Westminster John Knox, 1991.

Westphal, Merold. *Overcoming Onto-theology: Toward a Postmodern Christian Faith*. 1st ed. New York: Fordham University Press, 2001.

White, Joel. *Die Erstlingsgabe im Neuen Testament.* Texte und Arbeiten zum neutestamentlichen Zeitalter 45. Tübingen: Francke, 2007.

Wikenhauser, Alfred. *Die Offenbarung des Johannes.* Regensburger Neues Testament 9. Regenburg: Friedrich Pustet, 1959.

Wildberger, Hans. "Das Abbild Gottes: Gen. 1, 26–30." *Theologische Zeitschrift* 21 (1965): 481–501.

Wiles, Maurice. *The Divine Apostle.* Cambridge: Cambridge University Press, 1967.

Wilken, Louis. *The Christians as the Romans Saw Them.* 2nd ed. New Haven: Yale University Press, 2003.

Williams, Ronald J. *Hebrew Syntax: An Outline.* 2nd ed. Toronto: University of Toronto Press, 1976.

Williams, Sam K. "Justification and the Spirit in Galatians." *Journal for the Study of the New Testament* 29 (1987): 91–100.

Williamson, H. G. M. *1 and 2 Chronicles.* Grand Rapids: Eerdmans, 1982.

Wilson, Gerald H. *The Editing of the Hebrew Psalter.* Society of Biblical Literature Dissertation Series 76. Chico, CA: Scholars Press, 1985.

Wilson, Ian. *Out of the Midst of the Fire: Divine Presence in Deuteronomy.* Society of Biblical Literature Dissertation Series 151. Atlanta: Scholars Press, 1995.

Wilson, Robert R. *Prophecy and Society in Ancient Israel.* Philadelphia: Fortress, 1959.

Wise, Michael O., and James D. Tabor. "The Messiah at Qumran." *Biblical Archaeology Review* 18/6 (1992): 60–65.

Wiseman, Donald J. "Abraham Reassessed." In *Essays on the Patriarchal Narratives,* 139–56. Edited by A. R. Millard and D. J. Wiseman. Leicester: Inter-Varsity Press, 1980.

Witherington, Ben, III. *Paul's Narrative Thought World.* Louisville: Westminster/John Knox, 1994.

——. *The Acts of the Apostles: A Socio-Rhetorical Commentary.* Grand Rapids: Eerdmans, 1998.

Wolff, Hans Walter. *Anthropology of the Old Testament.* Translated by M. Kohl. Philadelphia: Fortress, 1974.

Woudstra, Marten H. *The Book of Joshua.* New International Commentary on the Old Testament. Grand Rapids: Eerdmans, 1981.

Wright, Christopher J. H. *Old Testament Ethics for the People of God.* Downers Grove, IL: InterVarsity Press, 2004.

Wright, N. T. *Jesus and the Victory of God.* Christian Origins and the Question of God 2. London: SPCK; Minneapolis: Fortress, 1996.

——. "Justification: Yesterday, Today, and Forever." *Journal of the Evangelical Theological Society* 54 (2011): 49–63.

——. *The New Testament and the People of God.* Minneapolis: Fortress, 1992.

——. *Paul: In Fresh Perspective.* Minneapolis: Fortress, 2005.

——. "Romans." In *The New Interpreter's Bible,* 395–770. Vol. 10. Nashville: Abingdon, 2002.

Yadin, Y. "A Note on Melchizedek and Qumran." *Israel Exploration Journal* 15 (1965): 152–54.

Yeo, J. "A Literary Approach to Biblical Interpretation: An Introduction to Biblical Repetition." Paper presented at Reformed Theological Seminary, Jackson, 2005.

Yeung, Maureen W. *Faith in Jesus and Paul: A Comparison with Special Reference to 'Faith That Can Remove Mountains' and 'Your Faith Has Healed/Saved You.'* Wissenschaftliche Untersuchungen zum Neuen Testament 2/147. Tübingen: Mohr Siebeck, 2002.

Yieh, John Yueh-Han. *One Teacher: Jesus' Teaching Role in Matthew's Gospel Report.* Beihefte zur Zeitschrift für die neutestamentliche Wissenschaft 124. Berlin: de Gruyter, 2004.

Young, E. J. *The Book of Isaiah.* 3 vols. Grand Rapids: Eerdmans, 1965, 1969, 1972.

Young, Frances M. "Alexandrian and Antiochene Exegesis." In *The Ancient Period*, vol. 1 of *A History of Biblical Interpretation*, 334–54. Edited by Alan J. Hauser and Duane Frederick Watson. Grand Rapids: Eerdmans, 2003.

——. *Biblical Exegesis and the Formation of Christian Culture.* Cambridge: Cambridge University Press, 1997.

Young, Kay, and Jeffrey L. Saver. "The Neurology of Narrative." *SubStance* 94/95 (2001): 72–84.

Zahn, Theodor. *Die Offenbarung des Johannes.* Kommentar zum Neuen Testament 18. Leipzig: Deichertsche Verlagsbuchhandlung, 1926.

Zakovitch,Yair. "Reflection Story—Another Dimension of the Evaluation of Characters in Biblical Narrative [Hebrew]." *Tarbiz* 54 (1984/1985): 165–76.

Ziesler, J. A. *The Meaning of Righteousness in Paul: A Linguistic and Theological Enquiry.* Society for New Testament Studies Monograph Series 20. Cambridge: Cambridge University Press, 1974.

Zimmerli, Walter, and Joachim Jeremias. *The Servant of God.* Rev. ed. Studies in Theology 20. Naperville, IL: Allenson, 1965.

Zimmermann, Christiane. *Die Namen des Vaters: Studies zu ausgewählten neutestamentlichen Gottesbezechnungen vor irhem frühjüdischen und paganen Sprachhorizont.* Ancient Judaism and Early Christianity 69. Leiden: Brill, 2007.

Index of Modern Authors

Alexander, T. Desmond, 237
Allen, Leslie C., 34, 35
Alter, R., 52, 54, 70
Anderson, Bernhard W., 67, 68, 72
Aune, David E., 181, 182, 183n15, 187, 193, 262, 264
Averbeck, Richard, 19

Baker, David L., 219
Bal, Mieke, 63
Barber, Cyril J., 75
Bar-Efrat, S., 52
Barnett, R. D., 10
Bauckham, Richard, 83, 93, 157, 182, 185, 186, 200, 224
Bayer, Hans F., 165
Beale, G. K., x, xi, xiii, xiv, xv, 3, 4, 6, 7, 10, 18, 19, 27, 63, 103, 108, 113, 115, 123, 124, 125, 141, 146, 147, 148, 163, 165, 171, 176, 177, 179, 182, 185, 186, 187, 194, 195, 196, 197, 199, 216, 223, 237, 255, 257, 260, 261, 265
Beasley-Murray, George R., 179, 186
Beavis, Mary Ann, 123, 165
Beck, J. A., 53
Becker, J., 259
Beetham, Christopher A., 237, 249, 253
Begg, C. T., 263, 264
Behrens, Achim, 150, 151
Benedict XVI, 200
Bergauer, P., 158
Bergen, R. D., 59
Bergsma, John Sietze, 133, 136
Berlin, A., 52
Betz, Otto, 173, 205, 257, 261, 264
Biddle, Mark E., 191
Billerbeck, P., 84, 100, 101, 137
Bird, Michael F., 135
Black, Matthew, 92, 137

Blenkinsopp, Joseph, 75, 127, 129, 130, 263
Bloch-Smith, Elizabeth, 4, 21
Block, Daniel I., 3, 4, 6, 9, 28, 156
Blomberg, Craig, 105, 158, 164
Bock, Darrell L., 84, 95, 137, 140, 141, 143, 144, 215
Bockmuehl, Markus, 259
Böhler, Dieter, 190, 191
Boling, Robert G., 65, 72
Booth, Wayne C., 66
Bordreuil, Pierre, 15
Boring, Eugene, 179, 185, 186
Bouma-Prediger, Steven, 11
Bousset, Wilhelm, 180, 182, 183n15, 185, 187
Bovon, François, 126, 138, 144
Bowley, James E., 259
Bray, Gerald, 113
Brin, Gershon, 260
Brisson, Luc, 201
Brown, Alexandra, 265
Brown, Raymond E., 75, 84, 95, 264
Brownlee, William H., 138, 260, 261
Bruce, F. F., 153, 260, 261
Brueggemann, Walter, 150
Buber, M., 53
Budde, K., 51, 52
Burton, Ernest de W., 153

Caird, George B., 52, 185
Callender, Dexter E., Jr, 4, 15
Calvert-Koyzis, Nancy, 152
Calvin, J., ix, 148, 159, 225, 232
Campbell, Douglas A., 103
Carter, Warren, 117
Cartledge, Paul, 205
Casey, Maurice, 164
Cassel, Paulus, 69
Cerfaux, Lucien, 255

INDEX OF ANCIENT SOURCES